The Faith of a Child

By Patti Boulaye

Published By Bipada Academy LTD

Contents

Foreword

Anyone who knows Patti would agree that this book should have been published years ago. They would also be aware that she could fill the pages of half a dozen more books full of fascinating and inspiring glimpses into her powerful and loveable personality.

Unfortunately, her modesty prevents her from putting pen to paper, or rather, her fingers to electronic lap-top and keyboard. She needs someone to bully her lovingly into turning her deeply spiritual convictions and inspirational life experiences into a book.

My prediction is that she will very soon become a household name as a riveting author. She is obviously destined to ride the chariot of fame not only as a singer but, as a writer with the power to change people's lives for the better.

Anyone fortunate enough to hold this book in their hand is in for a real treat and new revelations, and a great deal of food for thought.

Dr Joy Philippou Phd. Dip. Ed. Cert Ed MBE (February 16th 2016)

All of us who think we had a difficult childhood must read Patti Boulaye's unbelievable life story. Her riveting story is a paramount example of what can be accomplished when insurmountable odds are overcome by positive thinking, spirit, vitality, never giving up, love and eliminating all excuses. I am an avid reader and could not put down this book written by this multi-talented lady which can help so many people that think there's no way out of a life of heartache, pain, disappointment, etc. She is the beacon light to having a successful life after experiencing impossible odds on the road to happiness and success.

Dale Brown
National College Basketball Hall of Fame Coach
Louisiana State University 1972-1997

Dedication

The biggest influence in my life has been my mother, the woman that God, in His infinite wisdom, appointed as my mentor and physical and spiritual guide through my life. I couldn't have chosen better, she had a great sense of style and decorum; she was a very strong and spiritual woman with a gentle personality, a sense of duty towards her eight children and society as a whole. As the Biafra war raged, she assumed responsibility for our lives and the lives of friends and neighbours in need of protection and a secure hiding place. For the rest of her life, each one of these was her child. Jesus was her best friend, she had this unwavering trust that He would shepherd and care for her children. That is why this book is dedicated to my mother and champion, Arit Dorothy Effiom Coco-Bassey Ikoku, who is now at peace and with her friend Jesus, the good shepherd, to whom I give thanks and praise for this book. T.T.G.O.G

Preface

From the minute I was born in a taxi, on the way to the hospital, to this day, as I begin to write this book, my life has felt like one big training exercise and preparation, but for what, I do not know. As I grow older I try to anticipate what the future might hold for me and what I am being moulded for. This is occasionally frustrating, but mostly a source of excitement, especially when I get a glimpse of what I think it might be, through my many encounters. The answer might come from anywhere, through my family or acquaintances or the world generally. I believe we meet each person for a special reason and I search for that reason, relentlessly with each encounter. So there is never a dull moment in my life, which so far has been filled with many highs and lows. During my low periods I try to find the positive in the situation, trusting that God is always in control; thus, when things go right or wrong, I believe it is all as He wishes. As exciting as these glimpses may be, I do believe that we must live for the moment and do everything that we have to do each day diligently and as though we were doing it for God. We cannot know when life will end and so we owe it to those who love us to give all that we can each day with an open heart.

Looking back now, I find it hard to find a time when I felt that I was in control of my plans; of course, at the time, I usually thought I was in control, but if I'm honest with myself, I realise that God always had a big hand in the way things went. The only thing I could decide on my own was what sort of person or woman, wife, mother or citizen I wanted to be and how I would affect the lives of others.

I have come to know that my prayers have always been answered, though not necessarily as I wanted, but nevertheless, they were and are answered. For instance, when I was a child I would tell everyone that I would have six children, which is not unusual in Nigeria. Speaking to my mother on one of her many visits to see me, my husband, Stephen and our two little angels; I lamented the fact that I always wanted more children, My mother laughed out loud and said;
"Since you were little you always said you would have six children and God has answered your prayers in His own way."
I must have looked puzzled, so she said:
"You now have six children to look after, Stephen's four daughters and your own two children with him."

It wasn't exactly how I had planned it, but I had learnt not to argue with my mother's wisdom or God's way of doing things.

The story of my early life from my toddler years in Nigeria to my time in Britain can only be described as an adventure. I would like to make a graph of my life, showing the highs and lows following my journey through living in villages to cities. Through a difficult, but happy childhood, kind and cruel people, through my parents nasty divorce, a stepfather who was to have the most kind paternal influence in my life, the Biafra War and my mother's brave stance, sacrifices and risks for her children and neighbours, attending a Catholic boarding school and finally to England; perhaps the graph would show that all these things have helped to form my character.

Acknowledgements

I cannot do anything without God. I would like to give God the glory for training me through the Holy Book all I have experienced. Only He, and not I, is responsible for all I have achieved.

A sincere thank you to my husband Stephen Komlosy, who has been my backbone and support for over forty years. I'm not sure he knew what he was getting into when he proposed to me. Or how much of a whirlwind and hard work I was going to be. I am grateful for his loyalty, calm, patience, gentleness, incredible generosity of spirit and unconditional love. I thank Stephen for not only encouraging me to write this book, but for spending many hours enthusiastically editing the book. I thank God for bringing Stephen into my life. I could not have asked for a better husband and friend.

My special thanks to Peter Cox without whose help this book would not have been published. Also thank you to Sebastian Komlosy, our son, for so lovingly designing the cover and for bringing old unusable photos to life. Special thanks also to our daughter Aret Kapetanovic for her support, encouragement and love. I thank Dr Joy Philippou MBE who spent the past eighteen years nagging and encouraging me to write this book and for her sterling work editing the book. I am grateful to author Lorna Byrne for her encouraging words and support and for confirming that my guardian angel is real, that "we are all, in fact, angels". My thanks also to my friends Les Saxon, Geoff Roberts and all the wonderful people who have encouraged and supported me.

Many thanks to His Holiness Radhanath Swami who, in his wisdom has made me realize that I have a lot to offer through my spirituality and experiences. That humility is a natural, peaceful and wonderful state of being.

Finally to my siblings to whom I have dedicated a whole chapter in this book because they have been a great part of my survival, my dealings with people in general and the woman I have become. They, like my late mother, have always been there for me and have filled my memories with love, strength and the power to overcome difficulties through great faith. Someone said; "no family is perfect" and that is true, but to me, my family is as perfect as you get because I would not exchange them for anyone else's family.

Chapter One: The Long Walk Home

Before I go into my history, I would like to tell you about the one single day in my life when I learned most of life's hard lessons. I was attending Reagan Memorial Primary School in Yaba, Lagos, before the Biafra War began. When I was eight or nine years old I was given a lift to school each day by our next-door neighbour, who was a teacher at the school; as this was convenient for Mummy. I didn't like going to school with this woman, because I could sense I was an imposition, but there was no choice, my school was at least ten miles away and the roads were dangerous. Also I hated the school where I was bullied. A girl, threw a pair of scissors at me, because I would not rise to the challenge to a fight with her, a fight which the whole class was anticipating. One of the sharp ends of the scissors pierced my back and drew blood. My class teacher seemed unconcerned and sent me to have it dressed in the dispensary. When I returned to the class, my attacker and I were punished and told to sit in silence in detention, after the end of classes that day.

As a result of this I was five minutes late for my lift home and the woman had driven away and left me behind. I recall seeing the car driving away as I came running towards it knowing she would be furious with me. At first, I had a sense of relief when I saw the car and then, I can't describe my emotions as she sped away and I realised that I was on my own I had no money for the fare home or to make a call to my mother. I would, in any case, not be allowed to use the school telephone. The school day ended at 1:30pm and without money and under the hot sun, thinking only of one step at a time, I began to make my way home on foot. I knew I would be afraid if I was to allow myself to worry about how far I would have to walk. I remained on the main Agege Motor Road just in case my mother came looking for me and, as much as possible, I walked on the tarmac away from the earthen verge so that she would be able to see me even though this was a dangerous thing to do on a Nigerian road where no-one abides by the rules. It turned out to be a journey during which I learnt many of life's vital lessons.

I had walked quite a way before I decided to risk getting on a Molue bus which were always overcrowded, hoping that if I could manage to scramble on, at least I would cover a little distance before the bus conductor realised I had no money, and threw me off . At the bus stops, there would be rows and rows of Molues, these are mini buses or large people-carriers, that are designed to seat thirty comfortably, but 70 or more would be squashed in, with some just hanging out of the windows and door. The busses had names on them such as "Blessing", "Hallelujah", and often the names were short statements like "God is good!" In the event I was discovered immediately, although I had tried to hide, the bus was jam-packed and bursting at the seams with people hanging out of the windows whilst others were clinging on to the roof rack for dear life. I managed to get on sandwiched between two adults who dwarfed me with their big, dusty and smelly parcels of food, which were, at least three feet wide and placed on their laps, making it difficult, or so I thought, for me to be seen. Unfortunately, the bus conductor had spotted me through the window and demanded the fare. The passengers were, understandably, not pleased with me when the conductor insisted I pay up or get off the bus, because, in order to let me get out past them, as small as I was, they had to struggle to stand up. Shifting their loads, whilst others categorically refused to get off the bus to let me out for fear of losing their tiny space. They all muttered with displeasure and some shouted abuse at me, as I pushed hard to get to the door with my wounded back throbbing, making sure I clung tightly to my school bag. When I finally got to the door, the impatient bus conductor pulled me off the bus. I lost my footing and fell on to the hard dry earth catching my knee. With all the commotion and the fall I was frightened and I sat by the side of the road and cried. I remember the heat and I began to feel hungry and my knee was bleeding from the fall. I picked myself up and tried to look on the bright side as I breathed in the dusty and hot air; at least, I was free from the suffocating body odour in the bus, mixed with the strong stifling smell of dried fish, peppers, herbs and cassava.

I picked up my bag and, brushing the dust off my uniform, I started my journey again trying my best to forget the abuse and madness of the Bus encounter. I knew now that no matter how long it took. I would have to walk home. The wound in my back was throbbing, probably from the sweat that was seeping into the thin dressing over the deep wound in the flesh at the side of my spine, and my leg was hurting from the fall The sun was beating down on the intricate partings in my hair that exposed the scalp between my plaits giving me a headache. I took off my socks and twisted them together to make a small round ring like a donut, placed it on my head and balanced my school bag filled with books on it. This was the way we were taught to balance heavy loads on our heads, leaving the hands free.

Along the main road, I came to a market place where there was an unusually large crowd of people and they were not the ordinary market crowd, the atmosphere was strange, there was something unpleasant about it all. There was a strong smell of something burning, like rubber; I could see the black smoke rising above the crowd. Being the curious child that I was, I moved through the people towards the smoke, weaving my way through the crowd trying not to lose my bag. It was not easy, but I persevered, pushing closer and closer to the front taking advantage of my size and gaps in the crowd. I was sure someone's car had caught fire. When I did get to the front of the crowd, I was stunned and shocked. I immediately ran back to the road and away as fast as I could run. It was not the burning car that I had expected, but the crowd had set a young man alight. They had pushed him into car tyres, doused him with petrol and set him on fire. From the evil conversations I overheard as I fled I gathered this was his punishment for stealing something. I wondered what he could have stolen to deserve such punishment. His twisted body was a terrible sight and the smell was indescribable and will forever remind me of that side of the human race that makes me wonder why God is so patient with us, His most destructive creation.

The lesson that no eight or nine year old child should have to learn so young is that there is an unseen force that can control a crowd, making it one entity which can do the most despicable things that no individual would think of doing.

In shock and frightened, I left the crowd and the area very quickly. Suddenly, behind me there was the sound of screeching tires and I leapt into the gutter narrowly avoiding being hit by a speeding car. My heart was pounding and the driver and a few onlookers shouted angry words at me. Tears welded up again in my eyes, but I wiped them away and continued on my way, making sure this time to stay on the verge and off the main tarmac highway.

Thirsty and hungry I tried, without success, to ignore the wayside food vendors around me as they went about their business selling their wares. Everyone seemed to be selling or buying something; bananas, watches, jewellery, homemade donuts, rice and stew, moi moi, and drinks, Pepsi, Fanta, Bitter Lemon and malt drinks. Vendors were shouting and holding up their goods, household cleaning products, towels and anything you could possibly want could be bought from one of these robust vendors, sometimes moving through the crowds carrying their entire stock on their heads, chest or balanced on their hips. I admired the way they kept their goods balanced, whilst manoeuvring the hazardous sidewalks riddled with broken bottles and other dangerous debris, not forgetting the cars whizzing by at speed. As soon as a car, bus or lorry slowed down or came to a stop, there would be a barrage of hawkers trying to sell the passengers, one thing or another. I wondered why the passengers did not just grab the goods and drive off, but no one did, at least not on this day.

The burning heat of the equatorial sun caused the men and women to walk slowly in order to reduce their body heat. Here and there people made makeshift sheds that offered shelter. There were beautiful and colourfully dressed women, I would stop and admire their slow undulating gait, and these women had buttocks that had a mind of their own! But they seemed unaware of all the chaos around them, moving through the market places with ease, hardly breaking a sweat with their charcoal eyeliner accentuating their sleepy eyes, full red or dark brown, even jet black lipstick intact. The body language of these women just gives the onlooker an impression of sensual calm in the midst of hell. Often, along the way, I observed men flirting with the women under the large Neem trees, something that would have caused much giggling at school. There was a certain female "come-hither" body language that I misread as 'get lost' which I later learnt to be the opposite and a very easily recognisable flirting ritual adopted by the Nigerian male and female. This often involves, what I call the "rolling of the hips" ritual. There is the undulating buttocks and gentle swinging of the hips movement. It is also the 'shakara' (the showing off) stance, which the men seem to find a great turn on beginning with the male making some sort of a pass or show of interest or admiration maybe whistling as the female goes by. Who would blame them; Nigerian women of most ages ooze incredible sensuality. In reply to the show of admiration, the female would turn her head slowly and slightly left or right, depending on which side the whistle came from, and then with hooded eyes, she would first lower her look, and then, ever so slowly she would look up in the direction of her admirer. Taking in his physique, perhaps status and attractiveness all in a second, and, if she liked what she saw, she would turn her head slowly back to the front and continue on her way, but now with an even lazier and more rhythmic movement of the hips, as if dragging her feet. If she is wearing slippers then these would become audible as clicking as she walked away. The male would see this as an encouraging sign and would now feel he could perhaps approach her, but with caution. Meanwhile, she is aware of the movement behind her, without so much as a turn of the head, but using only a slight look to the side, just to make sure he was hooked. Even when he finally got as far as to speak to her, she would play hard to get.

On the other hand if her survey of her admirer indicated that he was unworthy of her, there would be a serious and loud kissing of the teeth and this was usually followed by a faster turning away of the head and the walk away from him assumes a different rhythm, that of a less sensual swing, but more aggressive and intense. This would usually result in other men around the admirer teasing him about the rebuff. It is all very amusing to watch and helped to keep my mind off my predicament.

The main road was tarmacadam, but on the uneven verges, the art of avoiding the pot-holes and other pitfalls had been mastered by one and all. The roadside was littered with junk, the metal shells of abandoned cars, stripped of every useable part, which were being utilised as shelters from the hot sun. Everywhere, there were hastily built shacks with stalls selling all kinds of goods, at the side there would be washing hanging on wires tied from one tree to another. Occasionally, a heavily laden goods lorry, would speed past blasting its horn making cursing people jump out of the way.

There would be long lines of stalls under rows of parasols selling piles of peeled oranges, carrots, tomatoes, dried and fresh fish, fresh Meat, fabrics and all kinds of goods. Almost always these stalls and shops on the main road would open out into a roadside market with clusters of parked vehicles in a clearing full of potholes. The buses and cars would be more than ten deep, always some would be moving, weaving in between each other and the shoppers in the confined space, with many near misses, arguments and abuse breaking out between drivers, pedestrians and vendors. These were difficult areas for me to negotiate on my own as a child and I had some very scary moments, but I adopted a strategy of staying close behind a woman (never a man) making her way through the chaos and just kept in close step with her. Unfortunately, my woman, on one occasion, suddenly hailed a car and got into it, right in the middle of this chaos, leaving me totally exposed and confused with people shouting at me to get out of the way or asking in pigeon English, if I had a death wish. There were five or six such close scrapes and so I would cross the road to avoid these busy roadside markets, as soon as I saw one up ahead. Of course, crossing the main road was also hazardous and not always a good idea as you would take your life in your hands. Once, as I crossed the road, a seemingly stationary vehicle suddenly decide to take off at breakneck speed on to the road, beeping his horn like a madman causing me to literally jump out of my skin. Every now and then families of three or four would be returning from a day at the market, typically with mother carrying a big basin on her head filled with some prized purchase with a sleeping baby on her back, followed by a daughter with a large plastic bucket on her head, behind her would be a smaller child, a little older than me, perhaps, carrying a large bundle on her head, and not far behind, bouncing along, a four or five year old girl carrying just a wrapped up piece of cloth which she swung rhythmically from one hand to another as if she could hear music in her head. The older sister would turn around and rebuke the youngest for falling behind and tell her to keep up. The little one would pull a face and grumpily run to catch up. I followed one such family for a while until they turned into a side road, disappearing into the mayhem.

I continued my long trek home keeping an hopeful eye out for my mother's car, though I knew how slim the chances were, of my catching her attention or stopping her car without being run over, I tried to stick as near to the main road as much as possible to be able to spot her or anyone she had sent looking for me. I wondered if Mummy would be angry with me, for getting myself into this situation. I was still hopeful that she might find me as I had no idea how far away I was from home, I knew only that I was tired and hungry. I was certain that she would be looking for me. I also knew there were two main roads to and from Ikeja to Yaba; Agege Motor Road, through Mushin which was my route, or via Maryland on Ikorodu Road and she might be looking in the wrong place.

Still, there was plenty happening on the Agege Motor Road to keep me distracted as I ambled along. I was fascinated by the men who sat on the tops of moving lorries, that were so packed with goods that they looked as though they would topple over as they sped around the corners, leaving the usual trail of billowing dust behind them. I walked past vendors who piled up used car tyres by the dusty road forming tables for their large trays piled high of fresh hot chilli peppers, onions, plantains, tomatoes and other fresh food stuffs. Occasionally, there would be the smell of rotting vegetation from the open gutters, full of stagnant water, which had been used as a dumping ground for rubbish, indeed, there was discarded rubbish everywhere you looked, broken bottles, tins, railway sleepers, shoes, broken furniture and dead animals, like the odd wild domestic dogs, run over by a vehicle. Seemingly unaware of the mess, the vendors would sit behind their wares fanning themselves in the heat, driving troublesome flies away from their goods.

All along the highway were giant billboards with adverts for Fanta, Star Beer, Heineken, Lucozade, Omo and Lux soap (years later I was to be the face of Lux Soap for 29years!).

Sometimes I would leave the main road, wherever the road narrowed, making it dangerous for pedestrians to pitch flesh and bones against speeding 3 ton, metal monsters. I continued my walk on the side roads, which were not tarred. The dry orange coloured dust from the earth clung to my shoes and clothes. As earlier in my long trek I would smell mouth-watering spiced stew or fresh fish soup or fried plantain that would torment my hunger, then I would tell myself that the food was probably covered in dust and goodness knows what else. I would imagine that the food would make me sick. It worked a few times when my mind convinced my stomach that it was not in need of such poison.

For distraction I would play at football by kicking a few stones or empty cans around trying to see how far I could kick them or whether I could hit a random target. After a while I would get tired of this game, sometimes I would stop because I had to cross the road or because someone gave me an angry look or an angry word. I had forgotten the pain in my back as my tiredness set in. I must have walked at least 10 miles by now, and for some reason I felt no anger towards the woman who left me behind and I let my mind wander.

I was woken up from my day dreaming by a young man tearing past me at great speed. He was being pursued by an angry mob, shouting "Ole", meaning thief in Yoruba. Instinctively, I froze, so no one would mistake me for the thief. This was the right thing to do, because when a lot of people are whipped into frenzy, anyone running away would be attacked as a thief. As the crowd ran past me I was almost knocked to the ground. So I decided to cross over to the other side of the road for safety, but again a car, whose driver hurled more abuse at me, almost knocked me down.

Towards the end of the day I felt really tearful and sorry for myself and I found somewhere to sit by a smelly gutter full of rubbish. I was about to be overcome by the fear of not getting home before dark, when I observed from afar, a small girl of about ten. Maybe she was older. Years of carrying large basins of oranges on her head may have stunted her growth. A man whom she assumed wanted to buy some oranges from her had approached her. She lifted the large basin of oranges off her head with bewildering strength, She bent her knees to get closer to the ground and knelt, then slowly, so as not to lose any of the oranges, she lifted the basin off her head placed it on the ground in front of her and started lobbing the top off each of the oranges as he requested. The big man went through one peeled orange after another with relish, squeezing the juice into his mouth and throwing away the skins. He must have decided not to pay for the oranges, because with lightning speed, the little girl was on the other side of the basin of oranges and had grabbed the man by the crotch! Taking him completely by surprise, she held on, screaming at the top of her voice that she wanted her money or she would not let go of him. Clearly in some pain, he begged her to release him, but he was unable to break free of her vice like grip as he desperately tried to reach into his pocket for the coins. I sat on the cement mound and watched, it was a very amusing and entertaining scene and soon a small crowd gathered and were shouting encouragement to the wailing girl and shouting abuse at the man, for trying to cheat a little girl out of her few coins. In the end, he dropped all the coins in his pocket on to the ground, only then did she let go of him. She picked up what she was owed and left the rest lying in the dust. Clearly having difficulty bending he struggled to pick up the rest of his money. With the fun over the crowd dispersed jeering at him, 'oloshi' they laughed, (which is a curse word loosely translated as "fool") amid much kissing of teeth as they walked away. I had been laughing, out loud which elicited an angry look from the wretched man grovelling for his money. I couldn't stop laughing, but felt it wise to leave with the crowd. This incident brightened up the day for me and I had a bit more spring in my step as I set out again to continue my struggle home. Of course, there was the reality of my volatile and dirty surroundings. To add to the problems I was now not sure which way to go as dusk began to set in, when I heard a bus conductor nearby shout "Ikeja market" as the packed bus came to a halt and some of the passengers alighted. I ran to one of them and asked for directions to the market, because I knew it was about one or two miles from home. If I could only get to the market I would be able to find my way to Adeniyi Jones Avenue where we lived. I walked about another mile before I could recognise the road that led to our street. I now felt a new surge of energy as I realised I was near home, but strangely it seemed to take forever to cover those last yards. I had imagined home would be just around the corner as it so appeared when being driven in a car.

By the time I finally walked into the gates of our house, it was just after 8pm and I had been walking for seven hours, I had left the school in Yaba at 1pm. Someone shouted that I was back, and the entire household and Mummy came running out to meet me, I don't know where she found the strength to carry me up the long stairway. She kept repeating "Abassi sosong", "thank You God" in her native Efik, she asked me many questions, gave orders for drinks and food to be brought to the dining room and with military precision, my wounds were dressed, I was bathed and fed. They had been searching for me for hours. Not a word was said about the neighbour who left me behind, but Mummy had made her feelings known to her earlier in the day. All I was grateful for is that I never went to school with her again and soon after that I was moved to Maryland Primary School. I then took and passed an early entrance exam for the prestigious secondary school Holy Child College in Obalende, near Ikoyi. I still have the scar on my back, of course, but thankfully it shrunk, as I grew older.

Chapter Two: My Maternal Grandmother

My grandmother, whom we called "Nne Kamba" (great-mother), did not survive the period of the Biafra war, but she died a natural death during the war. Before the war, my holiday visits to her home in the village, Ikot Efa, are my fondest childhood memories. Nne Kamba did not like the hustle and bustle of life in the busy Nigerian cities and preferred her simple lifestyle in the village. The village had fifteen or twenty thatched roofed mud huts of which Nne Kamba had the largest with white walls, a large veranda, four rooms to sleep in, a living area for entertaining guests, an outside kitchen and a pit toilet about ten meters into the forest at the back.

Nne was from a village called Etigidi and married our grandfather, Obong Effiom Coco-Bassey, who was the local King of the area in Calabar which included the village Ikot Efa, This village was situated in the estuary of the River Niger as it meanders its way through south eastern Nigeria, meeting the Atlantic Ocean just east of the Niger Delta in the Bight of Biafra. The village was surrounded by thick equatorial forest and experiences long rainy seasons and short dry seasons; the rivers provided fresh water. It had good and fertile soil, mangroves, giant trees and thick foliage that lined the waters. The local trade was mainly fishing, farming, ferrying passengers to and from the numerous villages and larger communities by canoes and boats. The water temperature would rise considerably during the dry seasons, which delightfully tied in with our school holidays; there were different kinds of vessels on the river waiting for passengers and traders. When in motion, each vessel had its own characteristics, from the canoes with one or two rowers, which glided in a gentle, but slightly stilted motion, to the small motor boats, whose passengers would have a quicker and smoother journey, including the luxury of a roof to shelter from the hot sun or heavy rain. There were also some steamboats, a lot larger, that would carry many passengers and their cargos, I only remember travelling one of these two or three times, probably when it's was raining too hard or when we were carrying too much luggage for canoes. At the time it seemed very luxurious. The steamboats had smoke constantly billowing from a tall cylinder stack painted in various bright colours with names like 'Blessing', 'Patience', 'Comfort' painted on them. The passengers would sit on benches made of very faded varnished panels of wood; the steamboats would stop and let off their passengers at the tiny ports that led to various villages.

When my grandfather married Nne the majority of his subjects were not pleased about his choice of bride from another tribe or his refusal to take other wives from his own kingdom, The trouble started when his best friend tried to arrange for his ambitious sister to be one of the King's wives, which would have given him more influence with the King. The King refused to marry her, preferring Nne, his beautiful, foreign, young, stubborn and wise Queen who was nobody's fool and who was producing heirs at an alarming rate, though only five survived. Not even the witchdoctor had the power to make her infertile.

When Grandfather's ambitious friend's plot failed, while Nne's children were still very young, King Effiom Coco-Bassey was poisoned by his friend who usurped the throne and determined to take revenge on Nne and her young children. The family was driven into poverty and abused following the usurpers' edict that Nne and her children were to be outcasts. They were ill-treated and pushed out of the village and starved. Finally, they were forced into servitude with another family in order to survive. The children had to work on a farm with the rest of the villagers before which, each day at sunrise, they had to go to a stream, about a mile and half into the dense forest to fetch and carry back the daily supply of water for the whole household. The water was carried in dried gourds; these amazingly beautiful, natural containers were fruits, which grew out of the trunks of the calabash trees, which populated the forests. They are shaped like giant yellow watermelons with outer shells, which become very hard when dried. The villagers would cut the gourds off the calabash trees while they are still soft and cut a round hole to empty out the sweet pulpy mass inside and leave the casing to dry in the sun.

Nne's older sons died mysteriously one after the other, as the new King who, to his annoyance, despite usurping the throne, had still not been accepted as the crowned ruler by the people. He was concerned that the elders might take it upon themselves to appoint one of the Coco-Bassey sons as the natural successor to the throne. After some time Nne made plans to send her surviving children, which included one son under the age of ten and her eldest daughter, my mother, away from the village so they would stay alive. Traditionally, she had to remain with her husband's people after his death and as the wife of a late King she was not allowed to remarry.

Chapter Three: My Mother

The oldest of the surviving daughters was my mother Arit Dorothy Effiom Coco-Bassey who was a very beautiful baby, doted on by her father, whilst he was alive, because she looked so much like her mother. She was very young, only about five years old when her father was murdered. She told us how, on the day he died he appeared to her and picked her up and carried her round the compound pointing out things to her and explaining what they were, what was their use and how and why they worked. This was something she loved him to do. When he carried her back towards the house there was screaming and shouting and she could hear a lot of people wailing. Her father put her down at the door and when she went inside it was explained to her that her father had been murdered in the night. She was amazed because she had just been with him only moments before and he had just put her down at the door. Mummy always wondered how it could be that her father was lying dead in his room when he had just been walking around with her in his arms. This traumatic experience was her earliest memory, but thereafter her father continued to appear to her in her dreams. Arit was distraught about the loss of her beloved father, but she had no way of knowing that for Nne and her children the future was to become a living nightmare.

At the age of ten, little Arit developed smallpox which almost took her life, Nne tried every medicine man she could find and nothing worked, herbalists tried different concoctions, but nothing could make the child better and in a few days she was very weak. Nne braced herself for the loss of yet another of her children, this time, her eldest daughter, whom her dear late husband had loved so much.

While Arit lay dying, she recalled later, seeing her father in a dream; she was standing outside very tall gates of glittering yellow metal. She wanted desperately to enter and while she was wondering how to get them to open, her father appeared at her side and said "Adi,' (this was his pet name for her); "what are you doing here? It's not time for you to be here." She pleaded with him to let her stay, but he told her to go back. Then she found herself back in her bed and all around her were a group of elderly people, more than ten of them, she describes them as being strange and not like the normal medicine men and herbalists. One of the men proffered a foul smelling medicine, which was an odd colour. She naturally refused to take the vile liquid, but then her father appeared standing amongst them and she heard him call her name: "Adi', do as I say, you must take the drink", but she refused and he stressed more forcefully, "you must drink it immediately, I want you to get better." She did as her father told her and drank the medicine. She told us that she was cured by that horrible medicine given to her in her dream, although she had some marks on her body from the small pox, of which she was very conscious, they were actually not visible on her face.

When she woke up the next morning, to her mother's joy, Arit's strength had returned and she was able to eat and was soon better, she was a beautiful and graceful little girl and by the age of eleven Grandmother had turned down a great number of proposals of marriage for her from families and matchmakers. I remember that people who knew my mother from her youth would say she was the most beautiful young lady they knew and she had so many admirers and suitors.

Nne had struggled to feed her children and realising that they were in danger, she placed them all with families in her old village and Arit was looked after by one of Nne's close friends who was very kind to Arit and brought her up as one of her own. After the usurper died Nne's position as the widow of the rightful King was restored, but by then all of her children were grown up.

Nne had four sons and five daughters, three sons died while still young, her only surviving son, (known to us simply as "Brother") had escaped to Cameroon where he lived for the rest of his life. Nne's daughters were my mother, Tim-Nma, Nma Nko, Mina (who was my favourite auntie), she had five sons and no daughters, so we became her daughters and we adored her, and finally there was Christiana. Christiana was very feisty and was always described as troublesome, always combative and was said to have made too many enemies because she faced off trouble (not always a good idea,) but a family trait all the same. She would not shy away from a fight, nor did she suffer fools gladly.

Tim-Nma and Nma Nko spent their lives living in villages near to Ikot Efa, and would visit us occasionally, especially when they needed financial and spiritual help, as our mother, who was wise and caring, was to become their lifeline in every way. I remember Tim-Nma and Nma Nko as very cute older women; they were like the "terrible twins" with mischief in their eyes. I had a great fondness for them, but sometimes felt a little reticent in their presence, because, though our mother was a devout Christian, I couldn't be sure that her sisters were the same. Life in the village can sometimes make practicing being a Christian difficult, since most of the villages were steeped in fetishes and witchcraft.

Chapter Four: My Father and Mother

When my mother met my father, Paul Mathias Ebigwei, he was a good looking, young widower and the local village postmaster. He was Igbo and my mother was Efik, both East Nigerian peoples. Mummy was well known for her natural flare for dressmaking and fashion. She had had only a very basic education, though her pedigree was Royal and this still showed in her demeanour. My mother was in her teens, when she met Papa (our name for my father) at the local post office where he worked and where she frequently posted letters to her brother in Cameroon. Papa was widowed and he had admired her from afar for many months before finding the courage to speak to her. One day when she visited the post office he was behind the counter; she went in to post her letter as usual, but this time he was determined to speak to her. Mummy described their first sweet and innocent conversation.

"Can I help you with the letter." he asked. She nodded.

"Thank you" she said, handing him the letter and coins.

"Don't worry about the money; is this letter for your father in Cameroon?"

"No," she replied. "My father died when I was a child, the letter is for my brother."

She turned to go, but he quickly rushed from behind the counter to catch her at the door.

"I will make sure it is posted for you." he assured her.

She was shy, but liked him and from then on he would always find an excuse to start a conversation each time she visited the Post Office, asking her about herself and her family and eventually he plucked up the courage to ask her for a date. Arit was secretly pleased, but she told him that he had to speak to her mother if he wanted a date and that he would have to get the approval of her people, because the Efik tradition was that if he went so far as to be alone with her on a date, then they would have to be married. He dutifully met with her mother and the elders, his position as postmaster was respectable and so he was considered a good prospect for Arit. The Efik elders asked if Arit would consider a marriage to my father and she was happy to say "yes". Mummy described Papa as handsome, skinny and foreign. He was a lot older than her sixteen years, but she chose him. She had no desire to marry into her own people, owing to their utter wickedness towards her mother. She and her siblings had suffered greatly at their hands.

Soon, it was clear that they would be married. To prepare her for marriage, according to another ancient local Efik tradition, she had to enter "Nkuho" (Ufok Nkuho), the age-old preparation for brides-to-be in the "Fattening Room" where she would be kept in isolation, cared for by elderly women. Apart from instruction from these ladies, she would do nothing, but eat several times a day, sleep and get frequently massaged and her skin polished with palm oils and herbs. The intention was that the Bride-to-be was to eat, sleep and grow rounded and healthy looking. She would be fed Ekpang NKukwo, rice, fufu, plantain, yam, gari, and Afang and pepper soups. (These happen to be my favourite dishes from Calabar.) The idea of the fattening room is to present the wife-to-be to the husband in the best possible state of health and he is then expected to look after her and keep her in that healthy state throughout the marriage.

While they are in the Fattening Room, the girls are mentored and trained by the older women in the marital skills of home cooking, bringing up children, sewing (my mother excelled in this), and how to respect and please their husband and his family. They are even taught how to sit, walk and talk in front of their husband. The older ladies give the girls advice and the benefit of their experiences in marriage to ensure that the girls have a good start in their new role as wives. The girls also learn beauty tips, cultural dances like Abang and Ekombi, they are also taught folktales, folklore, Efik songs and many other forms of entertainment. They may sometimes also go through the Mbobi training, which involves the girls being taught the art of sexual pleasure and, of course, special skills in the bedroom!

Rather like the debutantes in old English society, there is a "coming out" ceremony at the end of the girl's isolation, invitations would be sent out to a great number of people who would be invited to witness the girl's coming out and to applaud her accomplishment in going through the rigours of the training.

For this coming out ceremony, which is also part of the wedding ceremony, the girl is adorned with a special new outfit, complete with ornate headdress, beads, bangles, scarves and body paints in readiness for the dance (Abang) which accentuates and exaggerates the size of the girl's hips and breasts. The graduation ritual is celebrated with much entertainment including the traditional Efik dances. This would last a whole day and well into the night with those invited, members of the family, well-wishers and friends bringing gifts and donations to the bride, to celebrate and rejoice with the family. Towards the end of the ceremony the bride is joined by her husband-to-be, the couple then embrace publicly and also dance to welcome and thank the guests as they cheer the couple.

Not long after my mother's ceremony and marriage to my father, Mummy became pregnant with her first child, Grace. Soon my father was transferred by the Post Office to another part of the country and that was the first time, to her surprise, that my mother discovered that my father was a widower and that there was a child from his first marriage and the child, Felicia, came to live with them. My mother, who was still in her teens, was now a stepmother!

When she was a few months old, their first child, Grace, developed a bad case of Black Water Fever, one of the deadliest forms of Malaria. Black Water fever is caused by malarial parasites. During the 1940s, Black Water fever had the mortality rate of well over 90 percent and it was more likely than not that the patient would not survive, especially if the patient was as young as Grace. She urinated blood. In desperation Mummy and Papa took her to see a German doctor in the local hospital, who treated the baby with every form of medicine he had available before sending her home to die. The doctor, had braced my mother and father for the death of their first child, telling them that there was nothing else he could do for the baby. But, curiously, on the second night after they had taken the baby home, there was a knock on the door of their modest home in Itu, in the early morning; at about 3.00am, my mother recalled, and there stood the doctor in his pyjamas carrying his medical bag. He told them he had been to the hospital laboratory to fetch an assortment of medicine, which he wanted to use to try to save the baby. A few days later Grace was better and had stopped urinating blood. Mummy and Papa took a small gift to the doctor to thank him for saving their baby. It was then that the doctor told them that he had a strange dream. In the dream the baby Grace came to him and told him which medicine to give her and since the combination seemed to make medical sense he thought that he would give it a try. He refused to take the gift saying that the baby had saved herself.

Grace also had another narrow escape from death. One day, neighbours caught Felicia trying to drown the baby in the water tub in the backyard! She had become jealous because the baby was getting all the attention from her father. Felicia stayed with Mummy and Papa until she had completed her primary school education, after that she was sent back to her mother's people.

Papa was constantly being transferred from town to town and he was sent to Onitsha, but his pay was not enough to sustain the family, so Mummy worked all hours making dresses and other clothes and furnishings that people needed, traditional costumes, corsets, wedding dresses, curtains, bed covers, bed sheets, shirts and uniforms in order to supplement the money coming in. She also was adept at making cakes for all occasions. She was very hard working and would often work twenty hours round the clock without resting; including cooking and caring for the family and house. She took on apprentices, training them in dressmaking as the workload got too much for her. Mummy had a great sense of fashion and the local women really appreciated her work. In every town to which Papa was transferred, they would come to her to have their Sunday best and party outfits made. She was very good at making wedding dresses and, of course, the cakes.

But things were not all rosy, my father's family hated my mother because she was not one of them, Nigerians are very tribal, my mother was Efik from the Calabar region and my father was Igbo, both were from the eastern region of Nigeria, but with no similarities in their languages or culture. The fact that she was extremely able, beautiful, the daughter of a King and strong willed, did not help, it created a lot of jealousy and resentment. If she had met my father's family before marrying him, I feel sure she would have reconsidered, but he was handsome, charming and had pursued her tirelessly until she agreed to marry him. She loved him dearly, but the pressure from his family, who had been accustomed to his late, submissive and traditional first wife, became unbearable and, worse still, their hatred was influencing my father and eventually turned him against her.

When my father was transferred to Asaba, not far from Okpanam village, where he was born, the move soon turned into a nightmare for Mummy, My father's family were spreading rumours that she had killed my father's first wife so that she could marry him and she deserved to die herself. They said my father had married a witch from Calabar. They had heard that Calabar was more infamous for witchcraft than other areas of Nigeria. There was scarcely a village, in Nigeria that was free from witchcraft, but women from the Calabar region were known for having some kind of power over men, which was threatening to other women. I believe a lot of this so-called power over men originates from lessons learnt while in Nkuho (the Fattening Room). Mummy was isolated and lonely, but would avoid contact with my father's family; to avoid confrontation. She threw herself into her work and started to worry about protecting her children. The elders of my father's village took it upon themselves to hold meetings in my parent's house, and sometimes they would openly debate the problem of my mother. It was amazing that they thought they had the authority to go to someone else's house to dictate what should be done and how the marriage should be conducted. Mummy kept quiet as she had no one on her side to protect her.

By the time I was born, Mummy had six children: Grace, Johnny, Anthony, Maggie and Rosaleen; her fourth child between Anthony and Maggie was lost whilst still a baby. After me, she had Samuel and my sister Eno with my stepfather.

Chapter Five: My Birth

While Mummy was pregnant with me, her seventh child, the Igbo elders put her under incredible pressure; there was a constant call for my father to marry another wife, one who would understand their culture. Mummy was far from her own people and without support. Finally, she told Papa that he should marry another wife to appease the elders and stop the constant barrage of attacks against her, but he refused. When her time was due to give birth to me she was taken by taxi to the nearest hospital across the River Niger, which was in the next town of Onitcha. Before she could get to the hospital I was born during the ferry crossing and then we were taken to the hospital in Onitcha.

It was a blessing when the family were transferred from Asaba to Aba away from the evil elders, but not far enough for their influence on my father to disappear. I was still a baby when Papa bowed to the elder's demands and started dating a woman of their choice called Regina, who was from his part of Nigeria. Men in Nigeria often have more than one wife, so this was by no means unusual. My eldest sister, Grace, who was old enough to understand what was going on, witnessed the verbal abusive attacks on my mother and how my father's family made her miserable and tried to get rid of her. Grace developed an understandable dislike for the paternal side of our family including Papa Shi Nne my Grandfather.

Plans to break up our parent's marriage had begun as Papa became estranged from Mummy and they would argue a lot. Additionally, there was a lot of stress on the whole family with my father being constantly transferred from one town to another, sometimes only spending as little as six months or less in each place. Wherever the family was transferred to, we would always live in government houses, which were modest but clean. When we were living in government quarters in Park Road, Aba, Mummy had acquired a boutique shop in Pound Road about a quarter of a mile from our house. Regina was doing her best to get rid of Mummy. She, started visiting the house, and Papa was spending a lot of his money on her, buying her clothes and shoes, Regina liked the glittery Indian shoes and dressed very well, she would sometimes spend the night at the house with Papa. My older siblings knew what she did for a living, because whenever they went to the cinema they would see her selling sweets on the side of the road; she was one of the sweet vendors outside the local cinema. There was now a lot of tension growing between my mother and father as Papa continued to spend money on dressing his new woman in all sorts of fine things and planned to marry her, while Mummy worked at the boutique shop, where she would sew and bake to bring in money to make ends meet. My half-sister Felicia had moved back into the house. Mummy had hoped that getting Felicia away from the village might help the two of them to get on better and enable Felicia to grow up happily with her half siblings. Felicia was not responsive to this. She did not get on with Mummy and had no desire to grow up with the rest of us children. She became very destructive, unpleasant and always miserable.

Mummy had agreed that Papa should marry Regina, but not before there was a huge row which ended with Papa threatening Mummy's life and Mummy running away with me when I was about one to hide with one of her sisters who was now married and living in Akwa Ibom. She did not expect Papa to find us, but he did. He traced her to the village and turned up wielding a shotgun, threatening to kill Mummy! Much to Mummy's embarrassment he caused a public scene in front of her family and friends shouting and threatening to shoot her. The entire village came out to watch as the village elders intervened, pleading with Papa to calm down. Mummy was very popular among the villagers because she always brought gifts to the people of the village when she went away. She was well respected and loved by the villagers. Later when we re-visited the village they always used to tell us children how beautiful and different our mother was. To them she was special and had a style unique to her royal background. Mummy felt that she had suffered loss of face and been disgraced in the eyes of her people. The elders finally talked Papa into going home, promising to talk to Mummy and settle the matter. Papa went back to Aba where Regina was now a permanent visitor to the house, though not liked by my siblings, for obvious reasons. But they were too young to voice their opinions.

Mummy decided that she couldn't keep running away or avoiding Papa who was now permanently behaving in a rather strange irrational and aggressive manner. So in order to be near the children, she plucked up courage and returned to Aba, but not to the house where Regina was ensconced. She took a room above her boutique shop in Pound Road, which was in the street behind Park Road where our house was. A wide tree lined path separated the backyards of the houses on both streets. Tradition dictated that all the children were to live with Papa, which was not unusual in that paternal society at that time. Mummy was distraught about this, but was unable to do anything about it. That is why at two years old I had to go back to live at my father's house and would be looked after by my sister Grace who was now 15 years old. My older brothers and sisters were occasionally allowed to go and visit Mummy and sometimes stay the night. Papa, who was now openly living with Regina, had learnt that Mummy had struck up a friendship with a dashing young rising local politician, known to all as SG Ikoku. This drove Papa to distraction.

One day, Papa sat Grace down and quizzed her:
"Would you like to see your mother come back and live here with us?"
"Yes."
"So would I" he paused for a while as though deep in thought, finally he spoke.
"There is something you can do to make your mother come home. If you bring me what I ask for, it will help bring your mother home."
"I want Mummy to come home, Papa. Whatever it is, I will do it" she answered, happy that Papa was at last making plans to get Mummy to come home.
"This is what you must do. I want you to listen carefully to me; when your mother walks on the sand, I want you to gather up the sand from the ground, from the footprints she has made, and I want you to bring the sand from the imprints made by SG's feet as well. Do not touch the sand with your hand, you must pick it up and carry it in a cup or a vessel of some sort." Papa said.
"Yes Papa." Grace replied, puzzled.
Grace was confused and wondered how sand could bring Mummy back, what would Papa want with sand? Although Grace was fifteen she had been protected by her mother from the practices of witchcraft and she knew very little about it. Grace was very reticent and quiet as a child and she told no one about Papa's request, but she was suspicious and she decided to give Papa some sand to appease him so she went into the back of the house where she found an empty sardine can. She broke off the key with the rolled up end still attached and carefully uncoiled a bit of the metal to use it to scoop up a little bit of sand from the corner of the yard, then she poured the sand into a piece of paper and took it to Papa the next day.
"Did your hand touch any of the sand?" Papa asked.
"No Papa."

The following day, Papa called Grace into the house, he unwrapped the paper and put a small amount of it on his tongue and said:
"You see, I just wanted to show you that the sand is completely harmless. Now I have something for you to do. I want you to put a little of this sand in your mother's soup! Do you warm up her soup when you visit her?"
"Yes Papa, of course, I warm up her soup for her when she is busy working." she answered.

She wondered what Papa was thinking, who would knowingly put sand in any food, how would Papa like it if someone put sand in his food? She knew Mummy would be angry if she tasted gritty sand in her food, so she decided not to do as Papa had instructed her. When she couldn't bear keeping the secret anymore she decided to speak with Mummy about Papa's strange behaviour:

"Mummy, I have something to tell you, but please promise not to tell anyone; if you do I will be in so much trouble"

She explained her father's instructions to her.

"Mummy I'm telling you this because someone else might be sent to put sand in your food."

Realizing that this was some sort of witch doctor mischief, Mummy was silent for a while, she looked a bit worried; but made no comment. A few days later she called Grace to her and said:

"Ok, this is what we will do. We will play them at their own game. I want you to put the sand in your father's soup instead and see how he likes it!"

She noticed Grace's reluctance and added.

"It will not do him any harm since any spell on it is supposed to damage me not him."

Grace decided to be neutral and threw the sand away. But as time passed and nothing happened to Mummy, Papa who had been spoiling Grace recently, suddenly changed his attitude towards her. He and Felicia seemed to be watching her closely and she was worried that maybe Papa had suspected that she had not carried out his instructions.

The plan was that something bad should have happened to Mummy by now, making her ill, and it had not materialised. As the days passed with Mummy in rude health, Papa became furious with Grace. He realised that Grace had told Mummy about their wicked plans. Then one morning without warning, Papa ordered my brothers to put Graces' things outside the house. So the boys reluctantly put her clothes into a suitcase and put them outside the house. Meanwhile, Papa was shouting at her;

"Come on, now pack all your things and get out of my house, go and follow your mother! All you are good at is wearing dresses and making iyanga (showing off)! He then threw some of her things into the street and slammed the door.

"Papa, please, I don't want to leave the house." she pleaded, sobbing uncontrollably. But the child knew he was too angry to listen to her; still sobbing she picked up the rest of her things from the street and put them in the suitcase and sat on it outside the house. She was the eldest child and was acting as mother to the other children in the house and she was reluctant to leave them in the hands of Regina and her father in this state of mind. All the other siblings were crying helplessly, begging Papa not to be angry with Grace. They were just children under the age of ten and couldn't do anything to help their elder sister for fear of being flogged by Papa. All they could do was keep out of his way and stand by the door or the window to check on Grace as she sat outside. Felicia, who had been helping Papa, to throw Grace's things outside, added her three-penny worth by hurling abuse out of the window.

"Why don't you go and join your mother, we no want you here!"

Mummy's position was untenable, her hands were tied, all her children, even her baby, had to stay with their father because of tradition. She was doing her best to get to the financial position of being able to take care of the children on her own and get them away from their father as soon as she could. But at this time, this was only a dream. Mummy knew the battle ahead was going to be difficult. It would take Divine intervention for her to get her children away from Papa, who, in the meantime with the vindictive Regina, was hell bent on making life impossible.

Papa had given instructions that no one was to give Grace anything to eat and no one was to talk to her. Grace sat outside not knowing what to do until it began to get dark, she was getting hungry and afraid, having had nothing to eat or drink all day.

One of Mummy's costumers told her she had seen her daughter sitting out on the street on a suitcase, so Mummy set off to find her and as it got darker Grace decided that she had to go to her mother's place, she put her suitcase on her head and went to Pound Road where she found Mummy coming in the other direction.

"I heard your father had put you outside the house since this morning" Mu

"I was getting very hungry and frightened." Grace explained.

Mummy, who was really pleased that her daughter could now be with her told Grace to put her suitcase in the bedroom. Of course, she was concerned about the rest of us still with Papa without Grace to protect us. Deprived of the chance to go to school herself, Mummy wanted her children to have the best education possible and she was concerned that Papa would now refuse to continue to pay for Grace's education, as Mummy would find it hard to find the money. To try to safeguard Grace's education, she determined to keep the peace with Papa. Mummy tried the get Papa to take Grace back for the sake of the other children, but he refused her entreaties, saying that he didn't want her back in his house. So Grace lived with Mummy and Mummy found the money to keep her in school.

"Your father is not interested in educating any of his daughters past primary school standard, because he feels it's a waste of money." Mummy explained to Grace.

As time went on Mummy was not able to keep calm with Papa as she heard that I was not really being looked after very well and she desperately missed me, her baby.

As I was a baby, I cannot personally remember the circumstances of the decision that took me away from Mummy, or how it was that I was living in Papa's house, but my eldest sister Grace tells me that before the divorce which happened when I was three, it was because the Elders of my father's people had decided that all the children including me, the baby, should be given to Papa. I do remember a few traumatic incidents of being taken back by Mummy. Later the matter was decided in the Divorce Court and the Judge, who was a friend of Papa's ordered that all the children should stay with my father. I do remember that one day Mummy came from behind the house sneaked in and tried to carry me away, unfortunately, Papa caught up with her in the wide tree lined walkway behind the houses. There was such a commotion that a crowd gathered, most of whom were on Mummy's side. They tried to prize me from Papa; he was pulling at my legs and Mummy was holding on to the rest of me! The women in the crowd were all shouting at Papa and trying to pull him away.
"Are you not ashamed to be fighting with a woman, how can you struggle with a woman over her child? Leave the child, let the child go!"
Papa was swearing and calling Mummy names.
"She is a harlot, a prostitute, a witch.........!"
"Thank you, husband, after all these years I've been your wife and had your children, it's now that you think this of me!" she replied

It must have been out of embarrassment that Papa let the crowd convince him to let me go, but he was so furious when he went back to the house that he got the police involved who backed him up and so I was taken from Mummy and returned to Papa, I can still feel Mummy's pain, I can't explain it, but I can recall so much of this and the sorrow remains with me.

On another occasion, Mummy came through the back of the house and must have been watching out for a time when I would be left alone. Often my brothers, sisters and all the other children from the neighbourhood would play at the back of the houses. This time it was getting dark and I was toddling about in the path and I remember Mummy grabbing me and putting me on her back, she tied her wrapper round me firmly as she hurried off. Carrying me on her back made it easier for Mummy to run faster. Someone must have alerted Papa as he appeared from nowhere brandishing his hunting rifle. Once again all the screaming drew the neighbours out of their houses, they must have been used to our family dramas by now; some of them hurried to intercept Papa who was chasing us carrying his rifle. He must have been aiming to shoot because the crowd was shouting at him not to shoot;

"Oga, don't shoot you will kill your child. Ah, ah, are you mad! If you shoot the woman you will kill the baby!" Someone else was shouting;

"I beg, make somebody call the police O!

The police were called, and, once again, I was returned to Papa.

One day, while the other children were busy with their chores, I must have decided to find my mother. It was a little before my second birthday, but I was able to walk unaided. Children in Africa walk at very early ages mostly, well before they are one year old. I must have memorized the way to my mother's lodgings during the dramatic comings and goings, because having set off I found my way there. I vividly remember that she cried when she saw me, and later she told me how shocked she was that a toddler had been left to walk unattended through the back yards all the way to Pound Road. She was amazed that I was able to find the house on my own.

They must have realised I was missing at Papa's and assumed that Mummy had abducted me. The police were called and when the police turned up to get me this time, I hid under my mother's white and gold four poster bed, there were so many things under the bed, because she didn't have much room to store her things, that it was easy for me to disappear. The police, out of laziness or just convinced that I was a missing toddler who would still be wandering around the streets, didn't bother to take a close look under the bed. I heard Mummy standing by the door and arguing with a policeman. I had the sense to keep still and not move or make a sound.

"Una no think sey, you for see de child, if de child dey for dis room. I beg una, go look for my child!"

No one had seen my mother in the vicinity of Papa's house that day. The police had been told that she had never left the shop and so the police left.

I remember being afraid to come out from under the bed even when Mummy said the police were gone and had started looking for me in the streets. Then I finally climbed out of the box full of dressmaking fabric ends and accessories, that I had squeezed myself into under the bed,

In the compound I could hear a lot of chattering among the adults, in which my name was mentioned a few times, but none of it made sense to me. I was bathed and fed. I manage to stay with Mummy for a few days that time.

Throughout the years to come, Mummy would recall this story, which served to keep the experience alive and fresh in my mind as she would often talk about how I as a toddler was able to find my own way to her.

Mummy's efforts with Papa were unproductive, as Papa and Regina had it in mind to distribute us children as house helps, to different people. Mummy had taken on Grace's school fees, adding to her struggles, but she did cause enough trouble to publically embarrass Papa into sending the boys to school. As for the girls, Papa argued that the girls should be married off as soon as possible.
"Over my dead body!" was my mother's answer.

Until Papa messed up and fell short of his responsibilities toward us, which he eventually succeeded in doing, my mother could not get us away from him, but through hard work and determination she later achieved her dream to be able to educate us all. As children, we may have sometimes complained about our strict upbringing, but as adults, we all appreciate the spiritual sense of courage, strength, faith and confidence that she instilled in us. She made sure we did not remain victims of the past, that we feared no one, looked down on no one and never felt inferior to anyone.

Chapter Six: The Divorce Court

I was about three. Mummy's relationship with SG Ikoku, was growing stronger. They had a lot in common as they were both going through a divorce; SG from his English wife and Mummy from Papa. As SG lived not far from Pound Road, they saw more and more of each other, SG would often drop in on his way home and sit and chat with Mummy. He was a very handsome, highly intelligent man with dimples and a great sense of humour.

Inevitably Papa took Mummy to court. It was a long drawn out affair with SG named as co-respondent. Mummy denied Papa's accusations of her infidelity. Even SG's English wife was called to the stand on Papa's insistence, but she had nothing to say. The court was always packed, there were many people including us children. The Courtroom was hot from the body heat generated from the crowd and the ceiling fan was struggling to cool the air. In those days the courts were considered to be places of entertainment where criminals were tried and where nasty disputes were settled. There was a good deal of "schadenfreude" and entertainment in abundance while the people listened to one accusation after another painting Mummy as a bad mother, wife and even as a prostitute. The spectators were often vocal, showing their surprise, admiration, shock, amusement, and sometimes anger as Papa laid it on thick with one lie after another. The case seemed to go on forever, Papa's lawyer spoke, the witnesses spoke and the judge had his bit to say. As a child it seemed to me that it would never end, time dragged and the stifling temperature made it seem like the whole world had something to say and each one was against my mother.

Grace was called to the witness stand, the people were whispering among themselves with the occasional "oohs" and "aahs". They were interested to see a young teenager called as a witness in her parent's divorce case, and they couldn't wait for the questioning to begin. They fanned themselves with pieces of paper or handkerchiefs and whatever else would cool their sweating necks and faces. They were not disappointed, Grace was not nervous, the crowd in the court room had given the whole procedure a festive feel and she felt as though she was about to speak her part in a school play. She relished being the centre of attention for a change, as my father's lawyer asked;
"Do you understand about swearing on the bible?"

"Yes, you must not tell a lie."

"Good!" he turned away from her.

"Who is this?" he asked pointing to Papa.

"He is my father."

"And who is this woman?"

"My mother." she replied.

And then the lawyer pointed to SG and asked;

"And who is this?"

"Ah, that's uncle." She smiled.

"Did you write a letter to uncle?"

"Yes."

"In the letter, you wrote 'Dear Father.' Why did you address the letter Dear Father and signed it, Your Daughter?"

"Oh! My parents said I must always show respect, if I am addressing someone older than me. If it's a man, it's "father" and if it's a woman then it's "mother", especially if they have done a lot for me. I was writing to thank him. That's why I called him Daddy."

There was spontaneous applause in the courtroom, Grace instinctively knew, the crowd thought she was a clever girl to have answered the questions the way she did and it made her more confident. The lawyer continued;

"Since this problem between your father and mother started, have you been going to school?"

"Yes, I have going to school……."

Papa, sensing that it was not going his way interrupted, saying he had something to say. The judge allowed him to speak and he told the court that he wanted to stop the case, saying that he had disowned Grace as his daughter and had done so a while ago and that he only has six children; therefore, he did not consider her testimony as relevant. The judge, Papa's friend, after a short deliberation decided that there would be no more of the children called as witnesses as they were too young to be aware of what was going on.

"Are you now admitting to only having six children?" asked the judge.

"Yes Your Honour." answered Papa

"So we are only working on six children"

"Yes."

The decision was made, since Papa was vehemently against us living with Mummy;

"Alright," said the judge. "To settle this matter, all the six children are to be placed in boarding schools and holidays are to be alternated between both parents."

There was a cry from the court as Mummy interrupted;
"What, even the baby?'
"Yes the baby too." answered the judge. Mummy was inconsolable.
"I agree, send them to the boarding house." shouted Papa.
Mummy became hysterical, she ran over to where we were sitting and grabbed me, Papa was equally as fast, Mummy had my arms as Papa was pulling me by my legs, both were shouting at each other and what with the noise and the pulling I became frightened and I started to scream. There was total chaos in the court. But we were all whisked off to my father's house. I remembered the pain as I was dragged away watching my mother sit sobbing helplessly after the judge's decision.

Papa, of course, had no intention of paying for any of us to go to boarding schools. Although he made a show in court of where he was going to send each child, this never materialised.

We lived with Papa and Regina. Mummy's friends advised her to be patient and see what our father did with the rest of us before taking any action that might jeopardise our safety or make Papa send us far away where Mummy would not be able to find us. Mummy immediately appealed against the judge's decision.

Mummy married SG, but Papa would not let go, he would send Mummy false messages about our illnesses real or imaginary, which were designed to upset her. Fights would start whenever Mummy came to visit as a result of these false messages and had come to make sure we were alright. On one occasion a message was sent to Mummy that one of us was critically ill. When she got to the house she found that nothing was wrong. Mummy was startled when Papa got out a koboko (a type of horse whip), which she did not know had been laced with poison. Regina and Papa had bought the whip from the witch doctor. Mummy tried to escape out of the house, but unfortunately the end of the whip caught her on the head. In her panic, while trying to escape, she had a very nasty fall. When she got home everyone was shocked at the state she was in. Her face and lips were swollen from the poison and she looked like a vicious gang had beaten her up. For over three months she was very ill, lots of prayers were said for her. Her head wound caused her terrible pain. After this her friends advised her to keep away from Papa and Regina. Her love for her children was being used to endanger her.

Shortly after this I was allowed to go to live with Mummy and Daddy (SG Ikoku) when Mummy was at last successful in making a number of appeals to the Courts.

When I was five, Mummy had Sammy, my little brother. Mummy would often recall how on the day Sammy was born at the General Hospital in Aba, the hospital main water tank exploded and there was no water in the building. Water had to be brought in from elsewhere by tankers, but only after great distress had been caused.

I thought Sammy was the most beautiful baby in the world and, according to Mummy, I made that clear to everyone. Mummy would often say that I was such a smiley child until Sammy cried and I would get very angry with anyone holding the baby at the time. I do remember a few incidents when I took my revenge on the nearest person to the baby after he cried. I still feel very protective of my brilliant younger brother and will not hear a bad word spoken about him.

Chapter Seven: Milverton Avenue, Aba

In the first year, after my parents' divorce, Regina was pregnant with her first child; the family had to move often to whichever town Papa was posted. Regina was getting more irritated with having Mummy's children around. During that year alone, Papa was transferred to Umuahia, Enugu, Warri and then to Owerri. Mummy used to handle previous transfers seamlessly and had a flare for transforming each accommodation into a home. But with our stepmother, each new home was shabby despite her best efforts, she was not coping well with the constant moves. To solve the problem of the children overcrowding the pregnant Regina, Rosie and, Maggie and the two boys were allowed to go and live for a year with Mummy and me and our stepfather in Aba. Though the older children were at Boarding schools in different parts of the southern region of the country, they all spent the holidays with Mummy. It was one of the happiest and most memorable times of my early childhood.

I was still about 4 years old when Mummy and my stepfather moved house to Milverton Avenue, Aba. This was where they were living when my brother Sammy was born. The house was opposite the railway. It was a beautiful building. My brother Tony was fascinated by birds and used to keep pigeons. For some reason, the birds chose to nest under the over-hanging roof of the neighbouring house. When Tony went back to school, at the end of the holidays, we always thought the pigeons would disappear, which they did. But once Tony returned for another school holiday, the pigeons would also return in their droves. They were not clean birds and Mummy would insist on Tony scrubbing the edge of the buildings, where they made a mess. Tony didn't mind doing this constant cleaning because he loved his pigeons so much.

We had wonderful adventures in Milverton Avenue. Across the road from the house, beyond the forbidden railway tracks there was a large compound where they manufactured products made from palm nuts and kernels. The place was permanently sealed off with barbed wire and was out of bounds to us children. Of course, this made it a challenge. The compound had a large group of mango trees inside the grounds just beyond the railway lines, which bore the most delicious mangos. When it rained heavily they would fall off the trees in their hundreds and we would sneak under the barbed wire, where bigger children had made a hole, and pick up as many of the fallen mangoes as we could carry. Sometimes the caretaker would chase off the children and if caught they would be taken home and severely chastised.

Mummy went back to work; she set up her sewing machines and apprentices on the veranda where she could see everything that was happening while we were playing. There were times when I wondered if Mummy had eyes at the back of her head! Nevertheless, we would often manage to break the rules and get away with it.

Mummy would try in vain to teach Grace to sew, but Grace was never interested, it just was not her thing, though now in retrospect, she wishes she had learnt the skill. Mummy tried to teach us all needlework. Rosie and I took to it, but Maggie and Grace were not interested. Even threading a needle was problematic and somehow Grace always managed to break the needle in the sewing machine. As for Maggie, she lost interest when she was rushed to the hospital because the machine needle had gone through her thumbnail! But it did not put her off being an enthusiastic follower of fashion, as she later became the most fashionable member of the family, attending the Sorbonne and becomes a "fashionista" in Paris.

Grace always thought that Mummy was too harsh on her and as she was the eldest and had all the responsibility for her siblings. She would complain to Mummy's apprentices who were mostly mature wise women;

"In my next life, I never want to be born as the first child, because I get blamed for everything and I'm always told I have to set a good example for the other children. I don't seem to be able to do the right thing. Every time I do something wrong, or even when it's not my fault, Mummy will scold me more than the others."
The apprentices told her:
"She is your mother; she wants the best for you and your brothers and sisters. We all want to run away from our mothers at some point or another. I promise you, when you grow up, you will all appreciate the training you have had from your mother. Your mother is a very strong woman, when you have your own children, you will think back and understand how hard it must have been for the poor woman, losing her children and having to fight a terrible man and his witch of a wife to get them back, and make a new home for her new husband. Just remember the way she has suffered and fought for all of you. She is working hard to make sure you all go to the best schools and can hold your head up in public. You shouldn't cause her any trouble."

Years later, while living in Ikeja, Lagos, like Grace, I remember feeling unhappy about the punishments, especially to do with homework, and the threat of the cane at school. But actually, now I can only remember one such caning at school. Mummy once gave me a smack for disappearing from Milverton Avenue. Now as an adult with my own children, I realise the anguish my mother must have gone through, imagining that something awful had happened to me. I was playing with other children and had not realised how late it was, until it began to get dark. Poor Mummy had the whole neighbourhood out looking for me. When they finally found me, I was a long way from home as I was not aware of how far I had wandered. I was not surprised when I got smacked. I knew I deserved it, after putting everyone through such anxiety. After that, I only had to be threatened and I would toe the line without arguing.

Chapter Eight: Nigeria Independence Day

As Nigerian Independence Day approached; there were many political gatherings at our house in Milverton Avenue, as Daddy was a politician, one of the leaders of the Action Group political party (AG). Dad was an intellectual politician, a very handsome man, a scholar who, fought for Nigeria's Independence in an honest way. He was more interested in helping people and working behind the scenes to improve the lives of people. He was not interested in amassing wealth. As an intellectual, what he wanted most was to acquire more and more knowledge, which he would communicate to others, starting with the family, he also lectured on economics and politics at various universities. Dad wrote books on politics, which are still being used in universities today. He had a great sense of humour and would amuse us with stories from different international political gatherings and quiz us during meals to test our wisdom.

"What is the difference between a wise man and a fool?" Dad would ask, but after we had all given up, he would say.

"A wise man learns from other people's mistake while a fool, learns from his own mistakes!"

Dad also told us years later that; "It is normal to be a socialist when you are young because it shows you have a heart, but to be a socialist after the age of forty shows that you have no brains!" I guess he was past forty when he said that! This was, nevertheless, confusing for me because Dad had obvious socialist/communist leanings and we had lots of copies of Chairman Mao Tse-Tung's 'Little Red Book' at home, with quotes like; "In time of difficulties, we must not lose sight of our achievements," and "Politics is war without bloodshed, while war is politics with bloodshed," also "Women hold up half the sky."

Even when he and Mummy went to a banquet at Buckingham Palace, Dad came home with amusing stories. What I remember now, is how much I admired Dad's intelligence, his mastery of various European languages and his ambition for all of us, which, of course, I fell short of.

There would be elections in 1959 to decide the Government to take over from the British at Nigerian Independence in 1960. I grew up with constant political debate and argument all around me. The guests at the gatherings, at our house were mostly leading lights of the AG. They had heated conversations about politics and the pending elections, which I used to listen to. There would be a lot of disgust expressed, cursing and spitting on the ground at the mention of corrupt British officials rigging the coming elections. It was thought that the British controlled the Northern Emir and his NPC (Northern People Congress) Party. There was outrage as it was rumoured that there had been a secret agreement imposed by the British on the Southern leaders, requiring them not to campaign in the North. All the NPC had to do was sit back, win the North while Parties in the Southern Regions cancelled each other out and vigorously campaigned against each other. This led to NPC election success giving them power over two-thirds of Nigeria and enabled them to form the first Central Government. The Country was split into three Regions which were to have selfgovernment controlled by a Central Government with a three hundred and twelve seat House of Representatives which decided national matters like the Economy, Defence and such like. The mostly Muslim North which had about three quarters of the land and half the population was won by the NPC who also won the Central Government Election with one hundred and thirty four seats despite polling less votes than the Action Group and the NCNC overall. The number of seats to be allotted to the Central House of Representatives was decided by the size of the electorate in each constituency. The Western Region was won by the Action Group which was the area mostly occupied by the Yuroba tribe. The Eastern Region, which was mostly Christian and covered the Igbo tribe, was won by the NCNC.

Listening to the conversations, the names of the iconic leaders at that time were etched into my mind, Dr Nnamdi Azikiwe, Samuel Okotie Eboh, Chief Awolowo, Chief Enaharo, Ahmadu Bello, The Sarduna of Sokoto, Abubarka Tafawa Balewa.

Although my stepfather was an Igbo from the East of Nigeria he was one of the leaders of the left leaning Action Group (AC) which was predominately based in the Western Region, making him unusual as most Igbos were with the NCNC based in the Eastern Region.

 Chief Obafemi Awolowo was Prime Minister of Western Region of Nigeria in 1959. He had built up AG (Action Group) into a national party. In 1962 he was accused of attempting to overthrow the Central Government with eighteen other members of AG and was arrested on a charge of treason. This was nonsense. My stepfather, one of the eighteen, escaped arrest as he was in Ghana.

Daddy, an Igbo, was the Action Group member for the Enyong Division of (Aro-Calabar) and was appointed Leader of the Opposition in the Eastern House of Assembly. He was a very clever and highly educated man and travelled a lot to other African countries especially Ghana where his university friend Kwame Nkrumah was President, he also travelled to Britain, US, Germany, Japan, Russia and later China, effortlessly picking up their languages.

In those last colonial days of the late 1950s we had permanent supplies of electricity, which powered the printing press on the ground floor rooms used as offices by Daddy and his staff. The printing press would churn out pages and pages of AG flyers, with its palm tree logo, to be distributed in different villages and towns. The room housing the large printing press could not be accessed through our living quarters so we were spared the smell of the ink. The walls of the house were so thick that you could not hear the constant chugging and swishing sounds from the printing press.

When Daddy was away, Mummy, who was an elegant and impressive campaigner, would often go on the campaign trail on her own, galvanising the women who were the heart and soul of the towns and villages. The Action Group was finding it difficult to penetrate areas where the NCNC Party, led by Dr Nnamdi Azikiwe, which was predominantly Eastern region based, had the support of the local people in the province of Calabar where my mother was from. There was also a lot of campaigning aimed at the Calabar Township where the people were more inclined toward the Action Group. The tribes in this area were all Efik speaking, which gave Daddy the edge as it was Mummy's native language. Action Group also had success in the county's middle belt and lower North, they successfully campaigned for a programme of free primary education, expansion of the medical programme, which included free medical care for children under 18 years of age and loans to farmers and entrepreneurs.

The AG Party leaders like Daddy, were from the rising professional class of Western educated and business elite, most were Christians and came up against religious discrimination in the Muslim North. There were very few Muslims among the early leaders of AG. In 1957 Chief Awolowo had announced that his government *would "seriously consider the enactment of a law which would make it an offence for anyone to exploit Religion for political ends."* Which has huge prophetic resonances for today. Chief Awolowo believed that a political party based on religion was incompatible with the harmony and equanimity of the electoral process.

***

We were living through one of the most important general elections to be held in Africa: in the most heavily populated country on the continent and one populated by the most ethnically diverse people.

Nigeria's landscape is extremely varied, ranging from thick coastal mangrove swamps and rain forests to dry savannah regions in the far North. It is thought that there are four hundred and thirty four ethnic groups in Nigeria, speaking three hundred and ninety five different languages. The major groups are the Hausa-Fulani, the Yoruba and the Igbo, (though in the South there is an often forgotten fourth largest group, the Efiks) and with about ten other groups they make up approximately eighty per cent of the population.

During the election campaigns in the late 50s, people would gather uninvited at our house, but these were not the serious AG leaders mentioned above, but people from the surrounding area. They expected to be served food, Kai-kai (locally made gin), Star Beer, palm wine to which flies are attracted like magnets. These gatherings were not planned, a well-dressed group of women would arrive followed by another mixed group, all in their Sunday best singing campaign songs of the AG, blessings and whatever else came to mind. We had stacks of chairs in one of the rooms, which would be set up as each group made themselves at home. I don't know how Mum managed it, but she would organise food, drink and chin-chin (biscuits) for these groups of supporters who would sometimes number up to a hundred men and women with a few grumpy looking children in tow. The adults entertained themselves by singing and dancing, led mostly by the women. The men would exchange jokes and stories as they drank and ate the rice and stew and fried plantain. Some of the women would go into the kitchen in the middle of the compound and help with the cooking and serving. I noticed that a lot of them would serve their husbands first before serving others. Some neighbours would seize the opportunity for a free meal and join the party. When the food and drinks arrived, one of the eldest would take it upon himself to say grace, blessing the owners of the house, the family, the election campaign, praising Mummy as a wife like no other, with the strength of a man, wisdom well beyond her years and the beauty of a goddess. Then as always, once he had the stage and a few "Amens" had been thrown in from the listeners there was no stopping him and the crowd was in for a 40 minute speech if no one had the gall to stop him. Usually, however, one of the older women, perhaps the speaker's wife would gently nudge him;
"Ozi go" ("That's enough")

He would obey and round off in five minutes, but not in time to stop a few heads nodding off to sleep. A lot of these people had had a long day at the market in the heat of the day and were tired and hungry. Electioneering politicians became a source of regular meals at least once a week. Whether these freeloaders would actually vote for the particular party or politician who was entertaining them was, however, suspect. Their main concern was the free food and drink that the campaigning politician was willing to provide in order to win their votes and support.

Throughout his life Dad would remain very vocal about the state of corruption and corrupt officials during several administrations in Nigeria, earning him many bouts in prison and house arrests.

I have one vivid and horrifying memory of these elections. One day, when I was five, the headmistress came into my classroom and interrupted the lesson to speak to my teacher. The teacher called out my name and asked me to follow the headmistress who led me to her office and said we had to go home and that a vehicle was waiting to take me and my sister home. She explained that trouble had broken out in town and we had to get home as soon as possible. I can't remember how many of us were in the jeep, but I remember that my sister Rosie was with me. We climbed into the back. It was one of the Action Group campaign jeeps with the large palm tree logo painted on either side.

The driver and one of the men who worked for Dad's political party explained that there were clashes in town and people were being killed by mobs wielding machetes, clubs and throwing stones. They were going to find another way home to avoid the mob. They would have managed it if they had not unwittingly brought the campaign jeep with the Party's logo emblazoned on it. To the angry crowd made up of supporters of another party and troublemakers, the jeep was an obvious target with 'enemies on board!' We turned around a corner and saw a mob of well-armed people carrying machetes, sticks, stones and knives all rushing towards us. The driver held his nerve as he realised they were supporters of a rival political party. He shouted at us to lie low and cover ourselves with the tarpaulin. The noise was terrifying as the crowd closed in around us, the thunderous roar of an ocean of hate. We were huddled under the tarpaulin paralysed with fear listening to the angry mob and their animal screams. People were pounding on the sides of the jeep. It seemed to last forever. I was frightened when I looked down and saw warm blood on the back of my arm and noticed that it was dripping from my face, yet I felt no pain. I thought: "dying is easy" and "there is no pain." The driver roared through the mob at great speed. But how we got away down a side road can only be described as a miracle! We arrived home in a battered jeep. It was then that we realised that our poor driver had had his head split open with a machete, yet he managed to stay in control of the jeep and got us home. His head had been struck in two places and his brain was partially visible. It was his blood that had splashed onto my head. He lost consciousness shortly after we arrived home and was rushed to the hospital, we were told that they managed to save his life, but the huge scars would be with him for the rest of his life. I don't remember seeing him again, but I have never forgotten his bravery that saved our lives.

Chapter Nine: Strong Sisters

I do not remember the Election Day for Nigerian Independence. All I can recall is the build up to the elections, the clashes between the supporters of the main political parties and, of course, the incident with our driver in one of those clashes. I remember that my older sisters were excited about the election and protected me from the crowds at the meetings in our house. I remember how they looked after me at school. I remember one ordinary school day my favourite teacher, who suffered from epilepsy, had an attack in the classroom while teaching us. All of us children were so frightened. For five or six year olds and under, to witness their pretty and kind teacher convulsing on the concrete floor and foaming at the mouth in front of us, without warning, was such a fearful shock that we will never forget. Hearing our screams, all the other teachers came in to help and I saw one of them push a ruler between her teeth; he seemed to be so rough with her, but now I know he had no choice if he was to save her tongue. They hurriedly ordered us out of the room.

There were two long buildings making an L shape, each of them housed three or four inter-connecting classrooms, mine was the Nursery One classroom, a typical classroom with a blackboard mounted on the wall. The classrooms were not painted; just rendered with plaster. Every morning, when we arrived, we would all play outside until the school bell rang. We would then form neat lines in front of our designated teacher. Classes ranged from Nursery One (for ages four to five years), to Primary one to five (for ages six to eleven years). I remember hating my early experience of school life because of bullies who picked on the younger children when the teachers were not looking. That was until my sister Maggie developed a reputation for kicking ass and being wild and fearless.

"I will tell my sister on you," became my favourite phrase for anyone who threatened and frightened me. Maggie in action was quite something to see. Once when we were on our way home, taking the usual short cut through a long tree lined walkway. The walkway was wide enough for a car to drive through, though no cars ever did, These walkways behind the houses were commonly used in those days as the rear entrance to each compound and afforded some privacy with low hedges, mango, orange and other trees. This was where a group of boys, loud-mouthed bullies, who were quite a bit taller than my two sisters, were waiting to taunt us. At first we tried to ignore them, but I think they must have said something that made Maggie snap, because suddenly, quite without warning Maggie and Rosaleen were laying into them, hitting, scratching, kicking and throwing sand in their eyes. When one of them tried to grab me for protection from the raining blows, I sank my teeth into his arm as hard as I could. It was all over in a flash and the boys ran off, although one ran the wrong way and had to come back passed my sisters who were on to him again like demons, he managed to escape brushing the stinging sand out of his eyes and mouth. I was so proud to have played a part in this fight, but later I felt sick with fear knowing that we would be seeing them at school the next day. I wondered what they would do, would they pick on me when my sisters were not around to get their own back. My sisters were so brave, so I didn't tell them about my worries and I kept my fears to myself.

"Stupid boys, they think they are strong just because they are boys, next time I'll kick them between the legs and see how powerful they feel." Maggie spat the words out between nervous laughter as we walked back home.

"Don't mind them," added Rosaleen, dragging air noisily over her teeth. I ran ahead laughing and imitated the boys like monkeys running away. My sisters have always been my heroines, after the bravura performance on the way home those boys and other bullies kept a safe distance between us and them.

Chapter Ten: Hospital Visits

I was a very thin child, my arms and legs were skinny, my eyes were big, but so was my stomach which protruded after a meal, much like a pregnant woman whose stomach has stretched almost to breaking point just before she is due to give birth. Mummy was worried that I was not putting on weight no matter how much I ate. The volume of food I ingested appeared not to have any effect on any parts of my body except my stomach, so there were quite a few inconclusive trips to doctors. My aunties and visitors would make comments about my big eyes and skinny body.

"Patricia, de no de give you enough food?" our visiting aunties would ask, to everyone's amusement.

"Maybe this child get tape worm oh!" aunty would continue.

"Sometimes I wonder myself and I have taken her to see the doctor many times, but they say she no get worms."

I would sit on the chair uninterested, with my back hunched, legs swinging, my head tilted to one side, they may as well have been talking about one of the dogs. I would frown at the mention of the word "doctor". My mind wandering back in time to past painful encounters with doctors, so much so even today it's hard for me put into words what the name, doctor, conjures up in my mind. I definitely had not had good experiences with doctors.

When we lived in Aba in the Eastern Region I had some terrible encounters with doctors. I am sure some of them were brilliant. I do know, however, that they saved my life a few times and it certainly wasn't their fault that anaesthetics and painkillers were not easily available in those days. I have to admit I was definitely more accident prone than my brothers and sisters. One time I got barbed wire caught around my ankle and a piece of the sharp end penetrated the joint on the inside leg. It took a very painful ten minutes before the children I was playing with managed to free me from its grip. The barbed wire was erected all around the Palm Kernel factory opposite our house and was out of bounds so, despite the pain, I said nothing to my mother for a couple of days because I knew she would be angry with me for disobeying her by playing in a forbidden zone. Every time Mummy saw me hobbling, she would say;

"Patti come here, why are you walking like that?"

"It's nothing Mummy." I would lie.

"Then stop walking like something is wrong with your leg."

"Yes Mummy."

I avoided walking in front of Mummy and would stand on one leg whenever she was about. The pain was steadily becoming unbearable and still I did not tell Mummy and I pleaded with the maid not to give me away. On the third morning I could no longer get out of bed, the inside of my ankle was swollen and full of puss, and a fever had set in, the maid had no choice, but to tell Mummy who was furious with her and me. I was bundled into the car and driven to the nearest hospital, Mummy was so angry with me all the way to the hospital saying:
"Are you trying to kill yourself uh?" and "Why are you always causing me so much trouble?"

To be any kind of trouble to my mother was the last thing I wanted. I was in too much pain to tell her, so I could only look at her apologetically, grateful for the ease of lying in her arms as she looked worried, gently rocking me back and forth in the back of the car. When we got to the hospital, the doctor told Mummy.
"Mrs Ikoku, we have no more anaesthetics left, normally we would need to put her to sleep for this operation. We must perform the operation immediately or she will lose her foot, but we have nothing to ease the pain for her."
"Do whatever you have to." said Mummy.
"We will need two people to hold the child down, it will be very painful for her, but I will try to be as quick as I can."
"My driver will help." said Mummy
She turned to the driver "Obi ngwanu!" ("Obi, let's go!")
"I will cut into the ankle to clean out the infection." continued the doctor, as he turned to wash his hands and put on a hygiene mouth guard. If I was listening I would not have cared, I just needed the pain to stop.

The doctor asked another male staff member to lend a hand. I clung onto Mummy as the doctor picked up a sharp scalpel, I remember thinking "What is he going to do with that?"
But Mummy very quickly turned my head away. A moment later I let out a piercing scream as the blade bit into my wound, I kicked out my leg, catching the doctor in the chest knocking him back on to the sideboard sending all the sterilised equipment flying in all directions. As he cut into my ankle the two men holding me down could not believe the strength of a five year old in pain. I landed on the floor and tried to get up to run out of the hospital. Everything happened so fast and in a moment I was back on the table, there were now nurses carrying fresh instruments and people holding me down as he cut and dug into the wound. I was still screaming,

but it was no longer piercing just hoarse and guttural, I would have sunk my teeth into the nearest person for revenge if I had the chance. The doctor worked through the wound, which was now a hole the size of 10p coin. The final straw came when he poured iodine into the wound. I could take no more and passed out. When I finally awoke, Mummy was sitting next to me in the hospital holding my hand. My leg was bandaged up and throbbing. I do not remember whether I had stitches, perhaps the hole was too large. My clothes were soaked through with sweat, Mummy was dabbing my brow, but I wasn't as feverish as I had been earlier in the day, I looked around the room, there were four ceiling fans blowing the smell of disinfectant around the room and mercifully cooling us down. I was calm now.

Outside, I could see the garden with different flowers of all colours, marigolds, bougainvillea, frangipani, hibiscus, even banana plants and lots more. It was still daytime.
"Patti, Pat, would you like some ice cream?" Mummy wasn't angry anymore.
"Yes please Mummy." My voice was still gruff and hardly audible.
Mummy went to fetch the ice cream and I tried to sneak a look at my throbbing ankle, but it was well bandaged up, neatly wrapped in white dressing.

Mummy took me home that day and I had to be carried around for the next few days and carefully bathed, Mummy did not let me out of her sight except at night, and even then I was in her room, on a make-shift bed. I was not happy with the pain, but I loved those few days of pampering and having mummy's attention.

I hated the visits to the doctor for him to clean the wound and change the bandages, but I was fascinated that the hole in my ankle was getting smaller after every visit. Soon I saw only the nurses as the wound got better. Some of the nurses were very gentle, whilst others were just brutal and then I would scream throughout the treatment. Eventually, the hole closed up completely and started itching as it healed.

As I got slowly better I was really looking forward to playing our favourite games like hide and seek, make-believe cooking etc. with my sisters and the children living in the compound and neighbouring houses. Our compound in Aba was a very large E shaped building, but without the middle bit. From the driveway the property was a double fronted house with large double wooden doors in the middle with two wide windows on either side of the doors. Above the front doors, on the first floor, were double doors onto the balcony. On the left of the double doors were two French windows leading from the living room (which we called the parlour) and from the dining room to the covered balcony which ran all around the whole house. The front doors were always open except at night, and led to a hallway with a mosaic floor leading to a wide and straight staircase up to the first floor. On the landing, to the left was a door that led to Mummy and our new stepfather's quarters consisting of a dressing room and bathroom, which led to their bedroom.

On the other side of the landing, were three rooms, a kitchen and shower room. Whenever I was ill, which was often, the maids slept on a floor mat in the room, which I shared with my older sisters, to watch over me. My two older brothers Johnny and Tony had their own rooms. Mummy would cook on the kerosene (paraffin) stoves, but none of the maids were allowed to use the stoves, owing to the danger of setting the house alight. Instead they would cook downstairs on wood fires with iron tripods in the kitchen in the side buildings, away from the main building. The front entrance was ours and so the families occupying the back had access to their apartments at the back of the building through a side gate that led into the inside of the compound. There were three other families living in the compound. The Balcony on the first floor made it possible and fun for us children to climb in and out of each other's windows even though this was not allowed.

My wound was healing fast and soon I would be joining the children again in playing outside instead of being stuck sitting next to Mummy while she was on her sewing machine. Even at the age of five, Mummy would involve me in the sewing, often she would ask me to hold the end of a folded fabric while she cut the fabric in two with a pair of scissors. She was so fast with the scissors that I would drop the end quickly before I imagined that the scissors would reach my fingers. Mummy would laugh at me and it became a game that we played. It was difficult for my little fingers to hold on to my end with Mummy tugging at the other end to keep the scissors and fabric in a straight line. I did enjoy helping mum do her sewing and continued to get better at it as I got older. However, I was always impatient because there were a hundred and one games I wanted to play with my friends, but bandaged up and not able to play much, meant I had to sit with Mummy and watch the other children playing outside.

Once in a while, I would be allowed to sit near and listen to the incredible His Master's Voice Gramophone with a brass horn and wind-up handle that produced amazing sounds from a vinyl turning on the turntable. The Gramophone was just inside the parlour by the door to the balcony and I could see it from where I was sitting. It would play my favourites

"Tennessee Waltz" by Jim Reeves or Louis Armstrong (Mum's favourite) and when Daddy was home it would be Benny Goodman, Tchaikovsky, Beethoven and others. The Gramophone had a picture on it of a dog that appeared to be listening, I assume to "His Masters Voice". I loved to watch the record going round and round and I would wait for the scratchy noise it mad e when the music came to an end. I would anticipate the next record, but I was not allowed to touch the gramophone, in case I scratched the vinyl, which would make the record 'jump' each time you played it.

In the rainy season, rain would come without warning and one day there was a sudden downpour accompanied by very loud thunder and lightning. The loud thunder did not frighten us as children because it was part of the monsoon rainy season and we were used to thunder and, we always greeted the storms with great excitement. On this particular day, there was more than the usual excitement induced by the louder than usual thunder claps and the heavy, warm rain creating huge puddles, which we were eager to go and jump in. Of course, in the back of our minds there were the falling mangos to secretly collect from the forbidden zone. Mummy was on her sewing machine on the balcony as usual, I can't remember what I was doing at the time, all I remember is that I got halfway down the mosaic staircase when lightning struck the house or rather it came through the open front doors and dragged me down the rest of the stairs through the open doors across the front drive on to the road, dumping me just before the railway lines. All I remembered was my mothers' screams; she later told me she thought I was dead, as I lay there unconscious, with my body in a strange and twisted position. I was bundled into a car and taken to the hospital where they dug out little pebbles from my legs and a small stone from my right hip. I didn't remember any of the treatment, thankfully, because this time I was anaesthetised. Most of my wounds healed extremely well with the exception of one caused by a small stone which had embedded itself deep in my right hip, just above the thigh where it left a lasting scar. Being struck by the lightning was a rapid and odd experience, "quick as a flash!" You might say, but the unpleasant ensuing treatments at hospital would stay with me for a very long time.

"Patricia is such a "tomboy", I don't know what to do with her!" Mummy would say to visitors as she slapped the back of one hand into the palm of the other, a gesture of helplessness.
"When will you learn to play like a girl, eh?" My mother would ask.
"Every time we see her, some part of her body is bandaged up. Even the boys are not so bad." remarked one of the visitors, as she fanned herself with a pretty round shaped fan decorated with fish of different colours. The fact that the ceiling fan was cooling everyone else in the room made me

think that maybe she was overheating because she had malaria. A disease I also had which caused a few hospital visits. I would feel hot one minute and shivering cold the next. I am still troubled by it today usually peanuts would trigger a bout. I would sit there wondering if this particular auntie was going to feel cold soon, but she didn't and so my mind wandered back to the noise of the other children playing outside.

"Ah, maybe she should have been born a boy." said the other visitor.

"Too late now." I thought.

"Come here my dear, let me look at you."

"Oh no, here we go!" I approached her slowly.

"Do you want to be as beautiful as your mother?"

I nodded in response.

"Then you have to stop playing rough games ah, or you will be covered in scars and nobody will marry you when you grow up."

I remained expressionless eager to go out and join the children or at least watch them play.

"You understand?"

"Yes Auntie." I lied.

This particular Auntie, like most of those that visited Mummy, either socially or to have a garment made, was not a blood relation, but in our custom it is rude for a child to address an adult by his or her first name, therefore, we address adults as auntie, uncle, sister, and brother, Mr or Mrs.

One day, I was playing with a few of the children of my age who lived in the compound. On some days when it was too hot and muddy to play outside after the rain had gone, we would often play on the balcony and chase each other or run from one end of the balcony to the other. Usually, we would leave the windows only slightly open giving us room to run and play unhindered. During such a playtime, as I came running round a corner, I was caught by the sharp edge of an open window causing a deep gash in my head; the impact would not have been so bad if someone had not secured the window in the open position. I was back in the hospital and this time they had to shave my head, and it required a lot of people to hold me down again for this treatment, which involved the dreaded iodine, stitching and a painful tetanus injection, after which I developed a deep and lasting fear of injections of any kind.

My visits to the hospital were interminable; I seem to have spent my early childhood getting to know the hospital buildings well. When I visited a village where there was no hospital I would be carried bleeding or moaning to some remote dispensary providing basic medical care to the surrounding villages where I would be patched up, always successfully. The nuns and doctors who ran these dispensaries were always so caring and kind to us.

***

As I grew older and into my early teens, I would often get into trouble with Mummy for ruining my dresses. For climbing trees I turned my pretty dresses into makeshift shorts by passing the front of my full skirt between my legs to the back and grabbed the edges to tie them at the front of my waist. It made the dresses look like baggy jodhpurs. This was the only way I could kick the ball or cope with the rough tackles without tearing my skirts during play times. On Sundays we would play outside the church, after service. While the adults were holding their meetings inside the church, the children would play outside until the parents were ready to go home. Mummy would be furious when she came out and found me with my Sunday best skirt tied up around my waist, covered in mud.

Chapter Eleven: Life in the Villages

My sisters and I went to the village, Ikot Efa, to visit Grandmother at least once a year from the time I was about five to eleven years old. After the usurper had died, my Grandmother had been restored to her respected position as the old King's widow and she lived in the largest house in the village. To get to the village we had to travel for hours, leaving the city at 6.00am. It was planned to arrive in the village before dark, having travelled by car through towns and villages where hawkers literally surrounded the cars as they slowed down in the inevitable traffic jams. We would make nine or ten stops before arriving in a town by the river where we were set to board three canoes. We arrived worn out from the long journey. These canoes were long and narrow and sat so low in the water that it looked as though they might sink under the weight of all our luggage and the big bunches of plantain and gifts for Grandmother bought on the way. When the canoes were laden, they were dangerously low, only about two inches above the water, making it feel as though, you were actually sitting on the river itself. Nevertheless, I still preferred the canoes to the bigger passenger steamboats, just so I could watch a canoeist skilfully jump on board having waded from the riverbank and pushed the canoe free of the sand and mud. He would then precariously balance at the rear end with a very long pole to push the canoe full of passengers away from the shore and into deeper waters. Once in the centre stream he would sit down at the pointed end and pull out a wooden paddle from the bottom of the canoe and start rowing, with every muscle on his arms and chest moving in an endless and perfectly choreographed dance. The canoe men were like athletes, slim and muscular, which was not surprising considering the amount of cargo and passengers they had to carry on a daily basis. We would chat with excitement whilst the canoeist looked on with a vacant and distant expression. As we glided down the river in the packed canoes it was great fun to leave our fingers trailing in the cool water as we made our languid way through the water. The powerful canoeist's paddles skilfully causing only gentle waves. The scary stories would start about crocodiles and snakes and other creatures that lived in the river and the forest, but we were not afraid, we had heard it all before. The river would reflect what little light was left in the day. The passing trees would grow darker as dusk started to settle to the strident constant murmur of the crickets, the laughter of the monkeys and the sounds of the jungle. An occasional large bird would clatter through the branches as we slid softly through the living jungle, as though carried on a gently swaying crib. After about thirty minutes into the journey, the canoe would be manoeuvred towards a clearing where three or four load bearers would be waiting to carry our luggage about a mile into the jungle to Grandmother's village. I remember wondering how they knew that we were coming; there must have been some kind of drums message system. I would remind myself to listen out for the drums next time we made this journey, but I always forgot to keep an ear out for them; I was too excited to be going back to the village and looking forward to freshly roasted corn on the cob, fresh fish, pineapple, pounded or roasted yam, plantain and palm oil, all my favourites to this day. There would be much noise and singing as the boats were unloaded and we would anticipate the happy trail into the jungle to the village. Our arrival would cause a great commotion and Nne Kamba would rush to greet and hold us. The first evening was always the best, as we all babbled together about our news and she roasted fresh fish for us on the open fire stove. Getting used to the pit toilets was easy. As a child; you take those things in your stride as you find them. I tried it recently as an adult on a trip to Africa to open a clinic for my charity and it came as quite a shock. I wondered for a moment why I had such fond memories of holidays in the village. But then I'm sure it was the dances and stories by the campfire or maybe the ethereal and musical singing on the way to fetch the water from the river in the very early morning. Or maybe it was the smell of fried plantain and fresh fish, barbequed on an open fire after the spectacularly colourful fishing festivals on the river. I am so glad Nne Kamba did not like living in the busy towns. She loved us all and was so pleased to have us with her during our school holidays.

I loved the times we spent in both my mother and father's villages. At my father's village, Okpanam, not far from Asaba, they spoke Igbo and at my mother's village, Efik was the language. These languages have nothing in common, but we children learned them both. While Ikot Efa was not far from rivers and springs, Okpanam was more inland, both were surrounded by jungle which made for lots of adventures provided by nature. In Okpanam the thatched roofed huts were mostly built with mud. Some consisted of one room and an outside seating area. However, our paternal grandfather's house was built with bricks and had a tin roof and a veranda, a large living room, and three bedrooms. The outside walls were painted a creamy colour, which had turned red in places from the rain throwing up the dust created by the red iron oxide saturated soil.

During the monsoon season the heavy rain used to cause a mud slide on a big slope in the jungle just outside the village. This was perfect for us children to go mud skiing down the hill. The village children would cut down leaves from the banana plants, which made very good sliding carpets.

We would place a giant leaf at the top of the slope on the edge and then sit on it and glide twenty feet down to the bottom. Most of us would be naked or just wearing knickers. We would climb back up to the top using the trees as leverage, our bodies' red with the sticky mud. Other times we loved to play kickboxing and wrestling and I became one of the best.

There were forbidden parts of the jungle, with its enormous trees, which were said to be full of wild animals, strange creatures, human bones and evil spirits. The older children told us about places where people, who offended the village headman, were beheaded, and the disobedient wives of the Obi's (Nobles) were killed. They said that, fatally ill people were left to die in the jungle. It scared us, but whether any of this was true, I doubt. Nevertheless, we were warned not to touch any of the offerings or the fetishes left in the bush.

Grandmother used to tell us stories similar to the European fables of vampires and witches that can take any form, mostly of animals, in the dead of night. She told us how the spirits of ancestors can takeover children. Such children are known as 'Ogbanje' (Spirit child) who are said to have a pact with the spirit world and, therefore, end up being sickly and die young. Those who live past a certain age are troubled and haunted by the spirits. Amazing myths and mysteries were woven around the spirit child who is said to possess prophetic and other powers. Such children were given tribal markings in an attempt to mark them so that they could be recognised should they be born again into the same family or village. To make these tribal marks, a mixture was made of ground charcoal together with the toxic resinous fluid, a poisonous acid notorious for causing blisters on the skin, known as 'cardol', contained in the cells found at the honeycombed end of the cashew nut fruit. An incision would be made in the child's skin and a small amount of the thick mixture would then be applied to the cut so that the scar would be black in colour and would widen to the shape of the original application. With care, the rest of the fruit is edible and is delicious. I loved the cashew fruit which only lasts for a day before it becomes inedible when the poison takes over, so I was always careful not to pick them myself, but to pay a small fee to a nearby vendor who may have picked them off the same tree, but had skilfully removed the toxic element.

As a baby I was very sickly and was therefore given a tribal mark just in case they lost me to the spirit world. Mummy was distraught at being told that her baby might be a spirit child and might not survive unless a ceremony was performed to break any bond with the spirits. I am grateful to her for not allowing them to cut deep marks or make a big incision because the place they chose for the marks was my face, but Mummy had the strength of character to put her foot down about the markings, They cut on both of my cheeks, which looked like tiny leaves as I was growing up, but they faded as I grew older and now only slight scars remain. Mummy apparently refused the usual negotiating of ritual offerings to the spirit world, which included a quest to find the binding tokens of the spirit world, sacrifices, offerings, making of promises, puzzles, gifts and other things. She considered all such things as demonic. She always said; "You never know what evil is awakened by such rituals." Although I almost died of malaria a few times and had many accidents, I was definitely not a spirit child, but my mother said that she sometimes wondered, because I was quiet, distant and a tomboy prone to accidents whilst playing with other children.

When I was no older than eight or nine, I witnessed a frightening Obganje ritual at Okpanam. It had been a hot sunny day, but the sun was just going down and the villagers had come back from a hard day at the farms and markets, the women had done the cooking, fed the family, the children had washed the multi patterned metal plates and had stacked them up in a corner of each hut together with the pots and pans. Food was cooked daily because there were no fridges, any left overnight would go off by the morning. The children were outside in the middle of the village playing; some were skipping and singing, laughing, clapping and cheering every time a child would continuously skip for more than the count of forty. We took turns at swinging the long rope, one at each end. The trick was never to let the swinging rope stop at any time and we all took turns running into the centre and jumping over the rope as it hit the ground. After a while we were able to begin to choreograph a jumping dance routine. It was great fun if there were two and sometimes three of us in the middle following each other's moves. Two or three children counted and the rest created a chant inspired by the skipping rope rhythmically catching the dry earth.

Suddenly the fun came to an end when a few of the mothers called their children away to mind their baby brothers or sisters. All the adults seemed to be walking hurriedly in the same direction. I asked the woman I was following, what was happening; she had just rushed out of one of the thatched huts tying a scarf on her head and shouting in Igbo at her children not to leave the baby alone at any time, she turned around and told me to go back and play with the other children. I turned away, but my childlike curiosity got the better of me and I hid behind a hut and then followed her at a distance.

A few days previously my sisters and I had heard the adults talking about a ceremony, which was to be arranged by the family of one of the children. Grandfather told us that it was all nonsense and that we should not listen to such rubbish. However, I was curious and on that visit to the village I had seen a baby boy circumcised and when I had cut my foot on a broken bottle my own wounds had been forcedly treated with a red-hot knife to prevent infection. What could be worse! I felt I had to go and watch, maybe someone else would be on the hot end of a knife. I wanted to see how bravely they would bear it.

I quietly followed the adults as they took a path leading to a clearing in the forest. There were many people there already standing in front of a hut, which belonged to the local witchdoctor. Outside the hut were all kinds of fetishes and carved images with dried blood on them, rings of white stones, jars and pots with dried up remains of food or something worse in them, fruits, animal paws, cowry shells, weather worn beads, which must have been once very colourful, hung around the necks of wooden dolls with white faces and staring eyes.

The crowd, that were already gathered, stood behind a ring of women all dressed in white, some of them wearing wrappers above the chest and some were bare-chested, but all had white painted patterns, bird shapes, dots, triangles, fish and other shapes on every bit of exposed skin. Some of the paint was getting smudged with their sweat. The sun was now behind the trees and disappearing into the horizon, the air was humid and still with little or no breeze. Just outside the witchdoctor's hut, three musicians were waiting, looking menacingly bored or spaced out. Their eyes seemed to be strangely wider than normal. Nobody moved except to swat the odd fly and there were many flies. Everyone seemed to be focused and silent. Another child had followed me. She was a little older than me and was one of the children from the skipping game. We hid behind a bush out of sight. I was glad of the company. We did not want to make a sound, for fear of being spotted, as the atmosphere was very menacing. There was something odd about the stillness of the adults, which added to our apprehension. My companion's eyes were wide with fear and confirmed the foolishness of my decision to follow the adults in the first place.

We had no choice, but to continue watching since any movement would have been seen or heard. Two women in white led a little boy aged about nine or ten, out of the hut. He was covered in white powder from his head to his toes with the exception of his lips. It was hard to see if he was frightened in any way. He was directed to sit cross-legged on the red earth. In front of him was a monkey skin with the tail still attached. On the skin was some food, bits of yam, plantain, kola nuts, a gourd containing palm wine, to which the flies were drawn and a bowl of palm oil. Two gong bells were placed one on either sides of the skin with another bowl containing a few beads. There were pebbles of different shapes and sizes, small animal bones, an empty broken clay pot and some ornaments. There was a live chicken lying on its side with its legs bound with white strings; it was twitching and its eyes were afraid.

The drummers began to drum a slow rhythm and the witchdoctor pranced out of the hut, wearing a dirty, uneven animal skin with lots of beads and all kinds of bits of dead animals hanging off his waist. His skin and face had weird patterns made with white paint. He had raffia around his neck some of which almost reached his waist. The raffia was strung on a string and tied at the back of his neck. He wore strange necklaces of all kinds of bones and teeth including a skull that looked like that of a baby, but was probably the skull of a monkey. All in all he looked like something out of a terrifying nightmare. We should have just run away at this point, but we were too afraid to move.

The witchdoctor muttered something then picked up a bunch of herbs and doing a jerky demonic jig, dusted his left and right shoulders with the herbs and began chanting. He sang in a nasty little voice through the ritual with occasional answers that sounded like 'doh' from the crowd. My eyes widened and my throat gave an audible gulp when the witchdoctor wrung the chicken's neck and stuck a knife in the neck vein and began sprinkling its blood around the boy and himself. When he put the chicken down on the ground it was still shaking and moving. The drummers increased the tempo.

The boy began to sway where he was sitting and soon his swaying became frantic and he was soon rolling and thrashing about on the floor seemingly with strength far beyond his age. The white powder, sweat and blood (his or the poor chicken's blood I couldn't tell), were distorting his features as he leapt to his feet and started cavorting around. The boy scratched his face and body as part of his frenetic whirling dance. The people began to chant: "ogbanje me ozigbo, ozigbo ogbanje, ogbanje", (make haste spirit child, make haste!)

The crowd began to sway to the rhythm of the child as if in a trance, and the drumming had become erratic and was now a cacophony of improvisations over the basic tempo, I noticed for the first time that the boy and the monkey skin were set in a big circle created by white stones on the ground.

The chanting from the crowd grew faster as the boy fell to the ground and rolled around spurred on by the tempo of the chanting. Then he was up again, dancing as if he was possessed. His eyes were closed and I wondered how he could see to throw himself about without leaving the white stone circle. Suddenly he opened his eyes, they were big and frightening and I thought he was looking directly at us. This was too much for us and we both took off like frightened rabbits. We ran through the forest expecting to be chased. We didn't stop until we got to the village. Shaking and panting with fear, we turned to see if we were being followed, but no one was there. We both felt that we were chased or that we were followed, but there was no one. I felt there were hidden eyes watching us from the dense forest. The little girl had apparently followed me to stop me going to the ritual, but had become curious herself and stayed on. I was so pleased to hug my Grandmother, annoyed as she was, that I had disappeared and not had supper with the rest of the family. I never told the adults about what I had seen, but it had frightened me and took its toll on me; I started bed wetting after this terrifying experience and it gave me recurring nightmares and a permanent fear of the dark. After that I was too frightened to go to the outside toilet in the village or even indoor toilets at home after dark. I began to see scary shapes in the corners of the rooms lit by flickering kerosene lamps. If I was sent on an errand when it was dark, I would prefer to be beaten for being stubborn and disobedient than to go outside or into another dark room on my own. My siblings would laugh at me and tease me about my fear of the dark and the bed-wetting, but still, I did not confide in anyone. I began to believe something was very wrong with me and that I had brought it all on myself. I became very obedient and would hang onto my mother's every word as if my life depended on it. I realised that if I had listened to her warnings in the first place about witchdoctors and fetishes and all that stuff, I would not now be so afraid of the hidden lurking horrors of the dark.

In the villages, everyone knew everyone else and the law was based on "an eye for an eye and a tooth for a tooth". Loss of face and bringing shame to the family name was avoided as much as possible. If a man got a girl pregnant, he married her, but not before she had a good hiding from her parents for bringing shame to the family and ruining her chances of a good husband, the pregnancy would forfeit her dowry. The rape of a young girl carried severe punishment. For instance, if a man raped a girl (which was a rare occurrence in the villages), the punishment for the man was severe and he could be deprived of his "accoutrements" via castration. Also because the girls were often betrothed to someone else at an early age, this would be a serious crime. However, I gathered from the conversations of the older women, upon which I used to like to eavesdrop, that the men were skilful lovers and I had observed anyway that the women were great seducers, skilfully using the promise of sex to get what they wanted.

Chapter Twelve: Port Harcourt

During those wonderful times living with Mummy at Milverton Avenue, Papa and Regina seemed so far away, arguments, fights and fear were forgotten for now. When they were transferred to Port Harcourt, Papa was still determined to cause as much discomfort to Mummy as possible. He suddenly arrived out of the blue and took all of us away, exercising his rights to have custody of us children even me. That was despite the Court Orders Mummy had obtained to have custody of me. Of course, Mummy was very upset because she knew that he wasn't capable of looking after us. After we arrived in Port Harcourt the girls were put into a school for only a few months, our brother Tony was sent to a school in Port Harcourt and Johnny to a school, Owerri. As for us girls, we went with Papa wherever he was posted and lived in different towns so often that we were never given enough time to get settled at any of the schools. Apparently our stepmother had decided that she wanted Maggie, Rosie and me to live with Papa, so that we could look after her first child. She needed us around, to run errands, do the cooking and things like that. Felicia had been sent back to the village of Okpanam.

I cannot remember the name of the school I attended in Port Harcourt, all I associate with it is the fear of grave yards, because the other children with whom I would walk home, would tell ghost stories as we were passing the graveyard. The stories were about how the spirits of the dead would haunt those who picked the graveyard fruits and how the spirits would reach out from the underground and grab them and no one would ever be able to find them. They said it was forbidden to pick or eat the fruits from the trees in the graveyard. The place was full of mango and pawpaw trees and once or twice with some other kids; I had thrown sticks at the branches causing the fruit to fall. So the stories terrified me and I began to imagine things happening to me as I passed the graveyard. At home, when it got dark, we would use kerosene lanterns, lamps or candles. Each room had a lantern on a table, but it was never bright enough and often we would carry a candle or lamp from one room to the other to brighten things up. I was still afraid of the dark after the Ogbanje encounter at the village.

I recall that, one night, I was sent to get something and I had to go into our small living room which was cramped full of bits and pieces and my imagination got the better of me, I thought I heard a sound coming from a large mirror as I was walking past and I turned to look into the mirror only to see a pair of red eyes watching me. I was riveted to the spot trying to decide whether the eyes were really there or not, they appeared to blink, which startled me and as I stepped back, the eyes appeared to come towards me as though they were coming come out of the mirror. I dropped the candle and ran out of the room screaming. Nobody would believe me, when I said I had seen a terrible creature in the mirror and it had tried to jump out at me. All they did was laugh at me, and one of my sisters said; "Didn't you know you should never look into a mirror at night as the spirits that dwell in the mirrors are visible at night!" I would like to think I imagined it, but since then, until recently, when I was on my own, I would avoid looking into mirrors at night.

Chapter Thirteen: Onitcha

The relationship between Papa and his new wife started to unravel. She was fair skinned, flirtatious, had a liking for purple or bright red lipstick and always wore a beauty spot. I remember her as being beautiful. To her, we were just house helps and we were at her beck and call. She had given birth to her first child, although I remember that there were murmurings about who the father of the child might be. Grace was sent away somewhere, I can't remember where, and the rest of us settled uneasily into the new and unpleasant domestic situation.

One day Regina asked my sister Rosaleen to heat up the straightening comb. The comb had a wooden handle and a metal-toothed comb. The process of heating the comb involved putting it carefully on a low tripod over a burning wood fire that was used for cooking in one of the outbuildings. It would normally take five to ten minutes to get to the right temperature, but five minutes is a long time to a child of seven or eight. Rosaleen carefully placed the straightening comb on the round metal tripod as she had done many times before. We all went out to play and forgot about the comb when, suddenly, our stepmother bellowed from her bedroom calling for the comb to be brought to her. We panicked and ran to the outbuilding that served as the kitchen and to our horror the metal comb with its wooden handle had fallen into the fire and both were red hot and the wood was burning. We tried to poke it out with a stick which itself caught fire. Rosaleen found a metal spoon and frantically tried to separate the comb from the burning logs, but instead she burnt her fingers. We froze with fear when our step-mother stormed into the kitchen. Rosaleen and I tried to explain and to apologise. We knew that there was going to be punishment, beating and goodness knows what else. But she strode over to the brazier, bunched up the end of her wrapper, pulled out the comb by the burning handle and hit Rosaleen with a vicious blow on her bare back with the comb, taking off some skin and leaving a ghastly weald six inches long.

Mummy use to tell us that when she was pregnant with Rosaleen she had a dream in which she was told that she was going to have another baby and she was shown two babies; one was a beautiful baby and the other was equally beautiful, but this second baby was covered in sores and mummy instinctively went to pick up the first baby, but she was told she had to have the second baby. So she said that was why Rosaleen had the most sensitive skin of us all.

Rosaleen screamed when the comb hit her and so did I. Regina ordered us out of the kitchen and told us to take our crying somewhere else. A couple of hours later my brothers came back from playing football and found us crying. When they saw Rosaleen's back they went looking for our step-mother Regina. There was a fight, Regina could give as good as she got, but she was no match for two angry brothers. When Papa returned it was decided that Tony and Johnny would be sent to boarding schools and that we girls would also be sent away.

Maggie, Rosaleen and I were sent to Onitcha to live with Nnewolie. She was Papa's aunt and was quite old. I vaguely remembered her; she had had long sagging breasts well past her navel. She showed us kindness, but was too old to defend us. I have tended to blank her out of my mind owing to the things that happened to us in Onitcha. Nnewolie lived in one room in a brick building within a poor compound with lots of families. She had a grown up daughter who lived somewhere else. The compound was home to all sorts of characters and a lot of quite unpleasant people. There was a Mr Thomas who would try to have sex with any of the girls in the compound especially when he was drunk and it didn't matter how young they were. Nnewolie was aware of such dangers and would try to protect us as best she could. For a while we were sent to a local school, which was very strict on clean nails and clean knickers. Whatever knickers we had arrived with were eventually torn or stolen from the washing line by people in the compound, new ones were not provided. We complained to Nnewolie that we had school inspections for clean pants, so she cut up some old wrappers into squares which she would place between our legs and then tie up on either side. She instructed us only to lift up our skirts in inspection, just sufficient to show only the corner of the front, so that the teachers would not suspect that our knickers were just pieces of fabric tied at the sides. I got into the habit of doing this as I had no other pair of pants. At night Nnewolie would make sure that the fabric was tied tightly in place to protect us against the likes of Mr Thomas who might be roaming in the night. All our spare clothes and shoes disappeared whilst we were at school, as we had nowhere safe to store anything. So we walked with bare feet.

Later I came to understand and appreciate this piece of cloth tied tightly by Nnewolie for my protection. All the women in the compound cooked for their husbands and children in the communal kitchen, usually after a long day at the market. I can't remember what the men did for a living, but I know the women were market traders, whose day began at five in the morning and went on until six in the evening when they would return home to the compound exhausted and often ill tempered. There were numerous fights between husbands and wives or between the women, mainly over their husbands or children. On one particular occasion I remember, one of the women was having a bad day in the market and had come home unexpectedly for something she had forgotten, but she walked in on her husband having sex with another woman and to make matters worse, an obviously younger woman. The affair was common knowledge in the compound, as nothing could happen without everybody knowing about it, the walls were so thin. The wife was not particularly big, but she came out of the house dragging the screaming girl by the back of her blouse. She had thrown her husband aside and dragged the girl out of her marital bed. The girl was half naked and was trying to cover her shame unsuccessfully with a wrapper, which she had hastily grabbed as she tried to get away,

The woman's husband tried to get between his wife and the girl, but the girl was seized by the angry wife who pushed her husband away from the girl before throwing a punch which caught the girl on the face sending her flying, She jumped after her and at the same time shouting at her husband that she would deal with him when she had finished with 'this harlot'. A crowd was gathering, children were giggling and pointing to the girl's hairy bush, Women's bare breasts are commonplace in Africa and so are not of any particular interest, every child, boy or girl has seen breastfeeding in the market and public places. But a completely naked woman in a public place was a very different thing, and was usually associated with mental illness, for no sane woman, above the age of puberty would expose herself beneath the waistline.

The girl tried to make her escape by running into the crowd, but the wife tightened her own wrapper around her waist signalling that the fight had only just begun and effortlessly, with incredible agility, caught up with the younger woman, pulling her to the ground by her threaded hair. To everyone's surprise and delight the girl decided to stand her ground and fight back. Now the crowd was in its element making room for the two women as they rolled on the ground, wrestling each other in the midst of the crowd. The girl was bleeding from the nose when some older women intervened, separating the two women who were now both exhausted. Someone handed the girl her wrapper with which she covered herself. Meanwhile the wife shaking and bopping up and down with rapid movements attempting to escape the restraint by the other women, her breasts bouncing to the rhythm. I squeezed between the legs of the crowd to get a closer look at the spectacle and to listen to the two women exchanging insults at the top of their voices. The older women now had things under control and dispersed the crowd, but just as we thought it was all over there was a sudden outburst from the wife who had caught sight of her cheating husband in the crowd and made a beeline for him. He doubled over cross-eyed, when she kicked him right between the legs. There was a groan from the dispersing crowd and those still gathered around.

"I will cut off your useless penis", she screamed as she kicked him in the face and the stomach as he huddled on the ground gasping for breath; he seemed to be unable to retaliate, still holding his midriff and moaning.

The other women joined her in shouting abuse at him. The wife stormed back into her house and the other women broke up into groups to discuss the fascinating proceedings.

The days were hot and humid and the flies were always a nuisance, out in their droves. Every day after school or during the weekends my task was to sit by a market stall outside the compound and drive away the flies or shout out if there was a customer. We were loaned out to some of the market traders in the compound and they put us to work. I imagine that they must have paid Nnewolie something for us. My sisters, who were two and four years older than me, had to go to the market first thing in the morning at about five o'clock carrying a basin of food stuff, including moi moi, plantain or cassava. I was lucky not to be able to carry the heavy basins even though I had to carry buckets of water from the pump to the compound every day. My sisters taught me how to twist a piece of cloth before rolling it into a firm circle and placing it on my head. At the pump I would ask someone to help lift the bucket of water on to my head. It took a few seconds for me to find my balance and adjust to the heavy weight of the water. The bucket was a third of my height and I was careful not to drop it because going back to the compound without water was out of the question and going back on my own for water to the pump meant there might not be anyone to help lift the bucket back onto my head.

Every day before school, we fetched the water for the day, before sweeping the compound, scrubbing the concrete stairs, pounding maize or beans in the pestle and mortar, washing rice, lighting a fresh fire, helping to prepare the food 'akpu' and egusi soup, fresh "bush" meat, pepper soup and cold drinks to be sold in the market. Then we would wash ourselves, using a bowl to scoop water from a bucket. I learned to pour water all over my body and then use the black soap and sapo (a sponge made from beaten bark of a tree) to scrub my body and wash my head, while one of my sisters would scrub my back and all the important places with the sapo. Then I would dry myself with one of my clothes and rub my body down with coconut oil before hanging the wet garment on a line to dry. Then I would ask one of my sisters to help tie on the makeshift pants before putting on my school uniform. This was all done in the open in the yard.

For breakfast we had a piece of yam fried in palm oil and, with any luck, there would be seasoned fried tomato or one fried egg each; sometimes we would have pap with fried plantain. Lunch and dinner were often non-existent. After breakfast we would help to set up the stall outside the compound and then walk to school for eight o'clock. If we were late we got six strokes of the cane, so we tried very hard to get there on time. When I caught lice at school, my hair was shaved off, which became problematic, because I caught something from the dirty blade used to shave my head and my scalp became infected. When my hair grew back it grew only in patches and my head was full of scabs from scratching all the time. At night we had to bunk down on a mat on the concrete floor in Nnewolie's room using an old wrapper to cover us, which became infested with bed bugs very quickly, we were often bitten.

School finished at 1pm every day, but, thankfully, homework was scarce, but hard to get done because of the work schedule at the compound, which left little time. Of course, we did, not forget the painful punishment at school for not doing our homework. In the evening, I would resume my duties of watching the stall, stealing moments to learn my times-tables; trying to do my homework while brushing away the flies from the food on the stall. I don't know why, but I remember how grubby my exercise books looked.

I was grateful for the makeshift pants/chastity belt when one day I was in the communal kitchen and one of the men came in, picked me up and placed me on his lap and tried to put his fingers into my makeshift pants. I called out, but he put his hand over my mouth. His fingers were coarse and felt rough like wood, I began to panic and kick at him, but he was much stronger than me and I felt I was suffocating. He removed his hand from my mouth to concentrate on untying my pants. Once he had done that he pushed his hand over my face again. I bit hard into his dirty finger, it must have hurt because he threw me down hard and I landed on the concrete floor on my back, just as one of the women came into the kitchen. She must have taken in the situation pretty quickly, because, as I sat on the floor crying, she picked up a log and hit the man very hard on the back of the head. I will always remember the sound of the log hitting his head making a sort of musical popping noise. He staggered for a moment and then ran out holding his head. The woman shouted after him:

"If I see you here again, I will tell everybody how small your penis is and we will cut it off for you. You hear me?"

She picked me up and carried me to Nnewolie who rubbed my back with a kind of deep heat balm known as Mentholathum. This is the only sign of affection I can remember from Onitcha.

On another day, just as the sun was going down, my sister Maggie came back from the market limping, but still carrying the big basin of goods on her head. She had stepped on a piece of broken bottle and was bleeding badly. The women in the market used rags to tie up her wound, but it bled through the thick covering of dirty cloth. When she arrived in the compound there was bedlam as the market women gathered around, they took the basin from her head as poor Maggie collapsed on the floor with the pain and loss of blood and exhaustion. The women washed her wounds, one of them put a knife in the fire and when it was red hot she poured oil on the knife with a practiced hand, it hissed and threw up a strong smelling white smoke. With this they immediately cauterized the wound on the sole of her foot. She screamed and we all screamed holding on to our big sister. Everyone who had gathered around said:
"Ndo sorry O!"
After her wound was dressed, she was given something to eat and allowed to rest.

One day, there was a great commotion going on as we returned to the compound from school. There was a beautiful maroon coloured convertible Opel Rekord Coupe with cream interior and white wall tyres, parked on the street outside the compound. It was pandemonium! The crowd from the compound and the town was at least twenty people deep in some places and they were all agog and chattering at once. We had to push our way through the crowd to see what all the fuss was about. Everyone was just mesmerized by the car, its smartly dressed driver and its beautiful glamorous passenger. It was Mummy! Everything about that day when our Mummy found us in Onitcha remains so vivid in my mind. Somehow I had thought I would never see her again, what with the topsy-turvy and unsettled life that we had led and the constant pressure on us day to day in the compound. Mummy looked a vision in her full flared polka dot, blood red and cream dress, silhouetting the full white net-laced petticoat. Her waistline looked minute for a woman who had given birth to nine children. She wore cream sunglasses pointed at the ends. As we pushed our way through the crowd someone shouted;

"Here are de children!" and pulled us to the front. At first, Mummy did not recognise us. It was not surprising! We were dirty and our clothes were just rags and we had no shoes. I had little hair on my head, just scabs mixed with dust. When Mummy saw us she collapsed on the seat on the passenger side of the car, put her head in her hands and wept in disbelief and shock. I gazed at her in amazement! She was so beautiful sitting there, her polka dot skirt silhouetting the full white net-laced petticoat. The crowd gasped as she
"This woman is the mother of dese children?"

Everything that had happened up till that moment had become a jumble in my mind; we had gone from relative comfort of the government houses provided for our father on his tour of duty around the country, to the big and well-furnished accommodation of Milverton Avenue with servants, interspersed with visits to both grandparents' villages and finally, to extreme poverty in Onitcha. Our current deprivation had become normal to us and we lived as best we could, as children do.

Mummy had searched for us relentlessly. With no co-operation from Papa, who had refused to tell her where we were, it had taken her months after her return from England to find us. She had been to college in England, the London School of Fashion, to improve her skills. This meant that we had spent almost a year in appalling conditions and poverty.

Of course, we had no possessions, but I had a tiny wooden box in which I had some coloured pebbles and other small treasures that I had collected, but I left it behind with the unhappiness and squalor. Without a word to anyone Mummy bundled us into the back seat of the car, just as we were, and we drove away. The nightmare of Onitcha was behind us.

Chapter Fourteen: Lagos

Not long after Mummy had found us in Onitcha when I was seven, we three girls moved from Aba to Lagos with Mummy. The boys stayed in their boarding schools and came home to Lagos in the holidays. We moved because Aba was no longer safe for the family, owing to the riots and killings caused by ethnic and political tensions, relating to Independence. Additionally, Papa's Eastern Region Court Order, giving him custody of us children, was not recognised or enforceable in Lagos.

In Lagos, we lived in a brand new house, bought by my stepfather, in a new residential estate in Ikeja. It was a detached house at 15 Adeniyi Jones Avenue, near the newly developed Ikeja industrial estate not far from the airport. We were also not far from a number of factories, which were being built, creating jobs in the area. The house was painted in sky blue and magnolia, the windows were glass slats, which opened and closed together. It had eight large rooms, each with electric ceiling fans, four of the rooms were upstairs and could be accessed via two staircases, one from the back of the house, which led to the upstairs kitchen, and the other at the side of the house, which led to the balcony outside the living room. The house had two balconies and two verandas, two bathrooms and two kitchens. There was a detached double garage to the left of the house, with windows to the back overlooking the servants' quarters, which were also painted in magnolia with sky blue windows. The servants' quarters consisted of two rooms, a kitchen, toilet and bathroom. At the back, at the boundary of the house was a dense forest full of crickets, bats, snakes, insects and other small animals of all description, but also mango, orange, banana, palm, coconut and other exotic trees. The forest was dense, but the servants soon found or cut a path from the backyard to the nearest market, about two miles away, through the forest. Mummy forbade us children from using this path. But, of course, our curiosity and the lure of fresh fruit got the better of us and we would wander into the forest with the servants when Mummy was busy or out seeing clients for her dressmaking business.

Hawkers were busy in our road plying their trade to the big houses. I often wondered how the hawkers, especially the women and girls managed to carry a whole store on their heads and also be able to lift them down and then up again after dealing with a buyer. Then I would think of the time when I was spared that hardship in Onitcha, because I was too small, but my older sisters were forced to carry large basins full of cassava and yams to sell in the market, but that all seemed a lifetime away.

In the evenings as I wandered out of our house to talk to the vendors, canaries would sing sweetly on the trees, while other birds squabbled over their nests. The beautiful butterflies of many different brilliant colours and sizes with long antenna shaped like a thin long shaft with a 'club' at its end, were now perching on the undersides of leaves, between the blades of grass for shelter from the night with their wings folded, ready to sleep. Some were sheltering under abandoned cement blocks, exhausted from their daily efforts to find nectar and avoid predators. Sometimes I would count as many as eighty of these beautiful butterflies on my way home from playing down the road. Some of them looked like they had huge eyes painted on their wings whilst others were just so beautifully arrayed that I would marvel at God's incredible creativity and how He could paint so many living things in so many different and colourful patterns. In the mornings on my way to school, I would be just passing at the right time to see the sprinklers come on in one or two gardens. I would be awe struck as I watched a cloud of butterflies rise from the grass. I would admire their different colours. Some of them had beautiful wings that measured almost two inches. I wanted to draw and depict them perfectly, but it seemed impossible, besides, drawing, I was told, was not considered a career and would not earn me a living. Later, I was to have nine exhibitions as an artist in London.
"Have you ever seen a rich artist who paints pictures and is respected?" My family would say.

I loved to daydream, as I walked at dusk while the sun was disappearing behind the trees into the horizon. It seemed as though she was slowly tucking herself into bed by throwing a blanket seductively over her brilliance, whilst allowing the world gently and silently to drift into darkness.

As time went by, very little, if anything, was mentioned about what had happened to us, while we were under Papa's care. I really don't remember Papa or Regina coming up in any conversations. However, we did hear rumours that things were not going well on that front, apparently. Regina was not the type of wife that Papa's family expected. The age gap between them was beginning to take its toll as Papa irritated and disgusted Regina in his old age. People would say that Papa was voicing his regrets openly, making comparisons between my mother and Regina, and saying that he wished he hadn't treated my mother so badly and should never have divorced her. This seemed amazing, considering what had gone before, not forgetting the months he made her search for her children. He even kept the clothes and other provisions that Mummy had sent us so we never got them. Papa had refused to tell her where we were, or to whichever town he had been transferred by the Post Office, so that she could not contact him. She had to go crying, to the local government offices, to beg them for information of Papa's whereabouts so that she could find us. The rumours of unrest in Papa's new marriage must have been true, because Papa started writing to Mummy and sending messages to her, trying to make amends.

I was never encouraged by Mummy to look back or to re-live what had happened in those times with Papa, or during those spent with the strange and ugly people that our Papa had farmed us out to. Mummy felt that looking back would create too much bitterness, and my mother was not going to let us add yesterday's worries to the present troubled times. "Sufficient unto today, is the evil thereof!" Owing to the troubled politics of the impending Nigerian Independence, we lived one day at a time and admirably, Mummy showed no obvious bitterness about Papa, for which I am grateful. She even allowed Rosie and me to go and visit my father in Zaria and Asaba, years later.

Mummy could read and write, but she did not have the opportunity for a higher education, and was determined that all of her children would be educated to the highest standard. After she had finally got her children back, she achieved this goal and created strict rules and boundaries, for her eight children, teaching us respect for ourselves and for others with a strong love for God and Jesus.

Despite all that we had been through and, indeed, were still to go through, Mummy made sure that, when we were with her, the household was disciplined, prayerful, happy and full of laughter. She taught me to count my blessings and focus on eternity. My prayer and wish is that I might achieve all this in my own household.

Mummy's sewing skills and thorough knowledge of fashion were to become very useful during our years in Ikeja. Daddy, my stepfather, was absent in Ghana working permanently as a political adviser to President Nkrumah. This was during Daddy's exile there after he was accused of treason. Communications between the countries was difficult, forcing Mummy to be self-sufficient and not relying on Daddy being able to send a steady flow of money. Under these circumstances, Mummy busied herself trying to provide for her eight children and three servants, in her husband's absence. She moved us all upstairs and rented the rooms below to an English businessman from Manchester, a Mr Harte and his Nigerian wife, while they waited to find a house nearby. They lived for about two years in our house and I remember spending a lot of my time in their part of the house playing with their newly born baby, Ann. Every day, when I got back from school, I would go upstairs, say Hello to Mummy, who would be at her sewing machine, change out of my school uniform, wash my hands and rush down to the flat below. I would play with the baby and help Mrs Harte with whatever she needed to do until Mummy sent one of the house girls to tell me that it was time to do my homework. Mr and Mrs Harte were a favourite with me. Mr Harte was softly spoken like my stepfather, unlike the loud voices of most Nigerian men. When they finally moved into their own house, when I was about ten years old, it was only up the road. I was pleased that it was arranged that I could continue to visit them. Just after they moved, Mrs Harte gave birth to her second baby, which I was thrilled about. One early evening Mummy was in the front garden giving instructions to the gardener, who doubled as the odd job man, while Mrs Harte was driving past, she saw Mummy and stopped to say hello. I was on the balcony doing my homework and could overhear their conversation:

"Good evening Mrs Ikoku."

"Ah Mrs Harte, how are you and Mr Harte settling in your new home?"

"It's a lovely house and we are happy in it. It's only round the corner on the next street, on the right."

"So you have not moved too far."

"How is your new baby?"

"He's fine, he's a good baby."

"You have a boy! We thank God."

I was wondering when she would get round to my visiting.

"Is it alright for Patricia to come and visit us and play with the babies, she is very good with the children".

"I know how much she likes playing with Ann, she can come and visit when she finishes her homework and daily chores."

"Thank you, she's a lovely little girl and the children like her so much."

"She always tells me she will have six children when she grows up." said Mummy, they both laughed.

"Let's hope she will not change her mind when she gets older."

I smiled to myself and wasted no time visiting the family the next day as soon as I had done my homework and my chores. Mummy had a policy that her own children should be able to do all the housework and cleaning tasks in the house better than the house girls or servants and this was done. However, I was lazy academically and I suspect that Mummy tolerated my visits to the Harte's family home most days because it encouraged me to do my homework and daily chores quickly and efficiently. Mrs Harte would always have a little bit of food for me and even though I had already eaten at home, I would always accept her hospitality with gusto. I found her cooking very strange, very European, like mash potatoes with tomato sauce on which she would melt butter, put together with peas and meat and she made many other meals that were odd to a Nigerian child. I would sing nursery rhymes and lullabies to the baby to make him sleep and then I would clown around, pulling faces to make Ann laugh and giggle, I would give her piggybacks or push her around on one of her moveable toys. When I got home I would be full of happiness, but exhausted.

It was during this period that we were finally able to go and see Daddy in Ghana. What a wonderful experience it was. Not only were we with Daddy again, albeit for a short while but, we were treated like royalty owing to Daddy's position. My best memory of Ghana is a day at the Presidential Palace when members of the OAU gathered for a meeting. There were well known African politicians including Julius Nyerere, (First President of Tanzania) Kenneth Kaunda (First President of Zambia), Jomo Kenyatta (First President of Kenya), Emperor Haile Selassie of Ethiopia, Gamal Abdel Nasser (President of Egypt), Joseph Mobutu of The Congo and others who were founding members of the OAU (Organisation of African Unity). President Kwame Nkrumah of Ghana and his beautiful Ethiopian wife were hosting the dignitaries and their families, which included us. This was to be one of those days that would be forever etched in my mind. Being with Mummy and Daddy dressed as we were all in our new clothes was wonderful, but of course, I had little concept of who all those people were or why they were there. We were introduced to some of the great leaders and I played with some of their children. The Children had a special film show in the Palace which was the first time I had been in an inside cinema and I just loved a colour film of divers diving off a very high cliff into clear waters (I think shot in Malaysia) and the music that was played, particularly an organ and guitar based record by an English pop group. Later when I heard "The House of the Rising Sun" by the animals I realised that this was the recording. The Palace had the most beautiful gardens. I'll never forget the long driveway, the peacocks, the banks of beautiful flowers and coloured birds of all different species. The peacocks were roaming freely and their piercing cries filled the air. The lawns were immaculate. As we drove up to the Palace, I remember having a sense of awe looking out of the car window down the driveway, which was lined with palms and brilliantly coloured flowers set off by the white walls. It may not have been the most beautiful Palace in the world, but seeing it through the eyes of a child, it spoilt other palaces for me, because nothing could ever compare with my first impressions of President Nkrumah's glittering Palace. As a result of this trip I developed a love for all things

Ghanaian including the food, spinach and smoked fish stew (Kontmomre), fried plantain, the maize dish, Kenke, with fried fish, tomatoes, onions and chilli, yam cakes and the red palm oil stews of fish, prawns, crab and snail. We delighted in a real fresh leaf salad, rather different from the so-called "Russian" salad out of tins, which was very popular in Nigeria.

President Nkrumah of Ghana was married to Ethiopian Fathia Rizk. They had three children. In his early years as President he united the four territories of the Gold Coast as Ghana and won independence from the UK on the 6th March 1957. He was awarded the Lenin Peace prize by the Soviet Union in 1963. Under his leadership Ghana adopted some socialistic policies and practices. He created and started various community programs, a welfare system, established schools, constructed Roads and bridges to improve communication. He installed tap water systems in villages and concrete drains for latrines.

President Nkrumah was a proponent of scientific socialism, economics, politics and a philosophy, which meant sticking to facts. He was like a magnate to the other budding African politicians and academics because of his promotion of Pan-Africanism and he was a founding member of the OAU founded in 1965 to enable African countries to play their role on the world stage. In 1964, he amended the Constitution making himself President for life. However, nothing lasts forever and despite his efforts, Ghana went from being the richest to the poorest country in Africa by the time he was deposed on Feb 24 1966 while he was away in North Korea. His people had begun to live in fear under the Preventive Detention Act which made it possible for his administration to arrest and detain anyone charged with treason without due process of law.

Chapter Fifteen: The Women

I was a very quiet child and this worked to my advantage. When my mother's women friends gathered in our house, they would often have wide ranging conversations. They would discuss other people's marital problems or trouble with youngsters, drunken husbands and lecherous men. They talked about polygamous families, bad or good choices of wife or husband, the latest gossip and whose husband was seen with his mistress. They talked about divorces, childbirth, which children did not look like their fathers, whose wife was supposed to be putting some potion in her husband's food (so he would only have eyes for her). The gossips even included; which wife must have put a spell on another wife to stop her having children. The conversations were riveting and often no one would notice my presence. I would sit quietly in the corner making my own judgement about the topic under discussion, to see if they would come up with the same conclusion. When I was younger, someone would say "little pigs have big ears" and the conversation would come to an abrupt end as soon as I was spotted or they would change the subject and send me on an errand. It took me a while to realise that "little pig" referred to me! Now that I was older, I would pre-empt their needs so that there would be no errands for them to send me on I would make sure they had drinks; or electric fans and, if they were eating, I would fetch the bowl and towel for them to wash their hands after the meal. I made myself useful so that I would be allowed to stay and listen with my piggy ears! I remember often feeling proud of myself for working out the solution to one or two of the problems then under scrutiny and knowing that I was right, especially when the subject was about relationships. I was good at that. It's incredible what you can learn from listening to a group of elders talking about life.

Nigerian women are fighters in every sense of the word and more in control of the society than is realised or apparent. I am always proud of the fact that Igbo women went to war, instead of their men. With their bows and arrows and spears these women terrorised the Red Coats, who had muskets, when they first arrived in West Africa. I feel I can do anything with the knowledge that the bold blood of these women flows proudly through my veins. The market women in more modern times, in 1929, were a force to reckon with. Women from the east and western parts of Nigeria played a major role in influencing and weakening the grip of the colonial power on the country by staging a successful revolt against a tax on their trade and bringing the whole country to a standstill.

I used to listen to the women for hours. They appeared to be fearless. They never seemed to talk about controlling men or seeking equality the way I hear modern women in the West talk today, yet they were obviously in control. They were aware of the special roll of the men in their lives, of their strengths and weaknesses, their positives and their failings. They spoke of men naturally, the way they discussed other women. They were not conspiratorial against men, but they certainly knew how to make them do what they required of them. They appeared to be able to manipulate their men, but they were aware how useful men are, given their role in the family. Although it was sometimes not to their taste, they would admit that getting married was a vital part of tradition and having children was a woman's biggest tribute to life and nature for the continuity of the community. The role of a married woman was seen, in those days, far more as an honour and privilege than it is in modern times. Being caretakers of the future was definitely not to be taken lightly. In regard to these women, who helped form my view of life, I would say being married defined who they were, above all other things, but additionally, most of them had either been activists on one issue or another or they were already respected pillars of their own communities. The women would say that no matter the heights you get to in life, your biggest achievement and pride should be the measure of how your children have turned out. In the Nigerian community the saying goes that "when a child is good, she is the father's child, but when a child is bad she is definitely the mother's child," so you know who carries parenting responsibility on their shoulders! As I have experienced it in Nigeria, the fact that the man is the head of the household is unquestionable and so is the fact that the woman is the decision maker. A man may aim to marry many wives as a status symbol, but I grew up wondering how men arrived at that daft idea. Their calculations were all wrong; say, for instance, a man has five wives, which means that he has five mothers-in-law. Who then runs his life? When they realise this, a typical authoritarian Nigerian male may try to start another family with yet another woman, but the more of them he marries, the more he loses control to the women! I believe this is why Nigerian men are desperate for sons, not only to carry on the name of the family, but also so that they could have another male ally in the family.

The women I listened to all those years ago had come to the conclusion that women are created with superior common sense while men have been created with the superior physical strength and the power of logic. They were very protective of their children and this was a prime consideration. I remember being amused when one of the women said "a man is strong of

course, until he tries messing with your children, then they will know what a superior animal the little wife is". Another added:
"And that is why the creator has given them weak points, just in case they get out of hand".
It was a long time before I could work out what the weak points were!
"Ah ah! What man go mess with your child, the one wey try, I deal with am proper?" exclaimed one of the women.
"That man dey craze o!" added another.
"Na waitin' you do am?"

The first woman told the story of how her husband got violent with her when he was drunk. She put up with this for many years and did not retaliate (even though there were times when she felt like poisoning him) because everyone would think she was not holding the marriage together which, as the woman, was her responsibility according to custom. But one day he came home drunk, as usual, but this time he took his drunken anger out on one of the children. She ended with a flourish.
"That na the last time that man ever touch me or my children."
The women laughed.
"Tell us what you did to him now!" They said, impatient for the juicy details.
"I went mad when he beat our daughter, so I kicked am between the legs so hard he fell to the ground and then I beat him till he begged for me to stop and then I threw all his belongings out of the window and threw him out of the house".
"No, you no serious, your husband no home, when he was sober?"
"Back keh! The man too shame to tell anybody what happened. Look at me now, I look like person wey fit beat big man like that?
There was much laughter as they all recalled various troubles with their men and other women and how they dealt with each one. Unfortunately, I was sent on errands and missed out on most of the good stories.

The women often discussed the polygamous family situation. Often, in large cities, if the man was already married, according to the Christian marriage ceremony in a church, and he got a girl pregnant; she would most likely be a servant or part of the household; she would be sent away to have the baby somewhere else, as a mark of respect for the man's wife and to avoid the shame this would bring to the family, not to mention the bad feelings it would cause. In some cases when the husband and wife were married by "native law and custom", the pregnant girl would have automatic rights of a wife, since she was carrying the man's baby. The man would be forced to either, move her into the house, creating a very volatile situation, or provide her with a new home, and accept her as his second, third or fourth wife. If he was wealthy enough, he would set her up in her own apartment somewhere else, where he would be able to visit her and the baby. She would then bare his name as his wife and possibly give him more children. This was a constant source of irritation for the women in the discussions I overheard, but it was the customary way, and some of them were that third or fourth wife!

Chapter Sixteen: The First Coup D'état

Freed from colonial rule in 1960; the exuberant free spirit of Nigeria embarked on a journey of slow decline, when Prime Minister, Sir Abubakar Tafawa Balewa and others were killed in a military coup in January 1966. The military took power and Major-General Johnson Aguiyi-Ironsi, an Igbo, took over as Head of State and about 6 months later he was killed in a counter-coup and Lieutenant-Colonel Yakubu Gowon took over. The first coup, which had been led by an Igbo, was followed by accusations of tribalism from the people of Northern Nigeria accusing Chukwuma Uzeogwu and his fellow coup plotters of staging an Igbo coup. Of course, politicians like Daddy, SG Ikoku, an Igbo, who had been prominent and vocal in the previous democratic Governments were treated with great suspicion by the military. In the following months and years after the first military coup Dad was still a wanted man. He was in political asylum in Ghana, which resulted in an uncomfortable life for my mother.

I remember the first raid on our house by soldiers when I was twelve. I was walking home from Mr and Mrs Harte's house nearby, after one of my usual after school visits. I remember noticing the workers, gardeners and hawkers huddled together in garages or gardens that I passed, listening to something on the radio. There was none of the excitement or jubilation that goes with listening to a football game, which would draw a crowd around any accessible radio. It struck me as odd, but I swung my arms quite happily as I walked home, oblivious that our lives were about to change. Then I began to notice that there must be something very wrong; everywhere, people on the streets, who were usually exuberant, loud, friendly, full of excitement and laughter, appeared distracted and tense. As I passed more people on the way, one or two of who would usually wave back with a smile when I greeted them, just stared at me without a word. One woman spoke to me in a hushed voice.
"Hurry home, the streets are not safe for you."
This was because we were Igbos living in an area of Nigeria occupied by Yorubas, a tribe, which was at odds with the Igbos at that time over the Coup.

I stopped for a moment not understanding what she was saying, it was my turn to stare and it was just then that the first lorry-load of soldiers passed me. They were all armed and silent, but there was menace in their spaced-out eyes that left me with a very uncomfortable feeling of foreboding as they stared back at me. A second lorry packed with soldiers sped past me churning up dust as they went. Somebody grabbed my hand and pulled me towards a nearby house. It was the neighbour who had told me to get off the street earlier on, although I did not know her well, I let her pull me along half running. She took me into a house and shut the door behind us. Once inside, she went to peer out of the window as if expecting trouble. I was frightened and confused. I stood where I was not knowing whether to run out of the house or stay put, oddly, I wondered whether it would be rude if I ran away, but before I could decide she said.

"Does your mother know that you are out?"

I nodded my head, not sure what to say. She appeared to be frightened. Her husband came into the room and looked equally panicked. Their fear spread to my stomach. From their accents I could tell they were Igbos, like me, from the eastern part of the country.

"She is one of the Ikoku children from number 15." said her husband.

"Do you know what is happening?" asked the woman

"What is happening where?" I said.

"How is she supposed to know, she is only a child!" said her husband.

I was almost twelve, but in those days that was young and I was naïve and innocent. The wife put on some slippers and hurried around from room to room. I didn't know what she was doing exactly, but the jerky urgency of her movements was unnerving.

I sat down and watched a wall gecko, a creamy coloured, translucent bug-eyed lizard, clambering up the wall. A little boy of about three years came out of one of the rooms followed by the house girl. I thought to myself, "I wonder how the gecko got inside the house." The house was similar to ours, and then I realised they did not have anti-mosquito nets on every window as we did. I knew all the while that I was trying to blank out the fear that was in my soul. The little boy was whingeing.

"Mama, Comfort don't want to give me Fanta oh!" he complained.

"Mah, e no let me…....." the maid began to explain.

"Make him ogi and get him ready for bed, I'll soon be back." She turned to her son,

"It's too late for Fanta and do what Comfort says."

Then she said to her husband.

"I'll take her home."

"No thank you, I can walk home alone." I protested.

"Not this evening. I'll walk you to your house."

I heard her husband's protests as she pushed me out of the door and shut it behind us, calling to her husband to lock it. I wondered if the world had gone mad, no one shuts the door to their house, unless they were going to bed and why were the streets deserted? Even the two permanent night hawkers were nowhere to be seen. They sold sweets, cigarettes and packets of chewing gum, that contained small collectable pictures of footballers like Pele or some faraway stars like Pat Boone or Ricky Nelson, Our street, Adeniyi Jones Avenue, was usually quite quiet with very little traffic, but the place was always alive with gardeners, drivers washing their masters' cars, house girls haggling prices with vendors selling plantain, meat, yam, fruits and all kinds of other food products, all done at a leisurely heat induced pace. But now the street was deserted, although I could see people hiding in the houses looking down into the street. As I silently hurried along the road with the Igbo lady (I learnt later that her name was Mrs Okafor), I could hear shouting and people arguing coming from the direction of our house. In another house, the mistress was yelling at a house girl in Yoruba. A lone night watchman sat on a stool set in front of a mat with his rubber slippers laid out beside him facing Mecca, in readiness for evening prayers. He swatted away mosquitoes as he followed us with his eyes. Fear rose in my breast as we drew nearer to my home and the sounds of shouting and screaming got louder and I could hear something crashing and breaking on the ground.

"Ah mba oh!" "Oh no", I heard the shock in Mrs Okafor's voice as she quickly turned pulling me back in the direction we had just come from.

"The soldiers are in your house, I want you to come home with me until they go away."

But I tore myself free, as she ran back towards her house. I ran on towards the gates of our home. Although I had run only a short distance, I had sweat pouring down my face burning into my eyes. I pushed away the sweat with the edge of my uniform. At our gates a lorry full of soldiers drove out narrowly missing me. I stopped in my tracks. One of the soldiers spat out of the lorry, his spittle was deep orange in colour and landed on the shirt of my blue school uniform. Normally I would have shown disgust, but instinctively, I did not react.

Once in the compound the situation was clearer, the soldiers had arrived unexpectedly and ransacked the house. We were now living in enemy territory with nowhere to go.

I ran into the yard and then I heard Mummy's voice with relief, she was somewhere in the house. I could hear that she was already busy supervising a clean-up. The front door was splintered and hanging off its hinges. There was fear on the faces of some of the house girls as I ran into the house, but Mummy sounded calm. There were pieces of broken glass, bottles and furniture everywhere, some of the house girls were crying as they swept and picked up the broken glasses, papers, chairs and china. There was such a mess everywhere and I had to step carefully over the debris left by the soldiers. It looked as though they had turned the place upside down. At least everyone was safe, though this was to be one of many such raids on our home.

"Where's Mummy?"

"She's upstairs."

"Is that Patricia?" Mummy shouted from the floor above.

"Mummy, it's me!"

I ran up the stairs as fast as I could to the first floor, through the kitchen into the living room. Mummy was now sitting in one of the chairs, with defiance in her eyes, which I mistook for anger. She did not look visibly shaken, but I instinctively searched for any signs that they may have hurt her and I was grateful not to see blood anywhere. She got off the chair and as she came towards me my instinct was to run from her anger thinking, that she was going to be cross with me for being late home, but she caught me in a warm embrace and hugged me. It was only then in her embrace that I gave way to tears as I realised how frightened I had been. Everything had been so surreal that evening, the events seemed to have unfolded in slow motion from the moment I left the Harte's family home, from the crowds around radio sets to the lorry full of soldiers, and Mr and Mrs Okafor, who had tried to shelter me. It was obvious that Igbos were no longer safe in Lagos or northern parts of Nigeria, the massacre of tens of thousands of Igbos in retaliation for the assassination of the Muslim Prime Minister, had begun.

"Pat, thank God you are safe."

"What did they want Mummy?"

"They were looking for secret documents!" she spat out the words in anger. "Foolish, idiots, as if I would be hiding secret documents!" she kissed her teeth, "they don't even know what "secret documents" mean."

For a moment, I could see that Mummy was actually severely shaken by the raid. She turned from me and dusted away shards of glass from broken bits of photo frames and from the furniture. Then she slumped down and started rocking back and forth humming. Slowly, she put words to the song. "Nobody knows the trouble I've seen, nobody knows, but Jesus. Nobody knows the trouble I've seen, glory halleluiah."

I came to know and love this song by Louis Armstrong as a symbol of my mother's strength and its words as one of the sources of solace to her. Years later, I sang; "Nobody Knows the Trouble I've Seen" with deep emotion at the Royal Albert Hall for BBC television.

It seems the soldiers could not find any "secret documents" and so they had decided to satisfy their lust for violence by breaking pieces of furniture, pots and pans, my mother's crystal glasses and china, many of which were wedding presents. Some of them had been bought in Europe or in England and were costly, but more importantly some had sentimental value for Mummy. But I learnt from Mummy not to cry over worldly goods because all that really matters is that the Lord protects the family and you fall into the arms of Jesus. Through Mummy's quick thinking my little brother Sammy and my baby sister Eno had been taken by one of the house girls to the neighbouring house to hide when the soldiers crashed in. Seeing that all was quiet, the house girl had returned with the two of them, leaving Mummy to worry about me. Fortunately, my sisters Maggie and Rosaleen were in boarding schools in Ijebu, Ode and Ibadan at the time, although Mummy did worry now for their safety in those towns. My older brothers were away in their schools, but Mummy sent for them to return to Lagos after the raid.

I remember the evening of that day as though it was yesterday. After the tidying up we bathed with Imperial Leather soap (what an odd thing to remember) after which we used mentholated dusting powder, which had a cooling effect. For dinner we had fried plantain with chicken and tomato stew served on the few remaining plates, which had not been broken and went to bed under mosquito nets. The mosquito coils were already burning and one or two drowsy mosquitoes were clinging on to the net. I hated the chemical smell from the coils, but as I was prone to malaria, with which I had been very ill, Mummy insisted I put up with it.

During this period we heard rumours of the retaliations and mass killings against Igbos in the North, in Lagos there were daily attacks in the streets, with bodies left by the roadside for two or three days. We were fearful because we were classed as Igbos as my natural father and stepfather were both Igbos, although my mother was actually Efik. Walking past those bodies on the way to school was a nightmare and has left a lasting impression on me. There is something unnerving about a dead body. I would avoid looking at the faces, in case it was someone I knew. Sometimes the bodies would be distended and bloated as they began to rot in the hot sun. The sight of them drove home to us that we were not safe as Igbos living in Lagos.

Known as a strong independent woman who got some respect from the military, Mummy was now being approached by Igbos seeking sanctuary and begging to hide in our house. These people were mostly introduced by the twelve or so tailors Mummy employed. Mummy took them in and hid them in our double garage. This had long been turned into a mini factory housing 14 sewing machines each manned by a tailor and this space served as a dormitory at night with some of the other rooms in the lower part of the house.

There were more military raids at the house.

Chapter Seventeen: Laxatives and Oranges

The soldier's raid and Igbo's being killed was forgotten, at least for one day when a basin full of oranges arrived at the house first thing in the morning. This meant it was the day of the month when we must all take laxatives. This was Mummy's way of keeping us all healthy and free from intestinal and stomach parasites. Castor oil was the favoured laxative. However the end result (no pun intended) was to be achieved either with castor oil or internal cleansing by means of a douche with medicine inserted into the rectum to empty the bowels. I must say I dreaded the enema, which was administered anyway following any complaint of a stomach problem, but I despised both equally. I would plead with Mummy that the mere sight of the basin full of oranges had already given me diarrhoea. She would ignore my pleas and make us children all line up and take two disgusting tablespoons full of the foul medicine. This was followed with lots of oranges already sliced into four or six pieces, ready for us to dive into them in our desperate bid to neutralise the ghastly taste and smell of the castor oil. Each of us would go through at least six to eight whole oranges until we felt we were over the nausea. The rest of the day we ate no food until we had been to the loo at least three or four times, sometimes even up to eight times. We did not play too far from the loos on the days of the laxatives. Every now and then, there would be arguments and desperate cries for access to the bathrooms or toilets.

"Patti how long will you be, everybody is waiting to use the toilet." my sister Rosaleen would shout
"Use the one downstairs."
"There's somebody in there already."
"Go and use the boys quarters then, I've not finished."
"Mummy, tell Patti to come out of the toilet."
"Patti come out of that toilet right now, you hear, and let your sister use the toilet."
"Yes Mummy!"

I tried to hurry as the cramp in my stomach gripped tighter, making me feel that I still had some castor oil to expel, but nothing would happen. I would hurry to open the door, but as soon as I turned the lock, the door would fly open and my sister would run past me to the toilet, sit down heavily with an audible sigh of relief. I would run downstairs looking for the next free toilet in which to relieve the mounting grumbles in my stomach, all the toilets were occupied and, outside the door I would repeat the threat to call Mummy I had just received from Rosaleen. This time it had no effect because the sister in this particular toilet was older and, therefore, outranked me. Bottom clenching never gave any signs of working and I would grab one of the Izal toilet paper rolls from the pantry in the kitchen and make for the forest behind the house.

I remember on one occasion, I was squatting down, watching out for snakes, when a millipede about a foot long made its way past me and disappeared under a leaf, I kept my eyes on the leaf hoping and praying that it did not turn around and head for my toes. I was told they are harmless, but I hate the look of them with their many legs all moving in a way that makes my hair stand on end. A red necked lizard scurried past and stopped to look at me, nodded his head and ran off into the forest. Two black ants ran up my leg, but I hastily brushed them off. It was now well past lunch time and the sun was beating down, the whole process was exhausting what with the lack of food, the disgusting after-taste of the castor oil still repeating and looking out for snakes and other scary inhabitants of the forest. I finished, went back to the house and sat on the bench against the wall of the garage, too tired to play and apprehensive of when the next attack would happen, wondering whether or not I could brave the forest again. I was soon joined on the bench by other members of the family no doubt feeling just as debilitated as I was.

Mummy had prepared a large pot of delicious smelling fish stew seasoned with mixed herbs and nutmeg and the aroma of the freshly made stew lingered in the air like an unseen messenger from Mummy, telling us it would soon be over and everything would return to normal. But at that moment the idea of eating after taking castor oil was far from tempting; not even Mummy's mouth-watering food could console me or compensate for the indignity of the process. Mummy emerged from the kitchen at the top of the stairs and called us, she gave us all lots of hot fluid to drink, which sent most of us scrambling back to the nearest toilet. Mercifully, this time it was short lived. To some of us it was a false alarm and then came the realisation that the worst was finally over and Mummy's fish stew began to have possibilities.

Soon we were all ravenous and Mummy, with the help of one or two of the house girls, would dish out the food with an amused look on her face as if she was trying very hard not to burst into laughter. We were too hungry and too weak to notice anything, but how much food was in our plates. On these occasions not even a basin full of food would have satisfied me because my eyes were definitely bigger than my stomach.

"Mummy can I have some more, please?" I would plead over my still full plate.

"Finish what you have and then come back for more," said Mummy.

After giving thanks to God for the food, we would eat in silence for the first ten minutes and then the good-hearted jokes, teasing and stories would begin.

"All Patti has to do is see the basin of oranges and her stomach goes into spasm."

"I beg, leave her alone, nobody likes castor oil."

"Mummy, Patti is the only one who should take castor oil, she eats too much and nobody can see where it goes." Everyone laughed.

"Don't mind them." Mummy would say.

Of course, I never did go back for more because there were so many of us and the amount that each of us could eat was always well calculated, so I knew there would probably be nothing left in the large pots of Mummy's tasty meal. I contrived to always be the last to leave the table, and finish off everyone's leftovers.

"Ah Patti! You are like a dustbin!" someone would comment as they all ran off to play shouting their thank yous to Mummy for the food.

Often I would look up at Mummy's face as she watched me rather thoughtfully. After cooking and dishing out the food, Mummy would go back to her sewing machine while the house girls cleared the table around me. I would finish the last pieces of fish and rice and run off to see what fun I was missing. We had survived another day of castor oil until the next month.

Chapter Eighteen: Mummy on her Own

Mummy visited Dad again in Ghana, during the time when there was disaffection with Nkrumah's administration owing to his Preventive Detention Act. She was shocked to find that Daddy had a new mistress. Mummy was subjected to a great deal of indignity and left straight away with Sammy and Eno and my two older teenage brothers. Her police escort delayed mummy and the children en route to the airport. She was taken to Police Headquarters for interrogation. My two older brothers were detained in jail for a short while. Mummy suspected that this was arranged by Daddy's new girlfriend that was a member of a highly placed family. They finally got to the plane, but before it could take off Mummy was ordered out of the plane at gunpoint and told to sit on the tarmac, while police off-loaded her belonging from the plane as the other passengers looked on. Mummy was upset and annoyed, but never showed it in front of my little brother and sister and the two teenagers. She did not want to give the soldiers any satisfaction, so she remained calm and straight faced throughout. The anxious moments as the soldiers searched her cases and radioed for instructions seemed to last for hours. Her personal belongings were then confiscated. Even the children's belongings were taken away. Eventually she was allowed to board another plane for Lagos. She realised then that this meant that she had to become even more independent and care for us eight children on her own. She felt she could not rely on Dad to provide for us, although she did not entirely give up on him. In any case the current situation meant that he would not be able to return safely to Lagos.

Mummy began to get much-needed contracts for her mini factory from local companies, including Vitafoam (whose young managing director has remained a close friend of the family till this day), to make their mattress and cushion covers, she also made wedding dresses, cakes and uniforms for the airlines like BOAC, especially ground hostesses and stewards. When Lagos airport was taken over by the military, she had to let the BOAC contract go, as it would have attracted too much attention to us as an Igbo family living in Lagos area. We were already under scrutiny as Igbos and Dad was wanted for treason and was a prominent member of Action Group, a banned democratic political party. It was hard for Mummy to get contracts, as some companies would not want to be associated with us because we were prominent Igbos. Mummy would have sleepless nights trying to think of how she would not only pay our school fees, but also feed the ever-increasing number of refugees sleeping in our home, especially in the servant's quarters or in the double garage. Of course, if they were able, some of them made contributions to the household. At one time there were thirty-five people of both sexes attending the daily five o'clock morning prayers, which Mummy conducted. Later she would help to build a church, which was named after her 'The Dorothy Ikoku Memorial Church', a wonderfully happy place.

I remember one morning during the school holidays, when the bell rang at 5am for prayers; the living room was so full of people that most of them had to stand. It was my sister Maggie's turn to read from the Bible. Mummy had chosen a reading about Wisdom, Knowledge and Understanding. The reading said that Wisdom was the greatest of these and, therefore, the greatest gift of all. I secretly prayed for the gift of Wisdom telling God I wanted nothing else but Wisdom, in its most heavenly form. Only a child could make such an ambitious request, but nothing is impossible for God.

To feed us all, Mummy started a veritable poultry farm in the backyard. It was at this time that we were befriended by Mr Ogbu, a very kind man who would accompany Mummy to her meetings with various factories when she was looking for contracts. One day Mummy and Mr Ogbu came back with a contract from Wahum,, a Chinese factory that manufactured matches. A precise number of matchsticks needed to be packed into each box. So the double garage was turned into matchsticks packing factory. Some sewing contracts had been withdrawn when the factories realised the political dangers they might be in due to the fact that we were hated Igbos. The Chinese couldn't tell the difference between the local tribes so they did not seem to care! They only knew my mother as 'Mummy', a title which stuck for the rest of her life, because not only was she a great mother to her own children, but she was also Mummy to all those who came to her, in their time of need.

I realise that Mummy had some great advantages which assisted her in the dire situation she was in, when left to fend for her eight children and look after many refugees. Mummy had little formal education, but had sharp instincts. She was beautiful, elegant and determined. She possessed incredible mental strength that came from her belief that Jesus Christ was her Good Shepherd and her best friend, therefore, she would lack for nothing. She was a brilliant seamstress and great entrepreneur, these together with her good looks and winning ways made it difficult to say "no" to her.

Since Daddy was living with another woman in Ghana, Mummy was not short of unwanted suitors, but there was one particular man (whom I will call Mr Jones), with his flashy car, who would persist in visiting without an invitation. More often than not, he would time his arrival to coincide with Mummy's afternoon tea break. He was so rude and pompous and irritated everyone, including the servants, but we were too polite to show this in his presence. It was obvious that he thought Mummy was rich because of her name. He was also aware of her ancestry as the daughter of King Effiom Coco-Bassey. That was where his knowledge of her life stopped! Of course, the truth was that Mummy was struggling to make ends meet and provide for the entire ever-growing household. She loved sardines or kippers or jam sandwiches for her tea. We children ensured that, whilst we had them, which was not often, no one touched our stocks of these, so that Mummy could have her favourite sandwich, when she took a break from sewing and supervising.

One day when my older sisters were home on school holidays, Mr Jones turned up in his usual fashion to join Mummy for her afternoon tea break. We girls wanted to put a stop to his unwanted attentions (or at least make it uncomfortable for him), but, clearly, we were not in the position, as an Igbo family, to make enemies of anyone, but the events at this visit were to grant us our wishes. The routine was to lay the tea on the coffee table with sandwiches, biscuits and cakes, if there were any (Mummy baked incredible cakes), the hot water would be kept in a flask because Mummy could often be delayed for a few minutes by one thing or another. She worked really hard and every minute was important. The Ceiling fan was switched on to cool the room; we still had permanent electricity at that time. The man and we girls were already waiting in the living room; he was draped in a brilliant white, lace danshiki and white hat. Mummy entered the room and greeted him;

"Mr Jones, welcome," she said and sat down to pour the tea. She unscrewed the top of the hot water flask and poured the water into the teapot. She then asked the house girl for more hot water saying the flask was only half full and there would not be enough for second cups. The house girl rushed into the kitchen and emerged carrying the kettle full of hot water; then, she tripped over the carpet pitching the kettle full of hot water into the air in a slow motion curve. Completing the arch some of the water landed in Mr Jones's lap. He leapt up and let out a scream, holding the outer layer of his danshiki away from his body to keep the scalding water from his skin! Thank goodness it missed Mummy. The kettle crashed on to the mosaic floor. The house girl, in a panic, ran into the kitchen and grabbed the nearest dirty floor cloth from the floor, ran back into the room and started wiping the floor. Mummy shouted.

"Don't worry about the floor get Mr Jones a towel to dry himself."
"Yes ma!" she replied and proceeded to wipe down his expensive lace white danshiki with the dirty floor cloth, leaving a great big dirty stain on the front of his rounded belly!
"You useless girl!" he shouted and slapped the girl across the face. We all gasped, nobody was allowed to hit anyone in Mummy's house and before he could hit her again, Mummy had hold of his hand. The house girl ran out of the room in tears, wailing more than the slap was worth. We all jumped up surprised and concerned and said so many
"Sorry Sir"s that Mummy was finding it hard to keep a straight face.
"These girls are so difficult to train, no matter how hard you try!" she said."
But Mr Jones was incandescent and with a toss of his head he said;
"I have never been so humiliated in my whole life. I refuse to come back to this house, as long as that useless girl is here".

Mummy saw him to the top of the stairs, with polite apologies; meanwhile the maid was still making a good job of wailing. When Mummy came back into the room, we were all quiet, afraid to laugh, the maid had stopped wailing and we watched Mummy walk to the settee, in front of the window and sit down.
"Go and see if he has gone" she said
We ran to the window, his car wasn't there and we ran back.
"He's gone, Mummy." we said
 Mummy started laughing; we were all relieved and joined in parading around the room mimicking the man's outbursts and fat belly. It was so good to see Mummy laugh her wonderful laugh. We never saw Mr Jones again.

I don't know how she did it, but one day, Mummy treated us to a black and white television set. It was such a wonderful day, imagine it, we had our very own television set and, better still, we wouldn't have to stand outside the window of our next door neighbour, peering in to watch our favourite programmes.

The neighbour was a lawyer, whose wife was the teacher who had left me at school to walk home for seven hours on my own. I suppose we were a nuisance, because they would often close the curtains, but the curtains did not fit very well and we were able to catch a glimpse of programmes like 'The Lucille Ball Show' and various Cowboys and Indians shows, it was so amazing! You would have thought that they might have invited us in to watch the television with their children for an hour or two, but they never did. Having our own TV set was such a revelation, affording so much fun and information about the rest of the world. Anyway, the television became a means of getting household chores and homework done on time, so that we could watch the programmes we loved. It was like torture to be interrupted and sent on an errand in the middle of any of your favourite programmes. Occasionally, the screen would go blank followed by lines of different shades of grey and a sign would be displayed with these words; "We apologise for the loss of your programme, normal service will be resumed as soon as possible". This would be followed by a loud "Oh no!" from all the children gathered.

I remember Boris Karloff and Alfred Hitchcock movies, 'The Twilight Zone' and who can forget Hammer Horror Dracula films, which frightened us all. I would watch these horror films through my fingers, so I could close my hand when there was a scary bit. Later I met the lovely Christopher Lee and he taught me to high kick, so not so scary really! There were favourites like Perry Mason, Dr Kildare, Ben Casey and Elliot Ness of The Untouchables. We would shout at the screen during scenes where some silly woman's husband or partner was being attacked and she would cower in the corner screaming instead of joining in the fight. This seemed so odd to us, surely you get out and fight if you are in danger! We wondered why white women were portrayed as weaklings in this way, when they should be fighting for their lives or virginity!

Chapter Nineteen: Dad Came Home in Chains

Another shock now awaited us, one that would change the course of our lives forever. Dad had settled in Ghana on political asylum with Nkrumah while Chief Owolowo and other members of AG were tried for treason and imprisoned in 1992. Dad was away on a special visit when the warrant was issued for the arrest of eighteen members of the Action Group including him.

Dad had been away working with President Nkrumah for four years, when on Feb 24th 1966 we woke up at dawn to the news of a military takeover in Ghana. Whilst he was out of the country in North Korea, President Nkrumah had been deposed and we had no news of Dad who had been appointed as Chief Political Adviser to the President. We heard about the gunfire and explosions at the Palace. Mummy contacted the Nigerian authorities for Dad's whereabouts and news, to no avail. Mummy was calm and prayerful as always, as we all waited for news of Dad. She telephoned Chief Enaharo to ask for news. Chief Enaharo was a friend of Dad's and a fellow member of Action Group and one of the eighteen who had been accused of treason. Chief Enaharo had been released that year from prison as a political prisoner. He had tried, like Dad to avoid the trial for treason in 1963 and escaped via Ghana to the UK from where he was extradited. Mummy rang him and begged for news, from Ghana. In the past, there had been news of assassination attempts and we were naturally afraid for Dad. During one of these attempts to assassinate President Nkrumah with a bomb, in August 1962, a little girl, who was presenting the President with a bouquet of flowers, was killed and the President was hospitalised for deep shrapnel wounds.
Chief Anthony Ehahoro told Mummy Dad had been arrested, that they plan to fly him back to Lagos and we had to thank God they did not kill him!"
"Ete ke arrest Ete Kamba, mmo esin eye ke plane, eye no ye edi Lagos. Abassi sosong ke mmo iwot ke eye!" Mummy explained the conversation to us, in Efik.
No sooner had she put the phone down than the lines to our house were cut.

In Ghana a gun battle had raged for the control of Flagstaff House, the President's residence, between the mutinous army and the Presidential Guards. President Nkrumah was away on a visit to North Korea and China.

Then it was announced that the Presidential Guards had surrendered when the coup leaders threatened to blow up Flagstaff House. Dad had been arrested in his home in Accra, beaten up and chained and at the request of the Nigerian government, was flown back to Nigeria and taken to prison in Kaduna. Mum feared the worst now, because this was in the North where Igbo's had been massacred: indeed this was the heart of enemy territory. Like Papa, Dad was an Igbo. For a while no one would say where he was being held. Finally the news came that he was held in prison with Chief Awolowo.

We lived in fear of bad news about Dad's safety and were fearful of further raids by the soldiers at the house, as we lived with our mother in Lagos, which was also in enemy territory. We children were shielded from the news as much as possible, but very often there would be looks exchanged between the adults with no words uttered which frightened us. "Careless talk is dangerous." People had to be careful what they said.

It was very difficult to predict the day, or time the next raid on the house by lorry-loads of ill-disciplined soldiers would take place so we lived in expectant fear. The day finally came. It had been a great day, I wore my favourite white organza dress, we had been to Church in the morning and lunch was about to be prepared by the ladies in the house with the younger children (which included me), doing the fetching and carrying.

We were to have my favourite Sunday lunch, rice and chicken curry, so hot it would make your eyes and nose water and set your mouth on fire. At the end of `church service, all I could think about was Sunday lunch, and the delicious prospect that after lunch, Tony and Johnny, our older brothers, would take us to the swimming pool in a nearby private club.

It had been a good day, until the arrival of the soldiers. They came without warning in three lorry-loads, this time. They drove in through the gates and before the driver had stopped, some soldiers were already jumping off the vehicles. There was a sudden deafening, frightening noise of hoarse shouting voices, all screaming in Pidgin English at the same time. They were threatening, unruly and waving their guns about. We were all shocked and feared for our lives, although we did expect them to come at some time, it still seemed so frightening. I held on to my brother, Tony's hand. If it is possible to feel panicked, frightened, confused and safe all at the same time, then that's the only way to describe my emotions at that moment.

Mummy remained calm and cool as usual, she was the "iron" head of the family group of eight children, two male servants, two live-in house-girls and our motley band of refugees, who had been sent into the bush at the back of the house as soon as the soldiers burst in at the front. Nevertheless, they would have been easily found, if the soldiers had gone looking for them. Of course, this was not the first time soldiers had broken in, to search the house. Mummy standing at the top of the stairs did not flinch as the soldiers scaled the stairs, two at a time, waving their guns at her, the first few thugs ignored her and pushed her aside, striding into the house and smashing all before them.

"What do you want with us? Just tell me what you want, so that we can help you find it!" Mummy shouted

"Shut up, woman!" was the reply.

The soldier who spoke was a junior officer. As he spoke, he roughly manhandled Mummy to the floor. Johnny, my seventeen years old eldest brother, who was being held on the landing by some soldiers, broke free and rushed forward to protect Mummy. Two of them set upon him knocking him to the ground with their rifles; it all seemed to be happening in slow motion. The screams of anguish from our Mother galvanized the rest of us and we leapt upon the soldiers, all fears for our own safety forgotten, in our blind efforts to protect Johnny and Mummy who was still on the ground. Tony and the three of us girls were all engaged in the untidy struggle. Tugging at trousers, arms, shirts-sleeves and anything that we could grab to hold back the men, fighting and biting. I sank my teeth into a soldier's arm. But still they were hitting and kicking Johnny who was desperately trying to protect his head from the riffle buts. Hearing the commotion, a senior officer came back out of the house and was confronted with the melee of soldiers and us battling, screaming children. He barked an order to call his men off and ordered them back to the vehicles. We all rushed to Johnny's side and held him tightly. He smiled through the blood, but made no sound.

As the officer turned to follow his men, Mummy stood in his way and wagged a finger in his face.

"Officer," she yelled.

"Would you treat your mother and family in this way?"

He hesitated before starting to speak, then thought better of it, took a step back and smartly saluted, and without a word followed his men to the vehicles.

It felt like a lifetime before they finally backed out of the gate raising a dust cloud in the heat, smashing the gate. We were all visibly shaken, Mummy pulled us together, however, breaking the spell, in her usual way, by delegating the cooking chores for lunch to us children whilst the grown-ups tidied-up the mess left by the soldiers and while she attended to Johnny.

He was bleeding badly from the head and a huge cut around his left eye and was taken to the hospital by Mummy and the driver. His face was unrecognizable. One of my elder sisters took charge of getting the house back to normal. She made me change my white dress. It was spattered with Johnny's blood. It was only when we went into the house again that we realized the extent of the damage done. There was so much to clean up, all that was left of my mother's best china was broken and the glasses, which had miraculously survived the last raid, were now all smashed, more furniture was broken and upended, not much had survived as far as we could see, still we would have our beds to sleep in.

By nightfall, Mummy was back with Johnny, at the time the doctors were not quite sure how much damage his eye had suffered, though he had taken some terrible blows to the head and body and would never fully recover. Nevertheless he later qualified as an aeronautic engineer. His head was all bandaged over the stitches. There was an atmosphere of confusion about the house, house girls running here and there, grown-ups ushering us away from broken glass. Hushed voices. I held onto Johnny. No chicken yet! Finally, all the broken glass was swept up and disposed of. The clothing that had not been ripped, but only thrown about was washed and hung up. Things got back to normal and in the evening we had our chicken, but I didn't like it.

Johnny, however, was not back to normal, he remained ill for weeks. All my twelve years we had been so close, his pain was my pain, and his joy was my joy. He had the gentlest of manners and a heart that topped the gentleness with kindness. I loved him so dearly. I just spent that evening hanging around him, hugging him every now and then and keeping watch over him. I tried so hard not to show my tears or my deep concern for the beating he had taken, so that, somehow I hoped that if I didn't cry for him it would all go away. As the oldest boy, he was expected to act as the head of the family in the absence of our stepfather, but of course he was far too young to have responsibility for us all in such hostile circumstances.

I was comforted then by Tony, who made all of us laugh again, aping the soldiers and that oh! So smart salute. I hated the soldiers and wished that I had the power to inflict some dreadful Biblical vengeance upon them, I hoped, with all my being that I had done permanent damage with my teeth to that soldier's arm. I hoped that I had at least drawn blood, ripped the skin right off and left my mark on him forever! But I doubt that he even felt it.

Perhaps it was just as well that our stepfather had been away in Ghana and was now in prison in Kaduna, the Military were to target us so often that had he been with us he would have almost certainly have been killed in one of the raids at the house.

Chapter Twenty: The Biafra War

In 1960, Nigeria gained its independence from Britain and was divided into three Federations as the Northern, Western and Eastern Regions. At the same time it joined the United Nations and the Commonwealth. Two years later in 1963 a new charter was declared, Nigeria announced itself to be a Federal Republic, during the same year, a forth region was created: the Mid-West Region. In 1966, the government was overthrown by predominantly Igbo army officers lead by Major Nzeogwu, who was from my father's village. The Federal Prime Minister and the Premiers of the Northern and Western regions were assassinated. General Aguyi Ironsi became the first military President of Nigeria. Six months later came the second military coup during which General Ironsi was killed. General Gowon became the next and longest serving military Head of State.

During the month of September 1966, tens of thousands of minority Igbos were massacred in the Northern Region by the majority Hausas, who, it is said resented their relative wealth. As a result, a million Igbo refugees moved into the Eastern Region, their natural homeland, and they started to expel non-Igbos or other non-indigenous peoples from the Eastern Region further enflaming the situation.

From the beginning of 1967, the Eastern Region was threatening to secede from the Federal Republic. Chief Awolowo, (head of the Action Group) who had been released from prison with Daddy earlier that year, regrouped his supporters, including our stepfather and demanded the removal of all northern troops garrisoned in the Western Region. He warned that the Western Region would follow, if the Eastern Region left the Federation. The Federal Military Government agreed to the troop withdrawal.

Lieutenant Colonel Ojukwu, who was the Igbo military Governor of the Eastern Region, had reached breaking point in the relationship with the rest of the military Government. Saddled with the cost of resettling Igbo refugees, who had fled the massacre from Lagos and Northern Region, Ojukwu rejected the plan for reconciliation put forward by the Federal Military Government. He announced the intention to retain all revenues collected in the Eastern Region as reparation for the resettlement of Igbo refugees. The Eastern Region Consultative Assembly voted to secede from Nigeria. Back in Lagos, General Gowon announced a State of Emergency and revealed plans to end the Regions as they were, and constituted the re-division of the country into twelve states. General Gowon also appointed Chief Awolowo and other prominent civilians as Commissioners in the new States and Federal Government to widen his political support. On May 30 1967: Lieutenant Colonel Ojukwu, was authorized by The Eastern Region Consultative Assembly, to answer the Federal Decree by declaring the Eastern Region a sovereign and independent republic under the name of Biafra. The Nigerian government's failure to protect the lives of easterners was cited as the principal cause for the secession. He described the secession as a measure taken unwillingly, after all efforts to safeguard the Igbo people in other Regions had failed. General Gowon, refused to recognize Biafra's separation.

The Military Government released Daddy, a year after his incarceration, he returned home to us in Lagos. I think, some understanding was reached with Mummy, bearing in mind that we were all in grave danger. We children were all thrilled that he was alive and to have him back with us. While the negotiations between the Regions were happening life went on in Lagos with Igbos being continuously targeted. After the massacre of the Igbos, we all seemed sure that Biafra was better off on its own, but we were fearful of a war. My sister Rosie and I had been allowed to visit our father in Asaba in the Eastern Region (Biafra) for a short holiday and we were just coming to the end of our stay when the war started. I shall cover the story of how Rosie and I got back to Lagos later in the book.

As hostilities broke out in July 1967 the Biafra troops were successful at first, but it wasn't long before the far larger and more superior forces of the Federal Government began to push Biafra's boundaries inward from north, south and west until at the end of the war only ten percent of its original area was left. Although the Biafra troops had inferior weapons to the Federal troops, they had the benefit of a very strong leadership and great determination. They were hugely outnumbered and outgunned, so they concentrated their efforts on exploring weak points in the Federal lines. At the beginning they made speedy strategic gains, carving off and surrounding advancing Federal Troops, and initiating commando attacks behind Federal lines. These were not reported in Lagos, but we got bits of news about the advancing Federal troops. By the 1968 Biafra had lost its access to the sea and was blocked inland. Its only access to supplies of any kind was by air and the people were starving and dying and fatal disease was rife.

Internationally, the OAU (Organization of African Unity), the Catholic Church and other organizations tried to bring about reconciliation. Federal Nigeria and General Gowon's regime was recognized by most countries.

The then Soviet Union and United Kingdom supplied the Federal Military Government of Nigeria with arms. Other African countries like Gabon, Tanzania, Cote d'Ivoire and Zambia recognized the Republic of Biafra as an independent State. France and Portugal supported Biafra and many brave volunteering individuals risked their lives to fly over Federal held territory to drop weapons, medicine and food into Biafra after pictures of the starving and sick children were featured in the press in the outside world. Frederick Forsythe was very highly regarded by Igbos due to his exposure of the plight of the people of Biafra. I have since had the privilege to meet both him and Martin Bell, both war correspondents, and independent observers of the war. They campaigned in Britain to get as much help as they could for Biafra, the children and for Biafrans stuck behind the enemy lines.

During the rest of the war we had no news of our relatives, because communications between those living in Federal Nigeria and Biafra were non-existent. My father, our half brothers and sisters, aunties, uncles and grandparents were all in Biafra. Some were in the Federal Government occupied areas and we heard unconfirmed rumours that great atrocities occurred in these territories.

Later we learnt that Papa had been pulled out of his house and lined up with other men, to be shot by the Federal soldiers. Fortunately, one of the officers, whom Papa had helped when the officer was a student, recognized Papa and spoke to him in Hausa, (the northern language. Papa was fluent in this language owing to years he spent as Postmaster to some Northern cities.)
"Papa, what are you doing in here?" the officer asked.
Papa explained that he had been dragged out of his house along with the other men. The officer then took him to his superior officer and after a short discussion Papa was saved from the firing squad, but he was unable to save the other men. Later, however, he was given a post as a local official overseeing the area by the invading Federal army.

Reports were leaked into Lagos, about how the invasion of the Igbo heartland and remaining rebel-held territory had stalled due to stiff Biafran resistance, but it was difficult at the time to know what to believe.

Mummy did all she could to get us children into boarding schools away from Lagos and the war areas for our safety's sake. The fact that her children had to pass the dead bodies of Igbos on the way to their schools in Lagos was giving her nightmares. Fighting broke out easily in Lagos and without warning in the volatile situation, with Igbos being hounded, but the federal Government was getting this under control, In Lagos it was obvious from the bodies on the roadsides that those carrying out the attacks were mostly targeting young adult Igbo males. Mummy was particularly worried about her two sons who were in their late teens and were an obvious target. Officially, they were deemed as security risks, their lives were in danger and they could have been interned. Thank God that through her political contacts and with Dad's help she managed to get Johnny away to Germany to study Aeronautic Engineering and Tony was sent to Los Angeles to train to be a Pilot, both their chosen fields. My oldest sister Grace was studying in London. Maggie was boarding at Our Lady of Apostle College in Ijebu-Ode, sixty-one miles from Lagos. Rosaleen was at St Theresa's College Ibadan, seventy-nine miles from Lagos. Mummy worked terribly hard to pay for us all, but she managed her business well and Daddy was able to help at this time. I eventually got into Holy Child College at Obalende, near Ikoyi, Lagos. The college was eighteen miles away. After one term of Mummy and me leaving home at 5.30am to get to the college for 8am, I moved in with a safe family near to the college. With all but her youngest children away from home Mummy had peace of mind and had more time to run her sewing business and mini factory.

Before I left home to be nearer my school we heard a lot of talk about the "final offensive" and from the refugees in our house we heard rumours of atrocities by the federal troops against the people of Asaba. This was the town where our father lived and where Rosie and I had spent our last holidays and had to escape from. We were warned not to give an opinion or even engage in any discussions about the war outside the house, the slogan "Careless Talk Kills" was everywhere.

Mummy made life for us as normal as she could make it. How she fed us all, and the many people, who came to find refuge in our house, is a miracle!

The war ended on Monday 12 January 1970 with the announcement of the Surrender of Biafra. The Biafra Head of State, General Ojukwu, had been persuaded to leave the embattled last enclave of Biafra and as an Igbo he remains a great hero of mine and of all the Igbo people.

Nigeria was blessed to have had General Gowon as the military Head of State at the end of the Biafra war. In General Gowon's welcome of the surrender, he famously said that there would be "no vanquished and no victors" and urged all Nigerians to come back together as one nation and re-iterated his promises of a general amnesty. Easterners were to be "welcomed with open arms" into one united Nigeria

I have always thought General Gowon's speech at the end of the war could have been a lot of empty words, but they weren't, he kept his promises. I have a lot of respect for General Gowon, whom I have met. At the point when the war ended, he had absolute power, but he showed integrity and wisdom in the re-integration of the Nation. In my view this was a fine example of how a Christian leader, whether military or otherwise, should act. I feel Nigeria owes General Gowon a great deal for the majestic, intelligent, compassionate and Christian way he dealt with the aftermath of the war and avoided further massive bloodletting. In my opinion he should be recognised as a great African Leader. That does not take away from the sufferings of the Igbo people, my people, (including me and my family) or the appalling number of innocent people killed. About two million people are said to have died in the Nigerian civil war between 1967 and 1970. Having lived through it, I have been affected by it in the way I deal with people and in my outlook on life. It has given me a great appreciation of life, a reason for being and an acknowledgment of the awesomeness of God.

Chapter Twenty One: Escape From Asaba

Before the war when I was thirteen, my sister Rosaleen and I were sent on a visit to our father in Asaba. Owing to the military road blocks, the journey of over two hundred and thirty miles took much longer than the average six hours estimated for Asaba. It was one of the few times Mummy had bowed to pressure from Papa to let some of us spend a holiday with him. We knew that there were negotiations about Biafra, and general unrest and killings in Lagos, but no one really believed that there would be a war, so, apart from its length, the journey to Asaba did not seem to be particularly hazardous. At this time Mummy had changed cars from her Opel to a Karmann Ghia and the car was not large enough for such a long distance journey, so we arranged to join a station wagon hire vehicle that was making the journey. She arranged for us to travel with an adult who knew the roads well and who had made the trip many times. News about Biafra was not much covered in Lagos at the time. As the town Asaba, was separated from the rest of the Igbo mainland by the River Niger, Asaba had declared itself 'neutral' territory hoping that, it would be in no danger of attack by the Federal Government troops in the unlikely event that war should break out.

We set off from Ikeja very early, at about 5am, in a "partly hired" nine passengers station wagon. "Partly hired" meant that the car would pick us up from home, but then be able to pick up other passengers on route. We picked up two or three at the bus depot and set off on our journey.

For a while we sped past villagers walking along the sides of the Lagos to Benin Road. Some of the villagers carried firewood or bunches of plantain or bananas perfectly balanced on their heads. A few of the older women had colourful wrappers tied loosely around their waists. One or two were topless exposing well suckled, sagging breasts. The men carried the heavier bags of rice or garri (dried cassava grains) and wore ill fitted trousers that stopped above the ankles. Some had short sleeved, sweat covered unbuttoned, shirts while others were bare-chested.

As we sped past, the villagers kept their eyes focused ahead for fear of tripping over the many potholes at the sides of the uneven road. The naked little children waved cheerily as we passed them. Rosie and I waved back. We drove past hawkers and their makeshift roadside stalls. The driver slowed down as we approached the hawkers to give his passengers the opportunity to buy something if we needed it. Young boys aged about seven and over, would make a game of racing the station wagon. They kept this up for about fifty meters or so after which they could run no further. They stopped exhausted. I watched them through the rear view window, as panting, they waved to us. They argued and teased each other about who was the fastest or slowest, but soon their naked forms disappeared from view. I wondered if they kept this up with every passing car.

After about two hours we started dropping off some passengers. We filled up with petrol and then picked up more passengers. A crowd of hawkers gathered around the station wagon trying to sell their goods. We had all kinds of products pushed through the windows to attract the passengers' attention. There were ground-nuts, loaves of bread, boiled eggs, cold Fanta, fresh ube (African pear), Bolli (roasted plantains), bananas, puff-puffs (local donuts) as well as gift items like mirrors, combs and blouses. All these were shoved at passengers, with gusto and a lot of shouting. There were all kinds of cutlery, biro ballpoint pens, Bournvita, Ovaltine, Tate & Lyle sugar, Peak milk, Cabin biscuits and Horlicks (my favourite). They carried towels, Omo washing powder, with the slogan *"Omo adds brightness to whiteness",* sandals and many more products. Rosie, our chaperone and I bought bread, tins of sardine, bags of roasted groundnuts and bottles of Fanta before setting off again. Most of the passengers fell asleep in the crowded station wagon now carrying far too many people. Nine was the maximum number of people the car was designed to accommodate, but at one point we had thirteen people squashed in. Travellers from stop off towns didn't know when the next transport would come along, so they were willing to sit among the luggage, even carrying some on their laps.

When, rounding a corner, the car suddenly came to a grinding halt, we all woke up wondering why we had stopped. In front of us was a queue of buses, cars and trucks. After about an hour uniformed soldiers unceremoniously ordered us out of our vehicle. We had hit the first of many military roadblocks on the way to Benin and Asaba. The soldiers or policemen carrying guns at various checkpoints, along the way took a few male passengers off the station wagon. No one said why the men were taken off, but they did not return to the station wagon and we were told to leave. The driver was uncommunicative and clearly did not want to talk about it. At each checkpoint the soldiers searched the vehicle. Most of the time, they would make us get out of the car while they carried out their search.

At some towns after the checkpoints we would drop some passengers and pick up two or three more and while the station wagon was stationary the rest of us seized the opportunity to stretch our legs and buy cold drinks from the street hawkers. It was always good to be able to get things from the small stalls outside the conurbation of makeshift houses and huts, which, at the time, passed for towns in the area and were dotted along the way. When the car was stopped, the heat inside became overpowering. It was wonderful when the car gathered speed, letting in cool air through the open windows. I managed to retain the window seat, which I shared with Rosie and I stretched my arms out of the window to let the rushing cool air cool off my underarm for as long as I could. As it was approaching midday, the Sun was directly overhead in its full glare, with not a single cloud in the sky. Whenever the car stopped, it felt like an oven. This was the part of the day when workers usually take a break for their siesta. Even the ever active hawkers sat down under the shade of the umbrella shaped canopies over the stalls at the roadside, made no movement and only watched passers-by and vehicles full of potential customers with a vacant and disinterested look in their eyes. They all had that familiar look of lethargic surrender to the power of the mid-day Sun. At this time of day, the costumer would have to call the hawkers over to the vehicle if they wanted to buy anything from them.

"Oga make una come now, you no want to sell anything? I beg make una hurry now, we no get time to waste!" The passengers would complain. In a couple of hours' time these same hawkers would get that second burst of energy and be up and at the passing trade. When the Sun finally began its descent from the high spot to down behind the tall trees, we overheated humans breathed a huge sigh of relief. The tall and dense trees mercifully threw welcome shade over the hawkers, stall owners and travellers alike.

I wondered that these small places in the middle of nowhere seemed to exist just to sell their goods to passing travellers. But when you have been stuffed inside a vehicle like sardines, with strangers, some of who were beginning to smell of a mixture of sweaty armpits and mothballs, the stops at these small communities were a welcome break indeed.

As we continued our journey, everyone became resigned to put up with the many road blocks and these interruptions to our journey began to be treated as normal, unlike the first two times we were stopped. However, the queues at the roadblocks got longer and more chaotic.

We had learned that our driver was not Nigerian, but was from Cotonou in the newly formed Republic of Benin, (not to be confused with the Benin in

Nigeria) a former French colony known as Dahomey. The passengers started chatting to him as they realized why the soldiers were not hassling him as much as they hassled drivers of other vehicles. His accent was undeniably French African.

Our vehicle finally got to the outskirts of Benin. The large town of Benin is over a hundred and seventy six miles east of Lagos on the Sagamu-Benin Expressway and just over eighty-two miles west of Asaba. At one point in Benin, there was a rather large crowd at the side of the road. Someone said something about a rampaging mob that had killed some people and had left their bodies outside their houses. Our driver shook his head;

"Every day, these killings are getting really bad!" he whispered in his French African accent. We couldn't see the bodies through the crowd, nor did I want to! We asked no questions and we drove on.

I am not sure exactly where we were when we saw soldiers dressed in two shades of forest green with soft crumpled hats. We realised that these were Biafra Soldiers. Their uniforms were different from those of the soldiers nearer Lagos. Some had helmets on. They stopped the car and peered through the windows into the car checking out each of the passengers in turn, as if hoping to read something in their faces. Other soldiers in the background carried on their conversations in Igbo, one soldier searched the back of our vehicle rather half-heartedly, while the one peering through car windows asked questions. He looked at me the youngest and asked:
"Na where una de go?" (*Where are you going?*)
"Asaba" said our chaperone, the older woman travelling with us.
"What is your name?"
"Ngozi Chukwu-Ka." the woman replied, giving him my Igbo name.
"I am asking the girl, not you."
The soldier searching through the boot of the car shouted from the back.
"*Hapu fa.* Leave them alone. Drive on!"

We drove on toward Asaba. Conversation amongst the passengers was down to a minimum and nobody asked questions. Who could forget the slogan among the Igbos in Lagos during the killings *'careless talk kills'*? Nobody said much and if they were afraid, they were careful not to show it. There was no sign of fighting between the two sets of soldiers on the way to Asaba. When the driver stopped for a call of nature, we all took the opportunity to do the same. We found a spot in the nearby bush keeping an eye out for snakes and other creepy crawlies. There were more Biafra roadblocks and between each roadblock, there were many Biafra soldiers in lorries. Some were sitting by the roadside looking bored. There were a few burnt out vehicles, but that was not particularly unusual at that time. Several times our car was ordered off the road to let the army vehicles and foot soldiers by. We finally arrived at Asaba at dusk.

The next few days everyone was talking about the start of the war and how Biafra soldiers had gone through Asaba and were advancing towards Benin. Some said Benin had fallen and the Biafra soldiers were marching on to Lagos. It never occurred to me that without knowing it we had probably passed quite close by some fighting on our journey, as we saw no signs of battle. Later I learnt there had been little or no resistance from the Federal side.

The town of Asaba had a relatively small population. It is strategically located in an idyllic and tranquil setting on the west banks of the River Niger on the main highway. The river separated the town from the rest of the Igbo dominated mainland, which had become Biafra. During the months of August, September to early October 1967 Asaba was first occupied by Biafra soldiers, as they made their way to Benin, then as the tide of the war reversed, the town was occupied by Federal Government troops of Nigeria. Later we heard that Asaba suffered a terrible massacre at the hands of the predominantly northern Federal soldiers. Almost 1000 men and boys were killed, but I have not had confirmation of this. The killing was apparently their revenge on the birthplace of one or two of the leaders of the first coup d'état, especially Major Nzeogwu (whom my family knew well), who were indigenes of Asaba and the surrounding areas. Also, there were a few high ranking officers in General Ojukwu's Biafra army, who were also from Asaba.

At the time, I was in my early teens, and was experiencing a delayed puberty. This, according to my aunties, was completely due to my fondness for playing football and climbing trees with the boys! I had begun to worry about why my chest was not showing any signs of sprouting breasts like my cousins and other girls of my age. At first, I was tall for my age, but I have stayed the same height ever since. Now that Mummy was not allowing me to play as much football with the boys, I had expected to develop physically, but nothing was happening. I had to stop climbing trees and had to help more with the sewing and baking. So I went back to my favourite pastime of listening to adult's conversations. But in Asaba before the invasion of Northern troops, the conversations were not of the usual wisdom or challenging lessons about relationships, matrimonial problems, whose gossip has backfired and so on. All the talk was about remaining neutral and whether General Ojukwu's secession of Biafra from the Federal Republic of Nigeria would really succeed. I felt that the rest of

Nigeria would not let the secession happen without a fight, especially with more oil being discovered in the south. Or the conversations were about whether the rumours were true that the Federal Government Troops, who were stationed in Benin, stood by and watched as Igbo families were targeted by mobs. There were frightening descriptions of the Federal troops (who were said to be predominantly Hausas), which painted them as tall demons with red eyes and jet-black skin. Before then, I had always thought the Hausas were beautiful, elegant, and softly spoken and the Fulanis were just simply beautiful, especially the women. As a child, the most beautiful woman I had seen was a Fulani milkmaid and now their soldiers were sounding more like the stuff of nightmares. People talked about how the Hausas had sworn to wipe out the Christian Igbos during the massacre in the Northern Regions. Nobody really knows the exact numbers of how many were massacred, but the official figures are thirty, to forty thousand but this was likely to be understated.

Even when more and more people came to the house to say their goodbyes as they headed East for Onitsha and the rest of the newly formed Biafra, with *"Ebe ka inu na eje?* Where are you going?" *"Ke o-mesiya,* goodbye" and *"ayin ga-afu unu,* we'll be seeing you" or "no si-mma, stay well," I still didn't take much of it in. I had developed a defence mechanism against all the negative talk around me and was taking things one day at a time. I began to wish that we could go home to Lagos. Nevertheless, apart from the heavy presence of soldiers in Asaba all seemed to be quiet. I had learnt somehow, to take problems as they came. *"Dying is part of living."* I heard that said many times.

Going in the other direction, from East to West, were non-Igbo people. They were travelling in from Onitsha across the river through the fear of retaliation by the families of those who had been killed in the Northern Regions. A lot of the Northerners had already left Biafra and now the western Nigerians, like the Yorubas, were afraid of being attacked by the Igbos. In Lagos before we left on our journey, I was not fully aware of the impact of the attacks on the Igbos across Nigeria. I was aware, however, that there had been intimidations, killings and bodies left on the streets and there were those who had sought refuge in our house. I was aware of the raids we had suffered from soldiers, due to my stepfather being an Igbo and taking political asylum and having a high status in Ghana. But now, being in Asaba, I became more aware that the killing of Igbos in Lagos was nothing like what had gone on in the Muslim North.

On a previous short visit to my father to Zaria, in the North where Papa was posted, I remember catching a glimpse of the beautiful Fulani woman and aching for days after having been thrown off a Sultan's horse. Now Papa had retired from being a Postmaster and become a Justice of the Peace presiding over lower court cases. At weekends, especially on Sundays, he would play the piano or organ at the Catholic Church during Mass. He was now living in Okpanam not far from Asaba. In allowing Rosie and me to visit our father, which we did not want to do, Mummy had listened to our protestations about not wanting to stay with our stepmother so we were to stay with a family friend that Mummy trusted in Asaba. Over the years I have forgotten the family name of our hosts. Out of respect we addressed them as Auntie/Mama Ngozi and Uncle/Papa Ngozi because their eldest girl, who was a little older than Rosie and me, was called Ngozi. I only remember this because Ngozi is my middle name, short for Ngozi Chukwu Ka.

"Nkechi, ezigbo nwa, e-wo, Ngozi, nekene unu, ke ku unu-me? Nno nu!" "Beautiful children, my goodness, look at you, how you have grown. Welcome!" Mama Ngozi greeted us.

She looked vaguely familiar to me, a smallish and slim woman. She was wearing a white laced blouse, cut low in a crescent moon shape to expose the neck and collar bone on the front with a colourful wrapper around her waist and a pair of slippers with tiny beads of different colours. I liked Mama Ngozi immediately. She reminded me strangely of my mother. Like Mummy, Mama Ngozi possessed an unusual mixture of effortless control of everything around her, yet maintained an outward appearance of vulnerability. Theirs is a mélange of authority and gentleness. A pair of safe hands! She was genuinely pleased to see us. And she had not seen us since we were toddlers. She called us by our Igbo names, Ngozi and Nkechi. She asked many questions about Mummy's wellbeing, the rest of the family and our journey, all in Igbo. Rosie answered in Igbo. I understood everything Mama Ngozi said, but my Igbo was very rusty as we habitually spoke Efik or English at home. The only times I attempted to speak the language it drew loud laughter from everyone.

Papa Ngozi, was an elderly man who spoke impeccable English and Igbo like Papa. When we arrived he was seated on an armchair in the living room and though the ceiling fan was on, he was fanning himself with a circular fan woven from raffia with simple patterns. The fan was a dried palm leaf colour. The patterns were woven into the middle of the fan in blue with red jagged edges. At his side was a horse-tail fly whisk just like the one Papa carried around with him. As is our custom, I genuflected in respect when I greeted him. He greeted us kindly and then sent a message to Papa that we had arrived safely. Our Papa referred to him as Di-okpa, (a title for head of the family or most senior male). He addressed Papa as

Ogbuefi (Chief).

There was little sleeping space in Papa and Mama Ngozi's large house just off Nnebisi Road. Older members of the family, who had escaped the massacre in the North, occupied the bedrooms. Rosie and I slept on mats on the floor with younger members of the family. Asaba seemed to be more humid than Lagos, which is by the sea and it was unbearably stuffy indoors. It was preferable to sleep outside on the veranda or balcony in the cool breeze. I would roll up my mat and join those already asleep on the balcony, finding a corner for my mat. As Rosie had such sensitive skin she slept indoors where the mosquito coils were lit to ward off the pests. I hated the smell of the mosquito coils so the Balcony was the place for me.

Papa brought Quinine tablets for Malaria when I complained about feeling feverish and I was forced to take the horrible and indescribably bitter pills in front of him. I never complained about feeling ill again until we left Asaba.

In the mornings I would fill a bucket with water from the tap in the compound and carry it to the enclosed wash area. We used Imperial Leather soap with a raffia sponge, which Mummy had included in our toilet bags. After soaping my whole body, with a bowl, I scooped water from the bucket and used it to rinse off the soapsuds before drying myself with my towel, which had large red roses on it. After the wash I rubbed perfumed pomade oil in my hair, coconut oil on my skin and Cuticura powder under the armpits before dressing for the day.

Rosie and I were well dressed and well ahead of the fashion of the time owing to Mummy's sense of style, which, thankfully, all her children have inherited. We saw a lot of Papa while we were in Asaba this time. He would take us with him to visit our 'Umu nna ayi' distant relatives and pay respect to the elders including Chief Osadebe (I remembered his name from the divorce court), the Odogwu, Edozie, Nwajei and the Okogwu families. These were some of Papa's long-standing friends or relatives. I was too young to appreciate who they were as I had probably only met them in passing once before. But I knew the protocol of greeting and paying respect and not allowing anyone to touch my head (Mummy's instruction). They would remark how very like my father I looked. I never minded as Papa always cut a dashing and slim figure. He was always smartly dressed, either in a western suit or in the white native attire 'akwa ocha', which he wore with a hat, a row of large red coral beads around his neck and wrist. He always carried a walking stick. Some of the dark and nasty memories about the divorce from our childhood were consigned to the past in our young minds. This was owing to my Mummy's determination not to make us victims, but to nurture a forgiving spirit. Papa was proud to show us off to his friends. Mummy made us such pretty dresses especially for church.

My favourite memory of Asaba was the trips we made to the fish market by the River bank. Once there I loved to watch the fishermen cast their nets into the Niger River. On the elevated land along the riverbank, were randomly built thatched roof mud houses, mostly occupied by the fishermen, and their families. Behind them, further up the hill were white washed or painted brick houses with corrugated iron roofs.

Very early some mornings, the mist on the river would be so thick that the approaching canoes and longboats would look as though they were gliding through clouds detached from the river, their prows cutting the mist and causing billows to rise as they silently passed. I would wonder whether the mist just rose into the sky as the day wore on, absorbed into thin air or just dissolved into the river. Such childlike curiosity would fire my imagination and inspire my own private folk tales. I would make up my own stories about gigantic unseen spirits that were swallowed up by the mist to help them to remain invisible to the human eye. These spirits controlled how much fish the fishermen could catch in the early hours of the day. Because the fish worshiped these River Spirits, they would gather at certain times of the day, in their thousands to pay homage making it easier for the fishermen. The mist was magical to me because, after a distraction like the loud cries of the fishermen unloading their fish, the mist seemed to rapidly diminish or be gone altogether as though affected by the noise. The sky would become clear blue as if the mist was playing a game of "now you see me, now you don't". I loved to sit under a tree and watch as the fishermen cast their nets in a swirling motion into the air. For a few seconds the nets created a pattern like a giant dancer's flared chiffon skirt before falling into the river. Moments later, the fishermen would haul up what looked like large schools of live fish still thrashing around, gasping from the sudden shock of finding themselves out of the water and in the dry heat and air. The fish were skilfully emptied into containers filled with water, inside the boat, to keep them alive. On the other side of the river, the rooftops of the houses of the much bigger and densely populated market town of Onitsha could be seen, especially the houses built on the hills. I was fascinated by the men on the shore, who took turns to transport the large basins of live fish on their heads up the banks to the traders. In a practised ritual preparation they squatted and readied themselves so they could absorb the full weight of the load, about to be lifted on to their heads, without losing their balance or injuring their backs. The heavy load of water and large fish was then placed on each carrier's head on top of a rolled up rag used to stop the basin from sliding off. The carriers would carefully and skilfully stand upright, turn to negotiate the steep steps up the raised bank from the river to the mini fish market at the top. I would sometimes catch a glimpse of the crammed live fish still wriggling in the containers.

At the fish market, the bartering would be in full swing, with people arguing over the price of live or dead fish in a mixture of Igbo and pigeon English. There were fish dried and displayed on round flat raffia trays placed over baskets or containers. The leftover fish were roasted and dried. The drying process preserved them for long journeys inland. But they still attracted insects and flies if not well packaged. Before cooking dried fish it was thought best to scrub them with salt, then rinse them in hot water to kill off any bacteria or insects. Different sized baskets were filled with giant mudfish with whiskers, catfish, medium sized fish and smaller ones like sardines. Some of the very large fish were gutted and cut into four or five pieces before being sold. The women sold smoked fish alongside dried or salted fish 'Okporoko' ('stockfish') imported from northern European countries. After buying some fresh fish, we would make our way to the car on the main road, where the driver would be waiting to take us back to the house. Behind us, were the sounds of traders haggling over the price of the freshly caught fish. The mouth-watering aroma of fresh fish roasting on open fires filled the air stimulating my senses.

Before the war, Asaba had been just a small, quiet town in which everyone seemed to know everyone else, a close community whose sons underwent very high levels of education. Many of them in high-ranking positions in the Nigerian Civil Service, like Papa. Now the town was unrecognizable, the population had swelled. The market places and streets were much busier with people uprooted by the war. But the growth had gone on before the war and I had noticed that even the villages I once knew were now small towns with more real houses than the traditional mud huts. The tiny village of Okpanam, I had known as a little child, had become a thriving town and was now completely alien to me.

At Mama and Papa Ngozi's house, there was a constant stream of visitors to whom kola nut and drinks were served. Some of them had escaped the slaughter in the Northern Region. Many had left lucrative businesses, and large houses behind. A lot had lost family members. In some cases they told of whole families who were wiped out. The women often cried uncontrollably as they recounted their experience and losses. Other women embraced them, understanding and sharing their deep pain. Sometimes they held on to the grieving women to prevent them from inflicting harm on themselves in their grief. Grown women would suddenly drop to the floor overwhelmed by the feeling of utter helplessness. The kindness shown to them in Mama and Papa's house seemed to cause total, complete surrender to the unfathomable pain of their loss. Often I found myself crying, even though I did not know the family concerned. Their pain was such that it was impossible not to feel broken hearted for them, not to share their grief. I hoped that somehow my tears might, in some small way, ease a bit of their pain. I would mouth "ndo, ebezi na" (sorry, don't cry) and "yali ba".

When I found the tears too much to bear, I went and busied myself with chores about the house, ran a few errands or fetched drinks for the visitors. Sometimes I would shut off the tales of horror and go out to play or sit outside the house out of earshot. If I was lucky someone would be cooking and I would breathe in the aroma of 'ofe nsala', my favourite Igbo fish soup. Sometimes, to get away I would let my mind drift and watch the birds as they flew in and out from the mango and guava trees and over the houses. There were so many species of birds that we did not see in the conurbation of Lagos, Sunbirds with beautiful yellow bellies, brightly coloured Kingfishers, Parrots of every hue, Kites, Egrets, Finches, Cuckoos, Guinea Fowl and the old familiar black Crows. The women would say, it was unlucky for an Owl to land on a house and, worse still, if it sang its mournful song. They believed this would mean death in the household. My favourite birds were the Long Tails, with tails about three times as long as the rest of their body. There was something very elegant about these birds. When they landed on a branch of a tree or a telegraph wire they looked like glamorous ladies wearing a long train at the back of their dresses. I made lots of sketches of such birds on any pieces of paper I could find. I'm not sure how good my sketches were, but I will never know, as the bits of paper did not survive the journey back to Lagos. I also loved the Parrots, they reminded me of the multi coloured wrappers of the Nigerian women at church, market place and on the streets. I always felt that my crayons or watercolours couldn't do them justice. When there were lots of Parrots gathered together in one place it took my breath away, they were such magnificent birds of different vibrant colours and shapes and sizes with a beak shape that is much easier for the amateur artist to depict. How anyone could think of keeping any one of those beautiful creatures in captivity is hard to understand!

We were lulled into thinking that things were normal. There were Biafran soldiers around, but that was usual as the whole country had been under military rule for years. But the visit to Asaba was cut short and we left there earlier than intended. Papa arrived very early one morning before we were

up and after a whispered conversation with Papa Ngozi we were told to gather our belongings, 'Kunie fa, osiso, osiso! Wake them up, hurry, hurry!' A car was waiting outside to take us to Lagos as Papa thought we should try and make our way back home that morning. 'Papa, ebe ka ayin na-eje? Papa where are we going?'
"I am sending you home to your Mother, God will go with you." Papa replied in English.

There had been a large movement of defeated Biafra soldiers crossing the Niger Bridge that night. Many crossed the river on army boats toward Onitsha on the day before, causing nervous speculation and talk about the defeat of the Biafra Army. They were fleeing from the advancing and dreaded Federal soldiers. Igbo civilians also fled across the River to relatives in Onitsha and the rest of Biafra. Others went into the bush. Those who left Benin for Asaba talked of atrocities and senseless killings of Igbos by angry mobs and Northern soldiers. Igbo families were beaten, killed and left in the streets. Women were raped, business premises were looted and properties burnt down. Some brave non-Igbos, who gave refuge to Igbo friends, were murdered by the Federal soldiers. Refugees spoke about fanatical Hausa soldiers killing young Christian men from non-Igbo tribes. Old enemies spitefully settled scores by falsely reporting rivals to the Federal soldiers. The advancing Federal Troops offered no protection to the civilian population and were themselves raping and killing. Recent arrivals talked about shelling and the heavy guns used by the Federal troops as they retook Benin and that they were now advancing towards Asaba. Those with nowhere else to go, like Papa, stayed in Asaba.

Papa and Papa Ngozi thought we would probably be safer travelling with a lady whom they knew and trusted. The lady, Mrs Johnson, was from Abeokuta in the Western Region. She had worked with Papa in the past. She felt it was no longer safe for her to stay in Onitsha where she had lived and worked as a teacher for many years. She was of the Yoruba tribe, but felt no longer safe in Igbo land. Her husband and children had left for Lagos and Abeokuta weeks earlier. She had crossed the River to Asaba with Papa's help and was now making her way to the West to her family and hometown on the Federal side. She spoke both Igbo and Yoruba so it made sense for us to travel with her. We said our farewells to Papa and our hosts; "O ga-adili unu mma! It will be well with you.' Papa Ngozi said.
Mama Ngozi called us to her; "Bia-nu. Nekene m, unu aburo ndi igbo, I nu go." "Come. Look at me, you are not Igbos, you hear!"
"Yes Mama Ngozi!"
"Ije oma! Ezibo nwa." "Safe journey! Beautiful children."
"Greet your Mother, for us!"

"Yes Mama Ngozi."

We waved as we got into the car with bags of drinks and other provisions. It was not long before we were on the main road travelling away from Asaba, heading west, with the blue early morning light bowing out respectfully into the horizon. It made way for the Sun's rays to rise slowly and majestically, engulf and cover the land with its brilliance and heat; enhancing the fabulously rich red earth of Asaba.

The road was unusually crowded with people heading toward us to Asaba or mainland Biafra. The people looked as though they had been walking all night. These were men, women and children who were escaping the advancing Federal Troops. Most were carrying their belongings piled up sometimes three feet high, on their heads. Some carried livestock, chickens and ducks with their legs bound together. Goats were pulled along on leashes. Women with their babies on their backs, their belongings on their heads, rolled up mats, bags of grain and other things. The younger children carried their even younger siblings on their backs. Some, just simply pulled the little ones along. There was a heavily pregnant woman who had a child strapped on her back with a dark green faded wrapper. On the wrapper were repeated photos of a young Queen Elizabeth 11. Each photo was framed in a circle, with words printed all over the rest of the wrapper in cream. For a few years I remembered the words on the wrapper, but now only the image of the Queen remains. The woman had a large basin of her belongings tied and piled up high, secured with a colourful wrapper of red, orange and black patterns, all of which were balanced on her head. Another woman was breastfeeding her baby as she walked or rather the baby was helping itself to its mother's milk. With one hand she held on to the load piled up on her head while holding on to the feeding baby strapped to her side, with her other hand. Some of the people were on bicycles while the lucky ones crammed onto cars, buses and lorries. Many of them were on the outside hanging on to whatever they could grip to keep their balance. Many sat on loads tied to the roof of trucks. Overcrowded trucks and buses were commonplace, but it seemed that the buses had five times the permitted safe numbers crammed in. I thought of the number of miles they must have covered, travelling in that position. There were many makeshift trolleys of wood platforms on old bicycle wheels, these were stacked with belongings and attached to a bicycle. One of the men rode a bike with a child, three or four years old, sitting sideways in front of him. On his wooden trolley sat a heavily pregnant woman with two young boys and a girl, sharing the small space with their belongings.

We drove passed the sign on our left, pointing to Okpanam, my father's

old village. As we slowly passed the mass of people heading into Asaba, the driver of our car tooted his horns a few times trying to clear people off the road. The large crowd of people caused red dust to rise from the soil, filling the air. There were very few cars travelling in the opposite direction like us, away from Asaba, towards Benin and with good reason as we soon found out. It was difficult for our driver to make much headway at a reasonable speed and so he suggested we should maybe leave the main road, it would probably be safer if we cut across the narrow roads through the bush. Mrs Johnson, the woman looking after us, asked if he knew the road he was suggesting.
"Yes Ma."
"Ok, if you are sure."
"I am sure Ma."

As soon as he could, the driver pulled off the main road on to an uneven potholed road that gave access to various villages and if followed for long enough would get us back on to the main road. I fell asleep again. We had been rushed from our sleeping mats very early in the morning. Now I had nothing to look at but trees and the small scattered groups of people walking towards us down the narrow road with their belongings on their heads and livestock dragged along behind then.

I don't know how far we had travelled, but I was fast asleep and having a nightmare about being in a crowd that was being chased by terrifying masqueraders, (these are people wearing raffia costumes covering the whole body, huge raffia masks representing animals. They are said to have powers and appear at various festivals mostly in southern Nigeria. Children are very afraid of them and pregnant women must not look at them for fear of giving birth to a monster.) In my dream the masqueraders were wielding whips, which they used to attack the screaming crowd as they ran for shelter. The whips made a strange muted war-war-war growl as they swung them in the air. I looked up from my hiding place and saw them suddenly take off into the air on the backs of giant birds. The birds laid eggs in mid-air as they flew away, and as each egg fell to the ground it made the boom, boom sound like an Udu drum. One of the birds turned its head and I looked into its flaming red eyes; it spotted me and turned and flew towards me. I panicked. There were more screams as the crowd shouted "Take cover! Take cover!' Someone grabbed me by the hand, at which point I woke up with a start, my heart was still pounding from my dream. Confused and disoriented, forgetting where I was for a moment; I allowed myself to be dragged out of the car into the bush and pushed face down flat on to the ground. Still drowsy, but with my heart still pounding, the noise of explosions in my ears, I was now awake, but confused, I could still hear the war-war-war growl in the distant and the booming sound of the bird's eggs smashing to earth was getting closer. There was confusion anyway, people were running and shouting. Suddenly there was a deafening explosion that shook the ground, making me deaf and set my ears ringing. Everything was in slow motion and surreal as I looked up and saw a person's head drop from his shoulders as the body seemed to continue running a few steps. Everything was silent now and the headless body tripped and fell forward on the uneven ground. I looked around me still unsure whether or not I was still in my nightmare. I could hear no sound, but there were lips moving and I could see that some people were crying. I looked around for Rosie and she was lying a few feet away from me in the bush, but she was safe. There were people lying flat on the ground looking petrified and confused. Nobody moved as one explosion followed another, although I could hardly hear them. It seemed endless. I closed my eyes and lay still, even though I could feel something crawling about on me. I was afraid to brush it away as if any movement I made might attract the shells. The explosions finally ended, but we did not move until the driver spoke, I heard him as though he was a long way in the distance;

"Madam, I think they have stopped. We are about ten miles from Agbor, maybe we should only travel through the small roads. I don't think soldiers will come through the villages. Should I try to reach Sapele Road?" This was the road to Benin.

"No!" replied Mrs Johnson.

"Sapele Road is too far, it will double our journey if we try to get to Benin, there may be soldiers on Sapele Road. We will drive to Agbor, I know people there."

"Yes Ma!"

My ears popped and I was relieved to be able to hear people speaking again even though, for a short while, it sounded as if they were still speaking from a great distance away. As people began to come out of the bush, I got up and frantically brushed and shook the insects off my dress and joined the small crowd of people by the roadside. I avoided looking in the direction of the headless body, not wanting to know whether it was real or part of my dream. A young woman with her wrapper tied over her chest, ran out of the bush next to me screaming! She was holding her head as she ran past us toward a young child lying in the open. I thought that the woman was hurt. The child was covered in dust or white ash and blood. The woman swept her into her arms making strange deep guttural noises as she cradled the lifeless and bloodied body of the child. The child was about two or three years old. Mrs Johnson and other women now surrounded the young woman with the dead child, doing their best to console her. Some people sat on the grass gazing ahead as if stunned, but others went over to the women with the dead child. We joined them with the poor sobbing woman to say, "ndo! Sorry!" We could hear a lot of voices wailing in the forest, but couldn't see anyone. A young man sat on the ground bleeding from the head, looking confused or in shock. All around us men, women and children wandered about picking up scattered belongings. Some had tears running down their cheeks, mapping lines on their faces leaving a trail of brown skin through the dust. We opened our cases and brought out clothes, which we shredded and used as makeshift bandages for those who had been wounded. There were bodies scattered everywhere, some charred and some mangled, lying oddly twisted like rag dolls. I tried not to dwell too long on the bodies and told myself that I was still in a bad dream. But really I knew the dream was reality. Somebody said;

"We have to bury the dead."

"Bring anything you can dig with or use your hands."

Silently, some of the men and women began to dig a shallow grave with whatever they could find; we joined them pulling up plants by the roots, clearing an area not far from where we had taken shelter during the shelling. When we finally got into the car it would not start. The driver looked at the engine and said it would take a long while to fix and he wasn't sure it would get us to Agbor anyway. Agbor was less than ten miles away, walking we should be able to make it before dark. But the people who had come from that direction said it was not safe for us to be travelling toward the Western Region owing to the advancing Federal Troops. After Mrs Johnson had explained that we had to make the journey to the West, they advised us to stay as far from the main road as possible. Those who were going to Agbor joined us as we set off. We walked along the bush path within hearing distance of the main road, carrying a few things we thought we would need from the car, leaving suitcases behind. Some of the men had helped us push the car into a ditch and cover it with branches, which had been cut from the trees by shrapnel during the shelling.

We started our journey carrying our loads on our heads just as we had seen the refugees doing earlier. After a long walk we took a chance and followed a path that headed in the direction of the main road, hoping, if there were no soldiers, to hitch a ride. There were no cars on the road, but we walked past a few burnt out armoured vehicles, cars and buses on the sides of the road. I don't know how far we had walked, when we heard what sounded like gunshots ahead of us. We all rushed into the bush and hid, the driver motioned that we should keep our heads down, but keep moving deeper into the bush. We all followed him crouching and hugging whatever we were carrying with us, he put his finger to his mouth and motioned to us to lie down. Just then we heard voices not far away from where we were now hiding. One of them shouted what sounded like an order. About five or six Federal soldiers came running, passed our hiding place, towards the main road, in the direction we had just come from. We stayed where we were, frightened and unable to move even after they had gone, in case there were more of them. After a while, we heard rustling in a clearing in the bush. The noises turned out to be two young girls, about my age or a little older, leaning on each other unable to walk properly. They were crying, both of them had blood running down their legs. Their dresses were torn and their faces were bruised and swollen around the mouth and eyes. I could see that they had been severely beaten and punched in the face. It wasn't until later that I realized that the soldiers had raped them. Our driver looked around to check that the girls were not being followed, before he dared to attract their attention with a whispered;

"Pssssh, pssssh!"

The two girls froze for a second and then they slowly turned around, wide-eyed with fear. When they saw our group, without making a sound, tears of relief ran down their faces, I found I was crying with them. They rushed noisily across the clearing towards us. I had never seen tears flow so easily without the sobbing or audible sound of crying. They were both shivering though the heat was stifling. We went forward to help them, but then the driver signalled all of us including the frightened girls to be quiet and go back into the bush to hide. We heard the sounds of more soldiers, trucks, and armoured vehicles approaching along the main road. The soldiers were on the move and there were many of them. They were mostly keeping to the main road, but some foot soldiers with guns were on the lookout peering into the bushes and making occasional little forays into the bush as they walked by.

"Ma, I think we are safe here, they can't see us!" whispered the driver.

Mrs Johnson nodded. We stayed where we were, about fifty yards from the main road. We were afraid to move for what seemed like an eternity before the adults motioned and whispered that we should go quietly further into the bush. We walked slowly in single file into the thick bush. One of the two girls needed to lean on someone to walk a little faster. We moved, away from the main road with the two young girls pointing out the direction we should take. We came to a path that led to a village with some of its huts in ruins. Some huts had been set on fire and one or two had taken direct hits from the shelling. When the shelling was done they had been raided by the Federal troops looking for retreating Biafra soldiers. As we got to the clearing of the village, a few people started coming out of the bush. One woman, the two girls' mother, shouted and ran to embrace them. When they saw her, they let their crying take over and began to sob loudly.

Strangely, neither of the girls could bring themselves to return their mother's embrace. They seemed to be bewildered and ashamed. I watched as she led them to a container of water, stripped them down and started frantically washing them. As they stood there shivering I realised that they were much younger than I had thought they were at first. The girls stood rigid as their mother cried and washed the blood from their bodies in the clear water that sparkled in the fading sun. In the middle distance we heard the sound of more shelling and everyone fell to the ground. However the "fumf" sound of the exploding shells, though loud, was not getting closer. We sat up where we were: not wanting to be too far from the ground, until the shelling stopped.

The people of the village spoke Ika, a language I had not heard before, which is not surprising when one considers that there are 300 or so dialects in the country. One or two of the words sounded like Igbo though I couldn't be sure. The driver and Mrs Johnson were led a short distance to where some bodies lay. Rosie and I were told to stay where we were. I could see from where I was, a woman lying on her back. Her stomach ripped open and her intestines exposed. Not far from her was a baby with a big gash to the side of its face as if it had exploded from the inside. Just for a second before the adults stood in front of the body, I noticed the umbilical cord still attached to the baby. I looked away and tried to distance my thoughts from what I was seeing and closed the windows of my mind to the shock of it all. I didn't really want to hear what the people in the village were saying. But I heard enough in Igbo to know that they suspected the Federal troops of killing most of the villagers for harbouring the enemy! Most of the people looked puzzled and shocked. After speaking to some villagers in Ika, the driver explained to us that the Federal troops had targeted the village because some of the villagers had accused Igbo villagers amongst them of having helped or conspired with the Biafra troops. The federal troops were not discerning as to who was or was not an Igbo. The shelling started again, we could hear the boom, fumf, boom, but they were now at a safe distance. By the time the villagers dug a shallow grave and the bodies and body parts were buried, it was dusk. As the sun was already going down it was felt that it was unsafe for us to continue on our journey. It would be too dangerous for us to be caught in the dense bush in the dark. It was suggested that we spend the night in the village and travel through the bush to Agbor the following morning.

As the few remaining villagers returned to their huts, or what was left of their homes, we were taken to a large rectangular mud building with a thatched roof. It was towards the end of the village. It had hardly been touched by the explosions and had just a few holes. Inside the building was an elderly man and his wife, he may have been the chief or an important man in the village. Mrs Johnson went in to meet them as we sat outside, until she came out and said we had been invited to stay until morning.

We entered the shelter of the large hut, exhaustion and thirst from the heat of the Sun, set in. My stomach collapsed even though I had not eaten for some hours. Both Rosie and I began to cry, one setting off the other. I could get no further than a few feet from the hut to relieve myself and did not make it to the latrine a few feet further. I embarrassed myself asking for water to clean up. Thankfully, it was cool in the hut. On one wall in the main room, there was a rather old looking calendar with a photo of an American pop star, next to other old and faded black and white framed photos. One was of a chief in regalia, probably our host. The room was tidy, the floor had been swept clean. There were some ornaments, but what stood out in the room was an old double settee set against the wall facing the entrance with a four foot carved wood coffee table in front of it. There were other doorways covered by faded curtains. Two of the doorways led to smaller sleeping quarters. The third led to the back, from which the man's wife emerged to welcome us. We helped her bring in a bench, chairs and stools from the bedrooms and the veranda. At the back of the building was another hut, which was the kitchen to the main house. I noticed that there was only one small room with a dirt floor. In the kitchen there was a raised area to the right on which were pots, pans, two tin buckets, white basins of different sizes, baskets containing, yam, and a bunch of plantains. Firewood lay on the floor to the left of the raised area. A couple of brooms leaned against the wall in a corner. To the left side of the kitchen on the floor, was the cooking area with large stones positioned in a circle and a tripod strong enough to take the weight of the large black iron pot lying on the floor next to the stones. There was firewood within the circle of the stones in the shape of a tepee ready for the fire to be lit for cooking. The kitchen's mud walls were partly blackened from the constant smoke even though the kitchen was more open plan than the house, with a very wide window about two feet from the ground, on the left side. The window was barred vertically with uneven sticks, placed fairly close together, enough to ward off any intrusion from animals, but airy enough to let out a lot of the smoke. When the fire was first lit, the kitchen was filled with smoke for a while until the flame was contained and the wood burned red. A little girl fanned the fire. We offered to help her but her mother said they could manage and I, for one, was happy to leave them to it.

We had boiled yam with dried fish and onions stew, cooked in palm oil for dinner. For some reason it tasted so good. Although Rosie and I would set each other crying again, it began to seem that some normality had returned as we all ate, mostly in silence. I almost began to forget the nightmare of the day. There was talk among the adults of Biafra soldiers dressed as civilians, hiding in the bush to avoid capture by the Federal troops. I was not looking forward to the darkness that was fast approaching like bad news. Or the nightmares that I expected to come with it. Two kerosene lamps were lit. The wooden doors to the entrance and the back were shut. A faded curtain was drawn over the doors to stop mosquitoes getting through the cracks. The dreaded mosquito coils filled the room with chemical smoke as we slept on mats on the floor.

We got up early and washed our faces, chewed on the atu (chewing stick) that our hosts provided to clean our teeth. We drank some akamu (pap or porridge). We offered some of the provisions we had brought with us from the car to the old man. He only accepted some tins of sardines as he said that we would need the rest of the food on the journey. Such amazing courtesy from a man whose village has been all but destroyed. We said our goodbyes, before setting off with farmers from the village who would lead us through the bush to Agbor. There were some horrible smells in the bush of rotting flesh as we made our way. Flies became a nuisance. I asked to go into the bush to ease myself. I had held on to a full bladder through the night not wanting to use the latrine a few yards from the hut we had spent the night in, for an irrational fear of attack from soldiers. But the smell from the latrine was unbearable anyway when the wind direction changed. Rosie and Mrs Johnson, whom we now called Mama, came with me while the others waited. We found a spot and even Mama squatted down. Relieved, we joined the others; it was a long walk to Agbor, along the way we met more people leaving the towns or their villages for the bush.

Exhausted we finally got to Agbor and the Benin-Agbor Road, where we were lucky to hitch a ride on a Mammy Wagon, which was a vehicle built on a lorry frame to carry both passengers and goods. We did not stop at Agbor as first intended, to see Mama's friend. Rosie had cut herself tramping through the bush and Mama was able to get a dressing for her at the roadside. On the way we encountered our first Federal troop blockade of the trip home. Mama passed us off as her children. She spoke Yoruba to the soldiers and the driver was Yoruba, so we were waved on along with the others. At Benin we got in a car provided by a friend of Mama's to Shagamu, where we parted company with her. We clung to her when it came to saying goodbye, but we knew we had to hurry home. Mama spoke to a few passengers to keep an eye on us. Then she paid for Rosie and me and we got on the mini bus heading for Ikeja in Lagos. I slept through the journey. I never saw Mama again. She was "Mama" to us for the journey from Asaba and I wish I had kept in touch with her, over the years. Rosie and I often spoke about her in loving terms.

Thank God, we finally got home to Ikeja before nightfall the second day. Mummy was very worried as she had expected us the day before and had no way of contacting us, or Papa, as Asaba had been cut off. In Lagos there had been no news of the Biafra soldiers getting as far as Benin in their initial incursion into Federal territory nor their defeat and withdrawal. Not much of the war was reported on the radio in Lagos, it had been assumed that Asaba and Benin were not part of Biafra. We told Mummy all that had happened. She sighed deeply and told us how kind God had been to protect us. She told us to put everything we had been through and seen out of our minds and leave everything in God's hands.

Being home was wonderful! Waking up at five every morning for prayers with our expanded family of refugees took on a different meaning. It was a few years at the end of the war before we even heard from Papa and found out what had happened to him in Asaba, soon after we left. After the war, our cousin Tony Jnr, who had been conscripted into the Biafran Army, told us about his experiences in the war. He said that when the Federal Government troops got to Asaba, and entered the town, they rounded up as many of the local men and boys as they could find. They accused them of conspiring with Biafra and then lined them up and shot them in front of their families and then forced their spouses and members of their families to bury them! There was wholesale rape and the stories from survivors were horrific! Rosie and I were at that time hiding in the bushes trying to make our way back to Lagos.

Chapter Twenty Two: After the War

Daddy had been released in 1967 and stayed with us in Ikeja during the war. When the war ended in 1970 I was Sixteen and doing my O Levels as a boarder at the Holy Child College in Ikoyi, Lagos. Daddy and Mummy drove us academically, which made life difficult for me. I wouldn't say I was backward or lazy intellectually, but it was hard to compete with the brilliance of my sisters Maggie and Rosaleen. Both of them would always come first or second in their class of thirty or so, while I was quite excited about an eighth position. I once managed a third place, which called for great celebration on my part, until I got home and found that one of my sisters was upset because she had only come second in her class! I felt like giving up then, but I still worked very hard and gave it my best shot. Mathematics was my bête noir! When it came to choosing subjects for the O level exams, the dreaded Maths was compulsory. Chemistry and Physics were the other subjects I loathed with a passion; I even handed in a blank exam paper with just my name on it, for my final Physics exam! Science was obviously not my forte. However, I excelled in History, Geography, English-Literature, the Arts, and was competent in Biology and Religious Studies, Daddy was not impressed. He knew I was going to fail in Maths and he challenged me by saying;
"If Patricia gets a pass in her maths O level, I'll buy her a Jet Plane."
I knew very well Dad could not afford a Jet Plane, but I really did try to accomplish a pass in maths just to watch him eat his words. But, yes; you guessed right, I failed, but only just!

I did like street parties. Live music was played and some of the parties lasted up to forty-eight hours in those days. In Lagos especially, it was commonly accepted that the residential street on which the party was being held, would be closed to traffic from the evening by the hosts. This was in order to be able to accommodate the hundreds of people that would attend. The musicians took turns to play hours of live music at these all night and all day long parties. They mostly featured Nigerian top musicians such as Sunny Ade, Ebenezar Obe etc. I know there were other music venue choices, which, as a schoolgirl, I was not old enough to visit. Places like Bobby Benson's Club where they played dance, pop and soul music by James Brown, Otis Redding, Percy Sledge, The Supremes, The Jackson Five, and The Four Tops were out of bounds. There was also Fela's Shrine, where Fela Ramsome Kuti was based, which parents frowned at. It had a bad reputation and was considered not to be a place for a girl who came from a good family. The gramophone and later on, record players, on which we listened to anything from African Highlife music, Jazz, Soul, Swing, Negro Spirituals, European pop to classical music, was my only window to the world of popular music. I was never curious about how American and European artists made money; I assumed they recorded in a studio, performed at parties like musicians in Nigeria or at open-air places to hysterical teenagers as we saw on the Television.

One day, Dad brought up the question of my career. It was decided, to my horror; that I was to be a lawyer. Like every teenager I felt that it showed how little my parents understood me. I was a quiet child and my mother often used to say;
"Nobody knows what is going on in Pat's head; all she does is look at you with compassion in those big eyes."

She was right; I was worried for her and the responsibilities she took on. Soon after the one-sided discussion about my career path, I had a word with my favourite nun, Sister Catherine, an American Nun of the Order of the Holy Child of Jesus. I discussed the possibility of going into the convent as a novice. I assisted her in the school Library along with Mary Elebesunu and Araba Okafor, who (apart from my cousin Jane Coco-Bassey), were to become my only close friends at Holy Child College. At first Sister Catherine was delighted, but after cross-examining me further, I unintentionally revealed that my parents' plan was for me to study Law and that I would really rather do anything else. Sister Catherine then gave me a lecture on how the Convent is not an escape route, but a calling, adding that God has a plan for each of His children and that I could serve Him in whatever path I found myself. However, she did agree to speak to Reverend Mother on my behalf to see if I could become a trainee Novice after my schooling was over. One day Sister Catherine got out the film of "The Sound of Music" and played it for Mary, Araba and me in the Library. I was hooked on the film and would request it over and over again thereafter, for the rest of my fifth year at the college. Perhaps as a precursor of the future, I was often cast in leading roles in plays and musicals at school and would appear as part of the choir on television at the Catholic Cathedral in Lagos. My favourite roles were in 'The Chimes of Normandy' an operetta by Robert Plaquette and 'Salad Days' by Julian Slade and Dorothy Reynolds. I also enjoyed the times when we had school events featuring dances from different parts of the world, taught to us by the wives of ambassadors whose children were at the college. We had Irish, Thai, Japanese and Spanish dances, which were fascinating and great fun. Many years later, I was to amuse Michael Flatley backstage at 'River Dance' with tales of us African children, trying to do the Irish Dance taught to us by the

Irish Nuns. I did, however, later include the Spanish dance in my own Channel 4 TV series, 'The Patti Boulaye Show'. In the end, my parents agreed that I could become a nun after I had thought the whole thing through during a holiday in England where my sisters Grace and Rosie were studying.

Chapter Twenty Three: Brothers and Sisters

Although this was the title of an all-black BBC drama series in which I starred, this piece of my book is not about the series, but about my real brothers and sisters, Grace, Johnny, Tony, Maggie, Rosie, Sam and Eno. I was the seventh after Rosie; we had lost a baby between Tony and Maggie.

Grace Coker

As a newlywed couple, Papa and Mummy lived in Onitsha, where their first child Grace Nwakaego was born. Two years later came Johnny my eldest brother and Papa's first son, followed by Anthony. Mummy and Papa then had another child, who died very young. Grace was seven years old when Maggie Obiageli arrived. Even at her young age Grace helped Mummy by taking care of the baby whilst Mummy got on with her dressmaking business.

Papa was transferred as the head postmaster to the area of Asaba and surrounding villages where my sister Rosaleen Nkechi was born. The pressures on my sister Grace, as are normal for first-born child, while we were growing up, were enormous. As the situation between Mummy and Papa got worse she lived through it all as I have related earlier. She was at the crucial age of thirteen when Mummy and Papa divorced. She bore the brunt of their divorce and was old enough to retain vivid memories of it all. Grace grew up being separated from us younger siblings for long periods at a time, yet she was never estranged from us. When she was away she used to send packaged presents to us with the little money she was able to save.

Mummy had an enduring, selfless love for her children and extended family. Her fighting spirit, strength, determination and refusal to be a victim rubbed off on Grace. It certainly affected all our characters. Mummy's example of her love for Jesus has meant that her children (hopefully) bear no grudges. Grace's strong faith and affection for her siblings made her the kind of sister we can turn to for spiritual and moral help. Grace is a trusted spiritual guide to me personally.

Grace has five children, fifteen grandchildren and still counting. She lost Tokunbo Coker, her dear husband and life-long companion recently. He was a wonderful brother-in-law and a kind-hearted man, who was always jovial. He was a veterinary surgeon. He encouraged Grace with her charity work. She does incredible voluntary work supervising the building and running of healthcare clinics in Nigeria and Cameroon for my Charity, "Support for Africa" and she does this without being paid even though it entails arduous journeys often under difficult circumstances.

My memory of the time I arrived in London to stay with her is that of perfect love and care from a big sister. To fill my time, she helped me enrol in a part time drama school and two weeks modelling training in Bond Street. During my early years in London I lived with Grace. When it was time for her to move back to Nigeria she gave me enough money to rent a small room in a house in Kilburn. She had opened an account in which she saved the money I had been giving her each week to help with my upkeep. I did not know that she had saved it for me. I was enormously grateful and thankful. In my early days in London she kept me on the straight and narrow and stopped my early success going to my head. Grace is a great eldest sister! She has done a wonderful job of being number one. She has five children, Yele, Akin, Yinka, Femi, Tope and grandchildren.

Johnny and Tony

Hardly a day has gone by when I have not prayed for my two elder brothers Johnny and Tony Ebigwei, since their deaths in the late 1970's. While we were growing up, it seemed they were always away. They were both in boarding schools and I only saw them during the holidays. They were very close and chose different aspects of the Aviation industry as their career paths. And when the time came, they went away to study in Europe and the US. Johnny went to Germany to study Aeronautic Engineering and Tony to Los Angeles to train as a pilot.

As a child I developed a great love for football because they were both so good at it and would let me join in their games. They both had a love for Martial Arts, but they were naturally gentlemanly and great characters, very popular with the ladies. They did not get into trouble with Mummy, except during the early days when the killings of young Igbo men started in Lagos and she was particularly worried about their safety. Once when they thought Mummy was asleep they drove to a party in her car without asking her. Mummy was very upset and they got severely reprimanded. Owing to her fears for them Mummy always waited up when they stayed out longer than her curfew and got very angry when they showed up and tried to sneak into the house. Once, she chased them down the stairs with a whip in her hand. I loved my two brothers and admired them greatly. They were as near to perfect in my eyes as can be.

Johnny was nicknamed "Johnny Weissmuller" after the actor who played Tarzan due to Johnny's good looks, physique and goal scoring skills. He was a very likeable character, gentle and kind. He couldn't bear to see anyone in trouble without helping, sometimes to the point of being gullible. Johnny was very dark skinned and had a winning smile. His time in Germany was fraught with trouble. He was picked on by the German police, locked up and beaten up just because he was black. This had a profound effect on him for the rest of his life. He had a German girlfriend with whom he had a daughter named Camilla, but their relationship did not work out, the cultures were just too far apart in those days. Being a black young man in Europe in the sixties was often very difficult and dangerous. After graduating in German, when he came back to Nigeria, Johnny was a different person, wiser and not so gullible, but not so open and his confidence was low, but he was still our gentle Johnny. He also has a son Onochie in Nigeria, who is a clone of his father, in looks, mannerism and voice. Painfully similar in ways that I find heart breaking! I was very moved to get a call from Onochie in the middle of writing this paragraph on his father! Johnny died aged only thirty six, we think due to a delayed reaction to the beating he took, not just during one of the times that the house was raided by soldiers but also, from the German police.

Tony did better in Los Angeles as a young black man probably because there were as many black people in the USA in the sixties as today, unlike Germany, where there were virtually none and Hitler's racist regime was only a few years gone, leaving most of the people adversely conditioned.

Tony was tall and good-looking with an angelic baby face, which made him the favourite for all the neighbourhood girls. He was very athletic and was serious about martial arts and football. He had a happy-go-lucky character and was always smiling. Like all my brothers and sisters he was generous to a fault and often took punishments for us younger ones when he could pretend that whatever had happened was his fault. Such an angel! He graduated in the USA and returned to Nigeria and became one of the first pilots to join the new Nigeria Airways. He died in a plane crash at only thirty-four when I was just breaking as a star in England. Tony left a son behind, who was named after him.

Dr Margaret Ebigwei-Ibru B.Sc (Hons) M.Sc M.Phil Laureat De La Faculte Des Sciences Pharmaceutiques et Biologiques, Paris

I have previously written about Maggie as my fearless champion and defender at school. Maggie was a wild teenager with a devil-may-care attitude. She was, and still is, incredibly brainy, generous, kind, caring and giving. Like all my siblings she is deeply spiritual. Everything she does has God in it. She is gifted with an amazing photographic brain and has an aptitude for languages. She is very stylish! When Stephen, my husband of forty years, first met her, he described her as being just like Sophia Loren, "top draw", I think he said, "and beautiful!"

In the early years Papa sought to marry her off very young. He thought it would be a waste of money to educate her and he reckoned that a husband would tame her. I suspect he was thinking more of the dowry he would receive. Little did he know that she was destined to be one of his most successful children! In those days fathers tended to expect the male child to be successful, never the daughter.

Maggie studied at The Federal School of Science Onikan Lagos, and then got her first degree at the University of Ife, Ibadan Branch before deciding to do her Masters in Pharmacology in Paris. She sailed through with Honours in French having learned the language from scratch to fluency in a matter of months. She attended Universite De La Sorbonne Paris, Universite Rene Descartes De Paris, Universite De Paris-SUD Centre D'Etudes Phermaceutiqus De Chatenay Malabry, France. Within seven years, Maggie had acquired B.Sc Pharmacy (Hons), a Diploma in French Language, M.Sc Pharma dynamics & Biological Essay of Drugs and Medicaments, M. Phil. Pharmacodynamics and a Doctorate in Pharmacokinetic (Cerebral Ischemia). She is a Laureat De La Faculte Des Sciences Pharmaceutiques et Biologiques, M.Sc in Dermo-Pharmacy, at Centre D'Etude Pharmaceutique Chatenay Malabry, France. Maggie is an entrepreneur par excellence and a former non-executive director of Nigeria Bank of Commerce and Industry. She is a member of the board of trustees of the prestigious Association of Private Educators of Nigeria. She founded and owns S.T&T. Regency International Schools that accommodates children from three months to eighteen years old. She is the owner of both Issyma Pharmacy and Issyma Children Foundation, which has educated hundreds of children and young people on scholarship and which she personally sponsors. Maggie has three children of her own, Teegee, Timi and Simi and a grandson from Teegee.

Her stubborn but caring character has sustained her through many hardships, heartbreaks and disappointments. Maggie does not suffer fools kindly. You can depend on her to tell the truth, which people often do not appreciate. Maggie seems to work five times as hard as anyone else. She is a perfectionist and expects the same from everyone around her, so the standards in her schools, which cover all aspects, are the very highest.

Maggie hates incompetence! However, she is sensitive and gets upset if she has been told she has hurt someone and is quick to apologise. She likes to help people to be the best they can be which makes her a great educator. I have learned and continue to learn a great deal from Maggie, her attention to detail, her fighting spirit (like my mother's) and her belief that God needs to be in all her endeavours.

To me Maggie is like a second mother and I am drawn to her because of the stoic way she faces her many challenges. I know where she is coming from and it's a good place and I love her dearly and deeply. She is always concerned about my wellbeing, for which I am grateful.

When her children were little, she started a nursery at home because her first child Teegee was a very sensitive baby. The nursery grew and soon she had an elementary school followed by the primary school and consequently College. ST&T Regency International School, GRA in Ikeja was born. The school building project overcame enormous opposition from powerful neighbours and companies who teamed up against her. Maggie, as I expected, fought back with gusto and no fear, seeking the help of her powerful friends, including the Governor of Lagos State. The school building was saved and she was given the permission to complete it. Maggie created scholarships for a quarter of the pupils, who attend free, which has been financially difficult for her at times. She knows how to build strength in a young person's character. She is an imposing figure and strikes healthy fear into the pupils and teachers alike. Maggie financially supports orphans that are being cared for in convents and other foundations. When the children are old enough, they are educated in her school free of charge. She provides their school clothing and equipment and keeps them in her School's boarding house.

She is very involved with her church and the Dorothy Ikoku Memorial Church, which is named after Mummy. She is a formidable motivational speaker on relationships and empowering women and gives lectures all over Nigeria and around the world.

I thank God for Maggie who, almost instinctively, knows when I'm in despair and in need of spiritual strength and guidance. Always, when I am low, literarily before I can think of whose shoulder to cry on, a long text message from Maggie pops up on my phone, which immediately brings me comfort and focus.

Rosaleen May-Nzeribe

I lost my dear sister Rosie to cancer when she was only fifty-six. Even at the end when the cancer had swept around her whole body I can remember only her beautiful smile. Rosaleen was beautiful, clever, wise, spiritual and full of light, which she radiated to everyone who met her. She had a smile that touched your very soul and I loved her so dearly. She was very allergic to bites and stings and if even a small thing like a mosquito bit her it would immediately develop into a large lump that could lead to further infection.

I remember the time when a bees' nest in our back garden was disturbed and the angry bees attacked everyone in the compound and beyond, the few stings that Rosie received from the attack developed into the most swollen and painful wounds. Rosaleen became an Industrial Chemist, graduating from Preston University. Later she became Rev. Dr. Rosaleen May- Nzeribe with a Doctoral degree in Theology just before she died from breast cancer. By sheer power of prayer, she was to survive for ten years with aggressive breast cancer. Her three children Emeka, Avril and Kicki, were the centre of her life. She had lost a number of children through miscarriages and she realised how precious they were. When she was dying she prayed to be allowed to see her children through university and settled, especially her younger son Avril, whose gentle character she loved, but who worried her as she felt that he would be taken advantage of in life. His father took hardly any interest in him. God blessed her by answering her prayers. But the price for the extra time she received was high, as the pain she had to endure was great as the cancer had spread uncontrollably. Still, I can only remember her smile and state of prayer, being grateful to Jesus and loving Him till the end. In our childhood we were together as one and I feel her with me still, especially in dark and dangerous days. During the last year of her life Rosaleen wrote a few unpublished books on spirituality. She was one of a kind and special in every way.

Sammy Ikoku Jnr

My brother Sammy graduated in 1979 as a Civil Engineer from the University of Lagos and in 1981 he graduated in Business Administration from the London Metropolitan University. He also attended the Haggai Institute, Oxford to study on their Advanced Management Programme, and the Aspen Institute. Like Maggie and Rosaleen he became known as a motivational speaker, working with large organizations and audiences. A top Nigerian TV personality who has had and continues to have a number of series of TV programmes of his own, he also publishes magazines.

From the minute Sammy was born in 1959 I thought he was the most beautiful baby in the world! Sammy was a special little boy, he had deep dimples, which I had never seen before and they charmed me to my boots. He smiled readily, bonded with me easily and hardly ever cried in my care. I was very protective and proud of him. Even at the age of five or six, as skinny as I was, I struggled to carry baby Sammy on my hip for as long as I could. Mummy would gently tease me because I cried if my brother was upset. By the time he was born as her eighth child, Mummy was no longer as strict as she used to be, so Sammy was spoilt a bit as a child, but he grew up with a very sensitive and trusting nature. His sensitivity meant he would have very tough time out in the world. In the family, much was expected of him and I understood the pressures of coming after two very bright big brothers and academically brilliant sisters (not counting me of course). For a young man growing up in Nigeria there is great pressure to succeed, not just academically, which Sammy achieved, but also in later life. He is gentle and softly spoken and natural and not loud like many Nigerian men. Poor Mummy had other problems while Sammy was growing up, so Sammy got his way most of the time as she struggled to educate and provide for her children and household. Whilst it is wonderful to be spoilt, it sends out conflicting messages to a child during teenage years. His father, SG Ikoku, had stayed in Ghana away from us for a few years. When Daddy was finally returned home to Mummy, Sammy and Daddy struggled to get to know each other.

Many years later, I read one of Sammy's inspirational books entitled "Trust God, Think Big, Act Dumb & Move Fast." I was heartbroken! In the book he wrote about the guilt he felt about his father moving out. I realized that for over 20 years Sammy had blamed himself for his father leaving home. He overheard an argument between Mummy and Daddy, the night before Daddy moved out. Sammy thought his rebellious behaviour had caused his father to move out of the house. This was far from the truth! Sammy, like most men, had kept his feelings and wrong conclusions to himself all these years. But he did get to bond with Daddy, grew ever closer to God using his experiences to inspire others. This is why I love these words; "Be kinder than necessary, everyone you meet is fighting some kind of battle."

In 2010 I visited Abuja at the invitation of the Universal Peace Federation as a Speaker at their conference. At the gathering of the religious heads and politicians I sang "Amazing Grace" to the thousands of delegates. When I was not speaking on the panel, I accepted an invitation to the NAN (News Agency Nigeria) headquarters. Whilst there, I mentioned Sammy's name to the head of the organization. She was full of praise for Sammy describing him as exceptional and charismatic. She said he was the best speaker they had had. I had seen Sammy on TV, but I took the opportunity to see him in person. He had none of the puffed out chest, unconvincing air of pomposity that Nigerian speakers, ministers and officials usually adopt. He was direct, very funny and brilliantly clear. I felt very proud! I know a lot about stage presence. I have observed and taught the topic enough times to clients to be very critical. I looked around, as he spoke, and observed the change of atmosphere in the room. Here was my baby brother looking every inch like a president! When he finished speaking, sticking exactly to his allocated time. I overheard two women sitting behind me:

"You see, when Sam Ikoku is speaking you don't want to listen to all the other useless speakers." said one voice.

"It is because of him that I came to this conference, just to hear him speak. The man talks a lot of sense. We have men like this in this country, but look at the useless people that are leading us." said the other, kissing her teeth.

I prayed secretly that Sammy would not go into Nigerian politics, which appeared at the time to be far too dangerous. I noted down what the two women had said so I could give him the feedback. When I read the words to him, he smiled his dimpled smile and said; "We thank God!" We thank God, indeed! Mummy would have been so proud of those words and her youngest son!

Sammy is famous as a TV pundit on a myriad issues on NTA (Nigeria Television Authority) Network News, and Current Affairs programs. Sammy motivates millions of Nigerians every Saturday on "Optimal Performance" and every Monday Morning on "Fully Charged" both NTA Network TV programs. He speaks at Seminars and Conferences internationally as well as at annual corporate events to inspire and motivate the workforce. His inspirational audiotapes and books are sold worldwide.

He is married and has seven children. God has used him many times to provide spiritual strength and comfort for me.

Eno Ikoku

Mummy was a disciplinarian, but then she had to be, what with eight children to bring up alone and keep alive during a civil war. She was also fiercely defensive of her children. Eno Ikoku is the youngest of my siblings. Both Eno and Sam were born to my stepfather, SG Ikoku. As I was under three years old when Mummy married SG Ikoku it came natural for me to call him Dad or Daddy.

From 1963-1966, during Dad's years in exile in political asylum in Ghana a lot of people saw Mummy as a soft touch or as a defenceless woman with five daughters and three sons to protect. One man to learn the hard lesson of how tough Mummy really was, where her children were concerned, was the headmaster of a primary school attended by my younger sister, Eno. It was during the mid-1960s. Corporal punishment was commonplace in schools, but Eno's headmaster over-stepped the mark. Eno, (who was seven or eight years old at the time) was driven to school every day, therefore, had no control over whether she arrived early or late. One day, she was unusually, late through no fault of hers. The headmaster took it upon himself to punish the child by whipping her twelve times on her back. The whip left vivid stroke marks on Eno's back! When she came home from school she was crying and in great discomfort. Mummy calmly rubbed some balm on Eno's back and tucked her into bed. I don't believe Eno, who was in great pain, slept that night, neither did Mummy. Early the next morning everything was prepared for a normal school day, except that day Mummy was going to take Eno to school herself. Poor Eno was terribly worried because when she and Mummy got to the school, the headmaster's secretary said he was conducting the school assembly and would be a while. This meant that Eno would be late again. Mummy said she would wait. She was then shown to the headmaster's office where she and Eno waited. Mummy's legs had developed St Vitus dance as she waited, a sure sign of impending trouble! After the assembly the headmaster entered his office, he was not exactly a small man by any standard. With unusual calm, Mummy rolled up Eno's school shirt enough to expose the stripes on her back. She showed the headmaster the wounds asking him who had inflicted these wounds on her child. Acquiring an intimidating air, the headmaster started to point out that the child deserved to be disciplined for being late. As he walked past Mummy to get to his desk she grabbed him by the back of his shirt with such speed and force, flung him to the ground and kicked out at him, while she was shouting:
"Nobody has the right to put a mark my child! You hear me! Nobody puts a mark on my child!"

When she had finished with him, leaving him cowering on the floor, she told Eno to get into the car. The next day she drove Eno to enrol into Maryland School, where I had spent some of my primary school days. With a mother like ours we learnt to be respectful, but not fearful of anyone. Like all my sisters, Eno is a formidable character, headstrong, loving, and clever like Rosie and Maggie, a great scholar. Eno became a medical doctor and is now a senior doctor with the US military.

My baby sister Eno, who has two wonderful children, Chudi and Nnenna and a grandchild, grew up to be spiritually strong, stubborn, but wise, full of compassion, though selfless, she does not suffer fools gladly. The youngest of nine children, I guess Eno was a little spoilt because mummy was not as strict as she had been in her early years or during the war. But Eno's stubbornness has served her well when it came to dealing with chauvinistic men.

Chapter Twenty Four: Trip to London

I was 16yrs old and I waited with anticipation and great excitement for my trip to London to stay with my sister Grace. Maggie was studying in Paris and Rosie was already studying in Preston in the UK. The idea was that I should think about my future whilst there and, in particular, to decide whether I wanted to become a novitiate at the Holy Child Convent in Lagos. Mummy got all my paper work and passport done by November 1970, but I had to wait till April 1971 to fly to London. I boarded the BOAC 707 flight with uncle Dele Nwajei so that I did not travel alone. It was a day flight; we left Lagos in the morning and arrived at Heathrow Airport in the evening. It felt as though it was still winter, though I was told it was spring and not as cold as winter. My sister Grace met us at the airport with a coat for me. It was a grey day in London and I was amazed at the rows of houses even though I had seen them in films and BBC news broadcasts, it was still not the same when seeing streets of tightly packed houses for the first time.

My sister's rented room in a house on Trinity Road, Tooting was cold and we had to feed 10 pennies into the metre before we could turn on the electric heater. There was only one bathroom for the entire house and the toilet was outside at the back of the house, which was a huge shock, I learnt to limit the amount of liquid I drank so that I would not have to use the loo at night. I was thankful, though surprised that we were the only ones who used the bath. When I asked my sister about this she pointed to the sink in the room and explained that each room had one and most people preferred to wash themselves than have a bath or shower. I didn't blame them, it was freezing in that bathroom.

The landlady was a surly woman in her 50s or 60s. She probably looked older than her years as her sour personality showed on her face. She was not happy that there were now two people in the room despite the fact that Grace had paid extra and had forewarned her about my coming to spend my holidays with her. We spoke in whispers and tiptoed to the bathroom in the mornings because everything we did annoyed her. She seemed to be permanently glued to the net curtains of her front room windows. I once ventured out to the corner shop to buy some bread and milk and she was peering through the curtains. I felt like my every move was being watched. "There are too many black faces." The landlady had complained.

My sister, whose husband, Dr Tokunbo Coker, was studying to be a vet in Germany, was pregnant at this time with her third child and was out working as a secretary until 6.00pm. Whilst she was out, in the first few days I was afraid to go out on my own and afraid to stay in, with the landlady and her husband, knocking at the door randomly to check if I had lit the gas fire heater or with some other excuse. I sat in the room dressed like an Eskimo and cradled a hot water bottle and, occasionally, I would boil the kettle and place my hands near the heat to warm them up. I began to wonder how I was going to survive the next twelve weeks. After a few days of asking what I did with myself all day, my sister Grace decided that we would move. I was very pleased and relieved.

We moved several times in the first four weeks taking in Clapham and Catford before finally settling into a large room in a house in Hewer Street in Ladbroke Grove. The house was in a sorrier state than the one in Tooting, but it was welcoming and had the great advantage of being owned by a Nigerian couple. We were much more comfortable in this accommodation even with rats and cockroaches for company.

I dared not even imagine how my sister managed it all while working in the daytime. Many times we looked up advertisements for rooms to let in the area we lived in, then we would call up the landlord and make an appointment to see the room in ten or fifteen minutes, but when we got there, the rooms were suddenly no longer available. One landlord was quite open about his prejudice, he said we didn't sound black on the phone and he was not going to have black people living in his house. This prejudice centred on one's skin colour was new to me as my school had children of all races and colours as most of the ambassadors' children went there. At home everyone around me was black, so you never came across this strange and ignorant idea. Being an African and looking for accommodation in London in those days was not for the faint hearted, which is why starving yourself to save up and buy your own property was very necessary. Even Caribbeans, referred to at the time as "West Indians", looked down on Africans and were embarrassed to be associated with them. Lack of education in the UK schools and ignorance about Africa promoted this attitude among the West Indians. Even Churchgoers of all colours were permeated with this darkness. As I was wrestling within myself about becoming a nun I tried several times to go to church and finally gave up. I was used to getting to church early to spend a quiet time with the Lord before the congregation came in, but each time I did this the row I was sitting in was left empty until the church was full and there was no other place for people to sit except in my row. Then and only then would someone sit in my row, but even then they would sit as far away from me as they could. Not even the priest would acknowledge me. This created a spiritual battle within me for a long time. Someone pointed out that the churches I had attended were all Church of England and that I was a Catholic. I learnt then that the Church of England also bore the names of Saints, so I had been confused. I reasoned with God that these so-called churches could not possibly be His because I did not feel His loving presence in any of them, all I felt was anger and hate and that was definitely not what a place of worship or the congregation should be like. I begged for His forgiveness and then I decided I would keep away from any kind of church and create one inside my spirit instead, so that I could worship and spend time with the Lord wherever I was. I was astounded, as I had always thought that England was a country of Christian people, but it did not seem to be so. I even became cynical about the campaigns to bring aid to the children back home in Biafra as self-serving and purely for show.

Our Ladbroke Grove landlord and his wife lived downstairs and rented out the rooms upstairs. Our room faced the front of the house. There was a bathroom and sink upstairs and we cooked on a stove in the room to avoid intruding too much on the couple's life. They had a lovely daughter who had sickle cell anaemia (a hereditary blood deficiency common among black people). They also had a son who was thankfully clear of the disease. The couple argued so much with each other most days and, even though they tried to keep their voices down, we still heard them battling it out through the floorboards and the noise just became part of our routine. My sister sometimes had to mediate and negotiate peace as they both came to her with their grievances one against the other. Our landlord was tall, strong and quite a handsome looking man, but he did not come up to his wife's expectations and everything he did irritated her, including his thick Igbo accent. I used to feel sorry for him. His wife was in England now and did not want to be tied to the old traditions she had left behind. This clash of the African and UK culture was too much for the relationship and this husband and wife expected so much more from each other. It was not easy for a black African man or any black man for that matter, living in England in those unenlightened days, and this poor man was married, with children, to a wife who expected him to live up to the false idea of life she saw daily on television. Even his sexual performance was constantly and embarrassingly criticized. Once, my sister commented;
"How can a man be expected to perform anything after such public and detailed criticism!"

His wife was no oil painting, but expected much from life. She would look at the way we were dressed, even though we lived in the same semi-squalor with them and she would try to emulate us, as we were comparatively well dressed, this caused more problems for the poor man. We had turned the large room we were renting into quite a nice little one roomed flat, but we couldn't do anything about the rats that would visit at night. We were model tenants and treated the landlords like family. They in turn did not mind our visitors and they joined in whenever we had guests. We cooked for all our guests, but sometimes the landlady would bring up some food when they joined us. However, I was not keen on her cooking which was an insipid watered down English version of Nigerian food. Cooking was not her forte, but, nevertheless, they were both good company, though the man was quiet and shy around us. Whenever my sister's husband came to visit from Germany or when Rosie came from Preston, we had the use of a small spare room facing the back of the house, which the landlord painted white for us. I liked them; they were both nice people who, perhaps, should never have been married to each other.

Living in Ladbroke Grove, I realised that my sister had some social life in London as she had quite a few Nigerian friends, who came to visit at weekends. We would all sit around in the room after eating and they would talk about their experiences in London. I remember once we were all joined by two of our regular housemates, the rats. We tried to shoo them away, but they wouldn't have any off it, which caused one of the guests to joke. "You see, that's one thing you have to remember about this country, even the rats are highly educated with university degrees!"
We all laughed.

Observing the audacity of the rats, I amused myself by imagining that somewhere under the floorboards and in the sewers, there were universities for rodents, run by professors who had been reincarnated as rats.

One day Grace decided that I should come into London with her on the bus. She was working in an office in the Strand, but she was concerned that I spent too much time alone in the room. Strangely, we had not discussed up to this point what I should do with my life. She asked what I wanted to do and I told her that Daddy and Mummy thought I should study law. Daddy would get me into the University of Lagos where he often lectured on Politics. I told her I hated the idea and that my suggestion of joining a religious order is what had prompted and earned me this three months soul-searching holiday to England. Mummy thought the holiday would give me time to decide the direction I wanted to go in life, adding that when I returned, if I still wanted to join the convent, she would not stand in my way. I had just turned sixteen and should have been in my preliminary year studying to get into university.

Was I serious about the convent? Well, to be honest it was a form of escape from Daddy's choice of law or architecture. I had five O Levels and Art was my favourite and best subject. However, there were no lucrative careers for an artist in Nigeria at that time. All my siblings were gifted in science, Johnny an Aeronautic Engineer, Tony a Pilot, Maggie a Pharmacologist, Rosaleen an Industrial Chemist, Eno a doctor and then there was Patricia the 'black Sheep'! But in truth, yes, I was serious about it as the idea of devoting my life to Jesus Christ was a real and inspiring concept. I related my conversations with Rev Mother and my favourite nun, Sister Catherine, to my sister Grace and found a kindred spirit. She suggested I took advantage of my stay by taking some lessons in shorthand and to learn to type. Instead, I chose a part time elocution class to improve my spoken English and remove my Nigerian accent. When we got off the bus at Temple, I walked along the River Thames and took a turning to find my way to St Paul's Cathedral. I noticed the Guildhall School of Music and Drama in John Carpenter Street and wrote down the name to show to my sister. The next day I rang the school and was asked to come in and join an adult class. The entrance was at the back of the enormous building and there were about ten to twelve people in the class. It was intimidating because all of them were accomplished and trained singers, so I decided to register for private lessons with the gentleman with a kind face, who ran the class. I told him I could not read music, but would like to sing some of the songs that had been sung so well in the class. He tried a few classical pieces with me and concluded that I learnt fast and had a good ear. The final piece we worked on together was "What is life to me without thee" from the opera Orpheus and Eurydice. This was my first flirtation with classical songs and I loved it. The next week I rejoined the class and received encouraging applause and great praise for my rendition of 'Eurydice.' The tutor said he would speak to the school to offer me a place as a fulltime student, but when Grace and I looked into it the fees were too high and anyway I was only in England on holiday.

Nevertheless, I had found my calling! I was smitten with the singing bug, I had sung so many times in leading roles at Holy Child College and in the school choir, but being a singer was not encouraged as a career. I was beginning to think that I should stay in England, if it were possible, and study singing and so I continued to study part-time at the Guildhall school whilst searching for another more affordable school. Fate led me to a small drama school and I enrolled at The London School of Dramatic Art (LSDA), which was founded and run by the elderly Miss Gertrude Pickersgill. Meanwhile at Guildhall, I began to be bolder in the classes for the first time and lost my shyness, because I thought I would never see these people, I was studying with, again when the course was over. I knew my parents would rather I did a secretarial course than join what they called "the vagabonds and strolling players" of the artistic world and I did not fool myself into thinking that I was going to be allowed to stay. Nevertheless, I was enjoying what I was doing and I decided to leave the future in "God's very capable and loving hands" as Mummy would say. I certainly didn't want to go back home and study for a Law degree.

The full time course at the LSDA was for two years and ignoring my parent's wishes, I paid up for a year with my sister's help and she applied for a student's visa for me. I was not due to start my course at LSDA for another month or so. I prayed that my student's visa would be granted. Meanwhile, I enrolled in a modelling school for fun and continued my evening classes at Guildhall School of Music and Drama. I kept these up for some time even when I started the daytime classes at LSDA. I was fast gaining life experiences as a grown- up.

One cold day I developed an abscess in a tooth I had broken about a year before coming to London. It was silly really, I was in the Girl Guides and we had one of our camping trips during which no one remembered to bring a bottle opener. The only option was to either break the tops of the bottles which would have rendered the drinks undrinkable or open them with our teeth. Having done it before, I volunteered and after many bottles my tooth gave in and broke in half. There was a little pain at the time, but it was bearable as my pain threshold is high. None of my family had ever needed a dentist thanks to Mummy's use of a Milton solution as our daily mouthwash, so that a dentist was not even on the radar. The tooth had not been infected until now. For days I took painkillers, but finally the pain became unbearable and got steadily worse by the minute. I found a number for Eastman Dental Hospital and took a train there. I had never known such pain; I couldn't speak without wanting to cry. When I got to the hospital, they asked me questions about next of kin etc and completed a form. I was given anaesthetics and was unconscious for the procedure. What a relief it was when I regained consciousness, I was grateful to be out of pain and profusely thanked everyone I could see. My legs were a bit unsteady and so I decided to make my way back to Ladbroke Grove station. By the time I got to Ladbroke Grove, the pain was back only it was decidedly worse than before. Now I was crying with the intensity of the pain, my head was about to explode and I was totally confused. I ran out of the station like a mad thing. Once I got outside the station, there was a slight relief from the pain as the cold air hit the tooth, making the pain bearable, but not enough to stop me crying. I was still groggy from my treatment at the dental hospital, but managed to get back to the house. As I entered the house and shut the door my head throbbed so that I thought I would die.

I couldn't wait to get back outside; I made my way back towards the station not knowing what I was going to do. I knew I had to stay out in the cold or I wouldn't be able get through the pain. I couldn't speak, the pain increased and the entire right side of my face throbbed more, so I scribbled on a piece of paper;

'Please tell me where I can find the nearest dentist, I'm in terrible pain and can't speak.'

Most people wouldn't even stop to look at the paper, I walked to the station still crying, one man finally read my note and told me there was a dentist two or three streets to the left off Ladbroke Grove.

When I found the street, I could just about make out a Dental Surgery sign more than a hundred yards away. It might as well have been one hundred miles as far as I was concerned. I hurried as much as I could to the surgery. Thank God the receptionist was visible from the street! I opened the door and as the warm air from the interior hit my face, the shock of the pain made me run outside. She must have thought I was completely mad. Once outside, I went to the window and motioned to her to come out, she ignored me and I kept knocking on the window and making pleading gestures. She finally came out when I fell on my knees sobbing. I handed her the paper now soaked in tears and she tried to get me to go inside, I got out a piece of paper and wrote;

"The pain is explosive in a warm environment, please ask the dentist if I could be given something to stop the pain so I can come inside."

It was a long shot but she disappeared inside and, after a lifetime, came out to the reception area with the dentist. Oh what relief! But he turned back and disappeared inside I thought my time had come and I would die on a London street, with no one knowing where I was. I was still kneeling and contemplating my death, when the door opened and the Asian doctor came out with an injection needle in hand.

"Please don't put me out, I want to be awake when you remove the tooth." I scribbled frantically. The dentist tried to explain some procedure, I was not listening "just take it out" I sobbed. He administered the local anaesthetics out there on the pavement. He returned to the patient he had been attending to, before my interruption, I waited on the pavement for the injection to take effect. Not even the sight of the injection needle bothered me as it had all my young life.

Greatly relieved, I walked into the building smiled and thanked the Receptionist; sat down and waited. I told the dentist I had just been to the Dental hospital and was treated under general anaesthetic. I pointed out the

offending tooth and kept checking to make sure he had extracted the right one. He did not charge me all he said was;
"You should never have been allowed to go through such pain! Go home, take these tablets and get some sleep."

Some years later, I found out that I had been used as a guinea pig at the hospital to teach the students. My famous Royal dentist in Park Street, Mayfair was shocked when he looked at the ex-ray of my teeth.
"Which dentist drilled all these holes in such perfectly good teeth?
"How many holes? I asked.
"Seven of your teeth have been drilled and filled for no reason."
"Bastards.' He said after I told him the story of my abscess.

What evil people they were, that had ignored my abscess and pain and unknown to me, drilled holes in my perfect teeth. Up to that point in my life I had always been able to see the positive side of everything, but now I was beginning to lose my sunny and childlike outlook on life. I left the gap where the tooth had been as a reminder of one of the most pain filled days of my life and how evil people can be.

However, my first few months in London, weren't all bad and were filled with lots of fun and adventure. I can't remember how it came about, but I once got a chance to be part of the Lord Mayor of London's Parade. A photographer singled me out and I ended up on the front pages of the newspapers wearing a white t-shirt with a large poppy in my hair.

My sister Grace loved to listen to records. Jim Reeves was one of her favourite singers; she was brilliant at ballroom dancing and even entered local competitions. I went to some of her classes with her and attended the competitions to support her at the Hammersmith Palais, which was the favourite entertainment hall of black people at the time. At one of the singing competitions at the Palais, urged by my sisters and friends, I sang *"All Kinds of Everything Reminds Me of You"* which had won Dana the Eurovision Song Contest about two years before, and won me a prize at the Palais. Later, I was asked to sing the same song, impromptu, at a Kneller Hall Military School of Music bash in Twickenham, to which we were invited by one of the Nigerians who was graduating from the School.

I was surprised that, after some persuasion from my sister Grace, Mummy and Daddy agreed that I could take the course at LSDA if we could get the Student Visa.

Chapter Twenty Five: Hair

My student's visa was granted and I started my course at LSDA, I kept very much to myself during the course. I can't remember why exactly, but I had a free day and so I got onto the underground to Oxford Circus, which was always my favourite tourist stop. I would normally walk the entire length of Oxford Street from Marble Arch to Tottenham Court Road and back, occasionally going into shops to look at the dresses. This time I decided to explore beyond the end of Tottenham Court Road by hopping on a bus to Holborn. It was my first venture into London's Theatre land, even though I did not know it at the time or even that such a place existed. My sister hadn't the time to go to the theatre, and we did not have the tradition of theatres, as such, in Nigeria. Back home in Nigeria, schools staged plays and musicals or performances were held on university campuses, as there were no standing theatres with shows that I knew of.

In London there was a lot to see and all of my sister's friends would show surprise that I had not yet been to Madame Tussauds. Every Nigerian visiting London had to see the waxworks and have their photos taken with the pigeons at Trafalgar Square. I had not yet got round to the pigeons, though I had seen tourists feeding and posing with the birds as I sat on the bus.

On this, my day off, from the drama classes, I was on the bus heading for Holborn from Oxford Circus when I saw a building that looked like Madame Tussauds with a long queue of people outside. On the rounded front of the building was a large colourful head of hair. I got off the bus at the next bus stop and walked back to join the queue, which went round the block. I was used to seeing Hippies in London and the fact that there were so many in this queue did not surprise me. Almost everyone in the queue was dressed in colourful flared trousers with very long scraggy hair and a scarf of many colours tied across the forehead. Some of the girls wore the kind of tie-dye dresses that were mostly worn by the poor in Nigeria. There were a few black boys and girls with perfectly rounded, large Afro hair, broken only by the scarf tied from the forehead to the back of the head. The whole queue was very colourful and cheerful. However, I was wearing a very demure white, black and grey patterned dress with knee length black and white, snakeskin boots like a very smart secretary.

Now I realize, how ridiculous I must have looked in that queue and I was aware of the curious looks I was getting at the time. It was a slow moving line, but I was patient as I wanted to see the waxworks. I had nothing else to do for the rest of the day, so I persevered. It seemed like a long time before I got to the entrance. The entrance was a door in a side-street at the back of the building above which was the sign 'Shaftsbury Theatre' above that was another sign 'Stage Door'. I was baffled. I was still trying to work out how this could be the entrance to Madame Tussauds and why it said Shaftsbury Theatre, when the door opened and a pleasant young man said "can we have the next three please?" I dutifully entered following the young man and woman in front of me. To the right, immediately inside the door was a man inside a cubicle who asked us to write down our names and telephone numbers.

"How much does it cost to go in?" I asked, confused. That was one of many embarrassing moments during my time in "Hair", but the day was still young.

Everyone looked at each other surprised and amused. The stage doorman said in a patronizing voice:

"This is an audition love. You don't pay to go in."

The others laughed

I wished the floor would open up and swallow me. I was hungry and tired and it had been a long wait. I was not quite sure I knew what he meant by 'audition', and I'm not sure I had heard the word "audition" whilst I was standing in the queue. If I did, I had not taken it in, besides I was used to "trying out" for a part at school, not "auditioning". I was feeling more and more like a fish out of water and very uncomfortable.

"What do I do to get in?" I asked reluctantly.

"You sing. Can you sing?" said the stage door man with a silly smirk.

"Of course I can sing!"

I was surprised he would even ask such a question, couldn't everybody sing?

"Just write your name and number down and you will be taken to the Green Room where someone will come and take you to the stage when it is your turn."

I was beginning to realise that I had made a mistake, but singing was something I liked to do and so I followed the others to the room where we had to wait. There was one other person, a hippy, waiting in the room as we entered in silence. I could hear someone singing over the sound system in the room. The door opened and a man called out a name and the hippy got up and followed him. Soon he was singing the same two songs as the one before had sung. They both sounded good, but I could not understand why they were singing the same songs. Afraid of going out there and making a total fool of myself I asked the other two to please explain what was going on, after letting them know I was there by default and had thought I was queuing for Madame Tussauds! They admitted I wasn't dressed like the type of person who would normally audition for the show, but I was encouraged when they said every young person in the country wanted to be in the show. Thank God they were chatty and gave me a brief history of the show, which was called "Hair"; it was the biggest hit show in the West End at the time. They said that members of the cast had become famous purely by being in the show. They told me about London's West End, the British equivalent of Broadway, I was familiar with Broadway from the movies shown on TV. By the time they had finished, my imagination was fired up, I looked forward to standing on the stage, imagining long velvety silver curtains opening majestically as each person walked on to sing.

Soon it was my turn to go on to the stage and I was somewhat disappointed as I walked out on to the stage. There were no curtains, to make it worse, there were graffiti all over the floor and walls and, well, the glamour I was expecting was absent. The stage was lit with strong white lights, which made it impossible to see into the auditorium. I heard people chuckling in the darkness of the theatre, and I became conscious of the way I was dressed.
"What is your name?" said a disembodied voice.
"Patricia Ebigwei."
"Are you a member of Equity?"
"What's that?" I replied
Great guffaws of laughter came from the darkness as I strained to make out some faces
"What are you going to sing?"
"I didn't come to sing." I was about to explain, when someone stopped me in my tracks by calling my name from the side of the stage. I turned to see the Musical Director.
"Do you know any songs?" he asked kindly.
"Yes."
"Well then, which one would you like to sing?"
I thought for a moment and said;
"The Sound of Music." There were louder guffaws from the auditorium.
"Ok! What key?" the MD asked.
"I don't know", I said almost inaudibly "just play it!"

The MD started playing and I went into 'The hills are alive with the sound of music....' in my best Maria Von Trapp voice, singing the first verse and chorus of the song, by which time I had decided I had made enough of a

fool of myself. I apologized and said I couldn't remember the rest of the song. There was a brief conversation among the people in the auditorium after which the voice from the dark said;
"Thank you, we'll let you know."

I was glad to get out of there and I took the train to Ladbroke Grove and arrived home thinking that it had been an insane and surreal day. When my sister got back from work, I gave her step-by-step account of my day. We were both laughing ourselves silly when the landlady called up from downstairs to say I had a phone call. It was the Company Manager from "Hair". He said that they would like me to come to the theatre to see the show and have a meeting. This was the beginning of a huge change in the direction of my life. One minute I was contemplating the convent, though that might have been for all the wrong reasons, the next I was about to appear on London's West End in the current biggest West End hit. I hadn't even been in London that long, where was God taking me?

The next day I went in to see the Company Manager after my drama class, I was asked to stay to watch the show that evening. I was completely mesmerized from the beginning. I fell in love with the incredible music by Galt McDermot. The show began with members of the cast making their way, to the stage, in slow motion, from every part of the theatre, through the Stalls, the Royal Circle and between the seats. I watched transfixed as they kept their balance whilst climbing over people's heads, sliding down the side pillars from the Boxes and up the steps on to the Stage. When finally on the stage, they sang "When the Moon is in the seventh house and Jupiter aligns with Mars…….. This is the dawning of the Age of Aquarius." Most of the message of the lyrics went over my head, but the show was great fun and I wanted to be a part of it. However, I crashed down to earth when it came to the part in the show, when the cast emerged stark naked from under a huge canvas. I was appalled, I had never seen such a thing and my enthusiasm about doing the show were immediately curtailed and I turned to the Company Manager.
"Sorry, I am not going to do that!" I blurted out, disappointed.

He was quick to explain that taking one's clothes off was voluntary and besides I would be under the huge canvass, completely covered singing 'Hare Krishna" and so I would not be required to be naked. I got the part because of my voice; as few respectable sopranos had auditioned, kept away by the nude scene. As the show continued, I was excited, moved at times, euphoric and bewildered by what I saw and heard. By the time the evening ended with "Let the Sunshine In" and members of the packed audience crowded the stage to join the cast, singing and dancing, I was in love with show business! My two favourite songs from the show were 'What A Piece of Work Is Man' and 'Eye Look your Last", but all the songs inspired such a mixture of emotions in me that I was enthralled.

"Hair", the wonderful show which changed my life, symbolized the Hippy movement, which was anti-everything taking in pollution, Government, materialism, the Vietnam War, parents or authority of any kind. All very well, but unfortunately the movement also promoted dope, free sex for all and lawlessness. The hippies wore, to my African eyes, strange looking Kaftans and, smoked disgusting smelling things they called spliffs. The black hippies wore cool, often oversized afros and large colourful earrings. They campaigned for peace through flower-power and love-ins which was hard for me to digest, also the idea of being squatters and taking over someone else's hard earned property never seemed right to me no matter how it was explained away. The lawlessness and lack of self-control among the cast seemed to miss the point and belittle the genuinely laudable aims of the Hippie Movement in a selfish and naïve way. I know that many of the cast did not approve of my conservatism and lack of sympathy for their lifestyles and they also thought I was "green". I was in the show, but my upbringing would not let me be completely part of all the hippie ideas. Still, I admired them for trying to change the future for the better and for taking risks to highlight the danger areas. I accepted that the young can and should dream of changing the world, it's only normal and many changes for the better have arisen this way, but the tendency was to go too far with it. The show expressed the view of youth by using the leading characters to highlight young people's worries for their future. There were some lovely people in the show including Richard O' Brien (Who later wrote "The Rocky Horror Show"), Diana Langdon and Paul Nicholas, though I didn't have much opportunity to get to know them better. I formed strong friendships with Ethel Foley, Vicky Silva and Joanna White. It occurred to me that, despite their good intentions, some of the cast might turn out to be the wrong kind of undisciplined parents and I wondered whether they were not laying down a foundation for a future that would be worse than that of the generation before them that they hated so much.

"Hair" gave me a great opportunity. Mentally, I was growing up fast, observing and praying to be able to separate the good from the bad, hoping everything I had learnt from the turbulence of my young life in Nigeria would see me through this brave new world.

The big nude scene in Hair was a public display of defiance. It was supposed to encapsulate what the protest part of the hippie movement was about. It amused me, however, as it put me in mind of those unfortunate people back home who walked about totally naked, and whom everyone referred to as being mad. Purposely showing nudity in public only draws pity in Nigeria and the exhibitionist would definitely not be taken seriously.

For a week, I went to the Shaftsbury Theatre after my daytime classes at LSDA learning the songs, watching the moves, by the end of the week I knew most of what the ensemble (Tribe) were doing, Marsha Hunt was leaving the show and I was to replace her. I found out, that the audition was held to find a soprano who could hit the high notes in "Hare Krishna". Whilst everyone who came to the audition sang the two most familiar songs from the show, my choice of "The Sound of Music" got me the job the minute I started singing. I found out that Equity is the actor's Union and the Company Manager applied for a preliminary Equity Membership Card for me, which was forthcoming. I took a few days off from LSDA for rehearsals before I joined the cast on the actual stage. The Management was nice to me and so were some of the cast members, but some were crazy and extreme in their behaviour. I was excited to join the show, a wild show with the best modern day music. This was beyond my wildest dreams, but I couldn't share my excitement with anyone except my sisters because I was on a student's visa and should not have been working! It was just as well, I know my parents would have been shocked by the show and would have ordered me home. Eventually my sister Grace smoothed out that end, assuring Mummy I had not joined a band of vagabonds or Fela Kuti type dancers although to see pictures of the show you might have believed that I had! Meanwhile, I set out to know more about the musical and show business in general. I was learning Shakespeare at LSDA, but nothing could beat cutting my singing, dancing and acting teeth on a professional and successful West End show.

Each day, I was getting home at about 11.30pm and waking up early for classes at LSDA, juggling classes and matinees. I came clean with the Principal of the school with the name out of Dickens, Gertrude Pickersgill. She was understanding even though she did not approve of the show, but she thought the experience would help me to get rid of my inhibitions. I was shy about reading out loud during the drama classes; the other students would snigger if I mispronounced words or placed emphasis in the wrong place in a sentence. It made Zieglinda, a German student and I feel very stupid. We consoled each other with the knowledge that the other students didn't speak any other languages except English, so we put it down to ignorance, but it did not stop us being self-conscious. It took me years to get over the inhibitions I developed at LSDA and some of the other private classes I attended afterwards.

As a show 'Hair' was a fascinating and extraordinary show to appear in. It was easy on the nerves as far as stage fright was concerned. On my first few nights I was allowed to run off the stage if I was unsure of what was happening or what I was supposed to be doing, and to run back on when I was sure. The script was loose and when I was comfortable with things I was given some minor roles to play. For instance, I loved being part of the trio of girls that sang 'White Boys', in which I and two other black girls would climb on to a ramp, step into a single gold stretchy sequined dress. It had three pairs of shoulder straps designed to accommodate the three of us. Each would put on a curly blond wig. Then the two at the end would stick out their bums as far as they could to stretch the uni-dress. The result was we looked like the Supremes in blond wigs when we were revealed and wheeled forward. We looked like a dream! The piece of stretch fabric was well put together to look like three gorgeous, glamorous dresses until we lifted up our arms and revealed a shapeless stretch of fabric, to gasps of delight from the audience. Such a brilliant idea and I got a taste for sequins from that little cameo and I loved the song.

There were a few downsides to appearing in the show. One was getting home after the curtain came down. I made my way by the underground to Ladbroke Grove Station, trying to get there before this one policeman would be between me and the flat. His footsteps gave me the creeps, they echoed off the pavement. I don't know why the sound of them alarmed me, but I had developed this irrational fear of him. The first time I heard him I hid until there was a safe distance between us then I ran all the way to the house. I made a point of getting home as soon as I could after the show to avoid those footsteps.

Once, a party was organised by a member of the cast and I thought it would be fun to attend, remembering all the fun parties at home with music, food, dancing and everybody being friendly and just simply celebrating. When I got to the party, I was over-dressed and out of place. The party was at one of the "squats" and everyone was sitting around smoking and passing joints from one to another. One or two people were rolling the joints, but apart from that, there appeared to be no movement. I hated the smell and made my excuses before leaving the party, which was like a funeral without a body. I knew by then that what they were smoking was illegal and the next day I learnt that there had been a police raid on the party and a lot of people were taken to the police station for fingerprinting and questioning. One of the cast members, who had been taken to the station, thought it was funny to recount how she had to flush a whole lot of the costly marijuana down the loo. I listened in horror to all their stories about the raid not understanding how being caught in a police raid of any kind could be taken so lightly, and I was thankful to my Guardian Angel, for making me leave the party when I did. Another lesson learnt 'avoid show business parties.'

I guess I must have appeared very boring to all the cast, as I had never tasted alcohol, except the Sacrament, nor smoked and I was not a party animal. I was just coming out of my mid-teens and only the company manager knew this. There were members of the cast who were obsessed with trying to get me to let my hair down, so to speak, strip, try drugs, sex, and use bad language, drink and smoke. On my birthday, someone baked me a marijuana cake as a present; it looked odd and smelt nothing like the cakes Mummy used to bake at home, so I refused to eat it. Before the "overture and beginners" was called, they popped open a bottle of champagne, which was very nice of them, but I also refused the drink especially before the show. There was tremendous pressure on me to drink the champagne. I was called 'chicken' and all kinds of names in an effort to make me drink, but I remained stubborn, besides there wasn't anyone I trusted to listen to. My main worry was that I did not know what effect a sip of alcohol might have had on me during the opening sequence where I climbed over the heads of the audience in slow motion. I might have lost balance and broken my neck or worst still, someone else's neck. It was only some time later, someone let slip that the champagne was laced with LSD because they wanted to see me stoned just once! I looked up what LSD meant and banned myself from ever socialising with young people in show business after work or letting anything pass my lips that was suggested by them.

I was told that drugs would bring me freedom. If only they knew how ridiculous that sounded to me. I was freer than any of them could imagine. I had been through terrible things they only saw in their nightmares. They had everything going for them, no war and life was easy and they were looking for freedom in drugs! The fact that no one in Hair succeeded in making me try drugs, sex or drinks says it all. If their movement could not persuade a sixteen-year-old naïve child from Africa to join in, then the movement did not stand a chance. I knew that Freedom comes from having rules, discipline and boundaries and has to be fought for. Freedom cannot possibly come from drugs or alcohol!

I didn't know, at that time, what I wanted to be, all I knew was I had to make the most of whatever life placed in front of me and hope I would live long enough to reap some rewards. Up to then, having respect for those older than me was second nature and yet here I was finding it hard to respect anyone in the show.

The wardrobe department tried hard to make me look like a hippie. The company manager was irritated with wardrobe because my costume looked like I was modelling it. I never felt hip. I recall the powder blue, patterned old blouse I was eventually given to wear. It had buttons down the front, but I was only allowed to do up no more than two buttons. The blouse was to cause me great embarrassment just when I thought I was settling in. One night, during a scene in which the cast had to sit absolutely still and cross-legged on the floor on stage, while the two main characters were leaping about in some other dimension and time. One of the cast, a man named Christopher, probably the most out-of-control person in the cast, who played a principal role; took it on himself to play a prank on me and tore open my blouse. It happened in the beginning of that scene in the show, when he knew I could not run off the stage. So I sat with my breast exposed to the audience. It was no big deal in the context of the show, but I was mortified and to me it signified cruelty and wickedness. I never did cry easily, but I was soaked with tears, and by the time I left the stage, I was inconsolable. The management allowed me to sit out the rest of the show in the long dressing room, which I shared with other members of the cast. I sat in the dressing room in shock contemplating what to do next. I sat there looking in disgust at the disarray around me and at the sink I never drew water from, because one of the girls habitually chose to wash her bottom in it. Apparently she could not have a bath as a squatter.

"I am in hell!" I kept saying to myself. My guardian angel was with me for sure, because when the show finished that night, I discovered I had two good friends in the Company, Ethel Foley and Joanna White. They gave me a pep talk and cheered me up, for which I was very grateful.

Hair was originally a Broadway Rock Musical, opened in London in 1968 when I was fourteen years old and a whole world away in a convent boarding school in Lagos. At first the show was declared "dangerously permissive" by the Lord Chamberlain, "unsuitable for the British theatre audiences". I would not only have described the show as dangerously permissive, but the hippie movement itself was very permissive. The Lord Chamberlain's powers of censorship were abolished under the Theatres Act in 1968 and the Show was allowed to open.

I am grateful to Paul Nicholas for casting me in the show; because career wise, it made me realise there was a vocational path in the arts for me. It gave me better training about the art of entertainment than any elocution/drama school could have taught me. I also learnt a great deal about human nature, the good the bad and the ugly. It made me grateful that the training I got from my mother and my past experiences had matured me mentally beyond my teenage years, certainly more than a lot of the older people I was working with. Yes, I seemed naïve to everyone else. I was a virgin and remained so the entire duration of my time in the show. Every night, I sang words in the show that had no meaning to me, like hashish, opium, sodomy etc. As a matter of fact it was in my thirties that I finally discovered the meanings of many of these words.

In the show, I observed people's emotional conflicts with life; their selfishness, greed, lack of understanding, meaningless self-importance and foolishness, but also their kindness, gentleness and wisdom. There were those who wanted to change tomorrow, yet lived today as if tomorrow did not exist. There were friends, who were not really friends, people were not truthful with each other and hypocrisy seemed to be the norm. There were people who were against the capitalist system and business as a whole, but who knew nothing about how anything inside or outside their own country actually worked. People to whom telling cruel jokes, at the expense of others, made them feel more important. I listened and deduced that the joke teller was usually in awe of or ashamed of the butt of his/her jokes. Either way, it said more about the joker to me. My five and half months in Hair, was worth twenty years' life experience in the outside world. I was green and fresh, as they used to say of me, and like a baby I took it all in. I was learning from other people's mistakes, vowing to avoid them if I was lucky enough to live past the age of thirty. The wise among the cast listened to their elders and the not so wise would only listen to and blindly follow their inexperienced, but fast talking friends. Like Daddy used to say; "a fool learns from his own mistakes, but a wise man learns from other people's mistakes". I saw that fools were only attracted to the foolish, even though there were a few wise members in the cast and they had a sensible management who was willing to guide them.

Personally, I felt that the more I learnt, the more I realised, like Newton that I knew very little indeed and could never know everything.

One of the artists left the show to appear in a play and, as the matinee was on a different day to that of Hair, members of the Hair cast decided to go and see her in the play. I thought it was a wonderful idea and reflected a sense of community and it would show support for her. It was the first time I had ever paid to go into a West End theatre. I can't remember what the play was called, but according to the others, it was not very good and the girl we had come to see was awful! Being so inexperienced, I couldn't say whether it was good or bad. Amongst those whom she regarded as her friends, there was a good degree of schadenfreude. It made me uncomfortable to hear such vitriol being said behind her back. I guessed they must also have auditioned for the part she was playing, but were unsuccessful. I got worried when they said we were all going back-stage to see her after the show, which they told me was the normal thing to do. Childishly, I believed her friends would give her good advice on how she could enhance her performance as they seemed to know exactly what she was doing wrong. I followed them sheepishly through the stage door to her dressing room.

"Darling, you were marvellous, fantastic!" They all said, as they air kissed her. My jaw dropped. Lesson number two; 'remember never to believe a word anyone says to you in show business!' There was not a word of their true opinions. The explanation I got later was that they did not want to hurt her feelings, besides this was a "dog eat dog" business. So much for 'Love-ins'!

I remember the day Mick Jagger came to the theatre to pick up his girlfriend Marsha Hunt. What a to-do there was! I had not seen such a fuss being made about anyone since the wedding of General Gowon, the young Nigerian Head of State. Mick was and is a phenomenal pop star; probably the brightest, and that, in the young adult world, gave him a demi-god status. Since I had not heard of the Rolling Stones until that moment, I waited with bated breath for a beautiful Elvis Presley look-alike or at least one of the Beatles or someone like that to come along. I let my imagination run wild; he must be the best looking man in England judging from all the fuss. I built up such a picture in my head that when I finally caught a glimpse of him I exclaimed:
"That is the ugliest white man I have ever seen!" Naive or what!
This is another lesson I learnt along the way; 'you are no longer ordinary or ugly when you become a star' and thank God for that!

When it was time for my sister Grace to move back to Nigeria she gave me enough money to rent a small room in a house in Kilburn. She had opened an account in which she saved all the money I had been giving her to help with my upkeep. I did not know that she had saved it for me. I was enormously grateful. The room in Kilburn was a tiny box room in a house where my friends Joanna White and Ethel Foley lived. It was so tiny I had to live out of a suitcase.

Chapter Twenty Six: Two Gentlemen of Verona

After a few months in Hair, there was a buzz about a new Broadway musical planned for the West End called 'The Two Gentlemen of Verona' with music by Galt McDermott the composer of Hair. The story was, of course, Shakespeare's, with script adaption by Mel Shapiro and lyrics by John Guare. The day Galt McDermott, and, I think Mel Shapiro and the producer came to London to cast their new musical, they dropped by to see Hair and sent a message back stage during the interval, which was handed to me by the Company Manager. The note said they would like to have a word with me after the show. I met them at the stage door briefly and they asked me to audition for the part of Sylvia in 'Two Gentlemen of Verona'. Two or three days later I auditioned. It was my first conscious audition. I can't remember what I sang, probably one of the songs from 'Hair'. I didn't get the part of Sylvia, it was decided that I was too inexperienced for the leading role, which went to the tall and very gorgeous Brenda (B J) Arnau, a beautiful woman who looked and sounded like Shirley Bassey with the longest legs I have ever seen. Sadly, this incredibly beautiful woman would shock my husband Stephen and me in later years with the speed of her decline due to drugs.

I got cast as part of the ensemble, which included Shirley Allan (my first true friend in show business), the lovely Helen Chappelle who had a voice that made me think I was only playing at singing. The American actor Samuel E Wright (the voice of Sebastian the Crab in 'The Little Mermaid") played the part of Valentine. The cast also included Diana Langton, Patricia Hodge, and Vicky Silver who was also in Hair with me. Away from 'Hair' I began to see some of my fellow actresses and actors in a different and more positive light, but I had already set myself on the path of never getting to know anyone too closely. 'Careless talk kills.' The unforgettable slogan during the Biafra war had stuck with me and had given me a fear of revealing too much about myself.

I liked and admired Brenda (B.J) Arnau very much. She was such a lovely lady, a great performer with an open personality and a smile that was sunny, friendly and vulnerable, which is rare in someone as drop-dead gorgeous as Brenda. I was extremely happy when she got the cabaret act part in the James Bond film "Live and Let Die" performing the title track by Paul and Linda McCartney. She was brilliant in the film and when I saw it, I was disappointed that her version was not used for the opening credits.

I supposed that they wanted to use the original McCartney version, but I thought hers would have been better, I guess I was biased.

Shirley Allen also got a dancing part in the voodoo scene in "Live and Let Die" and while she was away I loved to babysit her gorgeous baby girl. The reviews for the Bond movie had been brilliant for Brenda Arnau and she was soon to find stardom. I then began to realize that the business was mainly pre-occupied with finding a new Shirley Bassey, or a new Diana Ross look or sound-a-like when it came to black female artistes rather than looking for something really new. It seemed that they wanted to stick to the tried and tested whenever possible. In my case, everyone, including Michael Jackson said I looked like Diana Ross. Frankly I couldn't see the resemblance especially after meeting her. In the middle of her success, Brenda Arnau, decided she wanted to be known as BJ Arnau, which kind of confused things following such a big break in a Bond movie under her own name. The film increased TV demands for Brenda to appear on popular shows of the time. She went off to Las Vegas for a cabaret season at Caesar's Palace and was flying high with a dance-hit song she wrote herself called "Electra Flash/Dance Electra Flash".

I didn't see Brenda again for over twenty years until I bumped into her one day in Bond Street. She had changed, and was not the glamorous and gorgeous Brenda that I remembered; the sparkle in her eyes that I so admired had gone. She looked so lost! Instinctively I made her come home with me to Richmond where we were living at the time. She did not object. On the way home, she said she had suffered from peritonitis and had almost lost her life. Stephen, my husband, was sad that she had ruined her life and career with drugs. She would come out with the strangest things like the Queen of England was not the real Queen and that she had been replaced by a dwarf, and other drug induced madness. In a way it was funny, worrying and sad all at the same time, because she was so serious about the things she was saying. I worried about letting someone from show business near my young family, but Brenda needed protecting. She didn't seem to have anywhere permanent to stay, so we made her stay with us. After a few days, she decided she had something she had to see to and that she had to go. I told her to call me whenever she needed someone to talk to and that she could come back whenever she wanted to. After that I would get the occasional phone call, during which I would try to boost her confidence and then there would be silence for a long time before the next call. It broke my heart to see her decline to such a state. Drugs are not good for anyone! Brenda was perhaps seven or eight years older than me and here she was completely out of her mind and in many ways, like a child.

After a long time I got a call to say she would like to come and visit us, we were the only family she had, she would often say. I arranged to pick her up from Richmond Station. When I got to the station I was shocked to see Brenda, she had lost a lot of weight and her hair was cut down to an inch in length and dyed pure white. It was winter and she had no coat on and was dressed only in a leopard print bras and loincloth with only sandals on her feet. I can't imagine what the other passengers on the train must have made of this six feet tall, still striking woman wearing next to nothing in winter on the public transport. She stayed awhile with us and I gave her some clothes and one of my coats when she was ready to leave. I never saw her again and had no means of getting in touch with her. Mobile phones were not readily available in those days and she always called from public pay phones. I felt terribly guilty when I heard later that she had died, perhaps I could have done more, but I did not know or understand the full effects of drug abuse. I did not want to pry into her business and thought she would tell me anything she wanted me to know, about the way she was living, when she was ready. I wish I could have done more for Brenda.

A few weeks after Two Gentlemen of Verona opened at the Phoenix Theatre in the West End, I decided to find an agent. I had an incident when an agent tried to get me drunk with whatever else in mind. I kept meeting people who promised to make me a star. I couldn't understand why a total stranger would want to do this. I was being naive, but this was a whole new world to me, one that I knew nothing about. I soon learnt how the lower echelon of agents operated, but not many shows or plays offered enough work for the growing number of black artistes, so having an on-the-ball agent was important. There were so many of the sleazy variety that I felt that I should give up searching for an agent as a bad idea. So far, providence had had a complete hand in the way my life in the theatre was going and it hadn't involved any agents. Still, I was advised that I would not survive much longer without an agent because I had to know what was going on in the theatre world in order to get auditions for new shows. I began to call agents that I found in 'The Stage', a newspaper for the entertainment industry. I learnt quickly to tell them on the phone that I was black and save myself time and money, as most of them didn't want to take me on, saying that they couldn't possibly find me work as a black artist. However, two agents asked me to come and see them. I went to see the first one and never got to the second. The agent I did see had a pokey little office somewhere off the West End, which was part of his tiny and dusty flat. He was unkempt with a potbelly the size of a full term pregnancy, but with a beard. He offered me a drink and I opted for water out of politeness, but he insisted on me trying something stronger, even when I said I had never had alcohol.

"If you want to be in show business you will need to develop more strength of character, take direction without questioning and you have to keep up with the trends." he said.

What bovine feces! I was not about to trust him with my coat, let alone have the odious scruffy man as my agent. I had seen the effect of alcohol and drugs; it had nothing to do with strength of character. He disappeared into the kitchen and re-appeared with a glass of water and sat down, too close to me for comfort and asked me questions about my drama schools and experience in the business. "You haven't had a sip of your drink." He reminded me after a while. Out of good manners I took a sip and knew immediately something was wrong with the water. I didn't want another LSD incident! I should have left then, but thought it would be rude despite the way he looked and his creepy demeanour. (He may have been typical of what all agents were like). Next to me was a dusty plant and when he went to the desk to get a pad for me to fill in my name and address, I emptied the glass into the plant and pretended to have drunk it all.

"Good girl, I'll get you some more!" he said, ignoring my protestations as he went back into the kitchen to get another drink. Whenever he turned away I would pour a little of the drink into the plant, being careful to make sure that my glass wasn't empty. The meeting ended when he came back into the room with his shirt unbuttoned, sweating and breathing heavily. He sat down and placed his hand on my thigh. I felt physically sick at the sight of him and to think that he was touching me. I pushed him away and got up, but he grabbed my hand as he stood up and forced it on to his crotch, saying dirty things about black girls being…..whatever. Without thinking I turned to face him, looked him in the eyes as I kneed him in the groin as hard as I could, grabbed my coat and quickly left the flat. It wasn't until I got outside that I felt panicked, wondering what would happen if he called the police. Was he really an agent? He had my address and number. I could be arrested, I had heard rumours about the police, and it would be my word against his. Who would believe a black girl against a white male registered agent? As I walked to the theatre my panic increased and for a few weeks I thought that every policeman I saw was coming to arrest me for assaulting a theatrical agent. Needless to say I never heard from him, but for me, the suspense about the police was hellish. I gave up on seeing agents.

Without an agent I decided to attend 'whites only' auditions that I found in *The Stage* newspaper, as there were no black parts advertised. It was madness on my part! One occasion sticks out in my mind. It was an all-day open audition for white singers/actresses only, held at one of the theatres, near The Strand. The audition said 9.30am, I was the first in the queue as I turned up before 9.00am with a carton of hot tea I'd bought on the way. The doors opened just before 9.30am, naturally, I received strange looks from the person taking down the names and a few nasty comments from the other actresses.

"She obviously doesn't know she's black!" or

"Poor thing, she probably can't read!"

The waiting area soon filled with women and each one was called by name to audition for the director and producer. This went on all day with a steady trickle of people and I was left on the bench too afraid to make a fuss. I was starving, and humiliated at being the first to arrive and yet for hours my name had not been called out. Yet if I was to leave they may decide to call my name, I wanted to disappear or become invisible. Perhaps I was, because each time the man came into the room and called one of the ladies, he never even looked my way and yet I was sure that my name was first on the list. At about 5.30pm those who had been asked to stay behind were given instructions and told that their agents would be contacted.

"Excuse me." I said, holding back the tears, to the very girly young man running the audition.

"I have been here all day and you haven't called me!"

"The audition was advertised as an audition for white actresses only!'

"I'm sorry; I didn't notice that in the advertisement!" I lied and pleaded be allowed to see the Director.

He flounced off and I heard the conversation through the open door.

"There is one more person here for the audition."

"Well she is too late. She should have come within the time stated."

"She was here before the doors opened this morning." The young man lisped. Did I hear something human in his voice?

"What do you mean she has been here all day, why haven't we seen her?"

"She's black!'

"I don't care if she is green, yellow or red, bring her in here."

He came back into the room;

"They'll see you now," he said.

I followed him on to a dark stage and a small light came on, after a short interview during which I was hardly audible. I was asked to sing. I sang "What a Wonderful World" unaccompanied fighting to hold back the tears of hunger and humiliation. When I finished, there was total silence, as I stood there defeated, head bowed wearing a designer dress my sister Maggie had sent me from Paris. Then the director came on stage and apologised that I had to wait all day and said they would either have sent me away earlier or auditioned me if they had known. He asked me to leave all my details, as he liked my singing, I had great stage presence, he added. I whispered my gratitude and he shook my hand. His kindness had made it worse and as I turned to leave the tears began to flow easily and by the time I got outside I was in full sobbing mode. I sat on the pavement around the corner from the stage door, in my expensive dress and sobbed until I had no more tears. I stopped at a nearby Wimpey and literarily inhaled a plate of sausage and chips and made my way to the Phoenix Theatre to do the show.

I moved to a room in Acton where Shirley Allen also had a room, but the house was dingy and damp. One late night in Acton, on my way back from working in the show; a weedy teenager, holding a knife, confronted me under the railway bridge. He wanted my purse. We had just been paid and, as always, I was on a tight budget. Again, without thinking, I kicked out at him instinctively and caught him high up on the thigh between the legs, I think, connecting with the groin. Then I ran away shouting for help, which did not come, of course, but he must have been in too much pain to chase after me. I had learnt all this self-defence stuff at the campfire wrestling, kickboxing games and competitions in my grandparents' villages as a child. I never had reason to use these long remembered skills until I came to England. I was glad to leave the room in Acton, I did not feel safe in the area and I was worried about the boy who had stopped me. I moved into a bigger room in a flat just off Harrow Road, near Westbourne Park, which I also shared with Shirley Allen.

My provisional Equity Card was coming to an end and so was my student's visa. But I had another six months to go before graduation at LSDA. I had applied for an extension of my visa through an Asian solicitor whose office was in the West End and whom I was told specialised in immigration. I paid him a fee. It was a lot of money and he said he would deal with it. He said he had enough time to apply for the visa and saw no problem. Knowing nothing about such things I trusted him until one day my passport arrived by post and with a note saying my visa had been refused because my application had been presented too late. I was to be deported! My world came crashing down! What would I say to my parents who were already disappointed at my choice of career? How could I face them with the shame of being deported like a common criminal? I had not been going to church and even my daily prayers had been neglected. I had been so ungrateful for the blessings I had had and I wondered if God was disappointed in me, perhaps even angry! Hopefully, He would forgive me. I felt that all I had to do was ask for help as Mummy had taught us. I knew the power of prayer and asked for help and, thankfully, God was listening and came to the rescue!

A few days after I got the passport with the frightening message, I had gone out to buy some milk and bread for breakfast. As I approached the house on my way back I just happened to look up to see Shirley Allen, at the window on the first floor, signalling frantically. It was then that I noticed the two policemen at the door of the house; I knew immediately that the police were there to deport me. I turned around and went back the way I had come and waited until they had gone. Shirley said I had to find a proper agent to take care of my work permit, but I didn't think there was much hope of that happening as my visa had now been turned down and I knew no respectable agents.

Thankfully, I was not left to live in fear of deportation for too long because a short while later Dick Katz, a Director of MAM Agency, came in to see the show and came back stage. I met him in Brenda's dressing room and he mentioned that he managed an American singing girl group who were auditioning for a replacement for a third member. He was a very well dressed, rounded, portly man with a friendly face, and had been a famous jazz pianist with the Harold Davidson Big Band before becoming an agent. He always seemed to have a cigar in his hand and possessed a set of smiling, kind eyes, and the kind of eyes that are always a window to a good soul. The auditions for the girl group were held at the Wigmore Hall. I bought the song sheets for 'Both Sides Now' and "Yellow Taxi" by Joni Mitchell from Chapels in Bond Street. Fortunately for me, I beat lots of girls and got the job.

The next day I went in to see Dick Katz in his office, he seemed even nicer than before. Talking with him was like speaking with one's favourite uncle and I liked him immediately. His smart office was a large room with a huge desk behind which he sat, behind him was a big window overlooking Conduit Street, directly opposite The Westbury Hotel. I told him I had visa and work permit problems and explained what had happened. He just nodded and asked for details. Then all he said was how much I was going to be paid, £75 a week when I wasn't working and £100 when I was. I promised him I would not let him down, to which he looked unconvinced and amused, as if to say, we shall see, a look that haunted me for a long time. I was not used to being doubted and I wanted to prove him wrong. As I left, he gave me a list of songs to learn and said he would sort out the visa and work permit. He got my visa extended and got me full Equity Membership and a work permit. God bless him! I would rehearse during the day and do the Show at the Phoenix Theatre at night. Dick Katz had such clout that he even got me out of my contract with 'Two Gentlemen of Verona', so that I could go on tour with the girl group. It was the longest nine months of my life! The nine months were filled with unpleasant experiences, which included copious insults from the other girls about my singing and my dress sense. I couldn't do anything right!

One day, I had finally had enough and left in tears after further insults and humiliation. I walked into MAM's offices still crying after being reduced to tears during a recording session with the group in a studio just off Edgware Road. I had no appointment. Seeing the state I was in, the secretary buzzed Dick Katz who was speaking on the phone at the time. He said to send me in. As I entered his office, Dick finished his call, sat back in his chair, cigar in hand, with a twinkle in his kind smiling eyes. On the way to his office I had tried to rehearse my apologies, but here I was in front of his smart desk spurting out words like;
"I can't take anymore, I am so sorry to disappoint you after all you have......."
Before I could finish, I heard him say;
"What took you so long?"
I stared at him in some confusion. I wasn't sure I had heard correctly what he said.
"Mr Katz, I don't understand! I know you must be disappointed and angry with me and I am really sorry. You have shown me so much kindness and now........"
He buzzed his secretary to get me some water. I was still distraught and miserable. He leaned back in his leather chair.
"The last nine months have been the most peaceful months I have had with that group. Usually there would be phone calls to this office with news about fights, foul language and a series of complaints. But not once, in the last nine months did I get a single complaint."
"Peaceful!!" I said laughing.
"Not the adjective I would have chosen".
"Yes, but I have heard from the musicians and others about what you have had to put up with and how you smoothed out trouble on a daily basis. I would like you to see out the next two weeks of bookings, I will see what I can do for you after that."

Well, the next engagements were torturous, made easier only by the thought that the end was near! During those two weeks I got on tape a tirade of abuse by one of the girls in my hotel room. I did not mean to tape the abuse, I was recording myself practicing when one of them knocked at my door, and I simply forgot to switch the tape off.

"We don't know where the f... you get the f...... money to buy the designer dresses you wear, we don't f...... pay you enough for you to buy those dresses....... You will never amount to anything........ you are a

talentless bitch… you probably walk the streets to buy these f......
expensive dresses!!"

The only thing that puzzled me was what she meant by "walk the streets",
though my command of English was good there were colloquial terms in
the language that were still foreign to me. Walking the streets was later
explained to me. Of course, my stylish sister Maggie, who lived in France
and married to a dashing multi-millionaire, was sending me the designer
dresses from Paris, but I never told them this. I just turned up to events
dressed to the nines!

While I was in the group, we toured different European towns and cities.
We were based in London where the girls favoured a small nightclub in
Mayfair called Gulliver's and it was in the club that I met Tony who was
the DJ. Up until then I had been saving myself for Michael, the brother of
one of my sister's best friends in Nigeria, on whom I had a crush. Tony the
DJ was a pleasant character with the Spanish looks. He was polite and a
safe companion. I was not in love with him and I'm sure neither was he in
love with me, but he was nice, kind and fun to be with. I was nineteen when
he became my boyfriend. I had felt uncomfortable being single because I
seemed to make other women feel vulnerable when I was invited out to
places on my own. Once, while I was in 'Hair', long before I met Tony, I
was invited to a ball at the Great Room of the Grosvenor House Hotel in
Park Lane, but I had no one to go with. I had to meet my hosts, a wealthy
couple that had taken a shine to me, at the Great Room. I could not afford
to buy a ball gown and I did not possess one, so I went to a fabric shop in
Berwick Street and bought two yards of a fabulous sparkly expensive
cream beaded fabric. I made myself a long dress using all the skills of a
seamstress taught to me by my mother. I knew it was a great success when
I got to the Great Room, which was an awe inspiring room packed with
people and I had to walk down its sweeping staircase under the fairy-tale
chandeliers. I stood at the top of the staircase trying to make out my hosts
in the room full of white faces. My nerves steadily got so bad that I was
shaking. It felt like everyone was now watching me and I wanted to turn
and run out of the building, when I saw my hosts waving. It took me
perhaps too long to take the first step down the interminable staircase. I
had to take it one step at a time and years later I finally got to the bottom
of the staircase where my hosts met me. I was told that women in the room
were giving me dirty looks while pulling their partners away from me as
we walked towards our table. It would have been less of an ordeal if I had
gone with a boyfriend.

I had a flat at Park West, a short walk from Marble Arch on Edgware Road in the same building the other two girls in the girl group had their flats. Tony eventually moved in with me and shared my tiny flat, which I had struggled to afford on my own. Ours must have been an uneventful relationship because I can't remember much about our time together, but he was a good companion. After about eighteen months of sharing the flat, the situation became uncomfortable because Tony now had a steady girlfriend, which came as a relief to me. While I was in the group and constantly touring, our relationship worked well, but when I started to work in London in "Jesus Christ Superstar" and then "The Black Mikado", I was around every day and the cracks began to show. Although there were never any nasty rows, it was just uncomfortable. However, though I knew he was seeing someone else, it was still good to have him around as a male companion when I needed one. When he finally moved out, I realised that I couldn't afford the flat with its convenient location, on my own. Luckily, Rita, a lovely lady and a friend of my sister Maggie, offered me the use of her flat in Chelsea as she was always in Nigeria and hardly ever in London. The timing was perfect. I took the opportunity and moved to Chelsea. She wouldn't let me pay rent and so I began to save up to buy a flat of my own.

What I remember most during this period was the IRA terrorist attacks in London, especially in September 1973 when a shopping-bag bomb was detonated by the IRA at the offices of the Pru on Oxford Street, injuring six people. Another bomb was detonated in the street in December that year, not far from the flat. These bombs were scary because you didn't know where or when the next blast would be! For me they were unwanted reminders of the Biafra War. I remember one taxi ride with a cabby, who had a thick Irish accent. I got talking to him and he said it was terrible being Irish in London with all the bombs going off. I replied:
"At least if you don't speak or if you change your accent, no one will abuse you. Try being black! You only have to be seen to incur the wrath of your fellow men!"
"I've never thought of being black like that before. It must be a permanent nightmare. "

It was at Gulliver's, the same club where Tony was working, that I first met the young Michael Jackson. I didn't remember much about meeting the rest of the Jackson Five; I was too mesmerized by meeting the shy, pimply teenager with the eyes and smile of an angel. I prayed that, if I were ever blessed with a son of my own he would have the same gentle spirit as this young man. I thank God that my prayer was answered when my son Sebastian was born with the kindest and gentlest of spirits. The Jackson Five were appearing at Wembley and I had gone with a small group of people to the concert. There was such a massive crowd, that after the concert, which was fantastic, I felt I might die in the crush of people trying to get out. It was a frightening experience! At one point my feet barely touched the ground in the tunnel as the people were so tightly packed. The pressure from behind was so great, pushing everyone forward. If I had lost my balance I would have been crushed underfoot. After that experience I developed a crowd phobia and never again attended such a large concert. We all went back to Gulliver's to meet the Jackson Five after the show. Michael was seventeen at the time and taller than me. He was very sweet, but he did not say much. However, I managed to get him to talk a bit. At the end of our chat he asked me:

"Are you related to Diana Ross?" He was a great fan of hers.

"No, I come from Africa!"

"You must be a throw-back, you look so much like her." He giggled and looked away shyly.

His eyes sparkled! His innocence and aura moved me. I have never met another truly shimmering Star like Michael! I have been blessed to have met him three times since then and been able to spend more time with him.

1.

2.

3.

4.

1: Papa and Mummy
(my parents) wedding.
2: Papa
3: My brothers and sisters
Left to right:
Tony,
Maggie,
Tony Jnr (cousin),
Rosaleen,
Grace (Standing),
Mummy, author as a baby
Johnny
4: Grace
5: Mummy's wedding
to SG Ikoku (Daddy),
6: Second from left:
Chief Obafemi Awolowo,
GCFR.
Sir James Wilson Robertson
(The British Governor General
of Nigeria),
Sir Ahmadu Bello
KBE.
Second from right: Daddy
Far right: Chief Enahoro.

5.

6.

1.

2.

3.

4.

1: Mummy 2: My brothers Johnny and Tony (Right) 3: Tony far right. 4: Me as a teenager
5: Eno and Sammy Ikoku 6: Dearest Rosaleen. 7: Me with my sisters and brother.
From left; Grace Coker, Sammy Ikoku, Dr Maggie Ibru and Dr Eno Ikoku

1.

1. My sister Maggie
2. Clockwise; My brother Sam, my sister Maggie, my eldest sister Grace, me and my sister Eno
3. Stephen's mother (my Mother-in-Law) and my Mother

2.

3.

Me and my husband Stephen Komlosy engaged and our Catholic church wedding after a special dispensation from Pope (Saint) John Paul II obtained by Bishop Howard George Tripp.

1.

2.

1-2: Me with my husband Stephen Komlosy,
my daughter Emma and my son Sebastian.
3: Me with my son Sebastian (Aged 16)
4: Me with my husband Stephen and grandson
Dante.
5: Emma with her son Dante.
6: Dante playing with his grandma.
7: Dante asleep.
8: Dante.

3.

179

4.

5.

6.

7.

8.

1: With Mickie Most and Tony Hatch, **2-3:** In 'The Music Machine' with Gerry Sundquist, **4-5:** In cabaret & in costume

BiSi
DAUGHTER OF THE RIVER

6.

7.

8.

9.

10.

6: Starring in
'Bisi Daughter of the
River'
(said to be the highest
grossing African movie
ever made),
7: As Yum Yum in
The Black Mikado at
the Cambridge
Theatre London,
8: As Carmen in
'Carmen Jones'
9: As Carmen in
'Carmen Jones'
10: As Carmen in
'Carmen Jones'

182

1.

2.

3.

1-6: Various glamour photos
7: As the face of Lux for 29yrs.

4.

"New **LUX** keeps my skin soft, smooth and beautiful"

PATTI BOULAYE

"Having a bath is a whole exciting experience with new Lux. I enjoy such a lovely feeling of beauty whenever I bathe with Lux. Its rich, luxurious lather gently creams my skin into smoother loveliness, leaving me with a new more pleasant fragrance"
— Patti Boulaye.

Standard size 35p

7. **LUX** - the beauty soap of the world's most glamorous women

5.

6.

1.

2.

3.

1: With Anita Harris,
Elaine Paige, Sir Cliff
Richards,Dame Joan
Collins.
2: with my OBE medal
receive from HRH
Prince Charles at
Buckingham Palace 2016.
3: HRH Prince Michael of
Kent, Stephen Komlosy and
me.
4: Stephen Komlosy,
Lorna Byrne and the me

4.

5.

6.

7.

5: His Holiness Radhanath Swami and Stephen Komlosy.
6: Me with Michael Jackson.
7: L-R Sebastian Komlosy, Sir John Major, KG, CH, PC,
Dame Norma Major and Stephen Komlosy

Top to bottom: Starring in my own show Patti Boulaye's Sun Dance.

Chapter Twenty Seven: Jesus Christ Superstar & The Black Mikado

When I left the girl group, Dick Katz got me an audition for 'Jesus Christ Super Star', a musical that was already running at the Palace Theatre in the West End. I got into the ensemble as one of the Angels. I loved the lyrics and music, I was happy! It felt more like going to church for me, more like saying a prayer, like coming home! Although this was a friendly company, I did my best to keep to myself. I was beginning to learn that for me, there was going to be no such thing as "friends" in show business. There was not much that I remember during my time in the show except that I developed an aversion to drinking my usual orange juice in pubs after watching, in horror the unhygienic way the drinking glasses were washed before being re-used. It was also the first time I had heard the word *orgy*. I had been invited, along with others, by the wife of a very famous pop star to visit their home for a party, but someone told me it would be an orgy. Not knowing what an orgy was I did not refuse immediately, but when I found out the meaning of the word, I refused the invitation!

I was in Jesus Christ Superstar when there was an audition for an all-black show "The Black Mikado". I had not heard of 'The Mikado' or Gilbert & Sullivan at the time, but went along with all the other black members of the cast of Jesus Christ Superstar to the audition. It was the day after I had had my appendix removed. I can't remember what I sang, but it was a dance audition for the chorus and after jumping about strenuously for a while I bled through my dressing plasters and had to be taken back to the hospital. At the hospital they were angry with me for going to a dance audition so soon after my surgery. I had to be opened up again and I opted for a local anaesthetic while they drained the blood and fluid. I went back to Superstar after the procedure, but handled the Superstar dance routines with much more care this time. At the theatre one of the girls had received a script to read for the leading female part of "Yum Yum" and it was assumed that she had got the part and everyone celebrated. When I got back to the flat after the show, I was surprised to see that there was a script waiting for me also with a note to read the same leading role that we had just been celebrating about, thinking that the other girl had got it. I rang a lovely girl in the Superstar Company, called Lorenza to ask what it all meant and to seek her advice as to what I should do. She encouraged me to read for the part as other actresses would also have been sent the script, and the part, which was the leading lady "Yum Yum", had not yet been cast. She said if I was sent the script it meant that the producers liked me and I should have a try. I was torn as to whether to audition or just not go ahead with it out of a sense of loyalty to the other girl. I went for the audition with the hope of being cast as part of the ensemble, but I ended up with the part of Yum Yum. The other girl saw this as an affront. I guess because she was embarrassed that the Superstar Company had previously celebrated her getting the part.

The Black Mikado

On the 24th April 1975 The Black Mikado opened in London at the Cambridge Theatre. My emotions on the opening night were muddled, full of uncertainties, fear and nervousness! The show had been through a turbulent tour of the UK before the opening night in London. This was my first leading role in the West End, but I was not enjoying working with the show's company of actors. I was finding out how cutthroat and full of jealousy it could be. Unusually I had tried to make friends, but there was so much backbiting, gossip and nastiness going on, it was overwhelming. I had to switch off and get into autopilot and just deal with it on a day-to-day basis and trust that there was a reason for it all. I felt I could not trust anyone in the show for a long time. Coming from Africa and knowing nothing about trade unions and such, I did not understand the politics involved in the struggles between the Producers and the Cast. But by the opening night in London I did have three or four people in the cast that I could rely on.

When rehearsals started, prior to the pre-London tour, I knew I was in for a rough ride. Without trying, I had run-ins with most of the ladies in the cast.

On the first week during rehearsals of The Black Mikado, a supposedly well-meaning member of the cast told me, that rumour had it that I had slept with the director to get the part of 'Yum Yum'! I guessed it was jealousy. My natural reaction to the rumour was that of disgust. At twenty years of age, the idea of sleeping with the director, whom I had only just met at rehearsals and did not even remember, meeting at the audition, was absurd and evil. They had judged me by their own standards! The director was then told, by the same member of the cast that I had referred to him as "the terd", a word I was not familiar with. This put me firmly in the director's bad books, which did not bother me until I realised during rehearsals that he was not interested in directing me. He would leave me mostly to my own devices.

Yum Yum was my big break, my first leading role in the West End and I had made an enemy of the director! But I did find it amusing when it was rumoured, probably falsely, that he was having an affair with the same young woman who had, in her own words and not mine, described him as 'the terd'.

There were 'Three Little Maids' in the cast. The actress who played Pitti-Sin seemed to be permanently angry that I was cast as 'Yum Yum'. Before 'The Black Mikado' came along I had considered her to be a friend. When we were in 'Hair' together I used to sit up all night to braid her hair. In order to make her hair grow, I added heavy beads, as we would do in Africa to stimulate the scalp. We were having one of those hair-braiding sessions when my appendix got inflamed and she took me to the hospital and stayed with me. I will not forget that! So I was and will always remain grateful that she was there and was kind enough to come with me to the hospital.

Then there was the understudy for 'Yum Yum'. Throughout the show I had permanent problems with both these two ladies. But, there was a member of the cast, Les Saxon and his partner Geoff Roberts, who became and still are close friends. The third of the 'Three Little Maids' was a young and sweet girl who played Peep-Bo.

In my desperation and lacking leading role experience, I prayed more often and turned to the Lord to direct me as Yum Yum in the show. Safe and confident that my prayers would be answered, I muddled through the uncomfortable and demoralising rehearsals. The nice members of the company were few, but I did not associate much with them in case it sparked off another rumour. To top it all, my character Yum Yum's love interest Nanki-Pooh, was played by Norman Beaton who was a wonderful actor and a lovely character, but Norman was more than twice my age and unfortunately smelt of a deadly cocktail of whisky and cigar with garlic thrown into the mix as the show went on. Norman Beaton was a nice man and a great Nanki-Pooh, but I hated the smell of cigar and whisky together! It was nauseating and torturous every time we had to sing together. Norman was obviously not aware of it and thought I was being unprofessional by refusing to kiss him on stage. I was told that his wife was aware of his fixation with the kiss. She thought her husband had a thing for me and so she purposely put garlic in his meals every day, so that the dreaded kiss would be kept at bay. The idea of it seemed to me to be worse than the oranges and castor oil episodes back home!

The kiss between Yum Yum and Nanki Pooh became an obsession in the ensemble. With everyone telling me I was useless in the part because I refused to go through with the kiss. In my defence I pointed out that in the village of Titipu the law was that if you were caught flirting or kissing in public the crime was punishable by death. Centre stage at the back was a guillotine covered in blood as a reminder. Kissing publically was not commonly done where I grew up, except between a bride and groom at their wedding. If anyone was to tell me that I would have my head chopped off for kissing in public, I would definitely not do it. Yum Yum was not dumb; she was an innocent teenager, but pretty smart. I had chosen to play her as a complete innocent, so I could stand out from the knowingness of the other characters on stage. I was constantly instructed by the director to kiss Nanki-Pooh and it made me more determined not to. The entirety of my direction such as it was, centred on the stupid kiss!

Act Two started with me as Yum Yum, kneeling alone near the front of the stage wearing my beautifully designed and rather sexy low cut wedding dress. My costume was white satin and had a heavily beaded bodice. The skirt part was split to the thighs on either side. As the curtains rose I was centre stage, kneeling alone with my skirt spread all around me. My opening words were; "Yes I am indeed beautiful!" leading up to the song "The Sun Whose Rays'. I was so frightened of this scene and embarrassed about the words; not knowing how it was coming across to the audience, that I would recite the 'Our Father' before the curtains went up. I knew my voice was weak, or so I had been led to believe, especially because at the start of the tour I had not been able to hit the high notes as purely as I would have liked. Within a couple of weeks I was able to manage the top notes and made it easily for the Cast Album recording.

After rehearsing in London the show opened in Edinburgh. There was a demonstration against the producers and the show by a women's group. I can't remember what their problem was: something to do with an all-black show, coming to Edinburgh. How times have changed! I do remember we had problems with finding accommodation as an all-black company. However, I also remember the show being a success in Edinburgh, but it was clouded by internal disputes within the company. There were lots of disturbances in the company of actors who made various demands, which I did my best to stay out of. I had no idea what it was all about. It was all alien to me; besides, I had my own problems trying to survive the internal hostility. I was definitely not going to add to my troubles by reading the newspaper reports of the dispute. I was sure they would mention my performance and only confirm what the cast had been saying about it.

During the tour owing to the nastiness it became a habit for me to go into my dressing room to have a good cry. It was the only way I could maintain some kind of dignity and not break down in front of the cast.

One night, during the tour, Anita Tucker, (a very large American singer, who was playing a brilliant Katisha) came into my dressing room to borrow my eyeliner and found me crying. Anita had not said more than two words to me during the two months or so we had been working together. Annie Belle "Anita" Tucker was 24 years my senior though she looked like she was in her thirties. She was an international vocalist, recording artist, actress and model from Memphis. Sadly she passed away in 2009. She was known as, the "Voice of Sheba" and travelled the world as an entertainer. She spent years entertaining American soldiers abroad and appeared in several movies and Broadway productions. I remember her very fondly. Anita had this wonderful rasping, gravelly booming voice! She was a big woman and a big character. A little scary until you got to know her! At the time I was desperately in need of a friend or someone to talk to. Anita listened quietly as I told her the whole story from the beginning. I told Anita I had thought the actress playing Pitti-Sin was a friend, how I beaded her hair and how I found it difficult to be angry with her because she was there for me and kindly came with me to the hospital when my appendix erupted. Anita remained silent as I wept through the painful and cruel rumours, which Anita had of course been aware of. Her reaction was instantaneous;

"Those damn girls made me think you were the evil one!" she shouted in her growling voice. She became my champion! A Godsend! Unbeknown to me, Anita had related my predicament to the gentle giant Val Pringle who played an amazing and awe inspiring Mikado with the voice and size to match. Val, was an ex-basketball player. You could fit my hand into his three times over, he was that big a man and almost seven feet tall. Val turned out to have a heart as big as his towering size. Even I was shocked when he picked up my skinny and weedy understudy and pinned her to the wall at least 3 feet off the ground informing her quietly that if she ever picked on me again she would have him to deal with. He put her down, turned to me and said kindly;
"If anyone in this company ever picks on you again, you let me know."

Valentine Pringle was first discovered on the Jim Backus' US "Talent Scouts," a show on which celebrities brought unknown performers to the public's attention in 1962. Harry Belafonte brought Valentine Pringle to sing on the show with his rich bass voice that gives one, goose bumps. I kept in touch with him and Anita for many years after the show. He wrote

"Louise" for Harry Belafonte and had leading acting roles on TV and films. He was the voice of Porgy in a recording of Gershwin's great opera "Porgy and Bess" produced by the Readers Digest. Years after The Mikado I heard he had moved to South Africa with his wife and had been murdered in 1999 by burglars whom he had confronted after they had entered his home. Val was a US Army veteran and such a goodhearted man.

I was blessed with these two new champions in the show and life was getting better. For a while no one openly picked on me. As the opening night in London drew near, I began to panic. I knew this could be my make or break. Luckily for me, there was a dispute between Amadeo the choreographer and the director of the show, which opened a door for me to approach Amadeo on how I could best prepare myself for the opening night. Thank God, Amadeo decided to spend a full day rehearsing my every movement. He watched the dress rehearsals with me in mind and came up with a long list of notes. I spent the night going through the notes over and over again. The press night came and went, no one fired me and no one mentioned the reviews to me and so I counted my blessings. It was thirty-seven years later that I was made aware of what the critics had said about me as 'Yum Yum'. They were all rave reviews for me. A Benedictine Monk, Fr Auburn OSB a great musician and lover of Gilbert & Sullivan based at the Ealing Abbey, where my husband and I attended Mass, showed me one of the reviews by the reviewer in the Gilbert & Sullivan Society's own Magazine, Gilbert & Sullivan News. It reads as follows:

"The Black Mikado (1975)

From the Gilbert & Sullivan News - Discography (Terry Lane provided the following review of this production):

"The cast included Patti Boulaye (under the name Patricia Ebigwei) as Yum-Yum. The first thing to be said about The Black Mikado is that it is the sexiest, funniest version of the G and S favourite ever produced. Patricia Ebigwei was a heart-stoppingly beautiful Yum-Yum. The sexual tensions that are implicit in the plot were exploited to the full. For instance, in the stage production — something that is hinted at in the music itself on the record — the entry of the Three Little Maids (three young women of exceptional beauty) from School was turned into a trio strip routine. The girls arrive from their proper English school, dressed up in uniforms of floor-length tunics, elbow-length gloves and straw boaters. As they come on stage singing of their release from the confines of the lady's seminary they throw off the surplus clothing. Patricia Ebigwei's version of "The Sun whose rays..." is, in the words of the Gramophone reviewer of this

recording, "the performance against which all others must now be judged". It is one of those remarkable interpretations that make all others pale and unsatisfactory by comparison. No G and S lover is unmoved by this sensational piece of music making. Her version is a slow, erotic, languid ballad of vanity and sexual self-satisfaction that makes the conventional renditions seem prissy and just plain silly."

I was not aware of what the critics thought of me at the time, but the critic I mentioned above was right about one thing. I was very much at home with the lyrics of 'The Sun who's Rays' especially;
'Ah pray, make no mistake we are not shy. We're very wide awake the Moon and I'. I investigated the other reviews of my performance and they were pleasing indeed, had I known that at the time, they would have given me a great boost of confidence. I was told later that the Cast were not just cruel to me, but were generally unkind to each other as well.

At one point, in the show, there were constant whisperings about one of the girls' lack of hygiene. The nasty gossip got so bad behind her back that I thought I would end it by having a quiet word with her. I meant no disrespect to her, but soon learnt that people don't like honesty, even if it is for their own good. She never smelt again and the gossip did stop! But I don't think I was in her good books. I put her reaction down to embarrassment at being told, but I was glad she took it on board and silenced the gossip. Amusingly, she told the women that had been making unflattering comments behind her back, what I had said and they were all disgusted at my audacity!

There were a few "stage door Johnnies", one of them, finally stopped pestering me when he sent a brand new cream Rolls Royce wrapped in red ribbons as a present to the Stage Door for me. Lucky for me I was in the theatre very early. I asked the driver of the car to take it back and explain that it would ruin my reputation if the cast or my boyfriend were to see it. The man stopped pestering, though I occasionally got flowers and saw him sitting in a box and sometimes in the front row; he must have seen the show a hundred times!

Months after the show opened in London, I got to know Dulcie Gray the wonderful 40's and 50's British film star. She was Michael Denison's wife; with whom she had starred in many great movies. He was playing a very British Pooh Bar, the only white face on stage. Dulcie and Michael had a deserved reputation of being the smartest and most glamorous couple in show business and the early British movies. I would sit with her in Michael's dressing room and ask for advice about show business. She told me that, surprisingly, vulnerability in a performer is what attracts the public to a Star. When I complained about my lack of confidence and not being out-going on stage like other members of the cast seemed to be; she told me I would be successful if I did not try to lose my vulnerability. She said it was the very quality that made the audience want to protect me and it was my vulnerability that would help to make me a star. It was all right to admire those who seem to be sure of themselves on stage, but unwise to try and emulate them. I took her advice and stopped worrying about what others around me were doing. I decided rightly or wrongly that star quality is an inside not an outside job. Dulcie also told me;

"It is wise to be kind to the people you meet on the way up the ladder of success because you will be meeting the same people on the way down." Good advice indeed! I loved listening to Dulcie, she was writing a book called 'Ride on a Tiger' at the time, which she related to me and I learned that she had been a successful mystery writer for years. She gave me a signed copy of the book. When I asked her if she had ever been a singer. She sang me a song: "You Tickle Me Spitless, Baby". I don't remember the tune, but the words were hysterically funny.

During one of my visits to Shardeloes, Dulcie Gray's and Michael Denison's Amersham home, they told me: "Fame brings out the character of a person. If they are already unkind it will amplify the fact. If they are users, bullies, malicious, nasty, kind, gentle, generous and so on, whatever their character it will increase with the power of fame."

Dulcie Gray CBE was a very well-known singer, actress and mystery writer of over twenty books. Dulcie's was my first signed book, later Lord Archer, Sir John Major, Mitch Murray and Radhanath Swami and other famous authors would add to my collection. I got to know Michael and Dulcie better as the years went by. We went to many events and charity balls together with my parents-in-law who were great fans of theirs. Dulcie attended my Royal Albert Hall Events after Michael had passed away. Michael had been very ill for some time and on the day he died Dulcie had gone out for a while and when she returned she found Michael dead lying on the bed dressed in his best suit and tuxedo, stuffed shirt and red bow tie! He had realised he was going to die and had dressed up for this final performance!

While in The Black Mikado, I was offered a leading role in a film called 'Brutal Syndrome'. I went for a screen test and got the part of an ex-model turned photographer. I was glad that the character I was offered was normal, but her model friends were the ones doing drugs, getting into bad relationships and being battered by their partners. I had heard that if you get a part in a film as a black actress it's usually because they want you to do nude scenes and then the character will be killed off. Here I was with a part that was normal! I could not believe my luck, there were no nude scenes in the script for my character! I was looking forward to my first movie role with excitement. I think I learnt the entire script so I could be ready for the read through. The day arrived for me to meet the director and talk through the characterization and scenes. In one of the scenes my character was sheltering a model that had been beaten up by her boyfriend and she had come to stay with my character at her apartment. It was a night scene and the model was sleeping in the room downstairs, while my room was upstairs. In the middle of the night, the model had nightmares and was screaming in her sleep. My character was woken up and ran down the stairs throwing on a dressing gown.

Oh! Oh! Here we go, I thought!

"What kind of nightie would she have on?" I asked.

"Nobody wears nighties anymore."

I do! I guess I can come running down the stairs wearing pants and bras!"

"Look, this character is an ex-model, she doesn't care about who sees her naked, she is used to it and, therefore, being totally nude would not bother her."

The look on my face made him continue;

"There will just be myself on the set with the cameraman if that makes you more comfortable."

"That is two too many." I complained.

I had decided the film was not for me. The idea of my mother, father, sisters and any children I may have in future seeing me naked in a movie was not on the cards. The director gave me a lift back to the Cambridge Theatre with the hope of persuading me to do the film. Thinking back now there must have been a lot of publicity surrounding me as 'Yum Yum', so he was prepared to spend a lot of time convincing me. Just for safety's sake, I had kept quiet while he talked during the drive to the theatre. When he stopped outside the theatre, I made sure I had the door open and one leg out of the car before thanking him for the lift and for considering me for the part, but nude scenes were a No No for me. As I had suspected, he turned nasty;

"I can tell you now; you will never amount to anything in this business because no one would waste money using a black girl in a film unless she is there to take her clothes off."

"I am quite prepared to give up the business anytime and choose another career, but you are stuck in your dirty mind and filthy business, you are more likely to amount to nothing, than I am."

I shut the door and went into the theatre with no regrets. I had made the right decision not to work with such a person, judging from his last words to me. I didn't find out who played the part or if the film was ever made and I didn't care.

After about two years at the West End Cambridge Theatre the show was struggling to stay open and the Producer wanted to move it to the USA. As the end of the show's run at the Cambridge Theatre neared I was told a show was planned for Broadway and a further UK tour was also planned. For me it was a, non-starter! The idea of another few years with a cast like this was not something I could contemplate. I refused the invitation to either tour or go to the US. I had no idea what I was going to do next. The Black Mikado was in its last month. Then there was a message and number left for me at the theatre by a Stephen Komlosy, who was a director of the company that owned the Cambridge Theatre. The message said he wanted to discuss the possibility of putting down some vocals on pre-recorded tracks. I rang him back the following day. My call was put through and we arranged to meet at the theatre at about 3.30pm the following day. When I arrived, I waited in the auditorium while he was buzzed by the box office. Moments later the most beautiful man I had ever seen walked towards me wearing a three-piece suit, smelling divine. He was too good to be true! "Let's talk about the recording over tea." he said and hailed a black cab and held the door open for me.
"The Dorchester Please."

We got to the Dorchester for afternoon tea; thank goodness I was always well dressed. During the meeting I realised I was with a "gentleman" in the true sense of the word. He was so different from anyone I had ever met before, in Nigeria or Europe. He spoke differently, quietly and gently. His smile was cheeky and shy. He had clean beautiful blond hair and looked like a film star with straight-off-the-screen polish. Yet he still managed to make me feel totally in control and at ease. My normal self-conscious nervousness soon disappeared. I watched what he did with the tea as he gently guided me through the etiquette without being condescending, so I copied whatever he did. By the end of the meeting I had agreed to re-voice the vocals on the already recorded album he had produced unsuccessfully with another actress. I was single, but I decided that Stephen was too polished and gorgeous to be interested in little me. After the Tea at the Dorchester we got a taxi back to the Theatre. In the middle of our chit-chat in the taxi, this immaculately turned-out man, whom I had only known for two hours turned to me and said;

"Will you marry me?" I swear I heard screeching breaks in my head.

"What? Are you crazy?"

This must be a joke or there is something wrong with him, I thought to myself:

"I knew he was too perfect, he must be nuts".

Two years later after a lot of regrettable heartache on all sides, we were married and Stephen turned out to be the best thing that could have happened me. My soul mate! Thank God he did not give up on me nor pay any attention to my continued rebuffs especially after he told me he was married already. For a very, very long time I felt bad and had a terrible conscience about breaking up a marriage and I make no excuses about it.

Chapter Twenty Eight: Stephen and Me

The Black Mikado came to the end of its run at the Cambridge Theatre. Soon I went into the studio to record with Stephen. Not a word was mentioned about his proposal in the taxi as we worked together for the next six months. One day, a few weeks into the session a beautiful woman, an ex-model, popped into the studio for a flying visit, Stephen told me that this was his wife. The ring on his finger should have told me something, but I hadn't noticed. Though he was charming and handsome, I had not really seen him as a possible love interest somehow he seemed so out of reach. He was 400 percent more polished and gentlemanly than anyone I ever had met. He never tried anything on while we were working, but he was attentive and clearly attracted to me. Though I was not a virgin at this stage, I took a long time before considering the idea of sex. An idea I was very uncomfortable with in any case as I now knew that he was married. Nothing happened between Stephen and me and the relationship remained purely professional although flirtatious for a long time. I dismissed his proposal in the taxi as just a joke and a compliment! It was only years later that someone pointed out that my reaction at the first sight of him indicated love at first sight. No other person has ever had that initial heart leaping effect on me. Meanwhile during the period we were working together I was introduced to his four beautiful girls whom he would bring to the recording studio to say hello or to listen to me singing once in a while. Sometimes he would ask me to join them for lunch at weekends. There were three children from his first marriage; his first marriage! Mandy aged 15, Alice 13, Annabel 11 and Anouska the toddler from his second marriage. Mandy and Annabel had blond hair while Alice and Anouska were strawberry blond. They were all very pretty children. As such a handsome man, it would be hard to imagine Stephen having anything but good-looking children. Sometimes I would excuse myself from lunch, but most of the time I would join them. They were good company and also the first opportunity I got to observe a British family. It was amusing! I got to know the characters of the children. Mandy being the eldest daughter got to see the 'Black Mikado' a few times. Years later she confided that she knew about her father's attraction to me, even before he introduced himself to me. She had known how her father felt about me even before I was made aware of it. I think the three eldest children already knew and I felt that they were fond of me. I found their teenage antics quite amusing. Mandy and Alice were very competitive. They had a wicked sense of humour, Mandy more so than Alice, sometimes going too far. I had put this down partly to their ages and their being highly competitive ballet dancers at the Royal Ballet School. I used to wear my hair in plaits because I had to wear wigs in the show. During the day, I would add a few plaited extensions for fullness and length. I remember the time when one of them playfully tugged at my hair and pulled a plait off. I felt the tug, but did not turn around. Instead I looked in the rear view mirror and was amused by the shocked look on their faces. I had already noticed how they liked to have their little secrets and I did not want to spoil their fun.

Annabel on the other hand was an angel, a very quiet child with a gentle spirit, she reminded me of myself at the same age. She was pretty and I got the feeling she had been through a lot of teasing from her older siblings which her little sister Anouska was now going through. The older siblings being teenagers just saw themselves as being amusing.

I admired the way Stephen was with his children. I had never seen a father like him. In Africa, the fathers I knew put themselves in the provider's position. Even though the mothers were also breadwinners, the fathers had little day-to-day quality time with the children. But Stephen was at ease around his children and loved them completely. Nothing was too much for them! The ambition of his three daughters from his first marriage was to be dancers. The two eldest were in the prestigious Royal Ballet School with the help of great dancers Sir Anton Dolin and John Gilpin. Sir Anton and John were good friends of Stephen and I later got to know them. Talk about a wicked sense of humour they were a wicked pair! The two elder girls were to be the first two sisters to pass through The Royal Ballet senior School together and Alice started at White Lodge, the Royal Ballet Junior School. Stephen's third daughter Annabel was too young for the Royal Ballet and got into Arts Educational School, which she loved and decided to stay there.

Sir Anton Dolin was an English principal ballet dancer and choreographer with Sergei Diaghilev's Ballets Russes and with the Vic-Wells Ballet in the 1930s where he danced with Alicia Markova, with whom he later founded the Markova-Dolin Ballet and the London Festival Ballet. John Gilpin danced with Roland Petit's Ballet de Paris and the Marquis de Cuevas Grand Ballet de Monte Carlo. He danced leading roles for the London Festival Ballet, where for over twenty years he was principal dancer until leg injuries forced his retirement. He was Guest Artist for the Royal Ballet between 1960 and 1961 after which he became artistic director of London Festival Ballet from 1962 to 1968.

When I was in my early teens, I wrote a personal and private letter to God. In it I requested the type of husband I would like; if it pleased God of course to grant me my wish. "My husband must love me as much as I love him, he must love my family and he must love children because we will have six of them and he must be gentle, kind, handsome, faithful and clean and always smell nice. He must not use bad words, he must be softly spoken and honest."

Would you believe my audacity, 'he must be this and he must be that'? I was very young when I wrote that letter. I firmly believed I should put in my request before the earthly queue for requests got too long. I did not know the population of the world. There were so many people in Nigeria and around me. So I knew God had an incredible number of children. Being seventh of nine children taught me how to choose my moment, how to wait my turn. I had no doubt my prayer would be answered, why would it not? I had strong faith in the promises of the Lord; "ask and you shall receive, seek and you shall find, knock and it shall be opened unto you." What could be simpler than that? I sealed the blue envelope and addressed it to God. I knew I did not have to post it because the Holy Spirit had already done that "spiritually" for me. God being God already knew about my cheekiness and was probably shaking His head at me. All the same, if you don't ask you don't get! Yet years later I found the letter, God is indeed true to His word! He took notice of the prayers of His child. He answered my prayers to the letter. I could not have described Stephen better. It gave me confidence and made me feel loved!

After the recording was finished and my album was being mixed I saw Stephen regularly at weekends to discuss plans including the photo shoot for the album. The children were always with us. Soon I travelled to Paris at the invitation of Amadeo the choreographer for The Black Mikado. Our final destination was Antibes, where I was to perform with three others in at a wonderful venue on the beach. We rehearsed in Paris before travelling to Antibes. I stayed with my sister Maggie, who lived in a luxury flat on Rue de Berri, off the Champs-Elysees, Paris. Her flat was on the seventh floor of a block of flats. One night while staying with her, I had a dream or nightmare. In the dream I heard what sounded like the jangling of chains at a distance and the noise got closer and closer until I realised it was the sound of someone walking with chains around their feet, rather like a prisoner. He walked through the walls of my bedroom as if they did not exist. He was a giant of a man, dressed in torn dirty clothes. He reminded me of the prisoners we see in movies about ancient times. His long beard was tangled, his wet hair was dark brown and longer than shoulder length as he walked toward my bed. I wanted to scream for Maggie, but I dared not, I feared he would notice me if I made a sound. He walked past my bed as if it wasn't there. Then he stopped, looked in my direction and with a loud booming voice said, "Je désire aller à l'école!" three times and then walked out of the room in the opposite direction from where he came. Only then did I scream for my sister. The dream was a mystery! A mystic told me I had a sixth sense that picked up a desperate spirit. Great! That's all I need! The world was proving hard enough for me without spirits thrown in as well!

It was the beginning of summer and we started off by rehearsing in Paris. One afternoon I was sitting outside a café with the other dancers when the waiter came over to me and said: "Pardon, you are mademoiselle Patricia n'est-ce-pas?" I nodded surprised. "You have a telephone call." I thought it was a joke. Everyone else was as stunned as I was. Nobody knew we were at this large café. When I got to the phone, it was Stephen at the other end.
"Why have you not called me? It has driven me crazy not knowing where you are. Why didn't you call to let me know where to contact you?"
"Hello Stephen, where are you calling from? Are you in Paris?" I asked looking around for any public phones in the restaurant or on the street, expecting to see him in one of them.
"I'm calling from my office in London."
"How did you know where to find me?"
"I have been trying to find you! I've called everywhere. I can't believe how much I miss you."
I have never forgotten that phone call. The other dancers thought it was incredible that Stephen could find me in one of the hundreds of cafes in the centre of Paris. Everyone thought it was romantic;
"This guy must be crazy about you!' Then they changed their tone when I explained he was my record producer, married to a very beautiful ex-model and had four children!

I wasn't involved with him yet. It hadn't crossed my mind until then, but that phone call to the Café made me think about him more often. I kept telling myself I was just fond of him! After all, he is such a nice man and so kind and natural to be around. After rehearsing in Paris we moved to Antibes in the south of France. It was great fun working at night and spending the day on the beach. We shopped for food at the local shops and sat by the pool most of the time. I tried not to think of Stephen. The more I tried the more difficult it became. He called every day.

We were two male and two female dancers performing as Amadeo's backing dancers. We also had a cameo spot of our own by the pool, in the open air at the exclusive venue. Stephen would call to say he was missing me. When would I be coming back to London? Then if he missed a day without calling I lost my concentration. According to everyone around me

I would withdraw into myself. Because he was white and married the dancers would say;
"You don't want to end up being some married white man's plaything. You can't take him seriously!" I wondered if they were right, but fate had its own plans!

When the Antibes show season finished, we all decided to stay on for the rest of the summer. We had the use of a most fabulous old style stately home accommodation with a swimming pool and incredible views. Stephen offered to pay for my flight so I would be back in London earlier than I had planned. At the time I was being asked out and pursued by a French man named Gaston, but thankfully, due to Stephen's persistence it came to nothing. Even after Gaston followed me to London, a few weeks later, I realised that he could not hold a candle to Stephen. I was beginning to realise that no one was like Stephen! Was I attracted to his persistence and steady attention? Gaston had the same tenacity and he was single, that's all he had going for him. I was really flattered to have two such driven admirers! Stephen oozed class, patience and gentleness! Gaston was well, French, and would probably have lost interest if I were to have slept with him. He certainly could not compete with Stephen. If Stephen had not been on the scene maybe Gaston would have stood a chance.

I was comfortable around Stephen, his face, his voice, his wonderful smell and his children. I could not resist the easy and sincere way he told me he loved me and missed me even though all we did was talk about the record and his children. While I was in France I didn't let him know how I felt. I was afraid to open up; I did not want to dampen his enthusiasm. I don't know why, but I loved hearing his declarations of love. At the same time, I kept him at arm's length and tried to find a reason not to love him. I even searched carefully for any sign of bigotry knowing that that would completely destroy our relationship. Bigotry was rife in Britain at the time and that would have turned any feeling of love I had for him to revulsion. But Stephen did not have a drop of bigotry in him.

I never came across his wife after our initial meeting at the recording studio. I should have realised then that Stephen must have said something to her about the way he felt about me. I remember meeting one of her friends, an actress who made it clear she did not consider me a threat or rival to his wife. I got the impression they saw me as a young girl Stephen was having his midlife crisis about and would soon tire of. He was only thirty-four years old at the time! We were not yet in a physical relationship, so the actress' comment sounded odd. Was this a challenge or a put down? Whatever the actress' desired intensions, I looked at Stephen differently.

Anyway, she fancied him herself! Someone else at the event told me, not to take any notice! It was common practice among married white women to dismiss any black girls their husbands may fancy as nonthreatening. Why would any wife tolerate or even take such risks with her marriage? Marriage is not a game! I was also told at the time that it was unusual for a white husband to leave his white wife for a black girl. So far nothing serious had happened between Stephen and me. These conversations were planting seeds in my mind and eroding my Catholic conscience. How could the women be so unwise! A good marriage takes work, strong commitments, nurturing and sacrifice of self. Not indifference! Did that mean they were dismissing Stephen's attraction to me as a silly fling? That was the 'Flower Power' freedom of expression gone mad!

Back in the South of France, my fellow girl dancer, who had become a friend, suggested we cut short our stay if Stephen would pay for both our tickets. She did not want to stay on without me. Stephen agreed to pay for our flights. When I got back to London it was obvious how much he had missed me. A big bunch of Red Roses! I was more pleased to see him than I wanted to admit. When we got to my flat even though he had always been shy, blushing easily around me, now Stephen was too eager, anxious and awkward all at once, but he kissed me with such tenderness and passion that the inevitable happened. It happened only once! He kept saying he was completely and utterly in love with me.
"Boo, you are so mean to me, but I'm sure you love me too."
Stephen would call every-day on the phone or would come to see me for a few minutes at the flat after work. He dropped by in the morning on his way home after playing tennis. I preferred to meet him for lunch to avoid a repeat of what happened. He was very open about his feelings.
"Boo, why won't you let me make love to you? I can't bear it!"
I blushed at his words and would giggle, which only made it worse for him. I did not tell him I was giggling out of share delight that he still desired me. Still I was not about to give in. I got so used to seeing him all the time. He had made sure he was part of every moment of my day. He touched my heart so easily! Whenever I thought of him my soul, my spirit and my heart smiled. I did not know there was such a thing as a "soul mate" at the time. Now I can say and I should have known that he was my only soul mate!

I remember the first time Stephen reached out and held my hand as he drove me home after a meeting with the record company. It gave me goose bumps. We did not know each other well at the time. We were practically strangers. I had never held hands with anyone before. Yet it was strangely natural and made me feel safe. It frightened me to know that such a simple gesture as Stephen holding my hand should send such emotion through me.

It wasn't a sexual reaction; it was very familiar, as if he had held my hand so many times before. When I pulled my hand away it was with great difficulty and reluctance. His patience and persistence, among his many other attributes was my undoing. I came to love him for it. I wanted to belong to him, to be protected by him and I wanted to protect him. Everything about Stephen was lovable! He brought out my strength, made me feel in control. Yet I felt like a child with him. It was a while before I would let him hold my hand again for any length of time. When we were in a crowded room or in public together I would be aware that he never took his eyes off me.

Stephen owned a gold hardtop two door Mercedes 280 SE 3.5 with cream interior, although this was quite new, he was fond of vintage cars. We shared this passion for rare and old cars. The Bugatti was my favourite car. I'm not one for wanting to own things, but I would love to own a Bugatti someday. I thought I knew all the cars on the road until I saw an unusual car drive by on Park Lane and I asked Stephen what kind of car it was.
"That was a Rolls Royce Camargue only about 350 were ever made." He said.
"That is a dream car! I will own a Camargue some day!" And I did!
The album we recorded was scheduled for release. The photo session was arranged and I had to make a decision quickly on a new stage name since I had decided to change my name. I did not want the album released under the name Patricia Ngozi Ebigwei because the radio DJs of the time found it hard to pronounce. Whenever a radio DJ played "The Sun Whose Rays Are All Ablaze" from The Black Mikado they would finish by announcing, "That was Patricia N… N… that was Yum Yum from The Black Mikado."

I had to change my stage name before I released another record and here I was about to release my first album. I even re-released Yum Yum's song as a single under the name Patricia Abigway, the right pronunciation of my surname Ebigwei, but this still seemed to confuse DJs. While I was trying every combination of names possible Stephen visited me on his way home. He had just had lunch with Evelyn Laye, a brilliant elderly actress known to her friends simply as (Boo Laye). He was so enthusiastic about her that, by the end of the day we had decided on the name Patti Boulaye. I changed Boo to Bou and shortened Patricia to Patti and kept the Laye. The printing of the album went ahead on ABC's Handkerchief label. After that Stephen took to calling me Boo.

Maggie invited me to come and stay with her in Paris for a week. I was negotiating to buy a basement flat in Hammersmith, which would need a lot of decorating. This would be my first property and I was a bit daunted by it all, so I was keen to get away from London for a few days. Before leaving for Paris I had a meeting at Samuelson's film Services in Cricklewood. It was the largest film and TV equipment company, in Europe at the time. At the meeting I met with a scriptwriter and two others who had flown in from Nigeria and were casting in London for 'Bisi Daughter of The River'. While I was in Paris, I got the news that the leading role of 'Bisi' in the film was mine and filming would be in Nigeria. I returned from France to get ready for the trip. I was glad I would be away again from England. I needed time to think about things between Stephen and me. How would I be able to continue working with him without feeling awkward about it? When I got back to England my suitcase was seized by the customs at the airport. Apparently I looked too opulent and they had to keep my case and its contents for further investigation. When they returned my suitcase to me, they charged me customs duty for my three new designer dresses and four pairs of brand new shoes. Before I left for Nigeria, I asked Stephen to please make sure the customs returned my new shoes especially. Apparently they thought I was going to trade four pairs of shoes and some used dresses, bless them!

I arrived in Nigeria 9 days ahead of the filming schedule. It was good to be home staying with Mummy! A few days after arriving in Nigeria I fell ill and developed a fever. I had all my usual symptoms of Malaria with severe bouts of nausea. Mummy insisted I saw the doctor before the filming for 'Bisi Daughter of the River' began. In the early evening, my big sister Grace got back from work and took me to a doctor. After examining me the doctor cheerily said he had good news and bad news. What could possibly be good about suffering from Malaria, I thought? Then the doctor said,
"Do you want the good news or the bad news first?" I just stared at him.
"I will give you the bad news first. You definitely have Malaria, which I will give you tablets for! The good news is, you are pregnant! Congratulations, and I would guess about two months!
"Pregnant! Pregnant? Are you sure? That's not possible!" I was confused, delighted, then frightened, all at once. Was it even possible?
"Are you sure I am pregnant?" I asked again.
"Oh yes, I'm sure."
Well, this was unexpected on all fronts! When I spoke to Stephen that afternoon (he had problems getting calls through to Nigeria), I had mentioned about feeling sick. I told him Mummy was insisting that I see a doctor she thought I may have Malaria. But Stephen only laughed and joked:
"You are probably pregnant, Boo!" without hesitation he added.

"If you are, it's likely to be a girl because I obviously don't make boys. We will call her Emma. It's my last favourite girl's name the others have already been taken!" Then he laughed shyly.

Stephen and his jokes!! Here I was pregnant and I was happy to be so! But how could the doctors in London get it so wrong? Granted I was not taking any contraceptives after being told I would not be able to have children. How could I be pregnant? Every time I had thought of breaking up with Stephen something always happened to stop me. The doctors in a London hospital had said I couldn't get pregnant after an ovary had to be removed during an operation on my appendix. I still don't know why they had to remove an ovary. I was told my second ovary was not functional and, therefore, unreliable! I had cried about this and accepted that perhaps motherhood was not my calling after all. Now I was to have a baby, this was my miracle baby! How would Stephen take this news? I couldn't think of any man whose child I would rather have than Stephen's. However, I would have been more careful if I had thought I was capable of getting pregnant! Still I was over the moon. I was whole, happy and complete. How would my strict Mummy react? I was too frightened to tell her!

What a disappointment I had turned out to be! I was in an inferior career of which no one, but my siblings approved. I had not pursued my academic opportunities, much to my parents' displeasure. One minute I wanted to be a Nun and now I was pregnant out of wedlock and for a white man! It couldn't get worse! I dreaded breaking this news to Mummy and seeing the disappointment on her face. Luckily my sister Grace came to the rescue! She said that if I was not going to tell Mummy then she would break it to her gently.

When we got home from the doctor my sister Grace said to Mummy:

"Patti has Malaria, the doctor has given her some Quinine tablets to take."
I held my breath as she paused for a moment before continuing,
"Mummy, you know we were all sad when the hospital in London said Patti would not be able to have children. Thank God they were wrong because she is pregnant!"

I was terribly grateful to my big sister, I wouldn't have thought to put it that way myself. Mummy danced for joy, the idea that I was not married did not bother her at all. The most important thing was the doctors were wrong. For her it was great news indeed! She had worried for me bless her.

Once Stephen worked out how to get through on the phone he booked the calls days in advance. When his calls began to come through to Lagos, he was in touch at least twice a day. He must have booked the first call to Nigeria as soon as I left London if not before. After ten days his letters were beginning to arrive at Ikeja. Mummy's reaction freed me to fully enjoy being pregnant! I was going to have a baby! Me? Suffering from malaria or morning sickness didn't seem to bother me much after that. I was on top of the world!

Mummy wanted to know what Stephen was like. I gave her a character description of Stephen as best as I could. Secretly wondering if his colour would disappoint her. Knowing Mummy it would not have been easy for me to pull the wool over her eyes. She listened intently! If Stephen was just a passing phase and I had not been in love with him, she would have picked it up. As I described Stephen to Mummy, I realized perhaps for the first time that I was totally enamoured of him. I assured her he was a complete gentleman, nothing like any European man she had met before. I left out the part about him being in his second marriage with four children! I did not want anything to spoil my joy of being pregnant. Mummy listened carefully watching me as I described Stephen and when I finished she said;

"Eyen mi (my child), from all the phone calls, I don't doubt how this man feels about you, but does he know how you feel about him?"
"No Mummy, not really!"
"Good. A woman should choose carefully when to show the contents of her heart to a man. A man should always appear to be more in love with the woman if the relationship is to work. He should be allowed to do the chasing for as long as possible. At least it should appear so to him. It's the same the world over, whether the man is black or white, young or old. So it is good to always retain a sense of mystery about you! It puts you in a stronger position."

Then she added as she slapped the back of her right hand into the palm of her left, a gesture that showed that she was worried.
"Your problem is your feelings always show on your face, especially in your big eyes! Even as a child your face showed all your worries."
"Thank you Mummy, don't worry I will remember that. I can reverse my expressions with words."
"Do you want to marry him?"
"I don't know yet Mummy. When I decide I will make sure you approve of him."
"Pat, always pray for wisdom and God will tell you what to do."
"Thank you Mummy! I've always prayed for wisdom."

I hated not being able to tell her that Stephen was married. It was obvious to the entire household how persistent Stephen was and whenever the phone rang they would call out;

"Patti, answer the phone, we know it is Stephen calling from London!"

If I was not home when he called, Stephen would pester the operator to keep trying or he would leave lots of messages, much to the amusement of the household. They had not met him, but they all liked him already. If someone else got to the phone before me, I could tell it was Stephen at the other end from their shy smiles and giggling as they handed the phone to me. Once he said;
"I am worried your family might marry you off to some rich Nigerian who would pay a hefty dowry for your hand in marriage".

It was almost an impossibility to make calls from Lagos and very frustrating to call from London. Some days he was not able to get through at all. I was not aware, of course, that it all served to make Stephen miss and want me more. Men are definitely hunters by nature; therefore, they want what they can't have. That is why a woman, as Mummy said, should always do her best to remain mysterious, play hard to get for as long as possible, if she is to keep the man of her dreams. Living happily ever after takes quite a bit of work from the woman, so why not start by making yourself a rare object of his desire. I was blessed in that no matter what I did, fate and a "set of curious chances" (The Mikado) were driving Stephen and me together. Though pregnant I was still playing hard to get. Every time the phone rang from Stephen. I took a deep breath and calmed myself so that I didn't sound too excited;
"Hello Stephen, it's me." I realised how much I loved his gentle and quiet voice.
"Darling, I can't believe I finally got through to you. I have been going out of my mind not being able to speak to you! It's so wonderful to hear your voice. Is everything all right? Are you not pleased to hear from me? I really have been trying to call you. Have you received any of my letters? Darling, is everything alright you don't sound happy to hear from me."
"Of course I'm pleased to hear your voice." Stay calm I told myself. "The phone lines have been down for a few days."
"I left a message at your sister Mrs Coker's, did you get it? I rang Maggie in Paris for her number. I didn't want you to think I wasn't trying."
"Yes I got your messages."
"Good! I miss you so much Boo!"
"I miss you too!" I said calmly.

After one of these calls from him, I allowed the smile that was swelling in my soul to break on to my face. I closed my eyes and hugged myself so I could see his face and smell his fresh clean hair and aftershave. I loved the way he hugged me with complete surrender of himself, resting his head on my shoulders, he always smelt so good. I would bite my lip to suppress my longing to see him.

The day after my visit to the doctor, I knew I had to break the news to Stephen, but I did not want him to feel pressured in anyway.
"Darling are you okay? Is something the matter?"
"I'm fine! But I have something I have to tell you. I don't want you to feel obligated in anyway or that this is a trap."
"Darling what is it?" he asked again, I hesitated.
"Boo, you are getting me worried, what is it?"
"I am pregnant Stephen and I.....!" I blurted out. He would not let me finish.
"Is that all? But that's great news! I told you, you were pregnant!" He began to laugh.
"Be serious Stephen I'm not joking, this is for real and I don't want this to create any problems or make things difficult for you and your family! I should never have let this happen!"
"This is my responsibility, it's not your fault. I wanted this to happen." he said.
"Why would you want this to happen, have you forgotten you are..." I couldn't finish the sentence in case someone was listening.
"We will talk about Emma when you are back in London! When are you moving to the hotel and which one are you checked into?" He was immediately referring to the baby as Emma.
"I'll be at the Eko Hotel in two days' time, I don't have the number with me right now."
"Darling, I am so happy about the baby, you won't be able to get rid of me now. I don't suppose they can now marry you off to some chief or whatever they call them over there."
"Thanks to you, I'm not even worth a bowl of rice now on the dowry front!"
"Well I'm not sorry about that. Darling I must go to my meeting. I booked another call for tomorrow. I'll call you before lunch. I love you!" He hung up.
More letters arrived;

21st Oct 1976

My dearest Boo

I have spoken to Maggie twice today........ I am sure she thinks I am mad because I keep asking her why she thinks you have not called or cabled, but she says it is often very hard from Lagos.

Maggie sounds so much like you I am tempted to call her all the time just to hear her speak! I do wish I could speak to you............ Your picture for the album is so adorable it makes me feel so warm when I think of you.

I am so afraid that your silence is an indication that you are annoyed with me – my God – I hope not...............

My darling I just spoke to you! I heard the warmth in your voice and I knew you loved me – I am so happy – Mandy was with me and she thought I had gone insane! I'm so happy and I will be speaking to you again tomorrow.......... You sounded so great and so near to me – I am a new man! Tonight I will sleep, I'm so happy.

I love you

Stephen xxx

Two days later I moved into the Eko Hotel, which was my first experience of a Nigerian hotel and what a mess it was too. The entire film crew and artists were booked into the hotel as a block booking and they just handed out keys to any room without making a proper note of who was in which room. Stephen couldn't speak to me for two days and he was worried when they kept putting him through to a man's room which had been booked in my name, there were only two actresses in the hotel's list of the film crew and cast, Janet Bartley and me. Stephen spent the two days being put through to rooms belonging to members of the crew until I finally rang him and told him what had happened. His relief was palpable, though it took him a while to understand that the hotel was incompetent, that it was less complicated to accept the rooms we had been handed or we would run the risk of confusing things further at the reception and probably end up with no room at all.

Stephen's letters began to arrive daily at my mother's and at the hotel. Everyone knew about Stephen by now. He had gone through the list of the crew's rooms looking for me before I rang him realizing what must have happened. It must have cost him a small fortune. A voice inside me kept repeating,
"If you love him, let him go."
I thought of what I had to do when I got back to England. How I would tell him it was best if we didn't see or work with each other. While filming I had lots of time to think. I had mixed emotions. I had to think for both of us. He had been twice married to English women; what would he

understand about my culture? If two older and perhaps wiser English women, with experience working for them, could not make it work with him, would I be foolish to try? That was that! My mind was made up.

My pregnancy was the answer to my prayers. The baby will look like Stephen! I was happy, but with a Catholic conscience, I hoped that I would not have to pay too high a price for my sins. That was my overwhelming concern. My guilt was so great; I was prepared to give up seeing Stephen if I had to. Despite his words of love I didn't think his heart could ever be fully mine. I knew he said so many times that he loved me and missed me. I wondered how he would be under the pressure of the pregnancy and having to tell his wife and everyone else. He was being so brave and reassuring in his letters to me. The situation was going to get harder for him. How long would it be before it all got too much? I couldn't begin to imagine what it would do to him. It would be better if I broke up with him. My baby will always remind me of how much I was loved and by a good man. All I wanted now was for the baby to be healthy. I battled day and night with my conscience trying to make atonement. I was grateful to God for giving me a new life to look after and for making sure that the baby was a part of Stephen. That was a double blessing! I didn't want to push my luck by expecting Stephen to leave his second wife and child. He had told me some time ago that he loved his wife. I needed to remember that in case I got carried away with his words. It was easier for me, because I was overjoyed at being pregnant. I had a baby to look forward to. Stephen's letters kept coming all of them so full of love and hope. HELP!!!!

'Bisi' Daughter of the River 1976

Taking the Quinine tablets for malaria was terrible, especially with the nausea and nervousness of the first day of filming. I had to kiss my love interest and I could not hold my breakfast down. The Quinine tablets repeated on me making my morning sickness worse. When the camera started rolling, I got desperate and tried to control the nausea, with great difficulty. When the director finally shouted 'cut!" at the end of the kissing scene. That was it! I threw up violently, just missing the leading man. Unfortunately, the crew saw the actor who was playing Dexter, the male lead of the film, a James Bond type character, as arrogant. My throwing up after the kissing scene was interpreted as a slap in the face for the poor man. I thought the film crew were rather childish at times with their warped sense of humour, typical of the show business types I had worked with in London. The actor was quite nice, but the crew liked to fill their boredom with gossip, character assassinations and one-upmanship on each other and the actors. I wanted to tell him that I threw up because I was pregnant, but that would have created yet more gossip for the crew to dine out on. So I had to keep quiet about it. The actor was quite rightly unforgiving! Filming was packed into a few weeks and the final scenes were in Badagry, where my character had to drown in the Lagoon, during a James Bond type boat chase. The Lagoon was filthy. For my safety, I had to have an anti-tetanus injection before filming the final scenes. I wasn't sure what effect this would have on the baby. I took a chance and confided in one or two of the crewmembers that were in the position to make sure I was not in the filthy water longer than necessary. They promised not to tell anyone, but would find a way round the scene to make it real without putting me, and the baby through unnecessary danger.

A double was used in the long shots of the fight scene on the speedboat. While they were filming the double, I took a tea break sitting outside my Winnebago. It was parked in a clearing not far from the river edge about twenty five metres into the forest, where it would not be picked up by the camera during the boat chase. I was sipping on a drink as I watched a group of four women walk past. They were on a path that was about ten metres into the bush from where I was. They were each carrying wood piled up high on their heads. I had seen them walk by earlier in the morning, going in the opposite direction. I had remarked how the pregnant woman among them looked due to have her baby any day now. I was amazed to see her walking back with the wood piled high up on her head. A moment or so after they disappeared out of sight I heard a commotion and raised voices. I knew she was going into labour. Instinctively I grabbed a towel, a knife and a small flask full of clean hot water that was on the table and hurried in the direction they had gone. They were less than a hundred yards away and as I got to them the pregnant woman was already in the squatting position ready to deliver her baby. Within minutes she gave birth to a baby girl. I was surprised how quickly the placenta followed still pulsating. The baby started crying even before one of the women had finished tying two double knots in the umbilical cord. I went to hand the knife to her but she held out the umbilical cord and I cut between the knots. They giggled at my knowledge of delivering a baby as they checked her. She had already started feeding on her mother's milk. The others buried the placenta and I poured water, which was hot, but bearable, from the flask on to their hands. They rinsed their hands, dried them on their wrappers, shared the extra wood belonging to the new mother among themselves and off they went. They waved and thanked me for the towel with which the mother covered the baby. It was so quick, so clean, no fuss! I stood there grinning with satisfaction. I wanted to hug myself with joy when a member of the crew came running towards me,

"They need you for the next scene. What happened? Someone said you ran off into the bush in such a hurry with a knife!"
"Just helping to bring a new life into the World." I grinned.
I picked up the empty flask, the hot water wasn't even needed for the mother or the baby, and she was born without much blood on her. What a miracle life is!! When I told the others what had happened, I'm not sure they knew what to make of it. There was the general shaking of their heads and someone said,
"That would not happen in England! The woman would have demanded her right to be taken to the hospital. As for walking immediately after giving birth, you must be joking! Not in a million years. She would be bed ridden for a whole day at least." one said

I became more pre-occupied with what was happening to me, as I got ready to return to England. I did some heavy soul searching.
"What am I supposed to do? How do I deal with this?
Stephen! Everything about him was familiar; I know it sounds crazy. It sounded even crazier at the time. When I was with him, I wanted to stay and never leave. But I knew that was impossible. I liked the fact that he never told me a lie. I later found out that he never lied to his wife either. He never promised me that he would leave her and I never asked him to. If I was to put the pressure on him to leave his wife, it might have backfired and so that was not an option. I felt guilty enough as it was. What if I was not as good a wife, as his former or present wife? Then it would end up in another divorce for him. I convinced myself that if I were to marry him, we might also end in divorce.

I no longer thought of myself as a good Catholic or Christian. I couldn't go to confession. The Lord died to save me from my sins He had looked after and protected me, and my family, in such obvious ways through the war and our difficult times. I always felt His strong presence, especially in my desperate moments. How could I now face Him in the Eucharist? Perhaps the fact that Mummy was happy and not disappointed was such a good sign. She always used to say that Jesus loves me more than she did. I believed what my Mummy said, especially about Jesus! I dared to hope that He also would not be disappointed in me.

Was I trying too hard to be good? Why was I failing so woefully at it? Christ said;
"With men, salvation is impossible, but not with God. Anything is possible with God."
As I battled on in my soul, I knew no one was really good except God, but that was not an excuse for being bad;

"Lord please deliver me especially from myself!" I prayed.
A lot of painful things happen in these situations. Things get said and done that cause great pain! My faith in God, as rickety as it often was, saw me through.

The combination of Malaria, pregnancy and the anti-tetanus injection left me feeling very ill on the flight back to London. My fever had returned with great intensity and I worried that I might have caught something from the filthy Lagoon during the last days of filming. I had no more malaria tablets to take and I could not sleep on the plane. I had decided that I would have no problem bringing up my baby and working at the same time. I would free Stephen of any responsibilities towards the baby and nip any further interactions with him in the bud. I would work hard on whatever work I could find while bringing up my baby. I made the decision to be strong, ready to face Stephen and to tell him that I wanted to break off all contacts with him. His wife would not have to know about Emma. I was delirious, but those were my plans when the plane landed at Heathrow Airport! Fate had a different plan and everything happens for a reason! Having made my decision, I felt calm in my soul, assured that all would be well no matter what the outcome.

My intention was to move into my new basement flat at Overstone Road, Hammersmith, when I got back. I had ordered a bed and a set of sofas from Selfridges. There was no carpet, phone, other furniture, wallpaper or cooking utensils. Stephen was arranging for everything to be ready in time for me to move into the flat when I got back. There was a delay and the furniture people said that everything would be delivered in two days. Stephen was at the airport to meet me as he had promised. I had only half expected him to be there, though I was relieved to see him. My fever was worse and I could hardly lift my luggage on to the trolley. My fur jacket had no effect. I was freezing! My joints ached and my head felt like it would split in two. Even the slightest movement made my head throb and any kind of bright light went straight to the back of my eyes causing severe pain. Without warning I would suddenly get too hot or too cold. Stephen insisted he check me into a hotel where I could have access to a phone. I was in no fit state to look after myself let alone be in an empty flat that was unfinished. I did not argue with him. He checked me into a room at the Hilton Hotel in Holland Park. He would arrange for his personal doctor to visit and examine me. In the room, I fell asleep for a few hours and only woke when Stephen phoned to see how I was getting on and to say the doctor would be with me at about 6pm. I struggled out of bed to have a bath and wait for the doctor.

The doctor arrived on time and I let him into the room. He was fairly short and stolid with a pleasant enough face, but there was something about him I didn't like. He asked the usual questions about my symptoms and gave me an injection! I was too ill to resist: besides, Stephen had sent him, so despite his unpleasant manner; he was sure to have been good at what he did. I told him that I had had anti-tetanus injections and anti-malaria tablets in the past few weeks: I was pregnant and wondered if it was safe to have so many medications. He did not answer my questions, but instead packed everything into his bag before giving me a cold stare and his parting words were:

"You are a silly girl and you are in over your head. I am doing you a favour by telling you this. Let me remind you that you are in a strange country and you should be careful for your safety's sake, especially if you decide to go ahead with having this baby. If anything happens to someone like you, no one would give a damn. As for this child you are carrying, I could arrange for you to get rid of it. There is no place in this country for such a baby. Sandra (Stephen's wife) wants you to get rid of it and I doubt whether Stephen is being honest with you if he tells you he wants you to have this baby. He has beautiful white children and does not need yours." Then he added;
"Black people like you have always had enough trouble trying to survive, it would be wicked of you to bring another black child into the world!"

I was in complete shock! I was frightened! I was still sitting where I was as he let himself out of the room. I didn't know what to do. What did he inject me with? How could Stephen do this to me, I was betrayed? Why did he send this evil and hateful man to come to inject me with whatever poison was now in my blood. I didn't know what to do. I got my note pad out and wrote down everything the doctor had said just in case he had poisoned me and whoever read the note would know what had happened. Not that anyone, but my family would care, just like the doctor had said. I rang my sister Rosie who was in Preston and told her where I was and that I wasn't feeling well. If she didn't hear from me the next day could she please come to London! I didn't tell her what had happened, but she knew something was wrong. When I hung up, I sat on the bed totally dumbfounded!

How could Sandra know that I was pregnant and how did the doctor know what Sandra wants. Stephen only made the appointment earlier that day. How dare this Sandra say?
"She wants me to get rid of it!"
It seemed to all point to Stephen and that's where I directed my anger.

"If I couldn't trust Stephen or even a doctor, who was there left to trust?"
I thought.

When Stephen rang I put the phone down on him, but he kept ringing. I got my things together and checked myself out of the hotel and took a taxi to my new flat, which was five minutes away. Once in the flat, I locked the door.

I couldn't sleep; I sat on the floor of the flat completely petrified for my life. It sounded as though the doctor had threatened me. I had been in positions of physical danger many times in my life and I had been able to cope with them. But this was different, somehow more frightening. The next day, feeling totally exhausted, but grateful to be alive, I walked to a pay phone and called Rosie in Preston to tell her I was okay, but she was already on the train to London. When she arrived at my basement flat she had to call out my name before I would answer the door. She asked if I had seen Stephen. I said I never wanted to see him again, I don't know why, but I did not tell her everything. She went to Shepherd's Bush market and got a few cooking essentials. The phone line was soon connected and the beds and sofas were delivered. I was mentally immobilised and I didn't want to leave the flat even though I had my sister with me.

I refused to open the door to Stephen. It was Rosie who finally let him in against my wishes. He was looking very pale as if he had seen a ghost. I was so angry with him I thought he deserved to suffer considering the hell he had put me through. Rosie and Maggie were very fond of Stephen. Indeed every one of my siblings and Nigerian friends who met him thought he was the perfect gentleman and a very unusual 'white man' even though they all knew he was married. Rosie and Stephen had spoken to Maggie explaining that he had no idea why I was so angry with him. They could not understand why I was giving him such a hard time. Stephen is one in a million and I love him dearly, but at the time I blamed him for what the doctor had said, assuming that he had set it all up. I don't know what he said to Rosie, but she ordered me, as my older sister to listen to what Stephen had to say. When I looked at Stephen, my eyes were filled with anger and pain, which he could see and feel. He folded his hands as he sat opposite me and bent over as if he had been punched in the stomach. I tried hard not to feel for him, but he looked like a lost little boy and I suddenly wanted to protect him.
"What's wrong with you?' I asked coldly.
"I can't bear the coldness in your eyes! Why are you looking at me that way? Why won't you tell me what I have done wrong so I can do something about it?" he pleaded. Supposing he had set it all up and then got cold feet

and was now pretending that he knew nothing, sitting there with his blue eyes and blond hair; looking pained.

"How does Sandra know the doctor you sent to see me?"

"She is my wife and he is our family doctor. I don't think she knew I had sent him to see you."

"What? You sent your family doctor to treat me! Are you crazy?"

"Why not, he is a brilliant doctor, what happened?"

I told him about the doctor's visit to my hotel room, leaving out some of his racial slurs, but enough for Stephen to understand why I was so angry with him.

"The doctor had no right to interfere. I trusted him as a professional."

By the end of the conversation, I realised that after Stephen had asked the doctor to see me, the doctor had spoken to Sandra before coming to my hotel, Stephen had told her about me and about Emma, the very day he had found out I was pregnant. He said:

"I face my responsibilities and the consequences head on."

The loathsome doctor had taken it on himself to try to scare me off, taking Sandra's part. When Stephen called him in anger the doctor said that he was Sandra's doctor before Stephen married her and he had no regrets! I started to feel terrible about all the anger I had directed at Stephen. My trust in him returned completely, he clearly had no knowledge of what the doctor was going to say to me and was shocked and very angry about it. Sandra had made Stephen break the news face to face to her father knowing her father had always hated Stephen. He was Chairman of a huge tobacco company and apparently his reasons for not liking Stephen were that Stephen did not fit into the huntin', shootin' fishin' rugby playing and equestrian set! When he had finished recalling his confrontation with Sandra's father my heart completely melted and it occurred to me that the actions of the doctor might well contribute to the undoing of Stephen's marriage, and so it was.

When he moved to hold my hand I pulled away even though my anger had subsided. I don't know why I pulled away from him as it hurt me to do so. I guess it was difficult to switch off the pain. I knew that he deserved my trust and support. Where was this going to end? Before I left Lagos I had come to terms with being a single parent. I had no idea at the time that Stephen had told his wife about Emma. She must have been devastated; it was selfish of me to think I was the only one hurting! Now things were getting even more complicated. I didn't want to cause Stephen anymore pain. Being in love was one thing, developing a strong protective instinct toward Stephen was another!

"What did her father say when you had told him?" I asked gently.

"He said it was a brave thing for me to tell him such news in person."
I agreed that it was a brave, but stupid thing to do. I reminded him that he had told me he loved his wife;
"Why would you want to make things worse for your marriage? I really do not want to put any pressure on you. I am over the moon with things as they are. I didn't tell you this before, but I was told four years ago, long before I met you, that my chances of having children were zero. To be pregnant is a miracle for me! I was not expecting anything from you. Because of you I am going to be a mother and I am grateful for that. So don't let this pregnancy break up your marriage. I don't want you to feel trapped, guilty or responsible in any way. Emma and I will be fine. But we need to make a clean break of it before we both get too involved and make things worse than they are now for everyone involved."
"I want to be with you Boo! I want to be a part of Emma's life!"
"That may be very difficult! Stephen, you have been amazing in all of this and taking all the punches! But you love your wife and the devil you know is better than the one you don't know!"
"I do love Sandra, but not in the same way that I love you."
"I don't understand that, but I can understand her anger and I still don't think you should have told her because I was about to break up with you, when I got back to England. Unfortunately, I was too sick and couldn't think of anything apart from getting to a doctor. Then your doctor came and changed everything. I am so sorry I blamed you! I should have trusted you!"

Eventually Stephen left the flat. I was not afraid of being hurt, but when Stephen wasn't with me the doctor's words would play on my mind. I did not like the feeling, which the doctor had brought out in me, it felt almost as though I had just been through another war. I wanted to get on with my pregnancy and enjoy it! I did not want my baby to come into the world with a whole load of baggage that had nothing to do with her. I longed to be in the blissful state of mind of a normal mother carrying a new life in her. I needed time to think things through, but the more thinking I did the more confused I got. I decided to have patience, more faith and wait on God, He would handle things His way and in His time as He had always done!

Once I had come to that decision, peace and calm returned. In the following months I made many trips to Maggie in Paris with Rosie, or sometimes on my own. Having Rosie come and stay with me, or going to see Maggie in Paris was wonderfully soothing. We got on well and I was so proud of all my siblings, they were all so clever, they all made up for my lack of interest in attaining high academic status. I paid many visits to Nigeria to see Mummy and the rest of my family. Maggie's husband Felix Ibru (respectfully referred to as Brother Felix) was very nice and his sister Mabel was like family and also my sister Grace's husband Tokunbo (Brother Toks) was very funny and kind. Rosie was not yet married.

I saw quite a lot of Stephen, almost every day. Agent Tom Layton sent me for a casting for the Bruce Forsyth Show, which I got. There were six of us girls in a TV Special called "Bruce and More Girls". We were fitted for very clingy and glamorous costumes and we were to shoot the programme in two weeks' time. I was now over four months pregnant and no one noticed at the fitting because I was not yet showing, but by the time we came to do the show my stomach suddenly popped out. I struggled to get into the dress. I had brought a corset with me knowing this would happen. The corset made the waistline fit, but only just. My baby did not like it one bit and in rehearsals I began to feel faint. After the first time I fainted, I told Pearly, the only other black girl in the group that I was pregnant and she covered for me. She told everyone that I had food poisoning and then she would disappear into the ladies with me at any opportunity to loosen the corset for a little while before fitting me into it again for the takes. Somehow, baby and I survived the filming.

I started talking to Emma. I started telling my baby that I would protect her always and would not let anyone harm her. Talking to Emma became an enjoyable habit. It was now my baby and me against the world. The whole doctor episode had fortunately helped to make me strong. I was allowing the Stephen situation to take its course as God saw fit. Friends were telling me: "All Stephen wants is to have his cake and eat it!" Whilst they raided my wardrobe of expensive dresses from Paris and costumes specially made in Thailand, which no longer fitted me because I was pregnant, none of which I got back!

One day, I started bleeding, luckily, Rosie was on a visit to my flat she called an ambulance and I was taken to Hammersmith hospital where they told me I was lucky not to have lost my baby and kept me in the hospital for five days. Those five days in the hospital were the turning point, my growing up days. No more friends only family! I gazed constantly out of the window, working out a way of living in an adult world full of the unexpected and false friends. Could I exist in this world without being false and mean myself? I asked God to help me. Then I swear I heard a voice inside me say,
"All these things are meant to toughen you up! But on no account are you to change who you are. Count your blessings and it will all become clear!"
"But who am I?" I whispered.

"You are my child. A very special child." I began to cry, but this time I cried for joy.

By the time I left the hospital I had made up my mind I was never going to let anyone change me and that I would rely on my personal relationship with God for all the strength I would need. I began to count my blessings. I was special to God and that meant He would be helping me to fight my battles. My attitude changed. My light would be bright and irresistible!

I believed Stephen was torn between his love for me and the enormity of leaving his second wife and child whom he loved. I realised that if he truly was my soul mate nothing would stand in the way. I knew my capacity to love was great, but could I allow my love to cause such pain to other people? I knew that I should not actively try to force the situation, but let God make the decision for us. With Jesus on my side who could stand against me? I had a new song in me, there was joy in my heart and it changed my perceptions of life,

While I was waiting for the money from the programme to come in I was short of cash. I had put all my money into buying and furnishing the flat in Hammersmith. I lived on potatoes for a while. I had never asked Stephen for anything and I was not about to start, although he constantly tried to give me money and was always buying things for Emma. I said nothing to Stephen, although I knew he would have helped and been worried for me and Emma if he had known.

For the final two months of my pregnancy I concentrated on Emma. I would play music to her and would giggle whenever she moved. It was as if she knew when I prodded my swollen stomach that I was teasing her and I would laugh with delight at her reaction. Sometimes I worried about the baby inside me being so receptive and judging my mood so well. My baby was my best friend, a miracle and the best thing that had ever happened to me. She wasn't even born and yet she was great company.

Mummy was planning to arrive in London for the summer before my baby was due to be born. She planned to stay until Emma was three months old. Loving Stephen allowed me to be less selfish and more selfless. I learnt from him that real love is to genuinely desire what is good for the object of your love and not what will be best for you, Stephen was the best thing to come out of my theatre days.

There were two male dancers, Carl Andrews and Les Saxon who would drop in occasionally and cheer me up; they were such good company.

When Emma was born

Mummy arrived two weeks before Emma was due. Stephen visited almost every day as usual. My mother instinctively knew when Emma would be born and started to give me laxatives a couple of day before the birth so that Emma would be clean when she entered the world. I was seeing a private gynaecologist in Harley Street. The hospital, Queen Charlotte's, had convinced me to pay for an epidural. I reluctantly agreed against my better judgement, I thought it better to be safe than sorry. I had seen so many women give birth and personally assisted in a few, nothing could be easier! Yet they were making so much fuss about danger to the baby.

The epidural was one of the worst decisions I had ever made. I should have had more faith, trusted God, who had given me the baby, to keep her safe. Unfortunately, I forgot to mention the epidural to my Mummy before we were in the labour room and it all gave her quite a shock. As I lay on the bed with bad labour pains it was decided I must have the epidural. I was rolled to my left side and told to assume the foetal position. This is not the position you want to be in when you are in labour. To make things worse I was told not to move, as the injection was going into my spine and it would be dangerous if I were to make any sudden movements. I looked round just in time to see the anaesthetist holding what looked like a thin knitting needle a foot long! I had been expecting a normal injection, which scares the life out of me anyway, but this! I wish I had hidden my fear from Mummy, because the look of horror on her face reflected my own. She exclaimed in Efik, her native language:
"Oh God help me! They are killing my child!"

I was worried about Mummy, who looked like she was about to faint, she had never seen anything like it. Neither had I! I felt a crack in my spine as the needle went in. I was totally gripped with panic, there were only white faces treating me, I thought of Sandra and the loathsome doctor as I went into shock and my whole body broke into involuntary spasms.
"Don't move." Somebody snapped.
"The baby is coming! I have to push!" I shouted.
I could see Mummy was traumatize as I turned around still shaking and started to push. Emma came out screaming, I didn't blame her. Compared to the no fuss natural births I had witnessed, this was crazy! I was still shaking as they gave Emma to me; "it's a girl!" As if I didn't know! They weighted her and I told them to hand her to my Mummy while they stitched me up. Holding the baby calmed Mummy down, but not sufficiently. Like me she was hiding her fear and distrust of the hospital staff. Later when we

got home I saw that she had been bandaged up, because when she left the labour room she had fainted and had fallen down some concrete stairs.

Emma was to be taken to the nursery where all the other babies were. I refused to allow them to take her; I wanted her with me as long as I was in the hospital. The natural experience I had so looked forward to in bringing my baby into the world had been ruined. The epidural only kicked in after she was born and after I was stitched up. Mummy, who had given birth to nine babies, was very unhappy with the way the birth had been handled, it was all so unnatural!

Stephen called my hospital room to see how we were. Sandra had banned him from coming to the hospital. I knew it hurt Stephen not to be there. The next day I went home with Emma and Mummy to start my life as a mother. It was wonderful to have Mummy with me. She made me sit in a bath of warm salty water for my seven stitches. Mummy's wounds took a while to heal. Naturally, there was a strong bond between her and Emma, which lasted to the end of Mummy's life.

Stephen came to see Emma as soon as we got home, and he visited every day. He loved the baby. She was christened Emma Aret Patricia Komlosy at a church nearby and her birth was registered in the same name. So she became the first grandchild to bear Mummy's name, Arit (I spelt it Aret for easy pronunciation).

The film "Bisi, Daughter of the River" was premiered in Lagos at the new National Theatre, which is built in the shape of a captain's hat. Emma and I were there. Mummy made me a fabulous red dress for the premier. I wore it over the corset she had made for me to help get my stomach shape back to normal. The film was a runaway success! Nigeria's first Film success and box office smash hit, which ran in the cinema for three years. I was already known as the face of Lux Soap in Nigeria and remained so for twenty-nine years, so the film made me an even bigger star in my own country. Not surprisingly, the film premier had brought me to the attention of many men. The one that sticks in mind was a well-known, if not notorious Chief and businessman whose company had invested in the film. He was very rich, but lacked social graces in equal measure. He was not at all easy on the eye, but had a self-deceiving confidence, that comes with massive wealth. He called me a few times and I was polite, but not encouraging. After a few weeks he had decided to follow up on his calls to me and come to London to offer me the position of wife number three! He arrived with a large white gold ring with diamonds in a spiral shape as an engagement present. I guess he most have liked the fact that I addressed him as 'sir' over the phone. He had no way of knowing there were more suitors like him and I addressed them all as 'sir'. It was an imposing ring and would have impressed any young girl who wanted, or was simply desperate enough, to be wife number three to a mega rich husband. The Chief's marriage proposal went as follows;

"You will to come back to live in Nigeria as my wife, I will buy you your own car and apartment"

Trying to stay serious through the proposal.

"You mean a house sir, not an apartment!" I corrected him seriously.

"Ok a house." I wanted to laugh out loud. He continued.

"I will give you £50,000 a year for life." For whose life I wondered.

"What about my career?"

"You cannot be doing this acting thing as my wife, if you want to start another business of your own I will pay for it!"

"Wow! That is more than generous of you sir." I said.

He nodded, pleased.

"This is the best offer of marriage you will get from anyone, I am a very rich man and you already have a child whose father has no intention of marrying you. I will look after your baby and pay for her education."

I studied him as he sat there, his ugly face and mouth looking smug. His unprepossessing suited figure occupied my chair. I stayed polite despite my jokes and calm, remembering that this is a very crude and powerful man, and I had my family in Nigeria. He made a movement with his head as if to indicate everything was settled. He was obviously used to having his own way. I took a moment to make sure I picked my words carefully.

"Wow, Chief, that is indeed the best offer of marriage a girl in my position could ever expect! This ring is magnificent!" He nodded and added.

"There is a bracelet that goes with the ring which will be yours when you become my wife." The idea repulsed me. I smiled and continued.

"Naturally I am very flattered and honoured by your proposal. But you see Sir; I could not offer my hand in marriage without my Mother's consent. If my Mother gives her blessing I will be indeed honoured to accept your offer of marriage."

The Chief looked satisfied with this. He reminded me of the potbellied rich man she chased down the stairs with her famous koboko whip, when he came looking for Maggie. When he left my flat, I booked a call to Mummy who was now back in Lagos. I told her about the chief's offer and price. I quoted the 'best offer of marriage" bit mimicking his accent. I told Mummy he was coming to see her to ask for her blessing to marry me. She made no comment, but changed the subject to Emma and Stephen and how I was coping. I was not worried about what Mummy would say to him. It was not the first time she has had to ward off such suitors and she could be diplomacy itself. The Chief was one of those men in Nigeria who were sure their money would buy them anything and anyone.

When the Chief visited my mother in Lagos, he was told that his offer of marriage to her daughter was generous. And though her children showed her the respect of asking for her blessing for marriage, the final decision was always their own.

The chief interpreting Mummy's words as a "yes" and blinded by his own over inflated self-importance he flew to London to see me full of confidence. It was a blessing that he arrived at my flat unannounced, one evening, just as Stephen was leaving. As I introduced them, I sensed a distinct change of mood in the chief. The man could not hide his surprise. Even he could recognise a handsome, well-groomed and polished man when he saw one. I felt the Chief was unsettled at meeting this good-looking and polite young man who was playing with my baby. Stephen looked impeccable in every way! He took his leave as he handed Emma to me and kissed me at the door.

"Who was that man?" The Chief squeaked

"That's Emma's father!" I tried to sound surprised that he should ask.

"You are still seeing him?" His indignation made him stutter.

"He is the father of my baby. Why would I not see him?"

"What are your feelings for this man?" His stutter got worse.

"Sir, I am so sorry that you misunderstood the circumstances, I am hopelessly in love with him! He asked me to marry him a long time ago. I just didn't say yes. If he was to ask me again, I would marry him."

The chief picked up his briefcase, which I imagined contained a marriage contract of some sort and stormed out of my flat.

By the time Mummy went back to Lagos Emma was three months old. Mummy's time with us freed me up to go for castings. I got my first part in a Christmas pantomime "Follow the Star" at the Chichester Festival Theatre. The director was the wonderful Wendy Toye. My first ever female director and what a change it made to the company, there was a more pleasant and caring feeling about the place. A blessing for me, because after a few weeks of rehearsals I became worried about the state Emma was in when I got home.

In the mornings I would have her food ready. I started her on solids when she was four months old which got her off breast milk at four and half months. I would bathe and feed her, pack extra food and water in her bottles ready for the day. A lovely lady, a widow, who was one of the neighbours who lived above my flat, was looking her after. When I got back at night Emma's eyes were all swollen as if she had been crying herself to sleep. Stephen often visited her to see that she was okay during the day, but I instinctively felt that she was becoming a different baby. Somehow her sunny disposition was leaving her. "Your baby is amazing, she never cries!" The neighbours would say, before I started rehearsals "No one would know you had a baby in the house." Now they were saying she was always crying. The next day I took her to rehearsals with me and with the help of the Chichester Company, I rented a room in a house for the duration of the show. My favourite person in the cast was actress Lynette McMorrough. She was wonderful with Emma and with some other members of the cast she would look after Emma while I was on stage.

The room I rented was freezing, but had a real fireplace. One morning I had lit the fire, dressed Emma who was now coming up to almost six months old, sat her down in front of the fire about five feet away and went to have a quick shower. When I turned off the water I heard Emma crying, I ran into the room to find her two feet away from the fire. She was over-heating, but not hurt. I couldn't believe she got herself that close to the fire. All I was thinking was what would have happened if I had not heard her and she had got closer and burnt her hand or set herself on fire. I sat there hugging her and crying at the thought of what could have happened. That day I called my Mummy and we decided that she would go to live with Mummy for a few months. Mummy had wanted to take her home with her anyway. This was a terrible wrench for me and I thought I would die when Mummy flew in to take her home. All of the traumas surrounding Emma's birth and now letting her go, left me bereft. She was such a happy baby and I knew I would not be able to live without her for long

I threw myself into work. I hardly went home, as the flat seemed very empty without Emma. She was safer with my Mummy than any nanny, nursery or babysitter. I just had to cry myself to sleep!
When people asked me how I could have parted with Emma. My answer was always; "It's not about me anymore, it was about what was good for her. I want her to be where being a baby is normal and natural. Within a few weeks of being in the sun and out of winter clothes Emma was walking at seven and half months. I went back to Nigeria more often to see my family now that Emma was there. Stephen also put in calls to Mummy to find out how Emma was doing.

My agent booked me a gig at the Sheraton Hotel Bangkok, in Thailand for two weeks. Stephen said he could not bear for me to be away again for that long, what if I met someone else. I joked that it would take more than two weeks for a stranger to make such an impact. I arrived in Thailand on the

21st Jan 1978. While in Thailand, I went to visit Pataya Village where I found some cone shells, which were bigger than the ones I had been wearing in my hair. Pataya was just a small village in those days; all I could buy at that time were seashells or blowfish lamps. I settled for the cone shells, which I wore in my hair and which became famous when I won ATV's New Faces. While I was in Bangkok, Stephen was in Spain on holiday with Sandra and the Children. When I got back from Thailand, Rosie and I visited Maggie in Paris more often whenever I was not working. I was lucky enough to get lots of singing work from various theatre agents. A lot of the work I was getting was from the people I had worked for before or knew. I fantasised and toyed with idea of starting my own dress design business or hairdressing salon, but I never seemed to get the chance. I went to Germany to sing at a trade show and when I got back to London, I went back to Paris. Sometimes I would visit Rosie in Preston though that was difficult because she was a student and her accommodation was not easy for guests.

Chapter Twenty Nine: New Faces

My agent suggested I go on a TV talent programme called New Faces because my new name Patti Boulaye was not known. All the shows and publicity I had been known for, as Patricia Ebigwei, were now not associated with the new name. He said he couldn't do much for me under the new name unless I went on New Faces. I watched the programme and found it scary, the judges were cruel and I felt sure they would hate me. But my agent convinced me. I had to encourage him to get me work, so I agreed and he booked me an audition for 11.00am at the ATV studios in Birmingham. On the day of the audition, I should have caught an early train to Birmingham, but I decided to just turn up a bit later; hoped the audition would be over by the time I got there.

As always, providence had its own plans. I did not get to the ATV studios until 1.30pm at which time I felt the auditions would either be over or they would not want to see me. But when I arrived at the venue the auditions had not started because there was a strike. I was the last person to register for the audition. It was also to be the last of the series. I got myself a cup of tea and joined the other artists who had been waiting for about three hours, I was ill prepared and sang one of the songs from Hair, I can't remember which one. I know there were quite a few novelty acts and comedians and not many singers, so I was lucky. When my agent called a few days later to say I got through the audition and gave me the TV date I was petrified and got cold feet.

About five days, before I was due to appear on New Faces, there was a news flash on television about a plane crash in Nigeria at Kano Airport in which over one hundred passengers and crew were killed. I tried to get a call through to Lagos, but couldn't. I tried one of the hotels at Heathrow Airport where I knew the Nigerian pilots always stayed. I asked to be put through to one of the Nigerian Airways crew and I explained why. I can't remember which pilot's room I was put through to. I told him I was concerned because my brother was a pilot and I had heard of the crash in Kano. The first name he mentioned of the crew who had died was Tony Ebigwei, my brother! I had not expected that! I screamed and became hysterical. I was on my own; I did not know what to do. I must have been in shock because the tears dried up too quickly. This was not possible, he was in his thirties and so full of life and so proud of being a pilot. I remembered all that we had endured as children, I tried to pray, but my prayer turned to anger towards God. I sat on the chair and rocked back and forth not sure about anything.

I had had a dream about Tony not long before the fatal accident and now I played it over and over in my mind. In the dream I was on a flight with Tony. I don't know where we were going, but we were sitting at the back of the aeroplane, as it was a full flight. Then the next thing I knew I found myself in a whitewashed village in the desert. Everything was white all the people wore white. I knew I had been there for a while, but I did not know how long. I did not see Tony, I was not unhappy being there! It felt quite natural to be in this village rather like being on holiday. Finally, I asked the man who seemed to be in charge who, like everyone else, wore a white coat, when he thought I would be able to get back to my baby. He said it was not possible for me to get back to my baby because I had died and was not able to return. He said she was now a year old. I felt he read my mind when he asked if I would like to see her photo. I was very pleased and eager to see my child when he reached into his pocket and brought out a photograph. But before I could look at the image, I woke up. Now I wondered about the significance of the dream, I was always sure it spelt my own end and now I realised that it foretold Tony's death not mine. Before Tony's accident I had been to a dinner party where the guests decided to dabble with Ouija board. I had at first refused to take part and sat in the next room, but then thought the better of sitting on my own and went to join them. The board pointed to me and had a message for me. I got up and did not want to know what it was. Ouija boards are against my faith and so I left very disquieted. As I sat in my flat with the awful news of Tony's death, I began to wonder whether I should have listened to whatever spirit was there. Would I have been able to prevent my brother's death? Memories of my dear brother flashed by so quickly and there were many, even the happy ones were now sad and unbearable.

My anger at the Almighty and at the incompetence of Nigeria (the accident had been easily preventable), intensified and I did not want to listen to the quiet voice in my soul that was talking to me trying to calm me down. I booked a flight to Lagos, but could not travel for another seven days. Finally, the quiet voice got through; "think about your Mother," said the voice. Another wave of pain and guilt engulfed me and riding peacefully on that wave, like a surfer, I was able to pray without anger, to pray for my Mother who had just lost one of her sons. Oh poor Mummy! What would she do? How must she be feeling? I had lost a brother, but she had lost the baby she carried, nurtured and protected as best she could until his manhood. She was so proud of his achievements! So very proud, that her son was a pilot. Then I went from near acceptance to denial. My brother can't be dead he was too young! Who dies in their mid-thirties? I had seen dead bodies, stepped over them often enough, but they were not related to me, they were not dear to me. I had avoided looking at their faces so that they would not be too real. Tony seemed too alive in my mind; if I believed he was alive the nightmare would go away.

I could not think about New Faces. All I wanted to do was go home and be with my family and prove this was just a nightmare. I had to wait another week before I could travel. Stephen, who was doing his best to console me, told me I might as well go on New Faces while I waited to go home for the funeral. He had been with me most of each day since Tony's death. He felt that the TV show would be a distraction. The word 'funeral' was surreal! I chose to sing one of the ballads from my first album "The People Some People Choose to Love" written by a country and western singer, Jim Weatherly. I would have loved to have chosen one of the pop songs from the album. But I was not in the mood for a jolly tune. I got ready for New Faces and went through the show on automatic pilot. I can remember only two things in connection with the show; one was during a camera run through. The cameraman kept looking at me and then into the camera and then back again, after him bobbing in and out a few times I asked if anything was the matter. He said;
"The camera must love you because when I look at you, there you are shaking like a leaf and yet when I look through the camera you appear completely serene and calm."

I was grateful to that cameraman, whoever he was, for giving me the strength and confidence I needed to see the show through. When I sang I was fighting back emotions. No one was aware of my pain, but tears had flowed at the emotional point in the song. The second good memory was when Stephen turned up at my hotel in Birmingham to be with me. I was so pleased to see him. I had been given maximum points by the judges, Tony Hatch, Mickey Most, Rosemary Horner and Jimmy Henney and was the winner of that programme. The whole experience was hazy, rather like living through a dream and now I wish I could relive it as reality, but the moment had gone forever.

On the flight to Lagos, a few days later, I kept thinking that I would give up everything if only God would bring back my brother. I had never lost anyone this close to me! Yes, we lost a sibling, but that was before I was born. I transferred my anger to Nigeria. What country would allow an air force flight to take off when a passenger plane was approaching the airport?

When I got home everyone focused on my winning New Faces though they did not know what it meant. It gave Mummy something to smile about now that my brother had been gone almost two weeks. From that day I have prayed for him every day. For about ten years I saw his body language in some young Nigerian men, but when I saw their faces I would be disappointed it wasn't him. I saw him so vividly in my dreams. I would not allow myself closure.

When I got back from Nigeria, New Faces had been aired and I was a household name overnight! There were photographers at the airport and I thought someone else had arrived at the same time as me. From then on things got rather frantic. Lots of press interviews and TV appearances followed. When the press realised I had a baby, as usual they linked her to whomever they could. For a long time I succeeded in keeping Stephen out of the press. I would pass him off as my manager whenever he was with me. After I had appeared for the eligible Prince Charles, the press tried to link Emma to Prince Charles whom I had only just met! As if he could conjure up a baby in two weeks.

But when all is said and done the press were not bad to me. I started working with brilliant Richard Laver the PR, introduced to me by Stephen. Richard was fun to work with. He had people like Joan Collins amongst his clients. We would cook up stories for the press to keep them from making up their own. I was offered lots of songs to record; one of them became a one off hit for someone else. I thought it was too gimmicky. I wanted to be a household name with longevity. I was not looking to make quick money. I wanted to learn everything I could about show business and to be known for excellence and integrity. This choice Stephen pointed out was the longer route and meant spending possibly every extra penny I earned to promote my image. I was now appearing on many TV programmes as a guest. Stephen was always with me. He handled any contracts that needed looking at. He was a Godsend at the right time! A few weeks after Tony's funeral, Stephen lost his only brother, Timothy, who was killed by a bull in a freak accident on his farm. I had to comfort Stephen as he had comforted me. I was appearing in Camden Town when he turned up looking upset, my heart bled for him. He had sought me as soon as he heard the sad news about his brother!

At this point, I didn't know how things were for Stephen at home, but I never brought up the subject as I felt it was best not to know and certainly not to interfere. I kept myself very busy until one day Stephen came round and asked if we could have a chat over lunch. He said Sandra had given him an ultimatum, it was her, or me, and he had to choose. I had always believed that forcing Stephen's hand would work against me.
"Never force Stephen to choose! If you do, you will lose him!"

I had entered this into my diary on a single page as a New Year resolution, in case I was ever tempted. At lunch, I found myself telling him again that the devil he knew was better than the devil he did not know! Therefore, he was better off with his wife and little daughter. Emma and I would be fine and he would not have to get used to a new and alien way of life. Stephen was silent, I didn't know if the look in his blue eyes were of relief or pain or guilt.

When I had finished with the advice that was cutting me to pieces, he moved to touch my hand. I moved my hand away, saying that for all our sakes we had to make it a clean break. I was dying inside! We drove back to my flat in silence. After he had dropped me off, I put on a brave face for Mummy who had come to visit with Emma. When she and Emma fell asleep I called Rosie who comforted me. Rosie said she liked Stephen, "such a special man". Then I got Maggie on the phone and she made me laugh by saying;
"You will live, no one ever died of a broken heart! If they did I would have died so many times!" Then she added, "I know Stephen is a good man and we all like him! But you will find someone and anyone who gets you will be a very lucky man."
Stephen called me, but I wouldn't have a long conversation with him on the phone. I just told him:
"You have to stick to your decision! You are making this hard for both of us!"

Two weeks after my parting lunch with Stephen, I got a call from his wife; she was hysterical on the phone. I was puzzled! I've always hated hearing anyone cry, let alone be the cause of it. I couldn't understand why she was crying now that Stephen had broken off with me. I had not heard from her except that one time through the doctor. I really felt awful at how upset she was and kept quiet as she vented her anger on me. She said many angry words, which included how much she hated me and I deserved that. But when she said I had stolen Stephen from her, I didn't know what to think. I felt terrible not being able to do or say anything to comfort her. All I could say was;
"I am so sorry!"
"I hate you!" she screamed before hanging up.
I was still reeling and trying to make sense of why she thought I had taken Stephen from her when Stephen arrived at my flat.
"I have just had a call from Sandra she is very upset, what happened?"
"I should have called you before she did." he looked very tired and upset.
He said the last two weeks had been the worst time he had ever had having to be without me. It made him realise that he wanted to be with me. He and

Sandra were now officially separated. She was filing for divorce and he had moved into the basement flat of their house in Royal Avenue, Chelsea.

I must admit I was worried! I might make his life miserable if he married me. And was our love worth the hurt we were putting Sandra and Anouska through? I tried to be brave to trust in God's will and wait for His time. I was now more worried about our cultural differences. When Stephen proposed to me again, I tried to put him off and warn him about what he was letting himself in for.

"Stephen you are not just proposing to me, there is a large pyramid of close and extended family out there behind me that you are also proposing to."
"I will take you and everyone and everything that comes with you."
"Are you sure? You are not used to having so many people in your family. And mine is a large family. A very large family!"
"Yes, I couldn't be more sure."
"Well in that case you would have to get Mummy's blessing. It is the only way I could marry you." The irony of having said that same thing to the unwanted suitor did not pass me by.

But this time I really needed someone wise who knew me better than I knew myself. Mummy would stop my heart ruling my head. Stephen was about to be twice divorced. I would have to take him and whatever baggage came with him, just as he was willing to do with me. But I really needed Mummy to approve so I could settle my soul.

I remember how nervous Stephen was when the appointed day came for him to ask for my Mother's blessing. He was petrified! He had great respect for Mummy. This was a good start. He took me aside as I was about to leave him alone with Mummy in my little basement flat so they could talk with no interruptions.

"Darling, what are my chances of convincing your Mother that I would make a good husband for her daughter. The more I think of it the more hopeless my chances appear. It's a no win situation for me, whichever way I look at it! I can't find a single thing in my favour. I am twice married with four children and I am white for goodness sake! What if she says No?"
"Well if she says No, then we will have to have a very long engagement!"
I saw his despair and just had to love him. I couldn't believe he was prepared to go through all this for me. He looked very pale. I tried to ease his nervousness.
"Mummy is very wise she has been to hell and back in her life and she knows that things are never ideal and she knows a lot more about a person's

personality than they realize! She will see through your colour into your heart. As for your four children, to her children are a blessing from God, not a curse. As for your two marriages well, let me put it this way, by the time you finish talking to her she will know your very soul. You can't fool her. Good luck!"

I left Stephen and Mummy alone and took Emma out shopping. Then sat in a café and wrote in my diary while Emma ate some chips. I wondered which way my life was going to go after this day. Was I going to marry Stephen or just remain in a long relationship? I was nervous, but I trusted my Mummy's instincts. I knew, no, I hoped, she would see the virtuousness in Stephen's character and his love for me. I was out of the flat for two hours. Slightly nervous and anxious about Mummy's verdict I returned to the flat. I was surprised to see Stephen's car still parked outside. I walked in to find them both watching television together. Emma had fallen asleep and I lay her down on the chair next to Mummy. Stephen's colour had returned to normal. He and Mummy looked at ease with each other. He smiled when he saw me and got up to leave thanking Mummy! He kissed her on the cheek, which raised a shy smile from her. I followed him to his car.
"Well?" I said.
"You're right, your mother is a very wise woman."
"Yes and?"
"Well you have been sold to me lock, stock and barrel." he was beaming.
"What is my dowry?" I joked and he shook his head.
"What not even a camel?" he shook his head enjoying this!
"A goat, maybe?"
"Nope!"
"A chicken?"
"Nope! Not even an egg!" We both laughed delighted. He kissed me and we hugged each other. He whispered in my right ear.
"You are mine if you will have me. I am the happiest man on earth."
When I got back into the flat I asked Mummy:
"Mummy what do you think of Stephen." I wanted to hear what she had to say.
"Pat, Stephen is a good man. He will make a good husband for you. Of all my children you will have one of the best marriages."
"Thank you Mummy!" I hugged her.
Stephen became like a son to Mummy and a favourite uncle of everyone in my extended family. Am I blessed or what!

Being with Stephen has been like drinking the best Champagne in the world. This is what happens when we meet that one person in life who makes even Elvis Presley, Mohammed Ali, Brad Pitt or Will Smith seem like supporting actors. I think this is what being in love does for you.

The Music Machine

In 1979 I starred in my second film 'The Music Machine', which was a British musical drama and also starred the late, great actor Gerry Sundquist. It was a privilege to work with such a lovely young man and talented actor. The film was set in a London disco in which a competition was held to search for two dancers to star in a film, leading to ruthless competition. I also enjoyed working with Clark Peters who starred and choreographed my dance sequences with Gerry.

The Press

For many years after winning New Faces, we were lucky with the press. With a top PR like Richard Laver as my PR, the media was wonderful to me and ignored (to an extent) my relationship with Stephen. For a long time, our relationship was passed off as a fleeting tryst, which most showbiz relationships were. A well-known and young, successful black girl not only dating a married white man publicly, but becoming engaged and married to him was infrequent, and would be unlikely to happen.

Immediately after my New Faces success, before my engagement to Stephen was announced, the Press realised I had a baby, speculations were rife. They even tried linking the baby to HRH Prince Charles. I had only just met the young Prince who was eight years younger than Stephen and still single at the time. Mind you being a Prince meant that every journalist would link any attractive female to the handsome, eligible bachelor Prince. Knowing the way the mind of a hungry tabloid journalist works, a black African singer having HRH's love child would be the sensation of the year! Whether it was true or false didn't seem to matter. I thought they could not possibly be serious. At first I did not know about the speculation among the media about who Emma's father might be until one of the journalists went too far and rang me directly about the silly Prince Charles story. The young man was convinced he was on to something big. Not long after the incident, Stephen was divorced and our engagement was announced. Until then, it had not occurred to them that the father of my baby could be the extremely quiet, softly spoken and gorgeously handsome man in his thirties, who was known generally to them as my manager, and who never seemed to leave my side. We did not try to hide the fact that Stephen and I were together, but we didn't make a public display of it either. Richard, my

PR, had fun leaving them guessing. He skilfully squashed any suspicions pointing at Stephen before his divorce had been finalised.

We made press announcements to coincide with each single record I released. Richard kept the press busy with lots of stories and champagne receptions without them getting to know any intrusive personal details. Richard and Stephen very carefully handled and quashed any potential danger of the press creating their own stories. Nevertheless, that did happen a few times. When the press camped outside the house in Richmond for a while we gave them tea and told them there was no need for them to remain there. All they had to do was ask any questions they wanted and we would answer them truthfully. I hoped that this would just make us utterly boring. They liked to think that we were hiding something they could sniff out, but after we answered all their questions they left.

Everyone had the same story and some were actually kind in their articles, calling us the "most beautiful couple" and carrying lovely pictures. They also covered our registry marriage in Richmond in 1979 registry office. I guess high profile mixed marriages were rare in those days. We kept the wedding simple. Apart from Stephen's former marriages, the press had nothing else to get their teeth into. There were very few glamorous black artists around in the UK at the time, so I had a fairly clear and long run of favourable publicity.

Of course, some journalists predicted that our marriage would end in tears. Someone told me, the press had thought we would not last a year! They followed us for about 18 months, writing stories from time to time from whatever angle they could come up with, but soon they got bored with how normal we were. We were not party-animals; we were comfortable with each other's company. Neither of us drank alcohol, Stephen is tee-total anyway and I was never drunk or behaved badly and I did not appear to have a death wish as some beautiful and brilliant artistes do. So, over time, I started to become less interesting to the press. Fortunately publicity did continue, but at a reduced rate. Film Premiers and such brought easy publicity and photo opportunities. If I could not find a captivating dress in designer shops, either my mother or later, Gloria, my seamstress at the time, or I would make a dress to my designs to attract the photographers' attention. I was blessed with a wonderful figure, but only wore revealing dresses for premiers and such to attract publicity, which was part of promoting my career. There were a few diehard journalists who began to inject more spice and twists in their articles looking for or creating new angles on Stephen and me to justify their interest in us as a couple. I believe they thought it was all about to unravel and they wanted to be there when it happened!

I was fortunate that my early honeymoon with the press lasted six years or more. Seeing no signs of troubles in the marriage, no pending divorce, it was time for them to move on. My favourite person, as far as the press were concerned, was Richard Young. Richard was a well-known celebrity photographer with a smile that would draw you to him.

Whenever I had to force myself to go to an event because I was told you have to be seen all around the place as an entertainer, I hated most of it. It felt false! A bitchy journalist joked about another celebrity to me; "She would go to the opening of an envelope." I hated him for it and had no doubt he would say the same of me to others. It was obviously his party piece.

When I got pregnant the second time, I decided to be mother and wife full time. But for nine months in 1983 I was a regular monthly guest on breakfast television, on David Frost's new TV station, TV AM. The presenters were very nice and sweet people, Nick Owen and Anne Diamond. They were the only people in show business invited to our church wedding. I appeared with other celebrity guests. The most notable was a very strange Eartha Kitt. She was a great favourite of my husband, but she was not in a good mood when we met her. Having read her autobiography, "Yella Girl" he was disappointed.

It was about that time that I had made my 100th TV appearance. I wanted to spend more time with Emma and my new baby at home. Actually, as far as publicity went, I felt that I had been very lucky and blessed. So I retired for the foreseeable future to look after my two babies, to live as normal a life as was possible and to enjoy my marriage to Stephen. I spent more time travelling back to Nigeria and to Paris to see Maggie. During the summer holidays our home was filled with my nieces and nephews visiting from Nigeria. Stephen was their favourite uncle.

The Patti Boulaye Show on Channel 4; 1982

My TV series for the new Channel 4 was called the "Patti Boulaye Show". It was one of the earliest TV programmes, which had a reality content. Each week, the series featured me trying my hand at various sports and situations. Apart from the singing, I had guest stars including Champion Ice Skater Robin Cousins. Robin had the unenviable task of teaching me how to skate. I say unenviable task because he had to teach me to skate in front of the cameras. I felt like an elephant on the skates and brought poor Robin down more than once. He was the 1980 Olympic Champion, European champion, three-time World medallist (1978, 1979 & 1980) and four-time British National Champion (1977, 1978, 1979 & 1980). The embarrassment of flooring an ice skating world champion made me very determined to learn to stay balanced. He was such a lovely person, but I have not skated since! Another guest on my series was Liz Hobbs the 7 times British Ski Racing Champion, European Champion and World Champion. She had to teach me to water ski. Did you know they race at 80 miles an hour? For a long time I struggled to get up and away on the skis at Thorpe Park, the fast boat kind of yanks you out of the water, but not me, I always sank like a led weight into the freezing foul-smelling water, swallowing a mouth full to boot! Then Reg King, the famous driver from the British Water ski Team, Liz's boat driver and a good friend of my husband Stephen, was brought in to help. With Reg driving the boat, I had no problem getting out of the water straight away and up onto the surface, he just had the knack. Finally I was water skiing! Yeah! In another programme I tried my hand at a stunt in a James Bond Film starring Roger Moore as 007. My stunt coach was the late great Bob Simmons, who taught me things a girl should never know about disabling a man! Roger Moore was very kind and we had a long chat on the set, what a charming man!

My biggest disaster was in the flight simulator, trying to land a 747 jet plane full of passengers at Hong Kong Airport. Thank God it was a flight simulator! I crashed into the ocean killing all passengers. It was scarily realistic! In another show I tried my hand at different dances, African, Flamenco dance from Spain and we had some super guests. My license and insurance did not come in time for sky-diving and Formula One motor racing, but if I do another series I will include them. I was lucky to be able to co-produce the series and got a huge amount of useful experience doing the production side.

Chapter Thirty: Touring

Stephen and I lived together in a temporary flat in one of the huge towers in the Barbican whilst we looked for a house, ending up in Queens Road in Richmond and I began to tour the UK as a solo star learning the art of entertaining as I went along, bearing in mind that I had had so little experience. We went, first around the UK and then Europe in all sorts of clubs and venues. There were lots of press organised and back-to-back TV programmes following my success on New Faces. I released a single almost every three months each with a press reception in various locations. Stephen was brilliant at promoting and making the best use of the tracks that the record company released of me. He had extensive experience as the Manager of stars like Lionel Bart, Johnny Leyton, Mike Sarne, Billie Davis, Long John Baldry, The Graham Bond Organisation and Mike Berry. All of whom had hits in the fifties and sixties. He did not leave anything to chance backing up the record company's promotions and launched a separate PR campaign with Richard Laver. I couldn't have been more grateful that God brought Stephen into my life at this point. The Lord really did provide! Stephen did not drink or smoke and had never taken drugs, he was so very clean in that sense and so was I: this meant we did not attract any hangers-on or drug dealers that often creep in with the kind of success I had at that time. A lot of people in the industry tried to convince me I would be a bigger name without Stephen, at the same time offering themselves as better alternatives. The chances of anyone successfully steering me away from Stephen either to do with my career or on a personal level was zero! I had seen and experienced all I needed to learn about people and show business. Giving the experience of my life to this point, nothing shocked or impressed me enough to turn my head, unless I wanted it to. I was so grateful and humbled by what was happening to me and, to top it all, I had been blessed with this wonderful man who not only loved me, but was equipped with the knowledge to help and guide me through an alien industry and a whole new world. I was not interested in being a bigger name or mega rich; I just wanted to learn all I could about all aspects of show business and to be known as a wholly professional entertainer and actress. Also I wanted to gain my parents' approval and respect for my choice of career. A career my father viewed as only good for vagabonds and strolling players, based on what was happening in the Nigerian entertainment world at the time! I appeared on most of the top TV programmes of the time including the Des O'Connor Show, Celebrity Squares, Jim'll Fix it, The Sacha Distel Show, The Tommy Cooper Show, lots of talk shows, Children's programmes, The Royal Command Performances at the Palladium etc. I appeared for various charities in Royal shows attended by most of the British Royal family with the exception of the Queen Mother, although, much later, I did attend her 100th birthday celebrations at the Horse Guards Parade as an invited guest. Princess and Prince Michael, Princess Margaret, Princess Anne, Prince Charles, Princess Diana and Her Majesty the Queen attended the shows. Recently my charity, Support for Africa was able to help Prince Harry's charity to build a school in Lesotho after a chance meeting with him. I also performed for Prime Ministers and Kings, the great Mohammed Ali and many of the world's Heads of State.

Through my extensive tour of the UK and Europe I was trying continuously to increase my skills on how to entertain live audiences. I was also familiarising myself with well-known songs, standards and an eclectic mix of popular and classical music, which I had missed while growing up in Nigeria. I liked the oldies that I learnt as a result of my sister Grace's love of ballroom dancing. I also acquired a taste for Daddy's love of Big Band sounds like Benny Goodman and classical music by composers such as Beethoven and Tchaikovsky and for Mummy's love of Louis Armstrong, Ella Fitzgerald and others of that era. I got to love Edith Piaf, Rogers and Hammerstein, Michael Jackson, James Brown and most of the old Jazz musicians, film music and so on, indeed a thoroughly mixed bag of music for all tastes that would be required for an all-round entertainer.

In 1979, the record company had entered me for the TV Sopot Festival in Gdansk, Poland. This was the Soviet version of The European Song Contest, although it was not restricted to Eastern Bloc countries because any European Country could enter. I was there as a British artist, representing Britain and my record Company, ABC. Warsaw airport was worse than Lagos airport; drab and chaotic it was like travelling back in time. We took a connecting flight, which sounded like a flying freight train, to Gdansk for the Sopot Festival. When we checked into the hotel, the rooms were basic, old worldly, musty and run down and the soap smelt of carbolic, the loo paper was hard, like the loo paper at EMI's Abbey Road Studios until John Lennon complained. And the room service, well, what can I say? We arrived at the venue, which sat about five thousand on rows of wooden benches arranged in a crescent moon shape and sloping upward toward the rear like a Roman amphitheatre. The venue looked magnificent, the walls were brilliant white and the stage was done Eurovision Song Contest style with a large orchestra arrayed around the back of the stage. At first glance everything looked amazing. Then a tired Stephen accidentally leaned on a wall, wearing a dark suit and when he stepped away his suit was covered in white stuff. Fortunately, it all brushed off and we realised it was all whitewash chalk. Apparently there had been no oil paint available in Poland for thirty years due to the restriction on the use of oil, which was very scarce. I had to admire their improvisations and creativity under such difficult circumstances. We warned everyone not to lean on the walls. Boney M were special guests in their magnificent costumes, it was the first time I had seen them perform and they looked and sounded amazing. It was the first time I met my good friend Maizie Williams, the lead singer. There was another competitor from Britain, a group of pleasant and typically British young men called Black Lace. Demis Roussos was also a guest artist on the final day. After the three days of competition and heats I was the overall winner of the Record Company Competition. I won thousands of Zlotys, the local currency at that time and I was given my own Polish TV special and they had lined up a lot of press interviews for me. We had to get up very early the next day to go to the television studio for the TV special. Stephen had to ask for a changing room for me, and it turned out there was none in the Studio. Stephen insisted they find me somewhere private to change and a broom cupboard was cleared out especially for me! Luckily, I had my signature plaits with the cone shells I had bought in Thailand, so my hair didn't need much attention. I wore silver glitter over my eyelids for the competition and the TV Special. The Polish TV presenter, who interviewed me between each song and translated, told me that the combination of plaited hair, with cone shells and glitter on the eyes, gave me a special glamorous uniqueness that the Eastern Bloc countries had not seen before. I was very flattered because it was the first time my braided hair, which I did myself, had been called glamorous; usually it was referred to in Britain as ethnic until Bo Derek's hairdresser copied it for the film 'Ten'.

The audience were already in the studio when we arrived in the early hours of the morning and they heartily applauded the all-day camera rehearsals until the early evening live broadcast. The temperature was in the eighties. When Stephen asked, at about 11.00am when the audience would be let out for a break and refreshments, he was told that the audience were not allowed to leave their seats and were used to it. Apparently they didn't mind and they would stay in their seats as they had been told! I sang my heart out for that audience when the show finally went live: in part because I was feeling guilty that we had at least been able to demand a cup of tea and a sandwich, whereas they had been sitting in their seats all day in the boiling studio. We took a flight back to Warsaw after filming the TV programme. The next day I was told that my Zlotys would have to be spent in Poland as I was not allowed to take them out of the country! Stephen and I went out shopping for silver, gold, jewellery or any sort of ornament that we would be allowed to take home. We found nothing. Evidently, the Poles were not allowed to buy gold or silver so there was nothing in the shops. None of those shops had been painted for thirty years. We walked the main street trying to spend the money, but the biggest store we found in Warsaw was the size of a local Boots and had nothing of value in it and so we gave up. As we walked around the drab, but once beautiful city, we discovered that the entire country must have been watching the TV Special the evening before, because I had never been so famous! Suddenly the stony faced people that we had encountered four days before were all pointing at me, smiling and even applauding quietly as we walked by. It was surreal until we realised there was only one TV channel.

We went back to the hotel not knowing what to do with all the money, which was apparently an amount equal to about the average annual salary. I'm not sure what I won the money for exactly, there appeared to be several other winners in other categories, but I was glad to do the TV Special, which was obviously the top prize. The hotel booked a taxi to take us to the airport. As we got out of the taxi we handed the taxi driver the entire pile of Zlotys. There was nothing we could do with it. At first he tried to argue that we had given him far too much. We tried to explain that it was a gift. Finally we gave up explaining and walked away with a cheery wave before he attracted too much attention to himself and all that money. When we looked back he was still sitting in his cab staring down at the money. I hope he didn't turn it in. I wish we had spoken enough Polish to explain properly, all I had picked up was "Dziękuję i dobranoc" meaning: thank you and goodnight! Inside the airport we handed in our passports, Stephen's was detained and he was questioned closely for half an hour before being released and his passport was not returned until just before we had to board the flight. The Soviets had invaded Afghanistan in 1979 and there had been a lot of spying activity and the Poles were suspicious of Stephen with his Hungarian name and British Passport. Sopot is near the Gdansk Naval shipyards, which made fighting vessels for most of the Soviet Block navies. As my MD and I waited for Stephen, we ordered fried eggs. The food was served with cutlery, which was made of plastic, coated with some flaking silver coloured metal. The detention of Stephen and his passport was a bit scary, as he did not speak Hungarian and they might have thought he was a fake sent to look at their dockyards. I travelled with a Nigerian passport so perhaps that helped to convince them that Stephen was not a British Spy. It was a relief to board the plane and land in London. Needless to say Poland was off our list of countries to visit until the Soviet Empire collapsed, because we felt Stephen had escaped being detained and we might not be so lucky next time. Nevertheless our visit to Poland was a great experience and the Polish people are lovely.

About two days after we arrived back from Poland the IRA terrorists assassinated Lord Louis Mountbatten by detonating a 50-pound bomb hidden on his fishing boat Shadow V. It was a very sad day; Lord Mountbatten was well loved as an elder statesman and a war hero. He was a second cousin of Her Majesty the Queen. He was killed with his fourteen years old grandson, Nicholas, while spending the day with his family in Donegal Bay off the northwest coast of Ireland. The killing of Lord Mountbatten was the first such attack against the British Royal Family by the IRA terrorist campaign. It was a great shock to us all. On the same day as this brutal killing there was another IRA bombing attack that killed 18 British paratroopers in County Down, Northern Ireland. There was a sense of anger and, thank God, a woman, Margaret Thatcher was in charge of the British government and was not about to take it lying down. The hearts of most of the country were with her. There was a sense that the terrorists had gone too far, especially with the death of Lord Mountbatten's grandson and a solution had to be found.

One very bad winter, I was booked to appear with an orchestra starting on Friday 16th March 1979 for two weeks at the prestigious Savoy Hotel in London. The day before, we were appearing on the island of Jersey. It snowed heavily throughout the night and I was to sing, rehearse and perform with another orchestra at the Savoy. England also got hammered with snow, there was at least twenty inches of lying snow and all the roads were covered. It was a steady, heavy snowfall for over twenty-four hours. The deepest snow from a single fall that I had seen since coming to England, literally all the roads were closed. It was the worst snowfall across Europe, all the airports were closed and no flights were taking off or landing. We had to get back to London and Stephen spent the day on the phone trying to find a way of getting my Musical Director and us back to London. I don't know how Stephen did it, but he managed to charter a flight from Jersey to take us to Birmingham Airport, which was the only Airport that would allow our plane to attempt a landing in the UK. It was not only a hairy take off from the airstrip at Jersey, the landing was just as scary with the flimsy little plane sliding about all over the place! In Birmingham we were lucky to find a brave driver with a black Cab who agreed to defy the treacherous snow-filled M1 and drive us from Birmingham to The Savoy in London. We did not pass one single car on the road from Birmingham to London except the odd stranded and deserted car almost buried on the hard shoulder. It was a white road all the way with no tire marks. Incredible really!

We arrived just in time for me to change and go straight on stage with no sound check or rehearsal with the orchestra. My MD had brought all the musical parts with him and the orchestra just read them for the first time as I performed. The show went really well and the management were thrilled that I had made the effort to get there at all and we were able to rehearse properly the next day. That trip was crazy, one I'll never forget. I learnt what a resilient and resourceful man Stephen is, not forgetting God's protection and the help of His angels.

After that engagement at the Savoy, I had three more weeks of travelling before being able to take a week off. I was very much looking forward to the time off. We seemed to have been travelling constantly round Europe and the UK. We had moved to a lovely house in Queen's Road, Richmond, which had its own heated swimming pool. The house was just opposite the park and had belonged to the family of Mark Lester, that beautiful boy who played the part of Oliver in the film of Lionel Bart's "Oliver".

It was on the afternoon of Monday the 16th September 1979 I had the first day's relaxation and was looking forward to spending time with Emma and doing a few things around the house, when I got a phone call from Richard Laver, my PR.
"Patti, what colour flowers would you like for tomorrow?" I was silent for a moment,
"For tomorrow? Sorry Richard, what do we need flowers for?"
"For the wedding reception, the florists want to know what colour flowers to decorate the room with?"
"Wedding? Who is getting married?"
"It's only your wedding day!"
"Oh no! Richard I forgot! I must go and find a dress in the shops before they close!"
I put the phone down, grabbed the keys of the car and drove from Richmond to Bond Street in a flash, thinking that at least in that street I would have plenty of shops to choose from. By the time I got to Bond Street the shops were closing. I parked the car in the first space available. Luckily, it was just opposite a shop called Christina and the lady was just locking the door as I got out of the car. I ran to the door and knocked until she came back to the door to say they were now closed. I pleaded with her and explained that I was getting married in the morning and did not have a wedding dress. I don't think she believed me, but she opened the door while explaining that this was September and she would definitely not have a white dress left. All the summer stock had gone. She was wonderful and gave me a drink as we looked at everything she had in the store and finally, just as I was despairing we found a cream coloured winter dress. It was a size eight!
"Yippee!" We both shouted as I tried it on and it fitted.

"I'll take it!" I said and hugged her, showering blessings on her. I had a wedding dress. How scatty can a girl get?

The next day Stephen and I were married at the registry office in Richmond, attended by a few members of my family, my stepdaughters and the Press. My wedding dress was simple, but that never bothered me I was just glad to have found it. Richard Laver, my PR, arranged the wedding reception at The Caviar Bar in Knightsbridge. As we wanted to stay in England to be near our baby Emma, we decided not to go abroad, Stephen booked the Bridal suite in Pennyhill Park Hotel in, Bagshot, Surrey, for a week, for our honeymoon. The hotel belonged to a friend of ours, a very sweet man called Ian Hayton and his lovely wife Pat. The bridal suite was in the old part of the building and had a real, very old walk-in fireplace and was delightful and stunningly decorated. It had big windows that overlooked beautiful grounds, landscaped with different levels and large areas of lawn over gently sloping hills. The first night we spent in the suite I had a dream, which seemed very real. In my dream, I was woken by voices and the fireplace was lit, there was a family seated around the fire, dressed in a Jacobean manner with maids milling around them. The maids wore black full-length skirts and white frilly bonnets on their heads. I could hear their voices, but could not decipher what they were saying. There were maids coming in and out of the room with serving trays, while a woman sat in front of the fireplace sewing an embroidery on a white fabric held together by a square wooden panel and pegs. On the floor a boy and a girl sat playing with wooden toys. The room seemed a lot smaller and was differently decorated and only the fireplace was in the same position. Something woke me up and they were gone. I woke Stephen up to say I thought the room was haunted, but he told me it was only a dream and to go back to sleep. When I finally managed to fall asleep the room transformed itself again and this time I felt like I was a ghost looking in on the same family. It worried me that they were so real and they could not see me. I was able to move around this time and followed one of the maids into what appeared to be the pantry. I came back into the room, though I do not remember walking, it was more like gliding into the room where I observed the family for a while before it all faded into day time when I woke from my sleep.

During breakfast I tried to explain the two similar dreams to Stephen, but it was hard to interpret them as anything other than dreams. But the following night I had the same dream again, but this time as I observed the family there was a commotion outside the window. The family and maids all rushed to the window. I followed them to see what it was and then I saw an enormous fire about 100 metres from the window. The flames rose very high and I could make out what I thought was a person tied to a stake in the fire. There was a bit of excitement in the room as they chatted away. The next morning Stephen and I took a ride to see the sights in the surrounding area. Back at the hotel we got our room key from the receptionist and I asked her if there was any history of witch-hunts, or executions on the grounds of the hotel in the past. She casually replied; "Yes, apparently they used to burn witches in the grounds years ago, but that was before the hotel was built and there was only a farm house here!"

That did it. I couldn't spend another night in the hotel and we cut our honeymoon short. We made up for it by taking Emma and the Nanny with us to Spain, where we hired a villa in the grounds of the Los Monteros Hotel in Marbella.

For the first five years of touring I was always petrified before going on stage and even days before I would be a nervous wreck. I would feel physically sick before going on. This was not helped by the fact that I was always learning new songs and dance routines and I never felt I was good enough to be where I was. I relied on Stephen to be my biggest critic and though his views were from his personal taste, they were based on experience. I found his criticisms more trustworthy than those of total strangers who would only tell me what I wanted to hear to my face, but were probably saying something else when my back was turned.

I had great opportunities and lots of fun along the way, like performing with the Scottish ballet for the re-opening of His Majesty's Theatre, Aberdeen for Prince Charles. It was 17th September 1982 the day before Princess Grace of Monaco's funeral, which Princess Diana attended. This, of course, meant that she missed my show. It was her first official visit outside the UK on her own. I was really looking forward to meeting the young Princess Diana, but owing to the funeral, Prince Charles attended the opening alone. I was honoured to work with the Scottish Ballet's founder and choreographer Peter Darrell, who was a perfect gentleman and who never once indicated to me that I was not a real dancer. Truth is that I was not a dancer, but I knew how to fake steps. Dancing with ballet dancers was an experience that belonged to another world. These were dancers with a capital 'D' and yet they couldn't have been kinder to me, leaving me humbled by an exciting and unforgettable experience from which my dancing improved no end. It was a variety show with me alongside the Scottish Ballet and other artistes making up the bill. After the show, all the artistes had to line up on stage and wait for the Prince. Stephen who always wore a three-piece suit was standing at the side entrance of the stage when the Prince came up to him and asked;

"Are you security?"

"No your Royal Highness, I am Patti's husband."

"Ha, of course, it's Stephen! Good to see you again" said the Prince.

Stephen was amazed; he could not understand how Prince Charles could have remembered him or his name after only meeting him the one time in Newcastle about two years previously. The Prince is amazing that way! I am proud to say I did get to meet Princess Diana many times later and even had lunch with her and Linda McCartney at the Commonwealth offices across the street from St James's Palace. We were all heart broken when she and Prince Charles separated and devastated when she died. I still remember my conversations and encounters with her, some of which I will mention later.

My touring continued for five years during which I also worked with one of my favourite director/choreographer, Dougie Squires in a Review, which toured the country starting at one of my husband's theatres, the Glasgow Pavilion, in which I played a Carmen Miranda type character. Dougie, like Peter Darrell, made me feel that I could dance like a star even though I was not a trained dancer. His encouragement made it possible for me to fake it better!

Dougie Squires was awarded an OBE in 2009. He had worked with so many top stars for many years. As a, choreographer he was involved in over ten Royal Command performances and staged the show at the annual Christmas Party 'Not Forgotten Society' at St. James Palace, attended in past years by HRH the Prince of Wales and HRH the Princess Royal. I was privileged to have appeared in three of them. Dougie changed the face of popular dance on television, with his groups 'The Young Generation' and the internationally acclaimed "Second Generation". He directed so many theatre shows including the show that I wrote "Patti Boulaye's Sun Dance" and my star studded "Reaching out for Africa" Concerts at the Royal Albert Hall. He was artistic director of Her Majesty the Queen's Golden Jubilee in 2002, directing the parade down the Mall. He and Sir Michael Parker KCVO CBE got me involved as a member of the Entertainment Steering Committee of this spectacular and historic event; with a public attendance estimated at 3 million and Global TV audience figures of over 200 million.

As a solo star I toured with two male dancers and a band in my cabaret show. The dancers changed from time to time over the years and at one point Anthony Van Laast was one of them. When he left he choreographed the others as they came and went. I continued to learn how to pick up dance steps topping up on my dance experiences as part of the ensemble in West End Musicals. It was a fashionable thing to have lifts in choreography where the star is thrown into the air or lifted up high and I had to learn how to be lifted by dancers. I wanted it all, even though it sometimes proved quite dangerous particularly on a yawing QE2 in bad weather! Apart from my two dancers, whom Stephen often checked into the same hotel as me, as they kept me company when he was not there with me, I also travelled with five or six musicians and a Musical Director (MD) in whom I invested heavily. It was an expensive way to tour, but if I could have afforded it, I would have toured with an orchestra! I kept my MD and dancers busy arranging and changing the show frequently. We would rehearse the new show at the hotel during the day, and do the old show in the evening. It was a very costly way of doing things, but worthwhile. Another singer told me that she toured the same show for three years before changing the music. I was changing mine every three months or less, which meant that my MD, who had to write all the arrangements, was very well paid. Everybody, my musicians, dancers, PR and costume makers were paid weekly. Thank God, Stephen who had by now assumed the role of my manager was not taking any commission. He was with me at the beginning and end of my stay in each town during the tour, having driven up or used the railway from London; I've never met anyone who could burn the candle at both ends like Stephen. He was running his own business and my tour at the same time. I was usually booked for four to five days a week in each town; I was reinvesting in my career and spent five years on the road juggling motherhood, step-motherhood, my career and marriage.

My favourite accompaniment is a full orchestra. I was in my element whenever I had an orchestra. With all that sound around me I could really feel and express the emotions of the composer. However, I had my worst experience with an orchestra at the Royal Albert Hall. It was very early on in my career, and the Royal Variety Concert had sold out the capacity of five thousand five hundred. A famous conductor was conducting a very large orchestra. I was to sing two songs and I had chosen one ballad and one up-tempo song. My sound check in the afternoon went fairly well considering I literally had just a hasty run-through of the songs with the orchestra. There was a long break between all the sound checks and the show, which meant a long time at the artist's bar backstage for the musicians. By the time the show started the musicians were very jolly. Before I went on stage I had an unusually higher anxiety level than normal. I was very worried about doing the up-tempo (dance pop) song with the orchestra, but I had not imagined what was waiting for me. When it came to my turn the conductor counted in the start of the music, but there was a dreadful and unbelievable cacophony of sound. I looked across at the backing singers and their faces confirmed to me that I had not suddenly gone mad. Different parts of the orchestra were playing both the ballad and

the up-tempo at the same time! I had no choice, but to say into the microphone:
"Can we please STOP! They stopped and I apologised to the audience.
"Which song are we doing first?" I continued.
This was followed by great rustlings of paper, they all found the right music and we continued with my performance. I do not recall my actual performance, but Stephen said it was fine and I was very brave to call a halt on my first show at the Albert Hall. Nevertheless, the rest of that evening was shrouded in shock. It took me a while to get over it. I have since developed a fear of being backed by musicians who have the music sheets in front of them as they accompany me on live shows; I prefer them to know the music by heart.

Touring was my university for learning about the entertainment industry and it was full of excitements and incidents especially from drunken or bigoted members of the audience. I remember once at the Watford Bailey's Club, which had the capacity of over a thousand, it was a very large room and they packed them closely together. I made a habit of going into the audience while singing one or two of the numbers. On this occasion I walked towards a long table of about fifty people, I judged them to be some kind of company staff outing. It was unusual to see a black face in the audience at these clubs and so, for that reason, I made a beeline for their table. I stopped at various tables, exchanged greetings, and even kissed the odd nice person on the cheek and complimented a lady or two. I approached still singing; I had read the situation clearly by the time I had worked my way through the tables to this large and excitable party. I was aware that this poor black guy was very uncomfortable. Their body language was clear, especially that of a Neanderthal-like man who thought he was a comedian. I finally reached the table, the Neanderthal said;

"Patti, come and meet one of your brothers." There was a roar of laughter from the rest of the drunken table. He cringed. I faked a surprise as I ran over to him threw my arms around him and said into the microphone.
"Oh my goodness, Uncle, I didn't know you would be here! Ladies and gentlemen please meet my uncle." I presented the poor fellow who was looking rather bemused, but pleased, then I embraced him warmly again.
"Uncle, I'll see you in my dressing room after the show. And please come alone!"

Needless to say the atmosphere at the table had gone from my new uncle being the underdog to suddenly being the kingpin. The bully was red faced as I shook hands with some of the people at the table, totally ignoring him. I picked up the song from where I had left off and continued singing as I made my way back to the stage. I glanced back as I walked away and noticed with satisfaction how my new uncle's demeanour had changed. He was now the centre of attention at the table. I imagined they all wanted to know why he didn't tell them he was my uncle!

Bailey's club in Watford was one of a chain of large workingmen's clubs, in big towns and cities up and down Britain in the 80s. They were large, usually well-equipped cabaret clubs. I played them all! I was performing to a packed audience at one of these clubs one Saturday and as usual Stephen was standing at the back of the room where he could judge the sound and how the audience were receiving the show. As he stood there a man weaved his way over from the bar turned and said to him:
"Coorr!!!! I'd like to give her one!"
"Yes I know what you mean, I frequently do!" replied Stephen, cool as you like.
The same man came back stage after the show and was shamefaced and very apologetic to Stephen when he realised he had been speaking to my husband. Stephen was amused and told the man he only took his words as a compliment.

I had to learn to handle all sorts of behaviour from drunken men when I was performing. Undignified behaviour in these public places was purely a man's thing. There was a certain quiet feminine strength amongst most of the women in the audience, which I respected. It gave me the feeling that I could count on them if I encountered nastiness from a man. I was singing at one of those very large smoke filled clubs, up in the north of England, one night, when a drunken giant of a man walked on stage to intimidate me by exposing himself to me. I think he was expecting me to be shocked or something because he walked right up to me, all of six foot four inches of him eclipsing the lights and engulfing me in his enormous shadow. I was a bit startled not knowing what he was going to do. At the same time, Stephen had seen the danger and bolted from the back of the venue to the side of the stage. Meanwhile, the big man undid his trousers and said;
"Get a hold of this!"
Is that all? Thank God, I thought! Well giant or not he was in my territory on my stage, which I command. In those situations I always followed my guardian angel's instructions and did the first thing that came to mind. Without hesitation I stopped singing and said:
"Oh dear, you poor man!"
"Can you give me full lights, please?" I said to the lighting man. I knew the blindingly cruel effect the spotlights in this particular venue would have. The lighting engineer obliged immediately as I quickly sidestepped

the man and got myself to the front of the stage so he had to turn and face the audience. There was instant laughter and whoops from the audience, much to his embarrassment and confusion. He could not see a thing through those wicked, white and blinding spotlights! He tried to shade his eyes with his hands, which only served to expose his dwindling manhood to the whole audience.

"This poor gentleman has busted the zip on his trousers! Could someone please take him back stage and *take care of him*!" I said to huge applause. A staff member came on stage and led the man off. I saw Stephen standing at the side of the stage giving me the thumbs up and I knew everything was under control and we continued with the show.
"That poor man! I think he was looking for the gents!" I said and the audience laughed again.

As an artiste, I had a policy of always being accessible to the audience, having bodyguards only created an "us and them" situation. If people have paid to see me, then they will have the best I can give them during my performance and my time after the show. Being a performer is giving a public service and even though you can often forfeit your privacy, you belong to the audience when you are on Stage. People are, on the whole, too shy to approach performers, so it is really not a problem. I remember standing behind Angelina Jolie and her little boy in a Boots Chemist in Gerrards Cross. There were a few double takes, but no one bothered her even to ask for her autograph. People will leave you alone and the odd request for an autograph is always such an honour to receive.

Earlier on in my touring years I had a run in with Ronnie Corbett of the Two Ronnies. It was in Newcastle during my first appearance in front of the young Prince Charles. The preparation for the event, to be attended by Prince Charles, was a pain. I was told was 'you must not do this, you must not do that'! I felt I was not allowed to even breathe from the moment the Prince entered the room! Stephen had already given me the Royal protocol and the curtsey, which I practised. I was told do not speak unless spoken to, which was natural to me having been brought up in an environment where I was constantly in the presence of Heads of State and the other elders. It was simple common sense and respect for the status of important people. As Mummy would tell me,
"Show respect for the position, but reserve judgement as to whether the person in the position deserves your respect".

I was curious to see what the handsome young Prince would be like and when I finally met him, he was charm personified, a great example of a gentleman. He entered the room and the whole place lit up, it's not just because he was the prince, I have met a few important people who only bring darkness into a room with them. I was so impressed by the young Prince Charles after my first encounter with him.

During the day at rehearsals and sound checks I found out that for some crazy reason, I was topping the bill, much to the dissatisfaction of one or two people. I had to perform for 15 minutes and had chosen four songs including "Memories" made famous by Barbra Streisand. I had timed my show allowing myself a few minutes to walk on and off and time to introduce the songs. Ronnie arrived for his sound check while I was rehearsing 'Memories' and ordered me to drop the song and choose another because he was going to sing one line of 'Memories' as part of his comedy piece. There was quite a fuss about nothing! My musical director had only brought with him the arrangements of the four songs I had chosen for the night. The three of us discussed it and decided that as much as I wanted to oblige, such an accomplished and respected performer as Ronnie, it was impossible to drop the song, which would have meant losing four minutes of my 15minutes. I said that I didn't mind Ronnie using it first and as I would be the one repeating the song later in the show. Stephen and my MD saw no point in dropping the song, as Ronnie would have first go at it and if I left it out, I would have to cut short my performance, which would be unreasonable. He and his wife would not return my greetings when we met them at the airport the next morning. But I later found out that he is the sweetest man you will ever meet.

During the line-up, the Prince struck up a long conversation with me mostly about my recent trip to Nigeria. Avoiding the true subject of my visit being my brother's funeral. I joked about needing to top up on my tan occasionally, which amused him and he said; "I hear even people with your skin colour do get bikini lines?"
"Oh yes, Your Royal Highness." I said as I pulled the strap of my dress slightly off the shoulder to show him. He laughed!
"You call that a bikini line?"
"Yes your Royal Highness. This is a very good bikini line on a black person; would you like to see more?" I teased. He laughed and said.
"That would definitely get them talking."
At dinner I found myself sitting next to His Royal Highness, he made me feel so at ease. We had conversations about my family and his many trips to hotter climes. I was proud of my general knowledge and was glad to show off a little to the young Prince whose general knowledge was vast.

My observation of some of the incidents in my career greatly amused him. I recounted the whole day even attempting Newcastle accent rather badly, which made him laugh even more. We even giggled together after the National Anthem was played really badly by a Brass band.
"Thank goodness that's over." He said as we sat down.

That was the third time he had heard it played that day, but not quite as badly as that. I had entirely monopolised His Royal Highness's time at dinner, which raised a few eyebrows. I had so much fun! When I finally got on stage I couldn't help being effusive about the young and charming Prince to the audience. "I have just met His Royal Highness for the first time and if this country has someone like Prince Charles as future King I am applying to extend my visa to stay in Britain forever." The audience loved it. When I got back to the table the first thing he said to me was;
"Flattery will get you everywhere!"
'Thank you Your Royal Highness, I meant every word."
Stephen and I got to meet him many times on various occasions after that. After many years I got to see Ronnie Corbett and his wife again and he turned out to be a very sweet man and had not remembered that I had upset him in Newcastle.

Show business was not always glamorous. I performed in one of the worst clubs you could imagine. It was in a place called Eccles near Manchester. The dressing rooms had slime on the walls and I dressed in the car the first day I arrived. For the rest of the week, my dancers, musicians and I changed at our hotel in Manchester. None of us ate or drank in the club.

When we started touring the country I had a Jaguar XJ6 two door, but soon changed to the larger and more comfortable ride of the Lincoln Continental Mark V from the USA. The car was over 18ft long and was a shiny burgundy and had a 7.5litre V8 engine. It boasted a large boot at the back and a long nose in front. The power steering was to die for, considering its width and length. You could turn the steering wheel with one finger. It was that light to drive. The Lincoln Continental Mark V was built for long journeys. Inside, the finish was not as good as the Jaguar, but it had everything, including cruise control, which my XJ6 did not have. The ride of the Mark V was so ultra-soft it was like riding on a cloud and I loved the car, it was simply awesome. I was addicted to American cars for years after that and we were grateful for it when we had to drive from London to Scotland and back. There was the odd drawback with the car, for instance we could only service it at the American Car Centre in Kingston, Surrey and if anything went wrong in any other parts of the country it would have been hard to get spare parts and so Stephen had the car serviced regularly.

It was a very thirsty car and did about seven miles to the gallon. Thank goodness it had a big tank for petrol. Luckily it was a sturdy car and never broke down except once when we had to drive back from Edinburgh to London at night and the headlights stopped working. What a harrowing journey that was. We were already on the motorway when it happened. The headlights were on a swivel and shut, so that they could not be seen when not in use. They just shut and would not open again, so no lights. We had set out just after midnight on the four hundred mile journey. We had to rely on the headlights of the cars and lorries in front of us and drove closely behind them, but at a safe distance. We would heave a sigh of relief when we saw streetlights ahead, then we knew we were approaching a town and wouldn't have to rely on the light from other vehicles for a short while. There were a few nail biting times during the journey when there were no vehicles to follow. It spooked a few drivers to see this wide dark ghost of a vehicle tailing them without lights at two O'clock in the morning. You couldn't blame them for driving off at great speed. A few cars let us tail them until they turned off the motorways. The lorry drivers understood what had happened and let us tail gate them for miles until they also turned off. We did this all night until we arrived home at 7am exhausted with the tension of it all. Incredibly we did not run into a single police car all the way from Edinburgh to London.

I appeared a few times in front of HRH Princess Margaret who had the most incredible and expressive blue eyes, a really startling azure. My first show for the Princess was at a very large club not far from London. We had fun when we were asked to join her after the show, with her ladies in waiting and entourage with the owner of the club, in a private VIP alcove. The Princess was full of life and such fun to be with! She obviously liked Stephen and me, which helped. Fortunately, I had included 'La Vie En Rose' and 'Milord' both by Edith Piaf in my performance that evening, as these were her favourites. When we joined her after the show she wanted to know if I knew any more French songs. I started to sing a French nursery rhyme, "Au clair de la lune" the Princess joined in and so did everyone else and she knew more of the song than I did. We all sang a few more songs together and we were all laughing and chatting while her bodyguard stood by. For some reason a large lady, who was obviously a little tipsy, started towards our group with a determined look in her eyes. Stephen had spotted her and I had seen her approaching. I saw the Princess use the tiny flicker of an eyelid to her bodyguard, a look, which I thought nothing of, but I noticed the bodyguard went into action immediately. He politely steered the lady away with a firm grip on her elbow. The lady never made it to the alcove. Stephen said it was so smoothly done, he felt like applauding. At the end of the night the Princess offered me a lift home to my flat in

Hammersmith in her Limousine, which I had to very politely decline as Stephen was taking me home. We were not yet married at that point.

The next time I sang in front of Her Royal Highness was at Longleat. It was a July charity event and tickets were £250 each and Princess Margaret was the Royal guest. It was one of those strange days when you know something was about to happen, but don't know what it might be. All throughout the day the animals at Longleat were restless and cried incessantly and when I asked if this was the normal noise level I was told it was unusual for them to cry all day. There were three hours between the sound check and the show, during which time my musicians, dancers, Stephen and I drove to the nearest town to get some food, but especially to get away from the disturbing cries of the animals. It was quite a distressing day! It was completely dark when we drove back to Longleat through the tree lined driveway, which had no lights and I had remarked to those in the car that the place had a strange presence of evil hanging in the air. The animals had quietened down by the time we got back for the show. Even though Stephen and I were not scheduled to meet the Princess, we were suddenly told we were to meet Her Royal Highness after the show, I guess she asked for us. It was a Black Tie event, but Stephen didn't have a bow tie with him, so I had to improvise by making a black bow tie out of a pair of my black knickers! Much to Stephen's amusement. It looked great and no one noticed. One of the charity people had not turned up, so Stephen had to look after the Princess throughout the evening with my knickers around his neck! After the show we drove back to London and just before we got home in the early hours of the morning we heard an announcement on the radio that Lord Valentine had hanged himself. We were so shocked. It had been a very strange day, but Lord Valentine had looked okay when we met him during the evening. What could possibly have gone wrong? Were the animals on Longleat aware of something in the air that day? Lord Valentine died by committing suicide on 7 July 1979 at age 41.

I toured Scotland, England and Wales extensively picking up lifelong fans on the way, even though I never thought I was much good at what I did. The truth is I never stopped long enough to see what other performers were doing and how they entertained. They were usually featured on television at the same time as I was on stage, and if I happened to be appearing on the same show as other artistes, I would be back stage trying to get ready or gathering my nerves. I met some nice celebrities and stars on the way.

One of my tour dates took me to Liverpool and for the first time Stephen and I decided to visit one of the sights, the new Liverpool Catholic Cathedral, which was less than twenty years old. The Cathedral, a fine example of Gothic Revival architecture, was known locally as "Paddy's Wigwam" and opened on the 14th may 1967. It was an enormous modern building, not traditional at all. The previous building had been destroyed in the war. It had been some years since I had decided not to attend Mass in England and to pray on my own. At this time Stephen and I were married. I had not expected the impact or spiritual experience awaiting me. I knelt down to pray, to make an act of contrition, I was truly sorry for the things I had done especially, in not going to visit Christ in the Blessed Sacrament, not going to confession or receiving the Eucharist. I was not married in the church and did not feel God was pleased with me. I had also caused Sandra (Stephen's ex-wife) and daughter Anouska so much pain. I also would not accept that the Lord had called two of my brothers and Stephen's brother to heaven. Even worse, I had been angry with God and had not been faithful to Him despite His obvious show of love, which I had taken for granted. As I knelt there in prayer I was overwhelmed by a great surge of emotion and suddenly, without warning, I started weeping uncontrollably. Stephen sat there cradling me as I wept. When I stopped, he asked if I wanted to speak to a priest. I nodded and he went off and found a young priest and I asked if I could have a face-to-face confession. After listening to my confession the priest blessed me, gave me my penance and I asked him to pray for me. Stephen had also had a cathartic experience in the cathedral and became a strong catholic thereafter.

When we got back to London I started taking Emma to Mass at St Elizabeth Church in Richmond. Phil Linnott of "Thin Lizzy" was always at Mass with his beautiful wife and child and we would often speak with him after the service. I was very upset when he died so young. It had been many years since I had encountered what I saw as the negative side of English church congregations. Things seemed to have changed or maybe it was I who had changed. I no longer thought that going to Mass was about the people in the church. Going to Mass would be more about my relationship with God and being in the presence of His Blessed Sacrament. Although I was attending Mass again, I did not think I was worthy of receiving the Holy Communion until I felt that the Lord had forgiven me. I knew He would find a way to let me know. The only way I could see the Lord's mercy for certain was if Stephen and I were to be married in the Catholic Church. This seemed actually impossible, since Stephen had been twice married and divorced. I knew God could do anything, so I prayed daily for this outcome and set aside one day a week to fast and pray, returning to a tradition my Mother had taught me. The idea of never receiving the Eucharist for the rest of my life weighed heavily on me, but I continued praying for divine mercy and intervention. At the end of each Mass, I left with the hope that I could in some small way serve God in my life.

In the middle of all this there was one dark and miserable day, when everything felt like an evil dark cloud was covering us and everything that could go wrong went wrong. It rained heavily and the sun seemed to be hiding its face. We drove with my two male dancers to the BBC Studios in Manchester where I was due to sing two songs. The Orchestra were already there and then I realised that we had left the music sheets back in London and there was no way of getting them to the studio in time for the show. It was awful and I was worried I would get a reputation for being unreliable, something I had fought energetically since I got into show business. I had never missed a show or turned up late. I was scratched from the show. On the way back I remarked:

"That has to go down as one of the worst days of my life!"

Little did I know, it was going to get worse! When I got home, I was greeted with a call from Nigeria. My eldest brother Johnny, who was an Aeronautic Engineer, had died that afternoon, of a suspected heart attack. He was only 36 years old! I couldn't cry, this time I was completely numb. Johnny was just so wonderful, the most beautiful sweet-hearted person I have ever met. Stephen booked us on a flight to Nigeria. We had been travelling so much and I was exhausted and did not want to bury another brother. As we sat at the airport waiting for our flight I watched the world go by while mine appeared to be coming to an end. I realised then that no one knew my pain, but that some of the passing crowd may be in the same boat as me, yet I could not tell, who knows another's pain? That was when I made up my mind I was never going to be knowingly nasty to anyone, as I didn't know what he or she was going through and I might be adding to their pain! I was going to do my best to be nicer than necessary, because everyone I meet may be going through one problem or another.

In Lagos, Stephen and I stayed at Maggie's place at Apapa. I had taken sleeping tablets because Stephen and I had not been able to sleep for days. I did not want to face what was happening. When the driver came to pick us up for the funeral, I could not move and could not think straight, Stephen was worried about me. He knew I did not want to go to the funeral so soon after Tony's death. I would not give myself closure. After the funeral we went to see Mummy at her house in Ikeja, I went into Johnny's bedroom and felt him embrace me as I stood there. It was such a gentle embrace and yet I could not cry or accept that he was gone. Stephen went in to sit with Mummy in her room. The doctor, to help calm her, had given her some sedatives. Stephen sat with her in her room for hours just holding her hand in silence.

At one point, something was said to me by my sister Maggie, as we all sat in the veranda of Mummy's house. Not thinking, I snapped back at her and everyone came down on me for talking back at my elder sister. I regretted it the moment I snapped back. Stephen was indignant as he watched every one tell me off, I had to stop him interfering.

"They can't talk to you like that! Who do they think you are?" he said.

"These are the people who know exactly who I am. I had no right to talk back at my older sister."

"I don't understand it, but I must say, I respect it! I can't think of any other artist that I have ever met or managed, who would have put up with that!"

There was nothing to put up with. This may sound strange to the reader and I can't say it enough! I love my siblings too much to cause any of them grief in any way and I had no right to be disrespectful. I do love and honour my family traditions, which had been set by Mummy as the matriarch. They are perfect for my spiritual and mental wellbeing.

On the flight back I asked Stephen what he spoke to Mummy about for so long when he stayed with her in her room.

"I said that I felt her pain as I had just lost my younger brother and we just sat and kept silently meditating. She is a remarkable woman, but what I don't understand is how she can still have such faith in God when He has taken two of her sons away from her in such a short time and so early in their young lives."

"God is all she has at a time like this. Where else can she go for help? No! Her two sons came from God and He has called them home to Him. She can only give thanks for God's gift to her of two such wonderful boys, even though she was only allowed to keep them for so short a time."

"I think it is remarkable to have that kind of faith. I still don't understand it." said Stephen

"Even as we mourned our loss, you may not have understood a lot of the conversation because everyone was talking about some poor woman who lost her five sons in one car accident! We have to be thankful for God's mercy!"

Stephen and I were quiet as we settled on the flight back. So much had happened. We had so much to think about. Losing Tony and then Johnny both in their mid-thirties was painful for Mummy and the rest of us, but we have a saying in the family. "We do not mourn like those without hope. Our hope is in the Lord, our Saviour!"

When we got back to London Stephen gave up his Sunday tennis and came to Mass with Emma and me and has continued until this day. Stephen had obviously been more affected by the trip and his time with Mummy than he had realised. During Mass he asked why I was not going to receive communion and I explained that as we were not married in the Church I was not in a position to receive the Eucharist. I had not realised how much this had troubled him until he asked the Parish Priest, Canon Davys, if there was a possibility that we could at least have a blessing. The meeting with Canon Davys did not go well. I knew it was hopeless and impossible for Stephen and me to get married in the Catholic Church following his two divorces. After our meeting with Canon Davys, I had only one option. I said to myself,

"Why am I going through the secretary when I have a direct line to God my Father" and so I continued to pray and fast for God's Devine mercy and intercession. I kept telling myself, the day I get married to Stephen in the Catholic Church is the day I will know fully the greatness of God's forgiveness, but for now it was not looking possible. It would definitely take a miracle and divine intercession for us to be married in the Church.

We were blessed with another baby, this time Sebastian our son was born. I didn't dare hope that I could get pregnant again, let alone give Stephen and me a son. For many years we continued to go to Mass on Sundays at St Elizabeth's as a family. We wanted our children to grow up in the Church so they would have a good, strong spiritual foundation and character for their adult life. After many years of attending Mass at st Elizabeth's, Emma and I were asked one Sunday, to take part in the offertory procession and we carried the Hosts and Wine to the Altar. At the Altar I noticed the visiting priest for the first time, he was dark haired and had one of those smiles that makes you think the sun was shining through it. We smiled back as we handed the silver bowl full of the communion wafers and the chalice to be consecrated. His smile was irresistibly friendly and approachable. When Emma and I got back to our seats at the back of the Church, we both said;
"What a lovely Priest!" at the same time.
"I think he must be a Bishop." Stephen said.
"How do you know?"
"He is wearing a scull cap."
He was right. I then noticed the small violet zucchetto or pileolus, (skull cap), when the priest bowed his head during the service. After Mass we found out that he was Bishop Howard Tripp of the Diocese of Southwark. Stephen said we should talk to him about our problem and we had a quick word with the Bishop, during which Stephen laid out our problem in his brutally honest way. Bishop Tripp was rushing off somewhere and accepted our invitation to dinner during the week.

I cooked the dinner and after the meal Bishop Tripp said he was impressed that Stephen was willingly pursuing the prospect of us being married in the Church. He added that usually the wife has to drag the reluctant husband along. Well, I have to admit I felt blessed, loved and proud to have such a husband, he was determined as if on a mission! Bishop Tripp collected all the information Stephen gave him including when and where Stephen was born and where his two marriages took place. Two weeks later the Bishop called to say that he had found the church at Shrewsbury where Stephen was baptised as a baby and it is a Catholic Church. Stephen was not confirmed in the church because his parents moved away and eventually became Quakers. Stephen had been married in the Anglican Church during one of his marriages and in a registry office only for the other and that might work in our favour. Now the next step was for Stephen to be confirmed in the Catholic Church. The Bishop arranged for Stephen to have Catechism lessons with him personally. This lasted a few months and both men relished their time together. The Bishop admitted to me that he was finding Stephen's questions challenging and that his degree in theology was being fully tested by his discussions with Stephen. I knew what he meant, I was glad that someone more qualified in Theology like Bishop Tripp was now answering Stephen's questions about faith. The pressure was no longer on me. I tried to let my character speak for my faith, to Stephen, and luckily my Mother and my siblings were good examples. Besides, we all considered Stephen to be a most gentle, kind hearted, considerate and caring man. Once he said.

"Why would God have time for me now, when I have not exactly made time for him, especially after all I have done and the ones I failed to do?"

"You have children of your own and sometimes they only remember they have a father when they need something from you, I have never heard you complain or turn them away. If you, a mere man, can be that caring for your children, think how much more love God would shower on you, when you at last go to him." I explained.

Stephen was searching tirelessly and I loved him even more for it. Bishop Howard Tripp was more like an uncle to us, he liked Stephen's relentless search for God. When Bishop Tripp visited Lourdes he turned up at our house with a container of Holy Water for us. During one of his visits to the Vatican he came back with the best present we could have ever asked for. It was the answer to my prayers and a confirmation that Stephen and I had found favour in God's eyes! To me it spelt the words our Lord Jesus said to a few people in the Bible "your sins are forgiven you, go and sin no more." Bishop Tripp had brought back with him a special Papal Dispensation from the Pope John Paul 11 (Saint John Paul), that Stephen and I had his permission to get married in the Catholic Church! God be praised forever! Halleluiah!!!!!!!!

We arranged the wedding for two weeks' time, notified the family and a few friends. Before we received the Special Dispensation from Saint John Paul, we had switched from St Elizabeth's Church to Our Lady Queen of Peace Church, East Sheen, in the Roman Catholic Diocese of Southwark where Sebastian was now in the nursery. The Parish Priest was Monsignor Anthony Reynolds. It was the perfect choice for our wedding for so many reasons. We were incredibly blessed to have had Howard Tripp the Bishop of Southwark, Canon Francis Davy's of St Elizabeth's Church (who was born on St Stephen's day) and Monsignor Anthony Reynolds from Our Lady Queen of Peace officiating at our wedding. Apart from the honour of having a Bishop, a Canon and a Monsignor as the celebrants of our wedding, it was a simple and no frills affair during which Stephen's Confirmation ceremony also took place. My seamstress, Gloria, made my wedding dress and the Bridesmaids dresses to my designs in record time. I made myself a beaded turban, as I wanted one physical keepsake of our Church wedding. On the day a few adjustments needed to be done to the dress, but it did not matter, I was getting married to Stephen in the Catholic Church. And, for the first time in many years, I was going to receive the Eucharist. After that, everything else was secondary. I did not want a big wedding. I hoped my simple wedding would result in a happy and lasting marriage. Stephen's father was his best man and my uncle Dele Nwajei gave me away, as it was too short notice to arrange for my father's visa. Emma, Anouska and Annabel were three of my bridesmaids the fourth, was the daughter of a police officer from Richmond police, Martin Webster. Sebastian was the ring bearer and pageboy and had to be carried by Stephen throughout the wedding ceremony. I was touched that Sandra allowed her daughter Anouska to be a bridesmaid at the wedding. Guests included David Roland, the famous financier with whom Stephen was working on a deal, the lovely Ann Diamond and Mike Hollingsworth, her husband at the time. The reception was held in the City of London where Annabel, one of my stepdaughters, had arranged the reception at a restaurant, which she managed.

When Sebastian was a baby and I wanted to be at home with him and Emma. I gave a lot of time to charities and ended up being busier than I would have liked. I ended up juggling too many things and gave lots of free shows for all the charities that I had chosen to support. There were many of them and mostly, I paid my own musicians when I did charity shows. The share numbers of shows made it financially crippling for me.

I was either a committee member or patron of charities including Terence Higgins Trust, Barnardos, SOS, Sickle Cell, Eastside Educational Trust,

Grandparents Association, Help the Aged, Stars Organization for Cerebral Palsy and many more.

During this period, I started various businesses including a fashion line, a jewellery collection sold on QVC with the help of my friend Karen Youdell. I had art exhibitions of my paintings in London Galleries, something that I continue to do. I made and beaded a lot of my stage costumes until I finally found Gloria, my dressmaker. Gloria was not married to the idea of using patterns for dressmaking, which fact appealed to me. It was fun working on costume designs with her. She was not greedy and had many smart customers, especially during the Ascot and Epsom seasons. When travelling on trains, I would utilize my time by beading and sewing sequins onto my costumes. I even beaded my jumpers.

When Emma and Sebastian's large room got so filled with toys, I decided to build a toy box at home. I went to the builder's merchants to buy planks. I could not find a toy box large enough, but mine was well built and it has so far lasted over 30 years and will be used for Dante, my grandson.

I did lots of cooking; I learnt to make Chinese, African, Indian, Mexican and other dishes for Emma and Sebastian for after school. Stephen made the casseroles and English dishes, especially cooking the Christmas Turkey. His Turkey stuffing is famous. With such a large family, especially when my nieces and nephews came to stay with us for summer holidays, Stephen's casseroles were very convenient and delicious.

I wrote songs, and even wrote my own musical "Sun Dance" along the way. Though I'm not a trained choreographer, I am fairly good at African dances, so I ended up doing some of the choreographing, designing and making costumes for the show. I even designed the costumes I wore as 'Carmen' in Carmen Jones. I produced and starred in "Blues in the Night" a jazz musical at the Bromley Theatre. I also co-produced my Channel 4 TV series "The Patti Boulaye Show".

When I developed a knee problem from the early days of the aerobics craze and step-exercise, I stumbled on to Pilates at Pineapple Studios. My first trainer was Michael King, but I soon switched to Gordon Thompson's Body Control Studios in South Kensington. Gordon used to be a ballet dancer and became the first close friend I acquired after twenty years in show business. Gordon was adored by Emma, Stephen and me equally, a very special man. His nickname for me was 'Brown Bear' and I called him 'Frog' as he had a love of frog ornaments of all kinds. I was in his Pilates class on the day before I gave birth to Sebastian and I returned to class 3 days later, stitches and all! I had to prepare for my appearance on a TV show singing in front of Mohammed Ali at Henry Cooper's 50th birthday celebrations at the Hilton, Park Lane. During the performance, I could have fed 12 babies with the amount of milk I was producing. I met the great man, my hero Mohammed Ali, with my costume soaked with milk! His was the first autograph I had ever requested of all the stars I had met.

The beauty and blessing of being in show business is the opportunity to meet some wonderful people and some not so wonderful. I met and appeared in Jimmy Saville's 'Jim will Fix it'. I can only describe him as a bushman (African term for an uncouth person) who thought he was the king of England or show business. A lot of people I met at the time were as empty and as big headed as he was. Charlton Heston was dislikeable, while Richard Attenborough left me not wanting to ever show respect again to any other older famous personality. He was so rude, however, the tennis champion, Arthur Ash, was unassuming and pleasant. I took on the, how shall I put it "old fashioned" comedian Bernard Manning during Bob Monkhouse's 'Celebrity Squares' and came out on top. It was a TV Christmas Special and all the celebrities were dressed up as Father Christmas. Bernard Manning had to guess the celebrity behind the disguise. When it came to guessing who I was, "It's Red Rum!" He joked, referring to a famous horse of the time. Without thinking I replied, "No darling, it's Black Beauty!" I got a bigger laugh than he did much to the silly man's annoyance.

I worked with Willie Rushton, a nice man with troubled, yet smiling eyes, he presented me with a sketch of the two of us arm in arm. I treasure the sketch he did! I met and worked with many others like Robert Powell who played the quintessential Jesus in the 'Jesus of Nazareth' TV series. He played the part so well that it's hard to imagine Jesus excluding his portrayal. It is a great shame that he seems to want to turn his back on the famous role. Des O'Connor CBE was fun to work with on his TV show, so was Nick Owen, and Ann Diamond on their programme, lovely people! I also appeared with my friend, Simon Callow and my wonderful friend Ann Mitchell, in a very "bloody" play and the hard drinking, but unique Tommy Cooper on his TV show. Others stars I have worked with and met include, Philip Schofield, Barry Cryer OBE, my favourite songwriters, Les Reed and Barry Mason, Des Lynam OBE, Bruce Forsyth, Jimmy Tarbuck, Cilla Black, crazy Freddie Starr, Roy Hudd, spiky but loveable Jim Davidson, Max Bygraves OBE, Stan Boardman, Ken Dodd, Gloria Hunniford, Roger Moore, Michael Jackson (my favourite), Sir Cliff Richard, Robert Stack (Eliot Ness), Sir John Mills, the gentle giant Steven Segal, Sir Patrick Stewart OBE (another favourite), Peter Cook and the lovely Dudley

Moore, Jonathan Miller, gorgeous Mel Gibson, adorable Elijah Wood, the lovely Joanna Lumley, the lovely and gentle Patrick Swayze, Linda Carter, Christopher Reeves, the lovely Adam Faith, Marie Helvin, Bianca Jagger, Frankie Howard, Diana Ross, Tom Jones, Denis Waterman, Lulu, Britt Eckland, Stephanie Beacham, Helen Mirren, Joseph Fiennes, Kevin Spacey, Stephanie Powers, Francesca Annis, funny and adorable Jess Conrad, high kicking Christopher Lee, handsome and charming Rob Lowe, Lord Jeffrey Archer, Dame Mary Archer, Frankie Vaughan and so many more.

Footballers who have helped me with my charity include the lovely Thierry Henry, shy and gentle Lauren Etame-Mayor (Arsenal's former Right Back). I met Julio Batista, gorgeous Robin Van Persie, Emmanuel Adebayor, Guillem Balague, big-hearted Didier Drogba who appeared in my charity concert at the Royal Albert Hall, Chris Hughes, John Barnes and lovely goal keepers David James and David Seaman.

Art Exhibitions

Following a favour by Karen Youdell, a friend of mine, I painted a personal thank you card for her. She was surprised I could paint. It so happened at the time that a friend of hers was planning an art exhibition in London's Golden Square. Karen was looking for a celebrity to open the exhibition. She asked if I would do it and also exhibit some of my work. Well I did not have proper paintings at that time. Having exhibitions had not entered my mind. I had six weeks to prepare before the exhibition. I worked hard at it, starting with postcards and then bigger cards. Eventually I went on to canvas using acrylic paints. This first exhibition led to another seven or eight in other London art galleries in Soho and Mayfair and Hampstead over the years. Lord Archer was kind enough to open my first exhibition in Mayfair during the time he was running for Mayor of London. He had to break his schedule and I will always be grateful, because we got some super press, including the Financial Times, and lots of pages on my work in a top poplar Magazine. Now all sorts of people have my paintings on their walls!

Burglary at Richmond 1984

Aret (Emma) was aged eight and Sebastian was six months old when we had an armed robbery in our home in Richmond. I was in the kitchen with my niece Yinka, who was staying with us at the time. It was early evening and I was cooking. Stephen was in London at work, when a strange man walked down the stairs to the kitchen waving a sawn-off shotgun! He was wearing a balaclava and black gloves. My first reaction was amusement. I thought it was a joke. 'Beadle's About' or 'Candid Camera' or some such pranksters. My niece was nervous. Sebastian was playing on the floor.

"Don't nobody move, this is a robbery!" said the man. He had green eyes, bad teeth and reddish hair. I could see some strands of strawberry blond hair through a tear in his balaclava. I laughed at his words. It was surreal! "Take off your jewellery!' I did as I as told. I handed him all the jewellery I was wearing, rings bracelets, earrings and my Cartier watch. Not recognizing what it was he handed me back the Cartier watch, I put it in my pocket. I did not show any reaction. He had obviously never seen a 'Cartier Santos'. Apart from my engagement ring, it was the most expensive piece I was wearing.
"Where is the safe?"
"I wouldn't be wearing this much jewellery if we had a safe" I said.
"Let's look upstairs." He said, aggressively waving the gun.
Baby Sebastian made a baby noise. He was crawling on the kitchen floor when the robber surprised us. I spoke to my petrified niece in Efik:
"Pick up the baby and stay calm".

Half way up the stairs, the robber doubled back to lock the front door. This set off the alarm system. Meanwhile, I was having strange flashes of Stephen coming back and finding us all lying in a pool of blood. I began to pray the 'Our Father" in my mind. I kept thinking; Stephen does not deserve this!
"Oh dear! The police will be here soon!" I said to the man as the shrill alarm bells rang, hoping to shorten his stay.
He got panicked! He scaled the stairs to catch up with me. Just when he got to the top, Aret came out of the bathroom. She surprised him! His reaction was to grab her by the hair. Instinctively I grabbed his wrist, digging my nails into his flesh. His hands were shaking. For some reason this made me feel in control.
"It's alright, it's only my child!"

As I felt his grip on Aret's hair loosen, I let go of his wrist reminding him he had set off the alarm. He ushered me into the main bedroom. I immediately noticed a very expensive gold necklace Stephen had bought me on the dressing table. It was next to a fashion pearl necklace of little value that baby Sebastian loved to play with. I covered the gold necklace and at the same time I picked up the necklace with pearls and handed it to him. My heart began to race! I hoped he had not noticed me cover the other necklace! It would have infuriated him! So far I was managing to calm him down. I tried to keep all my words friendly and conversational. I joked about it not being his day, told him he had not planned it well. I even suggested he should take all that he wanted; "They are all old and used, pity you couldn't squeeze the entire house, into your bag and take that with you! That way you can rob it at your leisure!' I was relieved he had not noticed what I had done! I was developing verbal diarrhoea as a way of covering up my fear.

I can't remember exactly how long he was in the house. In the end he locked us all in the front bedroom, which was Aret's room. We heard him break the back door as he made his escape. All he had to do was turn the handle! The back door was unlocked at the time. We raised the alarm by shouting to a woman walking by with her daughter. They got our neighbour to call the police who got to us in record time. The police informed me as they arrived that they had received a call from a national newspaper about the robbery. Apparently, the robber had called the newspapers. Shame he hadn't given his name. Though he did come back to the house. This time he was intercepted when Stephen spotted him stalking by the pool and shone a powerful torch onto him, he ran away! According to the police, criminals almost always return to the scene of their crime. He claimed to the press to have robbed me of £100,000 of jewellery, but that was nonsense.

Chapter Thirty One: Politics

At one event in the late 70s, Stephen introduced me to Sir Basil and Lady Feldman. They both had smiling eyes, which matched their kind spirits. Stephen had known Sir Basil through Laurie Marsh, a property tycoon who also had a distinguished career in theatre, cinema ownership and filmmaking. Stephen had sold the lease of the Cambridge Theatre and was working with Laurie to float Laurie's company on the stock Market through a "shell" company Stephen had controlled. Laurie's company owned the Classic and Essoldo Cinemas chains in the 70s. I became very fond of Lord and Lady Feldman. I was comfortable in their presence, which was a rare thing for me in those days. Lord Feldman, as he later became, introduced Stephen and me to Conservative Party events. I sang at a few of these events and even gave a speech in the main room of one of the Conferences with an African point of view with Mrs Thatcher present. We had met Prime Minister Mrs Thatcher and members of her cabinet earlier. At one of my visits to Number 10, I was impressed that Mrs Thatcher served us tea herself and was as concerned about the drivers left outside in the cold as she was about her guests. She made sure that the drivers were looked after. I was amused that her husband and Roald Dahl were hunched up in a corner with their gin and tonics whispering away interspersed with the occasional guffaw.

It was not until John Major became Prime Minister that I showed much real interest in politics. Quite frankly, I hadn't really given the differences between the Parties any thought. Mrs Thatcher was still Prime Minister when John Major, the then First Secretary to the Treasury, was being interviewed on television. I was in the kitchen when Stephen called me in to watch his interview. There was something about him, a freshness and integrity, which came across. He looked vaguely familiar, as if I had met or seen him somewhere in Nigeria when I was a child, which was possible as he had been with a bank there for a short time. Here was a man who obviously cared and meant what he was saying, not many people, especially not politicians, could come across as sincerely as he did.
"This man will be Prime Minister! He is brilliant!" Stephen predicted and I agreed with him.

Sir Basil had invited Stephen and me to sit on the stage behind Mrs Thatcher when she made one of her speeches at Wembley. The speech was aimed at families. I learnt one vital thing from her. How important time keeping is for an effective public speaker. From where we were seated behind her, I could see and observe her actions; the way she placed her left hand so she could keep an eye on the time. She delivered her speech timed to ten minutes exactly. I was used to African leaders who, once in front of the microphone, would go on until their audiences were asleep and no one could remember what the speech was about anyway. A good public speaker can say all that needs to be said in ten minutes!

Michael Heseltine had challenged Mrs Thatcher for the leadership of the Conservative Party towards the end of 1990. After Mrs Thatcher ended her 11 years as Prime Minister by abandoning her plans to contest her re-election, John Major announced he would stand for the leadership of the Party and won and was duly appointed Prime Minister the next day. A few years later, in 1992 I was back at Wembley, this time supporting John Major to win his second term as Prime Minister, he had taken over from Mrs Thatcher and became Prime Minister in 1990 without an election. From the minute I met John Major, I knew I was in the presence of a sincere and different politician. I had met many British politicians of all parties during Mrs Thatcher's government and something always bothered me, they either appeared too hungry, too mean or too eager. They never seemed genuinely interested in anyone for longer than a few seconds before their eyes wandered in search of more interesting or more important persons. But John Major was different his Integrity was palpable. I made many enemies in the entertainment industry as well as the media for turning up and being photographed at Conservative events. I was not invited to either Labour or Liberal events, until years later. I was simply interested in the British people not their politics, but soon learnt how vicious British politics can be. One Party saw me as being too posh and above my station for a black person and the other I was told invited me because they saw me as classy, intelligent and different from the norm. It was flattering not to be told I had to be a certain way as a black person. That appealed to me.

When John Major took over from Mrs Thatcher as Prime Minister I wanted to be able to vote for him and I was glad that I was a British Subject by then. When he stood at the General Election in 1992, I was proud to have been invited to attend his final Rally before the results of the General Election were announced. The General Election was called for 9 April 1992, we prayed that that John would win and when the opportunity came to support him I jumped at it. I liked his natural down-to-earth approach. Unlike most of his critics I felt that he was not a hypocrite. Experiencing, after my arrival in Britain, 'the winter of discontent' during James Callaghan's Labour Government, I was not personally convinced by the

Kinnock slick campaign and neither was Britain. Yet, even at the last minute, on the night of the election, everything pointed to a slight Kinnock lead.

Lots of celebrities were invited along with me to John Major's final Rally, but on the day, in 1992, the celebrities stayed away, believing John was going to lose. For whatever reason, The Times Newspaper used a picture of me greeting the victorious John Major on its front page the next day. I could not have foreseen the negative impact which that photo of me, as a black artiste, publicly supporting a Conservative Prime Minister, would have on my career particularly with certain sections of the media. For an otherwise forward looking generation they permanently looked back to Enoch Powell, painting all Conservatives with the same brush. It's like condemning this generation of white people for the slave trade of the past. Anyway John Major won and we were very happy in our household!

I had developed a love for the British people whose good points far outweigh the bad. As I travelled the world, it was easy to appreciate how the Brits with their character came to conquer most of the world and create a huge empire. They have such discipline, fortitude and inventive genius. It was also easy to see how they came to lose it all. The respect, strength and unity that the Queen, as head of the British Monarchy commands worldwide, has sustained the country's reputation to a great extent, but, sadly by ridiculing it's old traditions, like the "for God and Country" spirit, whilst trying to appear cool, the country has slowly lost a lot of the respect it once had.

I was just beginning to understand British politics and the differences between the Parties, but in reality I had supported John Major, the man. I was amazed at the aggression and nastiness he had to put up with, not least from his own party.
"Are these people fighting to make a difference in the lives of their constituents or is it all about the interests of their Party?" I asked Stephen. "They are fighting for both, but, in truth, most of them have good intentions." Was his answer and it stuck in my mind especially since modern politicians in my own country, Nigeria, appeared to have different and financial reasons for going into politics. I had no interest in being in politics myself. Being a politician is not for the faint hearted! You can't please everyone all the time.

As always wisdom lies with Her Majesty the Queen: following the death of Diana, Princess of Wales, in 1997, John Major was appointed as Special Guardian to Princes William and Harry, with responsibility for administrative and legal matters. He became chairman of the Queen Elizabeth Diamond Jubilee Trust In February 2012.

After the negative re-action to the picture of me supporting John Major, you would think that I would have learnt to stay away from politics. But, as always, I go wherever life leads me, trusting God. When William Hague became leader of the Conservative Party soon after they lost the election, I was asked to help promote the Party to ethnic minorities. The Party's reputation since Enoch Powell had been greatly damaged as far as the black population was concerned. Some members of the party under John Major's leadership were already trying to change the Party's attitudes and he even appointed the first black Lord, Lord Taylor. This was lost on the black population at the time. Now William Hague, as leader of the Party, wanted to introduce more MPs from the ethnic minority. I was asked to help the party promote this new outlook. I am against telling people which party to vote for, but it seemed there was, at that moment, a chance for Black and Asian people to interact with the Party and gain access to the Houses of Parliament as individual members. It was an opportunity to break barriers and become part of future governments of this country and so I was happy to do what I could. Michael Ancram was Chairman of the Party at the time. I liked him, he had a fun side to him as a musician and he does a wicked Buddy Holly! After my meeting at Conservative Party Headquarters, a press call was arranged. There were many more press than I would normally have attracted. I got nervous! First question: "Are you going into politics?" I knew where this was going! I explained my reasons for being there and that I wanted to encourage the ethnic minorities to be more involved in the campaign for the first Mayor of London and the London Assembly. The next day, the headline in one of the papers screamed, "Patti Runs for Mayor". This was followed by many requests for interviews. I asked Stephen to make sure that he taped my answers so that I could refute further misrepresentation of my words. The next interview was for a left wing broadsheet newspaper, it was clear that the paper believed that any black person who supported the Conservative Party was fair game. They libelled me, I sued and they had to pay damages and destroy all copies of the article in every media. I am also bound not to give details.

Months later, a journalist let slip that the order had come from Tony Blair's Number 10 to dig up everything negative they could find on me. The fact that I had been in the notorious show 'Hair' led the journalists to think that there was bound to be some drug story they could unearth. When nothing could be found the newspaper resorted to making up outrageous headlines for which they had to pay. The headlines were meant to be very detrimental to me. When the Conservative head office was told about the headline,

Michael Ancram called me to verify the quote. I rang the Newspaper's editor to tell him I had a taped copy of the interview. But he said he was going with his headline and the mud would stick even if they were forced to withdraw the article later. When I put the phone down I prayed that whatever the editor and the journalist had planned for me would be their own destiny! Their article made my children's life hell! Not surprisingly the black population and black newspapers wanted to believe what the newspaper had said and a few Africans and Afro-Caribbean people berating me in public. Some left wing people were very aggressive and believed the article. But many people said it was a badly written article, and the front-page headline, which was followed by a two-page article, had no connection with the headline. The honeymoon that the new government was having with the press would not last forever and I have lived long enough to see it all unravel and crumble as all such things do. My transcript of the interview was sent to the Court. I was grateful to be represented by Edward Garnier QC, a brilliant and wonderful man. It took just a few minutes for the Judge to order that the article be struck off all records with damages paid with an apology to me by the newspaper concerned.

Despite such venom from the press and the government's spin doctors, it was nevertheless decided between Sir Richard Ottaway MP (who had taken on the role of my fairy godfather), and some other members of the Shadow Cabinet that I should run for the London Assembly. This was to keep the press off my back. The journalists were looking for any signs of racism towards me from the Party. There was none! I found the shadow cabinet to be very welcoming and helpful. Members of the Shadow Cabinet with the help and support of William Hague, Sir Richard Ottaway and Michael Ancram helped to prepare me. The training and advice I received from Richard Ottaway and Jeffrey Archer, who was a candidate for the first Mayor of London during William Hague's leadership, became a blessing for the future. I will always be grateful to all of them for helping me lose the fear of public speaking.

Lord Archer and Lord Basil Feldman became my referees during the campaign. My name was put forward to the 14 constituencies. I sailed through nine of them with ease, causing a bit of irritation among the longstanding political candidates. One particular black female candidate for The London Assembly was vitriolic. Of course, I am glad I quietly dropped out before the final election process because I definitely did not want to be a politician, but the experience was beneficial and constructive for me.

Chapter Thirty Two: Being a Mother and Grandmother

"There is nothing more powerful than the prayers of a mother for her children!" Anon.

Like most modern parents, after I became a mother I had to work a lot of the time and suffered the usual guilt feelings. We employed nannies, but that only made the guilt feeling worse. Mummy scolded me about employing nannies and not being there, so I gave up travelling, though Emma had travelled with me quite a lot of the time before she started nursery and school. I tried to structure our relationship and instil boundaries. The habits she had learned from the nannies were not helpful, so I became a little too strict! But she was such a beautiful and loving child. At six years old Emma was young enough to learn new rules. She was not allowed to waste food, watch adult television or visit friends' houses if I didn't know the parents, but she felt the benefit of having a two-parent family. Stephen was well practiced at being there for his children, even if it meant burning the candle at both ends! His energy, sense of duty and patience was very helpful. I was determined not to do what guilt-ridden parents often do; make ourselves feel better by making up for being away by letting the children get away with everything they want. It wasn't easy, but I stood my ground and enforced the rules. I tried hard not to be a typical tough Nigerian mother, but in the end that was what I was comfortable with. That was what I respected because my mother was wise, strong, strict and full of unconditional love. That's the kind of mother I wanted to be. She had inherited one stepdaughter and loads of hostile in-laws. Here I was in my early twenties blessed with four stepdaughters and two ex-wives!

I wanted Emma and also Sebastian to be able to stand their ground, be strong enough to be able to sit on their own, even when they are in a crowd of people. Emma had four half-sisters who, with inevitable sibling jealousies, were sometimes a bit cruel to her, but she was learning that it can be tough out there.

Both our children had to learn good manners and to be on their best respectful behaviour out of the home. But we also had to let them know how much they were loved. Emma was getting stricter rules at home than her other classmates, and naturally this seemed a bit excessive to her at the time, compared to the free spirited approach of some of the other parents. Being in show business, in a mixed marriage and very high profile at the time was a drawback for both Emma and Sebastian. People automatically assumed that I would not be a good mother and that my children would be spoilt and acted accordingly. Teachers' expectations were based on this assumption and some of them picked on my children for no reason. But, without fail, they later had to admit that they had been wrong.

I didn't want my children to rely too much on other people, if possible they had to be independent. I relied on help from my own Mother, drawing from her past experiences in bringing up her own many children and other people's children in the most appalling circumstances, as I had recounted earlier.

I took motherhood day by day and tackled each new experience at a time and I wanted the children to be able to stand up for their own principles no matter what others were doing or saying around them.

Being a mother myself helped me to understand why my mother would have taken a bullet for me. There can be no greater gifts than my children, the love of my family and my husband. Like my mother, I felt the same way about my children and still do. I had no idea, that this was obvious to my daughter, who, when at the age of eleven, her class was given an assignment to do a drawing of an animal; that best describes their mother. My daughter, who is a very good artist, painted a black panther. When the teacher asked why she had chosen a panther, she said;
"My mother is black and beautiful, but would tear anyone to pieces who messes with her children, just like a panther."

Emma (Aret) Komlosy

When Emma (who prefers the name Aret, which is her middle name and her grandmother's Efik name), was six years old, one early evening, she and I were shopping after school. We ran into one of the mothers and her six-year-old daughter whom Emma liked to play with. I was shocked to hear the child rudely interrupt her mother during our conversation. Emma froze when the child said, "oh shut up" to her mother. When they walked away an amazed Emma was confused by the fact that the child's mother did not scold her for such bad behaviour. She looked up at me;
"Mummy, she said 'shut up" to her mummy, she was very rude!"

"I know she was darling, her mother is a silly woman not to tell her off. I know you wouldn't think of saying something like that to your Mummy"
Emma shuddered at the very thought of it.

"I am proud of you darling. You were wise enough to know it was bad of her to be rude to her mother." I added.

I loved taking Emma on shopping trips. They presented many opportunities to learn and teach my child commonsense and moral lessons. Emma had ballet lessons at Madame Vacani before finding her forte and excelled in swimming when Stephen started teaching her to swim at home.

There was a child Emma played with while she was at St Catherine's Junior School in Twickenham. I was not comfortable with this child who seemed to be eight years going on twenty. She was a bit too knowing for her age. I kept my eyes and ears open. One day I realized why she was so forward. I gave her a lift home after she had been for a pizza with us. That poor little girl at the age of eight had the keys to the front door of her house. Her parents were still not back from work. She was being brought up by the television! Her parents were usually still at work, hours after she got home from school. That was the end of that friendship. I felt terrible for the child. My traditional African instinct was to take her home with us every day. Get her and Emma to do their homework together. Let her parents know where to collect her after work. "Every woman should be a mother to every child!" I remembered my mother's words. If the child was African, that's what I would have done. But this was a different culture.

Emma easily passed the 11 plus secondary school exam and got a place in Putney High School. After nine months at the school, she had her twelfth birthday. I knew she had two close friends. I drove her to school each day. In the car, I asked questions about school and her friends. I had no time for the headmistress, of the school. It was obvious she had already judged Emma as being a spoilt child without having the sense to observe the child before passing judgment. I had advised Emma after meeting the head of the school to avoid the silly woman.

As for her classmates, we invited the entire year to Emma's birthday party, hired a bus to take them to the 'Rolling Stones' Sticky Fingers in Kensington and then a swimming party afterwards. This gave me time to observe the behaviour and character of the girls. At the end of the day, I sat Emma down and told her that the only real friend she had was Arabella, her friend from junior school. Arabella had joined St Catherine's toward the end of Emma's time there and her parents were lovely and so was Arabella. The two friends that Emma had taken to at Putney High were not to my liking.

I felt my job was to protect my children while I could. I had been to hell and back in my childhood and seen some of the pitfalls that lay ahead for children. Sadly, we learned years later, that one of the girls Emma had taken to was heavily involved with drugs, which ended in suicide! The school was just typical of a lot of modern schools, full of regulations, while any attempt by teachers to care about students' behaviour was quashed. Putney High School fired a teacher because the parents had complained when she called the rowdy bunch of badly behaved pupils 'ruddy kids'. When we received the letter about the silly incident, Emma told us the students had deserved stronger words than that from the teacher. When we came out in support of the teacher, we were the only parents without complaint in the entire class according to the headmistress. The teacher was fired.

Years later, when my children were in their 20s, I worked with members of once notorious rock bands. I was shocked to see bottles of gin and whisky on stage from which they often drank during the show. I wondered how they could keep a clear head, enough to give a performance. When we came off stage I was quite taken aback that after consuming so much alcohol they were still coherent. They simply laughed and said the bottles were filled with water.
"But why?" I asked.
Well, since they had this "wild boy" image in the media, this was one way of not disappointing the fans and spoiling the image. I didn't know whether to be angry or disappointed. All I could think was, thank God I had the sense to teach my children that things are not always what they seem. Some young people could easily have been misled and could have put their lives at risk as the result of copying such musicians' example. It's a dishonest and difficult world for children to survive in!

I was once advised that by teaching my children politeness it would make them subservient! Those who have good manners have peace and, confidence and they are usually welcomed wherever they go. Good mannered people, whether rich or poor, command respect.

As we are what we read, see, watch and hear, I banned adult television. We had to fill the extra time with activities. Emma did not take to ballet at Madame Vacani's unlike her older half-sisters who ended up at the Royal Ballet School. So we took up swimming when she was ten years old. For five years we spent almost every weekend at swimming pools from Twickenham to Crystal Palace, Bristol, Brighton and many more towns in the UK so that Emma could take part in the weekly competitions. The discipline helped Emma get homework done on time. Emma was training every day after school so she had to complete her homework before the training sessions. I'm sure this discipline was partly responsible for her achieving the best result in Britain in Legal Reasoning during her second year as a Law student at Westminster University. She won trophies and medals at Surrey Championships and at the Nationals at Crystal Palace at the age of eleven and gold medal as the British Junior backstroke champion. As a swimmer she was graceful and beautiful to watch and very strong. Her elegant style had been taught to her by Stephen at home in our swimming pool. During competitions she would make the sign of the cross on the starting block. I used the opportunity to point out that everyone else in the competition is God's child. The one that works the hardest gets the extra help to win.

Being a poolside mum was a lesson on interesting parents. I liked the parents for their selfless dedication to their children's interests, but of course, every competitive situation has its dark side and some of the parents were a little too pushy.

I had given up working and travelling at this time to concentrate on Emma and Sebastian, but I was doing lots of voluntary charity work, whenever I could. Stephen and I took turns taking Emma to her training every morning at 5.30am and after school from 6.00pm. Some days we drove for an hour to Crystal Palace's fifty meters pool, but mostly just to Ealing Swimming Pool, which was nearer. It was tiring, but meant the four of us were always together as a family at the weekends because Emma usually had a competition to go to. I was so very proud of her, it put a lot of pressure on her, but it was a great opportunity for her to learn endurance, hard work, faith and how to handle failure as well as success. She learnt how to be competitive and remain kind. She took it all head on. She has a wonderful sense of humour and can mimic anyone without being bitchy. Sebastian grew up spending most weekends at his sister's swimming competitions. He loved it and we took lots of toys with us so that we could play with him during the boring waiting times.

As she turned fifteen I noticed the boys' reactions around her at competitions. At one of those 5.30am starts at Wandsworth training pool a parent joked about her son taking a fancy to Emma. Her tone annoyed me. It wasn't an innocent remark and I certainly wouldn't let her son near my daughter. It was too early in the morning. I was irritable.
"If he comes anywhere near my daughter, I'll castrate him!" I said.

The words came out before I had time to think, but it had the desired effect. I decided there and then that we would wind down on the swimming. I was still contemplating whether it was time to bow to her wish to quit swimming. Her name was on the list for the British Team trials picked to try for the next Olympics. Emma was good at all the strokes and had won over 100 medals, gold, silver and bronze, for backstroke, breaststroke, front crawl, the butterfly and the medley. She had developed swimmer's shoulders and was beginning to hate it. Her GCSE' Exams were around the corner. We decided together that her education had to come first. She had learnt all the lessons and discipline she needed from the competitive experience. She now had time to prepare for her exams. She became good at cooking and looking after the house and her baby brother.

I did not allow any sibling rivalry between Emma and Sebastian. The first time they got into a big and tearful argument, I punished them both. I didn't want to know who was at fault. I made it clear that fighting or argument equalled punishment for both. There was a tearful reconciliation when I told them:
"In the end we are all alone! You two only have each other to rely on. Emma, God gave us Sebastian, so that you would not be alone. Sebastian, if anything happens to me, Emma is the only mother you will have. It's the two of you against the world! If I should die and you two don't get on, I will not be at peace. That means I will come back and haunt you! So if you don't want an angry ghost following you around, you better get on!"
I was hoping that the ghost thing would be effective. I had not banked on mention of my dying being the most effective. They both started crying, hugging me;
"Mummy you are not going to die!" cried my two babies. I was moved and sorry to make them cry. I promised I wasn't going anywhere as long as they never quarrelled. It worked and I thank God that I have never heard them quarrel since then. I am proud of the love and consideration they have for each other. That's more than any mother could ask for!

I did set a rule for Emma about boyfriends. No boyfriends before the age of seventeen and half. She kept to that even though as a beautiful girl she had started modelling with a top agency. One day Emma complained about her friends describing their mothers as being their friends.
"Darling, God willing, there will be time for all that! But right now my job is to be your mother."
While Emma was studying Law at Westminster University, she worked hard for days on her thesis. The night before she was due to hand it in to the university, she lost the entire work she had written when her computer went down. She cried as if her world had come to an end. I understood her pain, but self-pity was not the answer. While everyone was commiserating with her I told her to stop crying and start again. At that moment I think my entire family hated me and thought I had lost my marbles. I ignored

their looks, went down to the kitchen, made a cup of strong coffee and took it up to her and said:

"Drink this. We will all sit with you, but you have to start writing your thesis again. You already know what it says, just write it down." She was horrified as was everyone else.

"Darling, you have written it once, you can do it again! I know it took you days, but now you have fourteen hours before you have to hand it in."

She did it! My clever angel did it! She stayed up all night and all day and we got her to the University in time to hand in her papers! She passed with flying colours. I knew then my daughter would be able to handle anything, any situation!

In 1996, Emma was chosen to represent Nigeria in Miss World at Bangalore in India after an accident at university landed her in Nigeria to recuperate. While in Nigeria, as she was an experienced and elegant model she was asked to help prepare the participants with the Miss Nigeria Contest, to train the girls to walk like models and answer questions. Then the organisers persuaded her to enter the competition herself and she ended up being crowned winner of 'The Most Beautiful Girl in Nigeria' and was entered into the Miss World Contest. After getting her Law Degree, Emma started her own Wine importing business with her boyfriend who became her husband. Additionally, Emma became the Director of Membership at the Café Royal in London. They have a son, Dante, who is the apple of my eye. Being a grandmother is the most fun you can have in life.

Sebastian Anton Komlosy

By the time Sebastian came along, I was desperate for a brother or sister for Emma. I had not expected to become pregnant again, but I prayed and hoped. When I finally found out I was pregnant it was during a severe mood change, the worst I have ever had. It was out of character for me to have a go at Stephen and even stranger that I went into a tearful mood for a few days. Unable to pin point what was wrong with me, I blamed it on being a stepmother, which was not easy. Stephen is a quiet man, who treated everything with calm, even the unpleasant side of managing his wife's travelling, his own business and children. On my side I accepted all that happened as God's plan, with the certainty that He had my back covered.

Dear Stephen desperately tried to find out what was upsetting me. We were in the car returning from dropping off my stepdaughters when I began to cry, which was a total surprise to me as it was to Stephen. He stopped the car and tried to console me. Nothing he said worked, no matter how kind

and gentle he tried to be. I just got more irritated with him. As he desperately pushed to ascertain the cause of my tears I announced.
"I want a divorce!"
"Of course you don't!' said Stephen amused, which infuriated me more.
"Don't tell me what I want and what I don't!" I yelled.
I sounded like a child that wants something, but does not know what exactly it is that it wants. Gently Stephen added.
"Why don't we discuss it when we get home?"
"I don't want to discuss anything when we get home!"
"Do you think you might be pregnant?"
"What?" I could not believe he had said that! It was so left field and far-fetched!
"Why don't you go and see Mr Malvern, he may be able to suggest something for irregular periods!" Stephen didn't know what else to say.

Once home, Stephen made an appointment for me to see Mr Malvern my gynaecologist at Harley Street the next day. I explained to him about my outburst and tearful day. He knew me well, and had delivered Emma. He said he would not count me as a tearful and moody type so he suggested that he examine me.
"Well, you will be glad to know that your husband is right! You are pregnant and my guess would be about seven to eight weeks! Congratulations!"
"What! Are you sure?"
"Very sure!"
"Poor Stephen, I gave him such a hard time and even asked for a divorce yesterday."
"I've heard of various moods and reactions in early stages of pregnancy but not of the woman asking for divorce." Mr Malvern laughed. "I'm sure Stephen did not take it seriously."
"Didn't I tell you, you might be pregnant?" Was Stephen's reaction.
"How do you feel about it?" I asked.
"I couldn't be more delighted, the only trouble is I've run out of girls' names."

When I told Mummy the good news and said I would like to have a son for Stephen, she told me to pray sincerely and have no doubt in my mind that my prayers would be answered. I prayed, gave thanks and trusted with the faith of a child, without doubt, I was carrying Stephen's son.

Sebastian was born at Queen Charlotte's Hospital in Hammersmith. My contractions started just after 8am. He weighed in at 8lb 13oz and I had to have thirteen stitches. Stephen and Mummy were in the delivery room with me at the birth. I chose a completely natural birth. Sebastian gave me a tough time trying to push him out. It was the first time in my life that I used a swear word! Mr Malvern had remembered the trauma of my first child and had made sure that everything was kept simple this time. As soon as Sebastian came into the world, I asked Mr Malvern to hand him to Stephen, whose delight at having a son at last, was written all over his face. Mummy said in her native Efik.

"Your wonderful husband deserved to be blessed with a son!"

I thanked Mummy for giving me the strong faith not to doubt. She replied by saying, "Abasi isi kponke ndito Esie. Edi eti ufan owo!" *"God never fails us! He is a true friend."* I remember going for scans during the pregnancy and one of the nurses wanted to tell me the sex of the baby. I said I already knew that the baby was a boy. But the nurse insisted:

"I think you may be disappointed!"

I was not going to doubt my prayer. I felt like my faith was being tested by the way the nurse insisted.

We had one boy's name in mind and that was 'Sebastian', suggested by my stepdaughter Anabel and inspired by Anthony Andrew's character in *'Brideshead Revisited'*. We were all also very fond of Anthony Andrews and his family, as an actor and as a person, such a charming man!

Sebastian, like Emma was a dream baby, hardly cried unless something was terribly wrong. Mummy's method of easing a newly born baby into the world was extremely successful with both my children and her method was also stress free for me. Mummy told me it was important not to allow the baby to cry from day one by pre-empting his every need, pains and discomfort. Knowing how to wind a newly born baby is vital. As I was likely to be working at the same time, it was important that I cultivated a baby who would not be distressed by travelling or a life with irregular patterns. Mummy made sure that he was easy to look after and did not become distressed. I listened and watched everything she did, asking questions and following her advice. Babies are designed to fit into the environment around them with ease as long as the mothers know to spend baby's first four to five days avoiding those natural painful experiences that babies go through, which makes crying a habit. Crying should not became a baby's only form of letting the mother know they are in pain or discomfort. It made me think that modern methods have created more of a problem for mothers and their babies, by overriding the mother's natural instincts. In times when a baby's cry would attract human predators from forests surrounding their dwellings, the modern advice of letting babies cry would have threatened the survival of babies and the whole family. I was grateful to have had the most stress free motherhood ever; I had my Mummy and the old tried and tested African methods to thank for that.

As with Emma, I was besotted with Sebastian and my protective instincts turned me into a tigress. As usual, Stephen was the best father ever, relaxed and natural. The baby's cot was next to our bed so most nights Sebastian slept on my chest or on my arm, soon, when he was almost two months old he learnt to find the nipple by himself and so I was hardly disturbed! My two children were so easy to look after, they hardly cried, both loved bath times, smiled when they woke up and were never grumpy. Their body language was clear and easy to read. Emma and Sebastian both weaned themselves off breast milk at four and half months old, just two weeks after going on to solids. Their favourite way to help their pains with teething was chewing on cooked chicken leg bones.

Whenever I found myself with a lot to do at home, the baby would be carried on my back, African style, and secured with a wrapper. It was hysterical when Stephen tried to do the same. He had no curved buttocks on which to balance the baby. Even with the wrapper tied around him and the baby, the baby would slowly slide down Stephen's back while holding on for dear life. Even after Stephen got the hang of tying the baby securely to his back, it was still such a funny sight! I loved Stephen for his determination to try to carry the baby African style. I have never seen a man try this method.

Sebastian was a very shy and sensitive boy and took a little while to settle down at nursery. It took him a year to settle down at St Benedict Abbey School when he was four and half years old. His first teacher was a Mrs Jeanerette in whose lap he spent the entire first day at school asleep. Genuine caring is hard to come by and we never forgot her! During that first year the drive from Richmond to Ealing took anything up to an hour and a half. Sebastian would cry every day when we got to the school so Stephen and I decided to go back to the school at his break times and peer over the fence at him. This was intended to give him the impression that we were waiting outside the school for him. It was during his second year at the school that he stopped looking for us during the breaks. This all meant that I could not go back to work, though I didn't mind at all, Sebastian and Emma were more important. Stephen was incredible in taking turns to be at the school, he sacrificed so much time away from work despite being a workaholic. I Thank God for His many blessings! Sebastian's confidence grew with his next teacher, Mrs Broadwick. He did have another teacher who started off nasty and reduced him to tears, in his first few days in her class. She called him a 'silly little spoilt brat' just because the five year old could not tie his shoelaces as fast as she wanted. I decided to go to the school girded for battle with the teacher concerned! Stephen intervened and had a quiet word with her. He was worried about what I might do in my anger. He was right. I needed to let my anger subside before I could speak to her! My children were well behaved and respectful and when I was calmer I told her as much.

"If you can show me another child in your class as well behaved as Sebastian at the end of this year, I will personally apologise and eat my words."

At the end of the first term the teacher was big enough to come up to me with an apology. I was proud when she said:

"If I only had two or three children like Sebastian in my class each year, it would make teaching worthwhile and more enjoyable. He is such a gentle boy! I would advise you to enrol him in a self-defence class so he will not be bullied in the future."

This was good advice and Sebastian eventually became a brown belt in Judo and also studied Karate and had very little trouble at school. I was proud when some of the mothers noticed Sebastian's behaviour towards me. How he ran to me after school, gave me a hug, and opened the car door for me before getting in on the other side.

"What are we doing wrong? Our sons don't even acknowledge us. We get the bags dumped at our feet as they run off to play with their friends. Sebastian behaves like the perfect gentleman," remarked a group of mothers to me.

It was hard for Sebastian to make friends, since we lived so far away from the school. None of the boys lived near us. For his ninth birthday we hired a coach to take 22 nine year olds to Kingston swimming pool and Pizza Hut in Richmond then playtime in our swimming pool at home before returning them to the school in Ealing where their parents collected them. A very exhausting day indeed! Not to be repeated in a hurry!

A short while after the party, a boy invited Sebastian to a party. His mother told me she was impressed to hear her son warn the others. "Sebastian is coming to my party, there will be no swearing!" I was shocked that nine year old boys would use swear words anyway.

The only time Sebastian got into trouble at school I was to blame. He hated having long curly hair because the other boys were cruel with their teasing. I was due to start filming for a BBC TV series 'Brothers and Sisters' in a suburb of Manchester. There was no time to take Sebastian to the barber and so I decided to cut his hair myself, not realising how difficult a task it would be. He looked dreadful, but went to school with the promise we would get him to a barber after school. The headmaster would not listen to reason and was unnecessarily ugly in his approach over my botched up haircut, even after I had apologised profusely. We took Sebastian out of the school and, much to Sebastian's delight he came with me to the filming in Manchester, which lasted a week. Meanwhile, Stephen and I wrote and complained to the Monks at St Benedict's Abbey who had known Sebastian from the age of four. They intervened and I returned Sebastian to school.

When Sebastian was a teenager, two years later, he came home from school saying for the first time, that he had been involved in a fight in the classroom. He explained that he had stepped in to stop the class bully, who is a very big boy, from attacking a much smaller boy in the class. He had aimed a punch at Sebastian, who by then was a Judo expert and immediately used the Judo 'Kasogi' throw as the punch came in, hurling the boy to the floor. Sebastian assured me he broke the boy's fall so that he was not injured; only his pride was badly bruised. As it happened, the next parent/teacher's meeting was that same night and I was battle-ready for the teacher's comment regarding the fight!

During the evening we had glowing reports from teachers about Sebastian academically, and especially about his manners and generosity of spirit. His French teacher told us that Sebastian touched her heart more than any other boy. One of the other teachers told us how, after her skiing accident, she had difficulty moving around between classrooms on crutches carrying books. She wasn't one of Sebastian's teachers, but she told us that when a crowd of pupils pushed passed her, as she waited for a safe opportunity to go through a busy doorway, Sebastian was the only boy to stop the others, hold the door open and carry her books to her next class. When we finally got to his form teacher, there was no mention of the fight Sebastian had been involved in. After he had finished his glowing assessment of Sebastian, curious, I asked about the fight.
"Oh that!" he said. "We all know Sebastian would never start a fight! He is too nice and too good at Judo for anyone to take him on! Besides, I'm told the boy concerned had it coming."

For Stephen, Sebastian being his only son after five girls was a special and wonderful gift. I knew he was going to spoil the boy and so I had to play the nasty parent now and then and tried to do damage limitation. When I confronted Stephen after my Harrods' fiasco where Sebastian had misbehaved in the toy department when he was only four, Stephen broke my heart when he explained that, at his age, he wasn't sure he would see his son grow up. Thank God he has! I eased off after that, but still tried to keep a tight rein on things. I needn't have worried, our son turned out to be a sensitive, respectful and considerate gentleman like his father. I am so proud of the man and the woman my children have become. Like any mother, I would defend them with my life.

I am proud to say that I have never heard my son Sebastian say a bad word about anyone. It makes me so very happy. Sebastian now has his own successful graphic design business and fills his nights by being a very popular DJ.

Dante (Grandson)

From the moment our daughter Emma (Aret) and her husband told us she was pregnant, I knew that an angel was about to be born into our lives. They lived in Surrey and we were in Buckinghamshire. I worried that I might not be able to get to their hospital in time in the event of a short notice birth. Aret had chosen the wonderful name of 'Dante'.

My prayers were answered towards the later stage of the pregnancy. Their landlord suddenly decided that he was going to sell the flat and they had a few weeks to find somewhere else. I registered her with our doctor locally and they moved in with us. So our grandson was going to be born in a nearby hospital. Dante was born and he was fine. Thank God! I looked into our grandson's blue eyes and found God smiling gently back at me touching my very soul.

When Stephen met his new grandson it was love at first sight for both of them. Dante was born with very fair skin and dark hair. His father has black hair and I am black, but at five months he had golden locks and by the time he was eight months old we had a blond grandson! Stephen's genes must be extremely strong! However, Dante has my toes. Poor thing! I will just have to get used to people thinking I am his glamorous nanny! He is the most beautiful child! I have been the typical African grandmother, taking care of the crucial first three to four days to make sure that Dante did not learn how to cry, so that when he does cry, we know that there really is something wrong. I made sure he loved his bath times and the massage that went with it to make his muscles strong. I introduced drinking water early and I carried him on my back African style and he would go off to sleep straight away. His potty training started early at three months and he took to it easily like Aret and Sebastian did. By three months his legs were so strong he tried to walk up my chest upright and was walking unaided by the time he was one.

At the end of each Mass at Ealing Abbey, I would take Dante to the Blessed Sacrament to give thanks. This was where I prayed for a special and precious spirit and soul to be given to our daughter. My prayers were answered!

Dante has giving us so much joy. He dances every time he hears music of any kind. He loves his daily walk with his grandfather. They bond well on those walks and I sometimes join them. During the walks we stop on a railway bridge and wait for the trains. The drivers toot their horns as they roll underneath us and we wave.

Dante was baptised by our favourite monk, Dom Andrew Hughes at Ealing Abbey. It was a glorious day and he tried to climb into the baptismal font. As a grandmother, I prayed that with this beginning, God would always command the wind beneath Dante's wings and be the light that protects and guides his steps. I am eternally grateful to have lived to see the birth of my first grandchild.

I have eight step-grandchildren and a step-great-grandchild all with different characters. One of them, William, at the age of four, came home one day from school where the teacher had been trying to find out from the children, whether their parents were Catholics or Presbyterians for the purpose of first Holy Communion. William shouted out "Mum, are we Catholics or Vegetarians?"

Another grandson, Beans, who was 15yrs at the time (he is the young actor, Beans El-Balawi, with some great films and TV series under his belt already, including being Demi Moore's son in "Half Light". Beans attended Westminster Abbey Choir School, where he was head choirboy, and was asked to say grace during the family Christmas dinner. We were delighted at his enthusiasm, but his grace was short.
"Bless this bunch as they munch their lunch!"

Chapter Thirty Three: Carmen Jones

In 1992, I took over the leading role of Carmen in Simon Callow's award-winning production of *Carmen Jones* at the London Old Vic. I went on the subsequent tour of Japan and the UK in 1995.

At first, Gary Wilmot was my Joe followed by the late and loveable Blair Wilson. As Carmen Jones, I was described in an article thus. "She sizzled on the London stage as an electrifyingly carnal Carmen Jones," and the Daily Telegraph restored the musical to number one in its London Musicals List as a result of my arrival in the part. Carmen Jones was the ultimate part for me. She is my alter ego. I was in my element on stage for the years I played the character. My dangerous stage persona thrilled my husband, but I never brought her home! I got very friendly with the second Carmen from the US at The Old Vic. She visited me at home, but was shocked to see me ironing everything from bed sheets, shirts to panties. She was too much of a star 'Carmen' to do the ironing. Hers was a modern Carmen, sexy and seemingly tough. I preferred to portray Carmen as one of the alluring market women I was used to seeing in Nigeria. My Carmen was sensual, mentally tough, beautiful and fatalistic yet oblivious of life's dangers. She was acutely aware of her feminine powers, but wickedly innocent in her application of them. She was emotionally dangerous and wild with men. Men chased her because she was a shameless flirt, but not easily available. This was her greatest appeal. That was how I played her character.

Carmen was the first part I had played apart from Yum Yum in the Black Mikado that I could completely identify with. The characters couldn't have been more different, from the demure, innocent, but ambitious 'Yum Yum' to the femme fatale 'Carmen'. Both characters matched my mental and emotional age at the time. Playing Carmen provided me with the necessary emotional and spiritual strength, a sort of devil-may-care attitude that I needed in order to hold my own as the leading lady in the top musical in London at the time.

I was wary of getting too friendly with the cast in Carmen Jones after my experiences with the other musicals but, at the Old Vic I could keep my distance from the rest of the cast. Not being a party animal I could go home after each show. Stephen was a great support and was always there for me. He attended almost every one of my 700 or so performances. My only interaction with the Company of players, apart from rehearsals was to request a full cast for my press night and a prayer with some cast members before my first press showing. They obliged, thank God! Before my opening night, I was horrified to count only 15 heads on stage for a performance. That was less than half the cast. I remember one cast member calling off sick for a few days then turning up just to collect his wages. I have never called off sick in any show. "The show must go on!" I believe in this because you never know how far people have travelled to see you perform. For a while I had no understudy. I even went on stage with Malaria for two weeks in Woking during the tour after the West End.

When I was first asked to audition for the part of Carmen Jones, I backed off knowing that it was an opera. The part required a superb operatic mezzo-soprano. I had not attempted a classical piece in over twenty years. Then, months later I met Gary Wilmot at an event. I was surprised to hear he was playing the part of Joe in Carmen Jones. I went to see him in the show, but by the end of the performance I desperately wanted to play Carmen. I went away and trained with a classical opera voice coach. I tried three vocal trainers before I found a coach who did not want to turn me into a stereotype opera singer. They wanted me to adopt the famous stance of one foot in front of the other, hands clasped above the belly button, before I could begin to sing the Habanera! I knew that I could not get my teeth into the way I wanted to play such a sassy character, while restricting my movement! It was six months before I felt I was ready to approach the Company for an audition.

At my first audition, it was daunting to listen to the operatic voices booming from the speakers in the waiting room. I was tempted to run away! Thank God my audition went well. I was invited to meet the director Simon Callow over lunch. Luckily for me, after seeing the show I had already formed a complete picture of Carmen's life and what sort of background she would have had. There were so many Carmens in Nigeria, especially in the market places that I knew the lady intimately. She was easy for me to understand. I could not fathom the overtly sexy, modern Carmen, who was then being portrayed without subtlety in the show, without regard to the 1940s date of the piece. I dared to tell the director as much. Simon, it turned out had spent a bit of his childhood in Nigeria and knew from personal experience how iconic the market women of all types can be.

Arrangements were made for me to audition for the Hammerstein brothers sometime in the future. I sailed past that. Then I had to have a session with the maestro Henry Lewis, whose wife Marilyn Horne was Dorothy Dandridge's voice in the film of Carmen Jones. I purposely had never seen the film as I felt it might influence how I envisioned Carmen, so I was not as worried as I would have been had I known who Henry Lewis was. I did know that he would have the final say. Whilst going through the songs and words with Henry Lewis, I wondered how anyone could mistake such a sensual woman for a sexy one. Two very different women! I knew I had the job in the middle of "Thinkin' about you all the time......" (This is when Carmen seduces poor Joe and convinces him to desert from the army and go to Chicago with her). Rehearsing this scene with Henry Lewis made it easy for me to get into the Carmen character. The lyrics cleverly told the story. Henry laughed and said; "In all my years I have never rehearsed a more dangerous Carmen!"

"Is that good or bad?" I asked.

"Oh! I would say more than good!" he replied.

"Yeah!" I thought. "I think I have a job as Carmen Jones!"

A few days after my opening night, Stephen and I had the honour of hosting maestro Henry Lewis at dinner. He told Stephen in front of me;

"Patti is the best Carmen I have ever seen and I have seen and worked with the best!"

One massive quote for the diary, probably as good as it would ever get! I felt proud, and relaxed into the part. Panic over! Henry Lewis' words came in handy when I had to be the sole Carmen in Japan and do nine shows a week.

On my press night in London at the Old Vic I was excited and petrified. Gary Wilmot was my Joe. As I sat on the Jeep waiting for my entrance, the cast members were on stage singing; 'Good Luck Mister Flying Man.' I was busy praying for courage and a clear head. Sitting in the jeep ready to make my entrance, I had not realized I was fiddling with a part of the door lock and my thumb got stuck. The heavy gates of the set rolled up revealing the Jeep as it rolled forward into its position almost on the edge at stage centre.

"Here comes Carmen!" they sing just as Carmen's bete noire taunts her with.

"Just in Time for lunch!" I attempted to rise, but could not free my thumb. I yanked it violently in character. A sharp pain shot through my arm and my shoulders to my neck. I continued with my first line;

"Every time you open dat ol prune-puss, you make sounds I don't like."

"You can't help the war efforts by staying home in your bed!"

"Dat's what you think!" I replied laughing.

I was in terrible pain! I had completely dislocated my thumb, but I was running on adrenalin and continued to the end of the scene. It was a long and painful scene during which I had to be tied up and manhandled. I went off stage to find Stephen waiting with an ice pack. He was the only one who had noticed what had happened and had called a doctor. Meanwhile I went on for two more scenes looking forward to the 'Aria' the "Card Song". The pain served to heighten the irritation and the emotional coldness Carmen needed for the scene. When I went to deal the cards my right thumb was so dislocated and loose, it suddenly faced the opposite direction. I knocked it back into place amidst gasps from those on stage who had seen what happened. The doctor was waiting. I had just enough time for a quick painkiller shot and a firm support fitted to my thumb to keep it in place for the rest of the performance. I suffered from the accident for over two years, but I had rave reviews the next day and the front page of the Evening Standard with a picture of my bent thumb. It was then that The Telegraph re-instated the show to its top West End Show spot much to Simon's delight. The next day, I was at Covent Garden raising funds for 'Help the Aged' charity, now called Stage for Age. I don't know how Simon found me. He came rushing up the street waving newspapers in the air.

"You clever girl you did it! You clever girl, you did it!"

"What's wrong Simon, what has happened?"

"The reviews are fantastic especially the Telegraph!"

"I don't read what the critics have to say." I enjoyed his excitement. I was glad that he was pleased. The critics loved my Carmen.

"You have to read this one!" Simon read the bit in The Telegraph. He was particularly pleased about The Telegraph! The main critic had sneaked in to see the show months before. He hated what the show had become, a show that he had so highly rated, he was sad that the standard had dropped. He had written a bad article condemning the show and removed the show from the Daily Telegraph ratings. That wasn't surprising, I understand that many of the cast were missing when he last saw the show and it had become lacklustre. The diva had taken the night off leaving the understudy to struggle through with a reduced ensemble on stage. I got the feeling the company of actors didn't care. But with the rave reviews, the Telegraph had returned the show to the top of its ratings. It was worth all the work to see the delight in Simon's face. Apart from loving the role he was the best part of the show for me!

Through the ordeal of my healing thumb in the following weeks, a get-well card from the Producer would have been nice, even if they were afraid of being sued. It seemed rather cold, but I understood their dilemma. Suing the company never occurred to me. I am not union minded or anti-bosses. It was my fault for getting my finger stuck. I was not a baby who needed everything on a metal Jeep cushioned so I would not hurt myself. Simon and Henry Lewis were the only ones in the company who asked how I was coping with doing the show with a gammy hand. I replied by saying as long as I didn't see the plaster, I was fine. The Wardrobe department made a flesh coloured glove without fingers, to camouflage the plaster cast. I never missed a show as Carmen in all the three years that I played the part.

The week I took over the part of Carmen at the Old Vic, I was advised by the assistant director, that four shows a week was going to be too much for my voice. Talk about putting ideas into your head! No wonder the Carmens and Joes wanted time off. Yet in Japan, towards the end of the tour, I had to sing 9 shows a week when the second Carmen was injured and the Japanese Management would not allow my understudy to go on. I did it all without a word of thanks or encouragement from the English producers. However, I knew I was blessed because my voice stood up to the test. What else could I have asked for? I just loved being Carmen!

"The Japan tour happened because of your interpretation of the character. The Japanese producers had seen the previous Carmens in London, but were not impressed." said a journalist who interviewed me. Michiko San, who was representing the tour organizers interpreted for me. I guess the journalist had no reason to make it up. This lifted my spirits.

Prior to the Japanese tour of Carman, I was in a musical playing Judy Garland in 'The Night They Buried Judy Garland' at the Shaw Theatre when the tour of Japan was being planned. As a result I could not go to Japan for the pre-tour promotion. A singer from London was cast to alternate the performance of Carmen with me so that we would both do four or five shows a week. I had asked to be cast opposite Blair Wilson as I had found it difficult to play opposite the second Joe in the West End. Blair had taken over from Gary Wilmot as my Joe at the Old Vic. He was a bit chubby for the part, but he was a lovely character and became a good friend. Blair taught me his idea of a voice warm up. He made the noise of a US police emergency siren followed by the 'fry voice', which sounded more like a male frog in heat. This was all the voice warm up he needed. He was an opera singer and had been for many years. But as for me, I needed the full warm up and training from Derek Barnes, our conductor, before each performance. Without a full warm up, I would be afraid to tackle the opera. The new Carmen got the muscle bound Joe I had difficulty with. I was over the moon to retain Blair Wilson as Joe after the irreplaceable Gary Wilmot. As I was not available to do the Promotional visit to Japan and Blair was otherwise engaged, the other actors playing Joe and Carmen were sent ahead of the rest of us.

Before going on the Japanese tour we broke the new cast in, at Plymouth. When I arrived at the theatre, I noticed that all the front-of-house photos were from past Carmens at the Old Vic. The management had been very careful not to have a photo of me, so as not to upset the new alternate Carmen. There had not yet been a photo shot on stage of her. Unfortunately, she had not taken a close look at the photos at front of house and thought that all the pictures were of me! She took umbrage at what she saw as a plan by the Management to portray me as first Carmen. She saw me as competition. This was silly as we were never on stage at the same time! We alternated the shows, so, to my mind there was no competition. Different audience, different show!

There was a video made during the other Carmen and her Joe's visit to Japan. We were appearing in Leeds when the Japanese film crew arrived to complete the documentary. Since the other two had gone to Japan they monopolized the crew and made a point of showing them round the theatre. Blair and I were completely and purposefully excluded. Blair came to my dressing room to tell me what was going on. When Stephen came to meet me I asked him to gently point out to the company manager that there were two sets of Carmens and Joes. The Japanese film crew then decided to interview me in my dressing room. I got Blair to join me. I wore a flowing pink satin dressing gown designed by me. Blair wore a smart red velvet smoking jacket, we looked really glamorous and the interview went really well.

When the time came to go to Japan, the other two left earlier, laden with gifts to be sure to get the Press Night. Which they did! I chose to see the New Year in with my husband and children and flew out the following day. When I arrived in Japan, mischievous cast members pushed Blair to get me to make a fuss about the Press Night. When I ignored Blair's conspiracy theory, he was told he had ended up with the wrong Carmen. As if they cared! The other two were welcome to have the Press Night. I would have been amazed if the Japanese could tell us apart, or know who was who. As long as the other two gave a good show we would all benefit.

There was only one Carmen and one Joe on stage at any one time, but rivalry was created seemingly for the entertainment of the company of players. I was seen as weak for not fighting for what they thought was my rightful place. It would have been a waste of time! The assistant director and young dance mistress had already formed camps in which I was not included.

The Japanese tour lasted two months, starting at the National Theatre in Tokyo, we visited the city of Osaka, Nagoya, Fukuoka and Hamamatsu; travelling variously by road. On the first day of rehearsals in Tokyo, the bus left the Hyatt hotel, where the whole company was billeted on time, leaving some stragglers to take a taxi due to their usual bad time keeping. I loved Japan. I liked their practice of respect, punctuality and discipline. At the first "blocking" rehearsals, the Jeep was parked on stage facing the wrong direction. It was not easy to manoeuvre. As soon as the mistake was discovered; twenty men appeared, picked up the vehicle and turned it around. No fuss. I couldn't imagine that happening in the UK!

The Japanese language sounded very familiar, almost Nigerian in places. I made a point of learning the protocol and key words before leaving home. I also got to know the kind Swedish manager of the Hyatt Hotel in Tokyo, as I wanted him to be able to differentiate me from the rest of the company. I had a sinking feeling that their behaviour (with some notable exceptions), was going to fall short of what was required. I had noticed few of them had any knowledge of etiquette or basic Japanese traditions or customs. After the first morning I avoided eating breakfast in the hotel restaurant with the ensemble, they were so noisy. We were given breakfast vouchers, which could only be used in the restaurant. I made friends with the Maitre D' of the restaurant. I requested he set aside a bagel, an apple (the apples were the size of a grapefruit) and bottle of water in a bag for me. The hotel manager told me his staff had formed a very bad opinion of the cast. He showed me the state of one of the rooms after a late night party. It was appalling and I was ashamed.

"Not even pigs could be this dirty. They kept other guests awake and the other guests were complaining about the noise!" he protested to me as if I was in a position to be able to do anything about it. The manager had a tough time cajoling his staff to clean up the mess. Looking at the expressions on their faces I begged the manager to tell them I had nothing to do with the party or company.

On matinee days the curtains went up at 9.30am for the first show. The second show was at 2.30pm and the last show 7.30pm. We alternated, if I did the morning show, the other Carmen went on at 2.30pm and I would then be back for the 7.30pm performance. Later on, during the tour, after the second Carmen was sent home from Fukuoka I had to carry all the shows on my own. As expected, I played all the shows with no help or even a kind word from anyone in the English producing company, but the Japanese backstage crew were very supportive. One of them was very handsome and looked like an oriental Gregory Peck! I knew I could have

292

played the Diva and pulled out to let the producers stew in it, but it was not my style. It was my job and also I just loved the role. The Assistant Director was a nuisance, I appreciate that he had a tough job but, he loved to gossip and relished any clashes between company members especially the principals. I was nice to him, but very careful to avoid any social encounters with him. It irritated him that I had no time for gossip. I did not take it to heart, as I knew what he was up to. I spoke to Stephen every day, he was busy with a stock exchange company flotation, but we spoke on the phone for up to an hour every day.

On the famous Press Night nothing much happened. The show was as usual. I stayed in my hotel room reading. I assumed that the management had naturally chosen the Carmen and Joe who had done the promotion in Japan for press interviews. It was up to the Company Manager and Assistant Director, which Carmen went on for which show. For ten days after my flight from London my ears did not clear properly from the pressure of the altitude during the thirteen hour flight which left me partially deaf. During rehearsals and earlier performances, the marvellous orchestra sounded as if they were playing in a distant room behind closed doors! I had to sing from memory. The next night, after the press night, it was my turn as Carmen. The entire cast got a notice to remain in costume after the show and to attend a reception to meet the Heads of the show's sponsors Horipro and Sony. Getting ready for the show, I asked Michiko-san about what the protocol was, who we were to meet and so on.
"It is a very important night". She volunteered.
"In Japan, the second night is more important than the Press Night. It is when important people and the important press come to meet the stars and the cast personally!"
The cast members were to be introduced to the guests after the show in a line up; hence the request to stay in costume. I noted with amusement that it would be hard for the Japanese to tell us apart without the costumes.

After the show, which was a triumph, I freshened up and changed back into the more recognizable red Carmen costume. I made my way to the line-up. Suddenly the other Joe and Carmen breezed in to great fanfare dressed in fabulous designer outfits, specially chosen for the occasion. I thought they looked wonderful, but they had missed the point of staying in costume. They pushed me aside aggressively to stand in the middle. I obliged and moved. Being the obvious Carmen in the line-up, I was picked out and taken round the room during the party to meet all the important investors and guests. Michiko had to translate most of the questions and compliments. One of the important guests had roving fingers, which came close to touching my breasts. As he spoke he was addressing my breasts not me and his fingers had a mind of their own. Not even in Nigeria had I seen a grown man behaving like a baby craving its mother's milk! The smile froze on my face.

"Michiko, please tell your boss, if his fingers connect I will punch him in the mouth!" I said

"I am sorry Patti-san, is because Japanese women do not have...." She began to explain.

"I don't care what Japanese women do or do not have, if he connects with my breasts I will deck him one in the eye."

She said something to him and moved me on to the next guest.

Blair told me, after the party, that our designer clad Joe and Carmen had left in a huff as they had been ignored all evening, due to the fact that they were not in costume and were not recognisable. After that, things went from bad to worse between the rival Joes and Carmens. It was obvious that not even the Assistant Director knew about the difference between the Press Night and the second night in Japan. He had unwittingly handed Blair and me the important night further deepening the chagrin felt by the other two. I got all the major press reviews and stories, which were ecstatic. Fate had dealt Blair and me a good hand on this occasion.

As I had suspected, it was clear that the Japanese could not tell us apart from one another. I also struggled to tell the Japanese people apart until I got to know them personally. The Japanese seemed to think that the promotion that the other Joe and Carmen had done prior to the tour was done by Blair and me; such confusion! Additionally the Japanese press and those that had seen me play the part in London had remembered my performance and booked interviews. They could identify with my sensual Carmen as being closer to a Japanese femme fatale. Sometimes it is better to let things be!

There was a public outburst against me by the other Carmen, in front of the cast during one rehearsal. She was obviously hurting and thought that she was being put upon. I told her not to behave like a peasant. It did not get any better, even when I tried subsequently to make peace and work out what was wrong. Since the rest of the company had behaved badly and left a pretty bad reputation at the five stars Hyatt hotel, I became a recluse and did my best not to be seen with the cast at the hotel. I confined myself to my room and only went down twice a day for a machine massage, after I had heard an amusing rumour about the blind masseure. I heard that she was very good, but had hands of iron. Apparently, there was a queue in her waiting room for her massage, but the place soon cleared following the painful screams coming out of the room from the first customer!

The other Joe and Carmen were keen to have well-developed muscles for the fight scene and took the opportunity to go pumping iron in the gym. Of course, I felt that this was not the right way to approach the character of Carmen. I did not see her as a tough modern woman. She was feminine, sensual and vulnerable. I spent my time doing Pilates in my room and occasionally went for a walk.

From my 25th floor hotel window I could see a lot of Tokyo. I watched school children in the cutest uniforms on their way to school. Early in the morning the adults would gather in the park to practice 'Budo'. I found their movements therapeutic. To the left of the park was a building, which had over forty storeys. Having read up on the vulnerability of Japan to earthquakes back home, I wondered how such a tall building could withstand an earthquake. I didn't have to wait long to find out! For a few days there were little tremors that felt like earthquakes to us foreigners. During two or three shows we had serious tremors and not a single member of the 1500 audience moved from their seats in the packed theatre. In the Carmen Jones Company there were eyes bulging with fear! But the backstage crew seemed to be unmoved and I took comfort from the fact that the audience was not afraid.

When we were still in Tokyo the massive Kobe earthquake struck on Tuesday 17th January 1995, early in the morning at 5.46 am. I was asleep in my bed on the 25th floor of the Hyatt Hotel. My curtains were not drawn. I knew that the whole building was swaying like a reed in the wind. I lay in my bed as everything not nailed down went flying around the room. "Do not take the lift during an earthquake" was one of the rules. Where could I go? My fingers dug deeper into the bed
"If I have to die now I would rather it was in the comfort of my bed!" Was my bizarre thought.

I caught sight from my window of the very tall building I had noticed earlier, swaying. I could not believe that it could bend so much as it swung back and forth. Avoiding flying objects, I jumped out of the bed and hid under the fitted desk pinned to the wall. Suddenly it all stopped. It cannot have been going on for long, but it felt like a lifetime! I looked at my alarm clock 5.49am. I climbed back into bed breathing heavily and just lay there, trying to calm my pounding heart.

The earthquake began at 5:46am and lasted for 20 seconds. It registered 6.9 on the Richter scale and, according to the specialists, it was equivalent to an explosion of a powerful 240 kilotons of TNT 20 kilometres from

Kobe at Awaji Island. More than 50,000 buildings were destroyed or badly damaged in Kobe and 300,000 people were left homeless. Across Japan 150,000 buildings were destroyed and 6500 people lost their lives and 25,000 were injured, most of them in the Kobe area. There were four foreshocks, one of which we had felt in the theatre, but there were 74 aftershocks felt. The damage done cost $100 billion, equivalent to 2.5% of the Japanese GDP. On the TV news I watched the collapse of a major freeway, the road on stilts bending and waving like a ribbon in the breeze. News bulletins featured uplifted streets, twisted and buckled railroad tracks. Fire raged all over Kobe. I looked out of the window at the ridiculously tall building that had been swaying earlier. Thank God it was still standing.

I wondered how far away Kobe was from Tokyo and learned that it is 427 kilometres about 265 miles away. Over six hours' journey! If it was this badly felt in Tokyo, I pitied the poor people of Kobe in their ruined city with aftershocks raining in. On the TV news items, there were shots of interiors of shops with people trying to stop things flying off shelves, trapped cars, burning buildings. When I finally got out of bed and ventured down the lift I felt that something profound had happened to me, I was badly shaken, but at least I was still alive. Would I see my husband and children again? Was I actually even alive? Was this some alternate universe and time zone?

Being in Japan began to feel surreal, as though I was in an alien world. Everything was so different, clean and super-efficient, but now so much laid waste. I felt disorientated, as I reached the lobby, the shock had left me curiously in disarray. My mind raced and I had strange thoughts. Would the Japanese replicate me? The poster for promoting the show was of a pair of eyes of a Japanese girl. I let my imagination run wild. There would be another me as soon as I left the country. I both admired and feared the Japanese. I had been watching too much Japanese TV even though I could not understand a word. I would watch the Japanese soaps, listen to the deep voices of the men contrasting the gentle high-pitched voices of the women. Now after the earthquake, I would only have CNN on the TV for normality.

I spoke to Stephen on the phone and relaxed a little; I prepared for my show and was grateful to get back on stage. The Kobe earthquake was the worst in Japan since the Great Tokyo Earthquake in 1923, which measured 7.9 on the Richter scale and killed 140,000 people. The 1995 earthquake was the greatest disaster in Japan since World War II. At the time it was reported to be one of the most expensive natural disasters in history. Apparently it was a very shallow earthquake. Shallow earthquakes are more likely to cause extensive damage, which was unfortunate, as the area surrounding Kobe was believed by many Japanese to be safe from major earthquakes. Kobe was one of the nicest cities in Japan and the residents were not prepared for a major earthquake. Some people had even moved there to escape earthquakes elsewhere in Japan.

I was even more aware that I was working with a hostile Carmen Jones company of players. Though we had a language in common, we shared little else. Looking back, I'm sure there must have been some nice people amongst the company, but I did not know them.

We still had the rest of the tour of Japan to accomplish over the next six weeks. We left Tokyo by coach on a long journey to the south toward the Kobe region. We were to perform at Fukuoka, Kyoto and Osaka getting as close as 45mins away from Kobe to finish up in Hamamatsu. We saw a lot of the devastation on the way.

The coach trip was a few hours of hell. The company members were devilish trying to get a rise out of me, but I ignored them. I carefully picked the very spacious seats at the back and made myself comfortable. Blair was frightened of the muscle bound other Joe and the company's aggression towards me and did his best to stay away from me when they were around, so he huddled down the front. Half way through the journey after the members of the cast had stopped their childish antics; someone decided to put the promo video made by the Japanese TV company on the bus's large screen. It was a sort of 'In Search of Carmen Jones' documentary. The first 30mins featured shots of an unknown black Carmen. Her identity was cleverly disguised as she weaved in and out of buildings. This was interspersed with long distance fleeting shots of the stage show. There was a three minutes shot of the other Joe and Carmen in a guided tour of the theatre in Leeds. This was accompanied with loud cheers and giggles from everyone on the coach. I saw the other Joe and Carmen swell with pride while poor Blair didn't know where to hide himself.

"Well, a few more weeks of this and it will all be over." I kept telling myself. I looked out of the window wishing I could be somewhere else. Slowly, I realised there was unusual silence in the coach; I turned my head lazily to see what had silenced them. I had not recognised my own voice, there I was on the screen in a beautiful pink satin dressing gown looking as vintage Hollywood as it gets. I looked amazing! Occasionally the camera would go to Blair in his smart velvet smoking jacket. If I had planned it, I could never have envisaged the impact the dressing gown would have on the screen. The interview lasted for the last 15 minutes of the video. Once again the good Lord had come to my rescue! The effect of those last minutes was devastating for the other Joe and Carmen. Things were never the same in the other camp after that. They began to quarrel between themselves and they seemed too pre-occupied with themselves to be aggressive to me.

During one performance, the other Joe finally let his rage get the better of him. He swung on the set as if he was trying to bring the whole thing crashing down. In the words of Gregory Peck-san, one of my favourite Japanese crewmembers; "He looked like a tiger in a cage!" During the rehearsals that followed, he almost strangled his Carmen. That same evening being over-aggressive during the fight scene, he cracked one of her ribs! She had to be sent back to England. The next alternate show, the understudy was on instead of the other Carmen, but after this performance the Japanese refused to have her back on, saying it was me or nothing! I had already sized up the situation and even toyed with the idea of being a Diva about it. I knew the Lord had looked after me so well within the company and I couldn't take the decision on my own. Before they approached me to do all the shows I prayed for guidance and total surrender to God's will. If I was to play all the shows God would give me the voice. If it is not His will, then the voice will cave in under the pressure and the understudy would just have to take over. I knew the silly Assistant Director would have to approach me cap in hand about alternating the Joes, which, since "muscle bound" was so aggressive, this was not a possibility for me. So I pre-empted the request by asking Blair if he had the stamina to do nine shows a week with me. He did not hesitate. He saw his chance of getting rid of the muscled Joe.

Not long after I had spoken to Blair, both the Company Manager and the Assistant Director came into my room. They presented me with the schedule and I said "No" to the muscled Joe. He would either have to follow his Carmen back to London or sit out the rest of the tour. Blair and I finished the tour of Japan together and all went well.

One thing the English producers did right was to fly the principals (stars of a show) in Club Class, considering the fee I was paid for doing nine shows a week was not great. When the plane touched down at Heathrow, there was a loud shout; "Home!!!" from the economy class. I was glad to be home, although Stephen and I had a great financial problem hanging over our heads. Stephen's deal had not gone well and he was struggling to clear the Banks. I would rather have to face up to our problems than be working with the company on another tour. Even the allure of Carmen was not enough to bring me to accept an offer of performing in a European Tour.

I worked with Simon Callow (the Director of Carmen) again in a straight play "Destiny of Me' playing the part of the nasty 'Nurse Hanniman.' I met my favourite actress and good friend Ann Mitchell in this production. She is now a star of "East Enders". For the first time I enjoyed working with and spending time with someone from my industry. When I went to audition for another show in the West End, to my horror I got to the theatre only to find out it was the same producer that toured Carmen Jones and worse still the nasty dance mistress was the choreographer. She made me do ballet during the audition, at my age!! I knew she did this to humiliate me, but I went through it because I knew she would one day have the same done to her when she was older. That is the circle of life: 'what goes round comes around.'

I recorded and released 'Christmas with Patti Boulaye' in November 2000. Just after that we started the charity Support for Africa as a tithe to say thank you to God. We, the whole family, poured whatever money and energy we had left into the Charity as a thanksgiving to the Lord, for looking after us and seeing us and our children through the many hardships we had in this period of our lives. It was only two or three years before we had another business success and we were back on our feet again.

Prince El Hassan of Jordan 1997

One of my most memorable shows was singing in Jordan at the 50th Birthday Party of the then Crown Prince Hassan and Princess Sarvath. Prince Rashid met Stephen and me at the airport when we arrived. Prince Rashid was informal charm and class itself, dressed only in jeans and without any ceremony he helped us with our bags into the limousine. He came with us to the five star hotel and saw us to our rooms. What a handsome and charming seventeen year old! On our flight was Her Royal Highness Princess Margaret, who was a Royal Guest for the party. The Party at which I was to entertain was filled with the world's Royals including the Aga Khan. It was to be held at the lovely Amman Citadel on the top of a hill with its romantic Roman ruins. I went to the sound check the next day, accompanied by a Jordanian Brigadier who was in charge of the entertainment. I had my own band with me and my show was a great success. I finished with a surprise by bringing Prince Hassan up on stage with me to sing his old school song from Harrow School. I had especially learnt '40 Years On' the famous song from Harrow School written in 1872. I invited all the ex-Harrovians among the guests to help the Prince out on stage. They were not shy! The stage was full of His Royal Highness and all the Harovians present. Apparently HRH was delighted. I was flattered when the Prince referred to me as "Crème Boulaye" in his speech after the birthday party. Each year since, Stephen and I have received Christmas cards from the Jordanian Royal family. Each year, it is a delight to spot the next addition to the family in their family photo on the card. After my show and the romantic Arabian Nights style birthday celebrations at the Amman Citadel, Stephen and I were invited to stay on in Jordan for Princess Rahma's wedding to Alaa Batayneh.

To entertain all the Royals and other guest for the wedding we were all taken by coaches with outriders to Petra and the Dead Sea. You do not want to swim in the Dead Sea; if you have any minor cuts or nicks on your body the salt is desperately unforgiving! The dust at Petra affected my voice rather badly, but what a privilege to walk amongst and touch the stones of that wonderful ancient City carved into the living rock. I had not minded about my voice until I was asked to sing at the wedding! When they came to me, I had to decline! My voice was just not there. It was hard to take the disappointment on the faces of the guests, but what could I do! I explained personally to the Prince and he was able to hear my croaks. It was the only time in my career that I have missed a show, albeit one which was not planned.

Chapter Thirty Four: Support for Africa - Healthcare Clinics

In 2000 I was invited to Nigeria by the then First Lady, the late Stella Obasanjo. She was once my teacher at the convent school, The Holy Child College, in Lagos. She wanted my help and advice on her charity foundation. Feeling honoured to have been asked, I paid for an economy class ticket and boarded a flight to Nigeria. I stayed at the Sheraton. I could ill afford this at the time, as Stephen's business had taken a downturn. I had retired from singing to look after Emma and Sebastian. It would have been wrong to waste the First Lady's charity's funds by asking her to pay for my flight and expenses. Perhaps that was naïve of me, but charity is giving not taking, that's what Mummy taught me.

"When you give to charity or when you do charitable deeds, know that you are giving to the Lord." she would say.

Besides, it would not have looked right if I was preparing to advise her on the proper use of charitable funds, I had to lead by example. When I arrived at the airport, my younger brother, Sammy, met me and so I dismissed the driver from Aso Rock, the President's principal residence.

"Will you be picking me up tomorrow for my meeting with Her Excellency?" I asked him.

"I don't know Ma, maybe another person will come for you."

I asked Sammy. "Should I have offered him some money?" Sammy shrugged.

"With official cars, it's best not to until you know what their status is. If they are with you for the duration of your trip, then you can use your discretion."

I checked into the hotel and had an early dinner with my brother Sammy before retiring for the night. The following day there was not a word from Aso Rock and so I went for a tour of the hotel and surrounding area letting the reception know where I was. This was my second visit to Nigeria's new capital city and there was not much to see as yet, although what was there was very smart. My first visit was almost two years before to sing at the President's Inauguration Party in front of the World's Heads of State. When I got back to the hotel for lunch I called Sammy.

"Have you heard from Aso Rock?" he asked, knowing the answer.

"Not yet."

"Now you know you are back in your country! This is what we have to put up with. Someone in the office is probably waiting for you to call in so that they can extract some money from you before they allow you through to see the First Lady"

"Well, in that case I hope they are not relying on money from me for their next meal, because they'll starve!" I said.

"Would they seriously think that I am in desperate need to see the First Lady? She invited me and I paid my way so I don't have to kowtow to anyone."

"The way their minds work is this, why would you come all the way from England if not to seek a favour? The First Lady probably does not know you are here."

"Are you kidding me?"

"I bet you she doesn't know."

The whole day was wasted. On the third day Sammy suggested we call the First Lady's office saying she probably had not been told I had arrived. I found this incredible, but he was right! Someone had decided that if I wanted to see the first Lady I had to come through him or her. They got the wrong person this time. I rang the number I was given and a man answered.

"Sorry Madame, I cannot put you through to Her Excellency."

"Then can I speak to her office please."

"Madame you need to make an appointment."

"Sir I understand that, but my appointment was yesterday."

"Her Excellency had a very busy day yesterday. If you would like to come to the office to make another appointment I will arrange another time for you."

"Thank you, that is very kind of you, but I don't need another appointment, I came to Nigeria at Her Excellency's personal invitation. She called me in London and invited me. I believe Her Excellency needs help from me, not the other way round. I would not have left my comfortable home to fly half way across the world leaving my husband and children to sit around in a less than comfortable hotel for three days. Please let Her Excellency know that I will be catching my scheduled flight back to London tomorrow morning. If she needs to talk to me about her foundation she has my London numbers." I was irritated.

"Please, what is your name Madam?"

"My name is Patti Boulaye and I would appreciate………."

"Please hold on Madame." I could hear him speaking to another man, but not what they were saying. Then he spoke to me.

"Madam, there will be a car at the Sheraton Hotel to pick you up in 30 minutes!"

I pleaded with Sammy to come with me. I felt like a total stranger, despite a lot of lovely and friendly people around me, including one very red-eyed soldier, guarding the hotel. The soldier broke into a wide smile when he saw me. He hurried over to me gun in hand.

"Ah, are you Patti Boulaye? Eh, you have made my day! Can I take a photo with you, please?"

The soldier went from being very serious and menacing to being an almost vulnerable young man in seconds. He spoke in a fast and clipped way and his accent was pleasant and light. He beckoned to another gun wielding soldier and handed him his camera, placed his gun against the wall and posed with me. He smelt of sweat, but not body odour.

"My friend, come now, take the photo quickly! I beg, hurry now!"

I have your picture on my wall in my room. I will tell my father, he will be very pleased. My father likes you too. I am so proud to be meeting you!" he enthused.

I felt shy and full of humility and this young man was lifting my spirit more than he knew. The other soldiers looked on with blank faces as he fussed over me. I was flattered to have a young soldier as a fan, but a little bit embarrassed at the attention it was drawing to me from passers-by. I half expected a senior officer to come around the corner and tell him off. After taking photos with him, I walked into the hotel and he went back to his post. The expression on his face was the highlight of my day. God certainly works in mysterious ways. I've learnt to thank Him for the privilege that allows me to arouse such obvious joy in another person's life. But especially at that moment: as I felt like an alien, among my own people.

Sammy, who always has a full day, was able to postpone all his meetings except one. He was with me when the car arrived to take me to the State House where we had to wait a short while before seeing the First Lady. As we waited I had time to reflect on my surroundings. This was the Presidential Palace. The approach to the State House was impressive enough, but not overwhelmingly so. The section we drove through had long rows of white pillars all linked together at the top. Once we were inside, it did not feel like a State House. It was not very impressive, a bit drab and unloved. It was then I noticed my baby brother was a man! I had not seen him for a few years and he was always my little brother. Now I was consumed with over-whelming pride as I observed Sammy's quiet dignity, the obvious class, wearing his pedigree with understated elegance and charm: very presidential! I suddenly appreciated what an extraordinary family our mother had brought up, children full of humility and light, a certain presence that inspires envy, even from those who consider themselves to have everything.

"What an uncomfortable life it must be living here, everything seems so dour and almost unpleasant with so many hangers on." I whispered to Sammy.

He shrugged and made no reply. I had the sudden realization that we could be over-heard as the seats may have been bugged and I said nothing more. I was warmly greeted by some of the staff, who recognized me from the film 'Bisi Daughter of The River', also from the long running LUX soap adverts and all the publicity about my success in England. How anyone actually takes notice of a face on a bar of soap always puzzled me! Perhaps it was the TV advertising. How long Sammy and I waited in silence was probably not as long as it seemed.
"Just go with the flow and let nothing come as a surprise." I told myself. Sammy's silence and calm convinced me that this was the norm. When we finally got to meet with the First Lady the atmosphere around her was strangely false. She was ill-at-ease and she had so many people just standing around looking unpleasant. It was as if she was not comfortable in her own skin let alone as being the First Lady of a major African country. As my English teacher at school, Miss Abebe, (as she was known then) was always quiet. She was pretty and shy in an almost vacant way. I was very fond of her back then, but here I was sitting in front of this lady not knowing how to greet her or what to say. I tried to use Royal Protocol out of respect waiting to be addressed first, but it was almost impossible to have a conversation with her. All I could do was answer her questions.
"Did you have a good trip?"
"Yes, Auntie Stella!" there was then a pregnant pause which I had to break.
"Your Excellency, may I introduce my younger brother Sam Ikoku."
"We all know Sam. You are welcome." she said, acknowledging Sammy. I guessed this was partly a reference to his weekly TV programmes.

There was almost the hint of a smile and I thought for a moment that I saw a glimpse, at last, of my favourite schoolteacher. Sam bowed politely saying nothing. She appeared to be playing the role of being in command rather than actually being in command, her words sounded scripted and carefully chosen. This was my favourite and respected teacher and I was sad that she seemed so disconnected and I mean no disrespect to her or her memory. What I observed and felt at the time was a woman trapped in a situation she could not control. Once we were all in her car she became a bit more relaxed. I accepted her apologies that she did not know I had arrived two days ago, no one had told her. I can believe that, I wanted to tell her that someone probably wanted a backhander from me before I would be allowed to attend the meeting, but I thought better of it.

We drove a short distance to the headquarters of the First Lady's Foundation, which she proudly showed off to my brother and me. An entourage of about twelve people followed her of course. The Foundation was housed in two large and magnificent buildings painted white and cream. But buildings don't matter, it's what does or does not happen inside that counts. At the offices of Her Excellency's foundation, I expected to be told about a lot of work being done across the whole of Nigeria from these two enormous buildings, but there was nothing. At that time there were just fourteen children with various physical handicaps housed in a part of one of the buildings and that was all. The other building was for the staff. I could see her hands were tied and that is why she sought outside help from someone like me. She set her heart on building a meaningful, charity bringing practical help to her country, but it seemed that she was restrained in some way. I know that she wished and hoped to achieve great things for the foundation. I felt for her, but I was deflated by the whole day and didn't know how I could tell her the truth. Outside help was impossible with so many hangers-on, making even a proper conversation impossible.

By the time we said our goodbyes, I had decided this was not a charity for me to get involved in.

Sammy and I were quiet on the drive back to the hotel in the official car. Once at the hotel I turned to Sammy and asked;
"What in goodness name was that about? How can the First Lady have more staff working for her foundation than the number of children they were looking after? With the HIV pandemic there should be an out-reach program to at least one million children all over the country. I can't believe God brought me all this way for nothing."
"God always has a reason." Sammy said.

His next meeting was waiting when we walked in to the hotel. Sammy introduced the two female lawyers to me and said.
"I want you to come with me for a short drive later and you will see how bad things really are, but first I have a meeting with these two ladies. After that, we can drive to the village, which is about an hour out of Abuja."
I excused myself and went to my room to freshen up. When I returned to the hotel lounge, the two lawyers were still with Sammy. They wanted to take the trip with us. Sammy's driver drove us to the village. He drove into a compound with sparsely painted walls. The sign over the door read 'Victory Children's Home'.
"This home was founded by a local doctor for abandoned children. She looks after the children with help from three paid workers." said Sam

We went inside to be greeted by sixty babies, some twins, triplets, and quadruplets. Beautiful babies, all sitting in cots crammed together in rows allowing just enough access to each one. There was not enough room for the babies to crawl if they wanted to, just enough room for a nursing chair and a stool for the staff. Two women who looked after the children greeted us. The doctor was not there when we visited. I could see from the faces of the two lawyers that they had not expected to see so many children all under the age of one. I remembered visiting motherless babies' homes in Lagos when I was at the convent, encouraged by the Nuns. In a city, you would expect a lot of abandoned babies in a home, but not in a small village. I wandered around asking questions and expecting the normal stories about single parents who couldn't cope, or that the young mothers had died at childbirth and the family could not be contacted etc. But I did not get these answers. On my rounds of the cots, I came across a little baby that looked like an artist's study of a skeleton covered with brown skin. His eyes were bulging, his lips were tightly pulled back showing all his baby teeth. His neck looked too thin to hold up his head, which appeared much bigger than the rest of his body. His ribs were visible; his arms were so thin that I wondered if they would break if anyone attempted to pick him up. I turned to the helpers;

"What is wrong with this baby, he looks like he is suffering from malnutrition?" I wondered why they did not feed him.

"Do you want to hold him? Victor likes to be carried." she said not answering my question.

"Yes, can I hold him?"

She wrapped a cloth round him picked him up and handed him to me. I have to admit I was afraid he might break or that his head would snap clean off his shoulders. I was amazed that he was able to wrap his skeletal form around me as I cradled him. He really did like to be carried as the lady had said.

"Why is he so ill? Won't he eat? What is wrong with him?"

"His name is Victor." She said smiling at him and taking his skeletal hand. "He is the first baby that was brought to the doctor. This place is named after him. He is one year old and he has full blown AIDS!" My eyes widened with shock.

I had met adults with full-blown AIDS! I had not come across a baby with HIV, let alone one that is at the stage of full-blown AIDS. It had never occurred to me to associate this stage of the disease with infants; we were all so ignorant of the disease in those days. I knew some adults carried the virus for a long time before reaching this advanced stage of AIDS. I could not believe what I was hearing!

"All these babies are HIV positive! Little Victor only has, maybe two weeks to live!" She whispered the last bit as if the baby would understand or be upset by it.

I looked around at all the babies. I was awash with emotions so confusing that I could not think straight. I could not see the babies through the tears in my eyes. The shocked faces of the two lawyers showed they were not sure what to make of it either. My thoughts went from disbelief to anger, to humility, to self-loathing and then loathing for anyone I have ever met who had thought themselves important or superior in anyway. Suddenly everything meant nothing, my life, show business became embarrassingly empty and vain. Images of TV, film stars, kings, queens and Lord knows what other title we give ourselves flashed before my eyes. It all seemed like nothing and crumbled to nothing in my mind! How could anyone feel important in a world where such things were possible, no matter how far away from you they were. Then reality hit me. It was not anyone else's fault. I was searching desperately for anything, anyone, any place that I could lay the blame on for this horror! It finally dawned on me that this was my country. As Mummy would say, "God has a reason for taking you to England the way He did. When He is ready He will reveal His will." Perhaps this was the reason for this visit, but what could I do. With eyes still filled with tears I finally submitted to helplessness. I sat down with the baby cradled in my arms trying to hold back the tears, then getting some strength back I asked:

"Why are there so many of these babies in this particular village."

"These are not all from this village. People are really frightened of HIV so that when their babies are born with the disease, they visit the witch doctor. He tells them that HIV is an evil spirit that would consume and kill the rest of the family unless the baby is buried alive! Of course, mothers of HIV babies can't bear to bury them, so they abandon them in the forest where they are found by farmers or hunters. Now that people know about this place, |the babies they find in the forests are brought here. These are the lucky ones and Victor was the first!"

I was completely incredulous and very angry now, my tears burned hot on my cheeks. I gently gave the baby back to the helper and left the building. I could not stand to be in there. My mind was racing: what could I do? I knew that I would have to do something.

I asked Sammy how he knew about this home in a remote village. He explained that a nurse he knew had told him about it. He supported the doctor by sending her 10,000 Naira a month to help take care of the babies' needs. That was a fair sum in those days and I felt so proud of my brother and respected him for what he was doing. On the drive back we all were silent with our own thoughts.

The next day my brother Sammy drove me to Abuja Airport for my flight back to London, we talked of Nigeria's political problems.
"Surely things can be run differently." I said to Sammy, in that way that all those in the Nigerian Diaspora always ask when they are confronted with the politics of Nigeria.
"Yes it can, but they don't know any different."
"A totally honest and charismatic leader like Chief Anyaoku (Ex Secretary General of the Commonwealth) and one or two others could change things, but I doubt if they will be given a chance."
"The people in politics here are crude and dangerous, someone with that kind of honesty and charisma would not survive."
"I guess those natural leaders don't make it precisely because they are principled and dignified." I said.

The thought occurred to me that my brother would make a great Leader, but the idea filled me with dread for his safety. Playing politics in Nigeria is a bloody affair and I suspect one would have to sell one's soul to the dark side to make it anyway. That would be impossible for one of Mummy's children.

I was met by Stephen at Gatwick Airport and during the long drive to Ealing, where we were living in a townhouse, while Sebastian was in school at St Benedict's across the road. I told Stephen about my trip and little Victor. I explained how I desperately wanted to save little Victor. Without even a beat, he suggested that we form a charity for the purpose and see what we can do to raise money for HIV medication. I loved him for his reaction. We were struggling financially at the time. Stephen was doing his best to get another public company business going in the tiny office in the townhouse.

Now here was Stephen in the middle of a financial struggle suggesting that I start a charity to help Victor. I was broken-hearted when the news came that Victor had died a few days after I had left Nigeria.

"Didn't you say there were sixty babies? Well we have to think of doing something for the other babies and God knows how many more all over the country." were Stephen's words of encouragement.

I began to make plans to start a charity with nothing, but goodwill and prayers, very desperate prayers. During the next 12 years we drew strength and endurance from our faith in God to continue the work of the charity, "Support for Africa" that I formed. For me it was tough not earning a living, but I spent the little money we could spare on travel, petrol and promotion for the charity. Stephen was grateful for God's help with his new venture, which was successful and he floated the company that he took over on the stock market where it has flourished. The charity was his way of giving thanks and I was full of love and admiration for him for putting others first.

At this time we became founder members of the Genesis Initiative supper club founded by Prince Michael of Kent, which met at the Dorchester Hotel to support small businesses. HRH is a Godly man whom I adore, but I was unhappy with the way some of the members were less than pleasant. After a couple of years I finally persuaded Stephen that we should leave the Initiative.

At that time the Combination Therapy for AIDS was terribly expensive and I realised that babies could not take the number of tablets involved daily. It was obvious the treatments with antiretroviral drugs would be toxic to babies. The side effects were extremely severe. In Africa the chances were antiretroviral drugs would be administered incorrectly anyway. Why was Victor's decline rather quick, less than a year? At that time I knew the speed of the progress of AIDS in adults varied and that the virus mutated and developed resistance to the antiretroviral drugs, sometimes faster than drug companies could come up with new versions of the treatment. The more I read about the virus the more frightening it appeared. My previous knowledge about the virus was acquired when one of Stephen's companies was working on an unsuccessful "interferon" treatment during the earlier stages of the virus' recognition; and through my work for the Terence Higgins Trust. It was an intelligent mutating virus that was able to resist treatment and replicate itself despite the application of drugs designed to repress such reproduction. An adult body can struggle against such an intelligent virus with the help of toxic treatments, but what chances would babies have? The answer was none! I prayed so hard for guidance. At first, I decided it would be quicker to set up inexpensive HIV education, information and awareness centres near villages. Through the centres mothers or parents would have had real information, so that they did not rely solely on the witchdoctor's assertion that the virus was an evil spirit. I knew we could not afford enough drugs to keep one sufferer alive for the rest of his or her life, let alone sixty or more babies. Even if we were able to raise enough funds for antiretroviral treatments of the time, Combivir and Trizivir, we still had the risk that the drugs might be administered incorrectly, and the recipient also had to have a good a nutritious diet, which was unlikely. I approached some companies for information including GlaxoSmithKline the makers of the drugs. The size of the problem especially the cost was daunting. I was used to helping charities raise funds for their various projects; but starting one, for Africa in particular, was a whole different ball game.

The next step was to think carefully, utilizing every bit of memory, knowledge and experience of Nigeria, my childhood days in villages and my voluntary work with UK charities, to find a way of being effective. There were a few problems to be overcome. We would be up against the witchdoctors and the very strong stigma attached to the virus due to ignorance. There were no words for virus or immune system in the local African languages; therefore any explanation of HIV would be lame and not understood. In the eyes of villagers not familiar with the sophisticated world of science, one thing is certain, if it kills, it is evil, therefore; it can only be an evil spirit. Talking with my sisters, it came as no surprise that in the polygamous family system, which exists in some Nigerian households, if one wife got HIV one of the other wives would be blamed. Or, in other cases, some unfortunate innocent rival would be accused of causing this evil in the family. Witchdoctors, oracles and herbalists found themselves powerless against the virus and struggled to understand it. They resorted to far-fetched and wicked solutions, as cures, including exorcism and, incredibly, sex with virgins for the purification of the blood. When these mad ideas did not work they reasoned that the virgin was not pure enough. This led to many reported cases of horrific sex with babies.

With such a strong stigma it would be a challenge to come up with some way for our charity to help. My first concern was how to fight the ignorance and safeguard babies' lives whether they were HIV positive or not. I wanted to be able to get to the mothers before they went to the witch doctor for a solution after their baby had got HIV. However, I realized that the HIV information, educational awareness centres, would be shunned and would be seen as the house of the evil spirit especially if they had signs saying they were HIV centres! It would be a place to be avoided at all costs. If anyone was seen going into the centres, for whatever reason, the assumption would be that he or she was HIV positive. They would be excommunicated and become like lepers in their local society. So my first ideas would not work. It was difficult to decide on some other way of helping, until one night while trying to sleep, the solution was presented to me. Taking my Mummy's advice, "if you find yourself tossing and turning at night, unable to sleep, ask God what He is trying to say to you, relax, open your mind and let your thoughts wander, then you will hear Him." She was right I did hear Him! I was to build Clinics, which would act as dispensaries, treating basic ailments like Malaria, cuts, dysentery and other basic, general tropical sicknesses and of course childbirth. HIV awareness and education would be offered alongside the basic treatment.

Before the Nigerian civil war, dispensaries were found within a few miles of a lot of villages in the Eastern Region. They were mostly run by religious orders, like Catholic priests, nuns, retired European doctors or missionaries. These were the lifesaving dispensaries I was taken to, whenever I had a bad malaria attack or got a piece of broken bottle stuck in the sole of my foot, when I was in a village.

The next morning after my revelation, I got the ball rolling. I told Stephen that the charity would be set up to build basic healthcare centres in villages. Through the centres we would be able to hand out awareness information on HIV while providing basic health treatments. We formed a charity and called it "Support for Africa". Stephen said we would need a good patron to enable the charity to move forward quickly and provide urgent help. John Major or Prince Charles, were his suggestions, making me laugh! If these were my two choices for patrons, then how was I to get it going? They would surely be beyond our reach. Two of the most important men in Britain at that time! Though we knew Sir John Major during his time as Prime Minister, he had lost the election about two years before and we had not seen him much. How could I even begin to think of asking him to be Patron of an unknown charity yet to be launched? It was now a few weeks since my encounter with baby Victor, which had already changed my life. Whatever our problems, those babies and their mothers had it worse, we had to do something.

Prince Charles was inundated with similar requests. I suddenly got cold feet and began to see this as a way out. Here was a good reason not to pursue an impossible charity project, a daunting task. Here I was thinking of starting a charity that would certainly cost us money during a bad time for us. Incredibly I had Stephen's backing. He was not going to let me back out and kept reminding me that whatever problems we were having, were nothing compared to what those babies had to endure. It is not in my nature to start anything that I won't be able to carry through to the finish. But I really felt I had to pass the buck on this one, so I did!

"Lord, if You really want me to pursue this idea, then You will have to deliver The Rt Hon Sir John Major or HRH Prince Charles!" I prayed. Having made this prayer request, I convinced myself that, I could not now be blamed for the outcome. I slept peacefully that night. I would start the next day making plans for more shows, art exhibitions and everything I could do to help pay our own bills. What was I doing even thinking about starting a charity? Despite my cop-out prayer as the day wore on, the charity became an obsession with me, every time I looked at my own beautiful children I was reminded of the horrible idea of even a single baby being buried alive or abandoned in a forest somewhere. Here I was doing nothing. I was not really relieved now that I had a way out; I knew, at the back of my mind, that I would have to do something. I began to hope that God would respond and I recalled that Dom Andrew Hughes OSB of Ealing Abbey, my favourite priest, once told me. "If anything appears impossible, it is in the Lord's domain!'

I tried to get on with my normal day. Just before noon, I got an unexpected phone call from Sir John Major's office to say that he was retiring from politics. A party was to be held in his constituency at which he would like me to sing. I was greatly honoured. Sir John is my all-time favourite person in British politics! Still I could not believe what had just happened neither could Stephen. Why did we hear from him just the very day that....... Well you get the drift! We were only discussing it the day before as impossible that we would get John Major to agree to be Patron of our new charity. God had His hands on me, on this project! I got on my knees again and prayed, I needed all the help I could get! My sister Maggie advised me that doing God's work is never easy because it rouses the devil's interest and re-action, so she was warning me of tough times to come. After speaking to Maggie, I was moved to tears and knew the charity was a reality for certain.

I entered in my diary a prayer: *"Father I give You thanks. All I ask is that You will bring the right people to help me. Please bless Stephen in ways that only you can and do not let our children suffer. Amen! "*

Nearer the date of John Major's party I requested that we be seated on the same table as John and Norma. Stephen always got on very well with Norma, especially when John Major as Prime Minister invited us, to spend a day at *Chequers Court,* the country house retreat of the Prime Minister. During the visit, Stephen encouraged Dame Norma to write the book she was planning about Chequers. At the party for Sir John's departure from politics Stephen sat next to Dame Norma indulging their mutual love of chocolate and I had the honour of sitting next to Sir John. During the course of the evening I explained my plans to start a charity. I told him in short hand about my trip to Abuja, about meeting the babies, especially Victor. I finished by saying it would be an incredible blessing if he was to be Patron. I promised there would be no waste of funds.

Sir John said he would be delighted to be patron of Support for Africa; he had spent some time in Nigeria at a bank and wanted to do something to help. What a wonderful man! May God richly bless him! I do not think I have met anyone else who had attained such high office that would not have thought himself too important to accept my request. John Major's "farewell to politics" party was the day Support for Africa was officially born.

When we got home in the early hours, I spent a long time finishing the painting of the design for the Support for Africa logo. I added the Hippocratic wand in the design, which the highly respected Nigerian High Commissioner Prince Bola Ajibola had suggested that I add at a meeting. The next morning I went to the local Kall Kwik and had the letter headed paper printed. Then I wrote a short letter to John Major thanking him for saying "yes" to being patron of the charity. I apologized for cornering him over dinner, presented him with a way out, in case in the cold light of day he had changed his mind. His reply came two days later, saying he meant what he had said. Oh what joy!

I started making plans, "blindly going where I had not gone before", but always with a child-like trust that God was well ahead of me on this one!

Through my work with Support for Africa I became very good at reading people's characters. A lot of people suspected my motives, I realized that people suspect you of motives that they themselves would have. Crooks would think you to be crooked. Honest people saw your honesty. Greedy people suspected you of greed. Godly people blessed you. Those with hidden agendas for helping you got impatient.

I knew with absolute confidence that the Lord had already set me up for the battle ahead. What a blessed battle it has been! After John Major's written confirmation, HE Prince Bola Ajibola agreed to be Patron as well. He even allowed me to hire the marquee at Abuja House in Kensington for a launch Party, with VIP guests including HRH Princess Katarina of Serbia, princes and various ambassadors. The most special to me at the time was HE Valentine Dobrev the Ambassador for Bulgaria, who turned out to be an incredible blessing to the Charity. The launch party took place in October 2000. The rain fell heavily that evening. It did not stop raining for months until it had set a record as the wettest year since 1954 with 56.6in of rain reported.

Having the charity gave me the opportunity for my next visit to Abuja to represent Dr Gerry Bodeker of Oxford University at the Conference for

World Scientists on the use of Herbal Medicine for HIV. The Bulgarian Ambassador was the most supportive Ambassador of our charity. HE Valentine Dubrev allowed us the free use of their magnificent building behind the Royal Albert Hall. It was at one of our fundraising evenings in the Embassy that I first met Dr Bodeker (Professor Bodeker), an Australian, who studied at Harvard. He was a senior faculty member in public health at Oxford University. He was also Adjunct Professor of Epidemiology at Columbia University, New York and a leading academic in the field of traditional medicine.

Dr Bodeker invited Stephen and me to an old master's ceremonial dinner at Green College Oxford University. Our main topic of discussion was HIV. I mentioned my fascination with the use of herbal medicine for HIV. My reasoning was that if the monkeys carried the virus, yet it was not deadly to them, perhaps there is something in the forest that might act as an antidote to the human variety of the virus, a bit like Quinine for Malaria. This line of thought always seem natural common-sense to me, worth investigating alongside scientific medicine. But of course it was not a popular idea generally

Not long after the dinner, I got a call from Dr Bodeker. He had been invited to be the main speaker at a conference at Abuja for World Scientists. The conference was about the use of alternative medicines for the fight against HIV/AIDS. He would like me to attend as his guest. I thought he was joking, but he was serious, adding that Stephen and I had more knowledge about HIV than perhaps many of those attending.

These were still early days in the fight against the virus. The knowledge I had acquired through reading Stephen's papers about the discovery of the virus in San Francisco in 1981 (which related to his business plan to float an arm of an American Company called Life Sciences on the stock exchange), was far more than I realized. My first-hand knowledge of the natural village environment with my common-sense approach to the crisis was appealing to advocates of natural remedies. But I did not see any reasons for attending the conference. However, encouraged by Stephen, I packed my things for the flight to Abuja. While I was getting ready, a call came through from Dr Bodeker. He was stuck in India and wouldn't be able to make it to Abuja after all, but he had instructed the organizers that I would be representing him. "You will be fine. They are expecting you. You will be well looked after. I'll see you when I return. Good luck." He was so matter of fact about it, a typical professor. He gave me a name to contact at the Conference and then the line went dead. Major panic ensued, followed by an unnatural sense of calm! The sort of calm one feels, which accompanies the certain knowledge that one is about to face a firing squad. Not that I have ever faced one. But I have seen the calm acceptance of those led away to certain death. I knew there was no escape. I will be attending a conference for world scientists and I will be representing Dr Bodeker. Surely, all I have to do is apologise for his absence and sit down. It can't be all that bad.

I caught the overnight flight to Abuja, arriving at the Hilton Hotel just as the conference's morning session broke for coffee break. I find it difficult to sleep on flights and stayed awake all night. I identified my contact, excused myself and went up to my room to change and freshen up. Fifteen minutes later I entered the conference room. The conference chairman met me at the door and asked if I would open the next session. Blood rushed to my head, I felt faint! My legs felt as though they would buckle under me. I was gripped with fear! I could not believe this was happening. He wasn't asking me whether I would mind. It was all so very matter of fact. I gazed at him in disbelief waiting for his next line, which should be. "I am pulling your leg, of course, do enjoy the conference." Nope, the man was humourless! I found myself saying.
"You cannot be serious! Is this a joke?' I asked. All I got was a vacant stare.
"Why don't you put the speaker after me on, to give me time to catch my breath and get over my jet-lag?" He agreed.
I went back to the coffee room and poured myself a strong coffee before taking my seat in the hall. I sat as close to the back as I could. I needed to hear what was going on, to gauge the atmosphere in the room. There were well over six hundred medical experts of all kinds attending. I wanted to observe the next speaker and the reaction of the room. Also, the long walk to the front when my name was announced would hopefully allow me time to compose myself, steady my nerves and assess their reaction to me.

My hands were shaking my mouth was unnaturally dry as I got out my note pad. I had nothing prepared. I had tried to make notes on the flight, about Dr Bodeker but nothing materialized on paper. What could I possibly deliver in front of almost six hundred scientists from all over the world? Nothing! I had always been afraid of public speaking at school. I avoided debates like the plague. I did enjoy performing because the script was written for me. All I had to do with a script was memorize the words and bring them to life.

Now there I was like a lamb to the slaughter. I suddenly remembered God, as I always do when I find myself with my back against the wall!
"Heavenly Father, You have not prepared me for this!" I whispered.

"Yes, I certainly have!" Came the answer.

"When, how……?" In the middle of my questions, the voice in my head continued.

"I chose seven members of the British Shadow Cabinet to prepare you for this day. Why do you think I forced you through the motion of running for the London Assembly, all those speeches in front of the London Constituency's Select Committees? What did you learn? You couldn't have had better teachers!"

"What did I learn?"

I got my pen out and looked around the room as the speaker before me began to speak. I observed half the room was already dosing off, the others were trying very hard to be attentive. The Speaker who was from one of the European countries was not holding their attention. He was a scientist, not a public speaker. He did not project his voice and spoke in a monotone. The ones still awake struggled to follow him without much success. I gave a quiet "thank you" in prayer for not having to follow a charismatic speaker. I scribbled on my pad: "Make them laugh!"

During my check in at the hotel desk, I had picked up a Nigerian newspaper. I got it out of my bag. The headline screamed; "Nigerian Dr Agbalaka's Aids Cure!!!" The article was damning. "But why can't the cure be found in Africa?" I asked myself. It didn't matter whether he had found a cure or not; the rapid growth of HIV was frightening and we owed it to the victims to listen to every idea. Nothing, no method natural or scientific should be discarded until it had been fully tested. I would speak about the difficulties of the likes of Dr Agbalaka and others trying to be creative. And also about the things I had learned from reading the first official papers in early 1981, on the HIV cases that were identified and reported in San Francisco. Those papers had grabbed my attention because it all pointed to Zaire in Africa as being the source of the first few cases. Two young men in the Merchant Navy were diagnosed with Kaposi's sarcoma, (a skin cancer) while still in their early twenties, whereas the disease is not normal in anyone below the age of seventy. Eating Mangabey Monkeys was thought to be the cause, although it was likely that these young men had caught the disease from sex with the local population who sometimes eat the monkeys. As a structure for my speech I jotted down 'beginning – middle – end'.

Just then I heard my name. As I was being introduced my nerves did not allow me the luxury of listening to what was being said about me. On autopilot, I got off my seat at the mention of my name. My thoughts were busy; "I would re-introduce myself when I get up there. I may not know much about scientific facts, but I probably knew much more about the early official unpublished information, concerning HIV than any of the scientists at the Conference. I also knew I could do better than the last speaker on volume and performance."

I arrived at the speaker's lectern, set down my notepad, looked to the back of the room. Everyone was focused on me, curiosity etched on every face, especially the few Nigerians who knew me as a singer/actress and the face advertising Lux soap! I looked too glamorous to be a scientist! I was in full makeup and a dress with a nipped in waistline. I could almost read their thoughts. With over twenty years in show business under my belt and taking into account my recent tutoring on public speaking by The Shadow Ministers. Not forgetting my eighteen or more speeches in front of the Conservative Party's *Blue Rinse Brigade,* this should be a piece of cake!

I smiled at the bored, stony faces and began; "Good morning Ladies and Gentlemen. My name, in case you did not catch it is Patti Boulaye. I am a singer by profession and have been in show business for over twenty years. Right now my thoughts are going in all different directions. But I have to say this to you and the Chairman of this Conference. Only a bunch of scientists would be crazy enough to ask a singer to address them on the most serious health matter of our time!" Laughter from the room! Yes! We are off to a good start!
"I am here at the invitation of Professor Dr Gerry Bodeker of Green College, Oxford University, who is either as crazy as you all are or he really believes I have something to contribute to this conference. Before I go into my speech, let me first tell you briefly about my life and how I happen to be standing here in front of you. My life has been a series of incidents and accidents! It all started when I left Nigeria for holidays in London................ "

They all found my story about how I stumbled into show business entertaining. My war background in Nigeria, how I came to know so much about HIV and my Charity, followed by my talk on the use of herbal medicine treating HIV. I cited the use of the bark of the quinine tree for the treatment of Malaria as an example. I concluded that since the original diagnose of the cause is pointing to Africa maybe, and only maybe, the antidote would be found in Africa.

I got loud applause when I finished. Not sure quite how seriously they had taken my speech, I had an over-whelming desire to escape to my room before the lunch break. But I went back to my seat to listen to other speakers. Delivery wise I scored highly, content wise I had no way of knowing until the Chairman cornered me at lunch time before I could escape.

"Patti, we would like you to chair one of the policy groups at the end of the day." Now I had had enough, someone was taking the micky!

"I am sorry, but I am not qualified to chair a scientific group on HIV. Do forgive me, I am honoured to be asked, but I feel someone else would be better suited to chair the group." I would not be persuaded to overplay my hand.

Later on I came across articles and extracts from the conference. I was amazed that I was quoted alongside the Minister of Health and the Chairman of the Conference and reported in the newspapers. This is an article covered on The World Bank Group website;

On Dec. 5 2000, the Minister of Health Dr. Tim Menakaya declared that: "After prolonged suppression in favour of conventional medicine, traditional medicine practice and practitioners henceforth would be accorded formal status in the national health system." Addressing the opening ceremony of an International Conference on Traditional Medicine on HIV/AIDS and Malaria at the NICON Hilton Hotel, Abuja, the minister also stated: "................" As if taking a cue from the minister's proclamation, United Kingdom-based Nigerian singer and international model Patti Boulaye has urged African scientists to look inwards for a cure for HIV/AIDS, especially through traditional medicine. The international model who flags off a two-day campaign against HIV/AIDS today in Abuja also plans to launch a charity foundation, Support for Africa 2000, to create awareness on the ravaging social menace which is already having Nigeria and Africa in a stranglehold.

Boulaye who flew into the country a few days ago, said AIDS was real in the continent. "Over 33.6 million people are living with HIV/AIDS worldwide, 23.3 million of these are in sub-Sahara Africa, representing 70 per cent of victims worldwide.

"The reality," according to her, "becomes more frightening because of the high rate of prevalence. And in 16 African countries, the infection rate is above 10 per cent of the population, and that rate is rapidly rising." She said South Africa had a prevalence rate of 20 per cent, Zimbabwe and Swaziland 25 per cent, while in Botswana it was 36 per cent.

The artiste disclosed that already, some countries like Uganda have "responded positively" to her NGO's campaign. Her campaign also enjoys the support of prominent figures like former British Prime Minister John

Major, former Commonwealth Secretary-General Chief Emeka Anyaoku,
Prince Bola Ajibola, renowned novelist, Fredrick Forsyth, among others
who are also patrons of the NGO.

Quoting Dr. Lester Brown, Chairman of World Watch Institute, Boulaye,
whose latest album: Christmas with Patti Boulaye, was released yesterday
in UK, said the need for urgent response to the danger of AIDS and malaria
in Africa was: "If we fail to respond, we will forfeit the right to call
ourselves a civilised society... and our chance to help save Africa."

Did I really say all that? Apparently I did. The Lord had my back covered
for sure! That is the only way I can explain my speech at the conference,
which was made possible by the mentoring of members of the Shadow
Cabinet.

Back in London, in 2001 we started raising awareness of the plights of
children like baby Victor. Everybody advised that the Charity should be
promoted with pictures of sick babies and aids sufferers. I refused to exploit
these poor sick people because I knew how dangerous such photos could
be to some of the victims and their families. There was a risk that the people
in the photos could be recognised by other people locally and cause them
to be discriminated against or worse. The Internet has made the world a
smaller place and though such pictures may tug at the heartstrings, we
could have unintentionally sentenced them to a life of hell in their own
villages. I once met a man in London soon after we had opened one of our
Support for Africa (SFA) clinics. The clinic was built in a very remote
village and this man was going home to spend Christmas with his parents
in the same village. That encounter convinced Stephen that it's a small
world and I was right about not using a visual image of aids sufferers. The
stigma in Africa was too deadly to take the risk. If we couldn't raise money
without the pictures, so be it!

The Bulgarian Ambassador, HE Valentine Dobrev gave us the opportunity
to raise funds through receptions at his Embassy with guests paying twenty
pounds to attend. Everyone was curious about the Bulgarians and so the
events were well attended! Our daughter Aret and son Sebastian were
always at hand to help and so was Mislav who became our son-in-law. As
successful as these events were, the amount we raised at the receptions
showed it would take many years to get the first clinic going. Architectural
drawings for the first clinic were drawn with the costs estimated at almost
a third of a million pounds. I was the only one that knew what an African
village dispensary had to be like. I modified the plans drastically so that we
would erect a building that was a third of the size and reduced the practical

cost to thirty five thousand pounds! In order to erect the first clinic within my target of eighteen months we had to do something big.

I was able to speak to the Head of Programming of the Royal Albert Hall, Lucy Noble. During the first meeting at the Royal Albert Hall, I was told that without a secretary and large committee, it would be impossible to fill the Albert Hall. I protested that I would find a way of filling it. But it seemed hopeless! They felt that the taboo subjects of HIV and Africa would never work at the Royal Albert Hall. She said; "There are other places more suited, like the Fairfield Hall for such events." Those words turned the Albert Hall into a challenge that I had to overcome with help from above. I asked if Stephen and I could take a look at the auditorium, she obliged. In the auditorium an idea came to me. For twelve years I had done BBC TV Christmas shows at the Royal Albert Hall for Major Sir Michael J Parker KCVO CBE. My idea was that Stephen and I would approach Sir Michael to produce the show at the Albert Hall. I took a copy of the layout of the hall with me from the meeting, which I studied carefully. The angels must have pointed out to me that three thousand people would fit into the stalls, dress circle and the choir seats.

We arranged to meet Sir Michael who had produced over thirty events at the Royal Albert Hall. He had also attended one of our receptions at the Bulgarian Embassy giving a very funny speech about his time as Her Majesty's Equery. Sir Michael asked Dougie Squires to attend and he kindly agreed to become the director of the show. A real top professional, he would make sure that we had a top quality show. During the meeting at his home in Earls Court, Sir Michael voiced the same concern about HIV/Africa at the Royal Albert Hall. "Patti dear, how can I say no to you? But I'm afraid we would find it hard to sell the idea to five thousand, five hundred people." I found myself saying; "What about if we had three thousand gospel singers?" I saw Sir Michael's eyes light up. I knew then I was on the right path. What Angel put that idea in my head? I would worry about that later. The angels were working with me!
"Where would we put three thousand gospel singers, the choir only seats six hundred?"
I produced the plan of the hall and pointed out that we could sell the dress circles, stalls and choir to the singers and we would only have to worry about selling the hospitality boxes and upper circle seats.

"Where are we going to find that many gospel choirs? The stalls are the best seats you can't give those to the choir! Those are the seats that would bring in most of the money." Sir Michael pointed out. I explained that we would invite all the choirs in the country and ask them to pay twenty-five pounds each to be involved. That would bring in seventy five thousand pounds covering the costs and producing a healthy profit before selling any other seats or boxes.

I could see he liked the idea of three thousand gospel singers. His shows for the military and Royal Family often involved thousands of soldiers Sir Michael just loved making huge crowds into a professional entertainment. At least we were now talking logistics instead of whether we would do the show or not. But we also needed stars to put a show together and we would have to work on that. I had no idea about gospel singers, except the lovely ones I had worked with on *"Joy to the World"* the BBCTV Christmas show from the Albert Hall produced by Sir Michael Parker. I wondered whether Gospel Choirs only existed in the US, although I was aware of a handful just beginning to sprout in England. Where was I going to find 3000 gospel singers? What in heaven's name made me come up with such an impossible figure? I worried through the night! The next day I didn't know where to start except in the only way I know how, on my knees in prayer. I apologized to the Lord, asked for forgiveness for running ahead of myself and His will and asked for help with finding three thousand gospel singers. I tried the yellow pages, no luck there. I had no idea how computers worked except how to press the "on" button. Panic set in, more prayers followed, I was agonizing over the problem of the gospel singers when the landline starting ringing. "Let it ring, they'll get tired!" I told myself. But the person at the other end would not give up. I picked up the phone. The voice at the other end was a cheerful young man.
"My name is Alistair, we met at an event about two years ago."

He must have gathered from my voice that something was wrong. I usually smile when I pick up the phone. I apologized to him and tried to reinstate a smile in my voice.
"I'm sorry it has been a long time."
"You don't sound like the cheerful person I remember. Are you alright?"
"I have set myself an impossible task! Unless you know anything about Gospel singers, you can't help me!"
"You need gospel singers? That's what we do. We book gospel singers."
"What in the UK?"
"Yes! How many are you looking for?"
"Would you believe, three thousand?"
"We don't have that many, but I'm sure if you speak to the pastors in the evangelical churches, also try the Elim and other evangelical Magazines you may find a lot more and there must be many more than that all around the UK."

He had called me to find out my availability for something or other. But how amazing was that! How could I complain! I was blessed! I got to work immediately; I was being encouraged and shown that I had to have faith. I was prepared to work around the clock. I did and for the next year I left no stone unturned. I never felt exhausted, though sometimes, as the date of the concert approached I would work through the night. My constant prayer was; *"Lord please bring the right people on board"*. Sir Michael's extremely efficient event coordinator Maureen Mele, was assigned to help me. Maureen was used to handling thousands of crowds and performers for Royal events and the Ministry of Defence (MOD) with Sir Michael. Maureen was a Godsend! Nothing fazed her. How did I get so lucky? What a stupid question! God was well ahead of my every move! Maureen was the best there was, the ultimate in event organizing. I learnt more from working with her than years at university could have ever taught me. Sir Michael and his team had just produced and organized the Queen Mother's one-hundredth Birthday pageant at Horse Guards Parade, on the 19th July. I attended the pageant with my son Sebastian as guests of Sir Michael. Unbeknown to me Sir Michael was preparing, as the Producer, for Her Majesty's Golden Jubilee celebrations in June 2002.

I started gathering gospel singers. I had little luck with the evangelical churches, so I gathered singers from wherever I could. I did visit a few evangelical churches, but they yielded very few choirs. Only one pastor was genuinely helpful. The others all seemed to have their own agendas and were too wrapped up in their own thing to back our plans. Sadly, the big name evangelical church gospel stars wanted to charge us, and the biggest name in gospel at the time from the US even quoted thirty thousand pounds! I made the decision with Maureen's help to widen the horizon in our search for singers. I gathered a list of groups, any groups that would sing. The word "gospel" derives from the Old English God-spell, meaning "good news" or "glad tidings". I appealed to any group of people that had the heart to help us save babies from being buried alive and would therefore be worthy of the name "gospel". Each of the singers was to raise twenty-five pounds to cover the cost of their seat, but they were welcomed to raise more money if they wanted to. This made their involvement more interactive and fun especially for the younger people; I felt that they held the key. There were about ten groups who raised funds for the charity through various activities. One young girl from Stage Coach (The Drama Schools) raised eight hundred pounds on her own. I learnt that; "Young people are not afraid of sacrifice" as St Pope John Paul 11 said. Her selflessness and supreme effort was touching and made me determined to build the clinic without wasting a penny on administration. I would have loved to do something for the child, but unfortunately I was already over working. I was grateful when the boss of JBPR, the PR for Stage Coach arranged for her photo to be in the Express Newspaper.

The process of putting on the fundraising concert and building the clinics was overwhelming. In the last three months I felt like I could hardly catch a breath, but I did not have time for self-pity. My focus was on the babies and I now apologize profusely to anyone who felt they should have had my attention or the star treatment and didn't get it! In the last month I was working sixteen hours a day, seven days a week with three hours break for Mass on Sundays. I ate on the move. Stephen was keeping up with me as well as paying the bills.

At the beginning of the Albert Hall project in 2001, I spent two to three weeks constructing the letter to the choirs. It had to read just right. I wrote the letter and prayed for guidance as I revised it a hundred times. I got welcome help from JBPR with writing the press release and finding choirs from drama schools. JBPR had two lovely helpful young ladies, Helen and Jo, organizing local publicity around the young people who were raising their twenty-five pounds and extra for the charity. They also helped design and print the charity's only publication. I say only, because I resent spending the charity's funds on printing information that would only end up in the bin and could be read on our Web Site anyway. We intended to build clinics, which would be self-sufficient structures that we would donate to the community to be run as basic healthcare centres.

I sent out the letters inviting all the choirs to join us at the Royal Albert Hall to help with the cause. Among the choirs that attended was a group of elderly jolly ladies from Birmingham whose average age was eighty-three years! JBPR introduced me to their client Stage Coach and they provided fifteen hundred students! The schools wanted to and could have provided all three thousand, but that was not the plan. I knew that God had already chosen those who would make up the rest of the three thousand. They came from churches of all denominations, schools, choirs, social groups, businesses and even the Metropolitan Police sent a hundred strong gospel choir! I also heard from a Muslim Choir and a Jewish Choir who were not on my list. Both wanted to know if they could join us. I was delighted to have them! The concert was about "Good News" and was about saving lives, if they were prepared to sing 'Amazing Grace' and 'Oh Happy Day' they were welcome to join us. I was very humbled and proud when they did!

Now I needed celebrities! And God found them for me. Before starting the charity I was a happy social recluse. I now had to network for the sake of the charity and attend as many events as I could. I was burning the candles at both ends. Stephen insisted that I take a ton of vitamins every day! At a show in London I met the beautiful and talented singer Gabrielle during the time I was gathering the choirs. She agreed in principle to be in the show. By the end of 2001 I had Gabrielle, my good friend Maizie Williams of Boney M, the wonderful Uri Geller and Rik Waller together with the three thousand gospel singers. I now had the tools to create a show and to promote the event. Sir Michael introduced me to Sir Cliff Richard at a later stage in 2002 and he was kind enough to agree to appear. We had no sponsors except Stephen and myself. I did not have the time to appeal to sponsors. That required a lot of work, which I would not have been able to handle with everything else at the time. I was keen to make sure that the initial deposit of sixteen thousand pounds, which Stephen personally paid for the Albert Hall was not lost.

Maureen Mele kept in constant touch with the choirs we were amassing. She was incredibly organized and she was simply brilliant at following up on every choir I found! This ensured that the choirs booked their seats early so we knew we could cover the total hire fee of £56,000 of the Albert Hall and the other costs. I sent out invitations to dignitaries including diplomats and stars. I asked the Albert Hall if I could use the Royal Box. The answer was no! I would have to ask permission from Buckingham Palace, but they were sure the answer would be no! I wrote a letter to the Palace having asked Sir Michael for the right person to address it to. Then I promptly forgot about it leaving it in God's hands.

Imagine how surprised, grateful and delighted I was, when the answer came back in about two weeks with not only a 'YES', but with a request to reserve 12 tickets for Royal staff. The show was to be on the 10th March 2002.

I mapped out the shape of the show as I saw it. I drew up a graph of how to build the show from the opening prayer up to the interval, retain and pick up the momentum at the start of the second half and keep the level rising up to the finale.

I invited The Descendants, a super children's group from Acton, whom I called the London African Children's Choir. I went to see the children and I took over the choreography with the help of one of the volunteers and organised their costumes. I also held auditions to find twenty female dancers. I called them the 'Sun Dancers' after a show I had written. They were to dance to African drums. I choreographed them with the help of my favourite female choreographer and dancer, Rashida Plummer, and I set the drum patterns for the choreography. I designed the dancer's costumes for the show. My dressmaker, Gloria Doolan, a real friend, made up the zebra fabrics into strips for the skirts. The gorgeous Debbie Moore, founder of Pineapple, donated black leotards. I stitched the zebra strips onto the leotards myself. I also saw The Dhol Foundation play at an event and recruited them for the Royal Albert Hall. Then I went into the studio to record the songs I had chosen for the choirs to sing. When we had all the star performers and choirs in place, I went into Premier Studio based in Hackney, with Nicky Brown. We produced a rough demonstration CD of the songs with me croaking through the routine songs. I gathered the recordings already recorded, like Cliff Richard's "The Lord's Prayer" and Gabrielle's songs on to one CD posted them to each of the Choirs for them to learn for the show. The Kingdom Choir was to be the leading voices in the show. These were all volunteers, as were all the choirs, performers, helpers and the VIPs who introduced the artists on stage. God bless every one of them! Michael Portillo, Iain Duncan Smith, and Freddie Forsyth were among those who introduced the artistes and Noel Tredinnick was the wonderful conductor who had to control all three thousand singers.

The children, the Sun Dancers and Dhol Foundation Drummers were magical on the night. But the star of the African Children's Choir was a little Brazilian boy in the Descendants, whom I had reinstated in the group. The little boy was originally left out of the children's group because he was too shy, but he warmed to me. Dougie Squires the director of the show, who naturally has an eye for what will work in a show, spotted the boy's potential and featured him, just long enough for him to wow the audience.

To add extra variety on the evening the Dhol foundation Drummers increased their number to over twenty. With their leader, Johnny Kalzi, they certainly raised the roof of the Albert Hall on the evening. Uri Geller was such a wonderful Star as generous with his time as ever, so was Sir Cliff Richard. Uri bent a spoon auctioned it for two thousand five hundred pounds plus a lunch at his home. This impromptu auction was the only one of the night.

We sold all the boxes and all the other seats and standing room on the top level. The Albert Hall was packed to standing room only. Having a top producer, conductor, director and lighting and sound professionals made it a very expensive project, which cost over eighty thousand pounds. Thank God I had no one to pay from the charity. All hands were on deck as we tried to feed and water the three thousand singers, bands and crew etc. I remember my dear friend Gloria Oakey, who had organized the John Major "farewell to politics" Party saying "if I never see another sandwich again it will be too soon!" She was joking of course, she was one of the people who just piled in and helped. I can't mention everyone in this book, as I would like to. So many people helped us achieve the five clinics and a school we have built in African villages. After the costs of our first Reaching Out for Africa event at the Royal Albert Hall were paid, we were left with sufficient money to build our first two healthcare clinics.

On the day of the show, Stephen, Emma and Sebastian worked like Trojans all day. We were there on our feet for seventeen hours. After my 6.30am SKY News interview about the event, my family and I arrived at the Albert Hall just before 8.00am to welcome the three thousand gospel singers. I needed help from above and prayed; *"Heavenly Father, you have handpicked every single person that will be at this event today. They are here because they want to help us achieve this task that you have placed on us as a family. We tithe this charity and this day to You Oh Lord"*

The choir was made up of people of all ages from ten to eighty-nine years old. They came from all parts of the country. The singers started arriving just before 9.00am and the production team, (especially Maureen) went into action. Each choir was colour coded with a specific seating area in the Hall. Everything was timed with military precision. There were no tantrums that I was aware of. Dougie Squires got rehearsals going. By 2.30pm all the choirs were rehearsed together with most of the show, then Sir Cliff arrived for his sound check. I had made sure that the choirs had learnt all the songs that the Stars were going to sing. This was designed to make the show easier on the star performers by keeping their rehearsals to a minimum, as they had been generous enough to agree to appear.

When he arrived Sir Cliff was taken aback and worried about the idea of rehearsing in front of 3000 singers. No singer, I don't care how great they think they are, would want to rehearse in front of an audience of 3000. I assured him it was a sound check with a difference; that the choir already knew the songs he was going to sing.

When Sir Cliff walked on stage for his sound check the screaming was deafening. The music began and he started to sing, the mass choir took over. Sir cliff could not believe the sound, he held out his mike toward the audience, turned to his left toward the ramp, where I was standing with Sir Michael and mouthed *"heavenly!"* I signalled thumbs up in return. Gabrielle's personal manager, who had become my point of contact with her, played up a bit, but I knew it was nothing to do with Gabrielle personally. Unknown to her, up to the day before the show, we weren't even sure that she was going to turn up, judging from my conversations with her manager. I had her in the running order as closing the show, Boney M as closing the first half. I made Sir Michael aware just a few weeks before, that Gabrielle's manager was being a pain. Sir Michael persuaded Bill Latham, Sir Cliff's Manager, to definitely put the show in the diary for Cliff. Gabrielle did show up, but with Sir Cliff there she had to drop to closing the first half. Maizie of Boney M being a Godly woman was wonderfully relaxed about the whole thing. Gabrielle was great, but she closed the first half and left. I got the feeling she was upset not to have closed the show. It was the only thing that marred a perfect day! I did not let on to her that we weren't expecting her to show up after my conversations with her manager. Anyway, I named the first clinic after her. The second clinic was named after Sir Cliff Richard.

During the afternoon, as there was such a buzz in the hall, Sir Michael came to me, troubled.
"Patti dear, could you get them to save their energy for the show tonight, I am worried they won't have any energy left for the show!"
"They will be even louder tonight." I said
"Do you think so?"
"I know so!" I assured him.
The teenagers from Stagecoach were having such fun nothing could dampen their spirits. They screamed about everyone that came on stage. It was like an all-day pop concert. I'm sure if I brought a chicken on the stage to perform they would have screamed their heads off! They were simply incredible.

We began the show with a prayer! I opened the proceedings with a song I wrote "Viva Africa". The Rt Hon Michael Portillo was proud to introduce Gabrielle. He was a big fan of hers. He remarked, that the choir had made him feel like a pop star. The Rt Hon Iain Duncan Smith introduced Boney M. Author Fredrick Forsyth introduced the Dhol Foundation. I restricted each introduction to two minutes exactly.

During the interval, Sir Michael came to me and said that we have a request. It was from someone among the Royal Staff in the audience. I can't remember the name, I know he ranked top in coordinating the Golden Jubilee celebrations. I had not had time to visit guests in the boxes as I was wearing too many hats. The Royal Staff were enjoying the show so much they wondered if we could reproduce this atmosphere at Her Majesty the Queen's Golden Jubilee celebrations in just over two months' time in June.
"Could I produce such a choir for that event", they asked?

"The timing is perfect, Sir Michael! I will make an announcement to the choir at the beginning of the second half. I will give them a challenge to increase their number to 5,000." I said

I made the announcement. The choir and the audience loved it.
"We have all been invited to take part in Her Majesty's Golden Jubilee celebrations at Buckingham Palace in June and we need to produce another 2000 to make us a 5,000 strong gospel choir. Can we do it?" They raised the roof! It was simply magic! I was on autopilot, exhausted by my own step-by-step schedule for the day. By the time I made the announcement, we had been at the Royal Albert Hall for twelve hours and with the Morning TV before that. The finale of the show was chaotic! The stage was packed with excited children. The ones that were charged with presenting the flowers to the star performers, held on to them when they came on to the stage. I don't think Sir Cliff got his flowers. In the finale I led everyone with 'Oh Happy Day' but don't remember singing it except when I watched the video. I remember seeing my daughter Aret and Sir Michael frantically trying to signal to a child to hand the flowers to Sir Cliff, but the child was having too much fun dancing. Aret and Sebastian were ever attentive and covered my back throughout. Stephen was acting as my personal producer and telling me where I had to be, who I had to go and see or speak to back stage. I believed everyone involved; Major Sir Michael Parker KCVO CBE and his team, Dougie Squires OBE, Alan Jacobi LVO of Unusual Logistics team and my family were all picked by the Lord, I could not have done it without them. Sir Michael, Alan Jacobi and Dougie all played key roles in Her Majesty the Queen's Golden Jubilee celebrations. Those who volunteered to make sandwiches for the three thousand strong choir like Gloria Oakey, even Maureen Mele, Emma Bagwell Purifoy (now Lady Emma Parker) found time to supervise and help. It was an awesomely big show run by ten percent of the physical manpower required for such a show, but with a thousand percent of heavenly power, which ensured its success. The help from above was confirmed when Iain Duncan Smith, the then Leader of the Conservative Party came back stage.
"Patti, I just wanted to say, what a wonderful show! What a wonderful evening. I am so overwhelmed and I know I am taking something with me. I don't know what it is, but it belongs here!" He touched his heart as he said that.
"I wish it was election night, I would have no problem winning!" He joked and everyone laughed.
"Thank you Iain, you don't realize what you have just said, perhaps someday I will explain."

I was sure that what Iain had said was the voice of God assuring me that He had heard and answered the prayers I had said when I entered the building sixteen hours earlier. I closed my eyes and said a silent prayer of thanks.

When everyone had left, they had to close the backstage area so we had to leave the building. I suddenly found both my feet had swollen and I could not walk. I had to be carried out of the Royal Albert Hall just before 1.00am on Stephen's back!

Starting a charity, even with the best intentions in the world, is not easy. Right from the start I had a few run-ins with Nigerian members of the House of Representatives. One such encounter was during one of my visits to Abuja. I was introduced to a member of the Nigerian government who, when I told him about my charity, said HIV/AIDS was "a western plot to discredit Africa." After seeing babies like Victor at the Victory Children's Home, his words and attitude infuriated me. What chances are there for the ordinary people if a member of the Nigerian Government shows such ignorance?
"Sir, I can assure you that this *western plot* is probably already creeping up on you." I warned him that his latest girlfriend might be a carrier. Something in his discomfort told me I had hit a home run. So I piled in.
"I hope she is loyal to you and you are her only lover. We all know how attractive uniformed soldiers can be." He fumbled for his handkerchief as I continued.
"Anyway, soldiers are not stupid, they know about condoms and must use them all the time, so there is no danger there." I sighed before adding.
"Then again Sir, I'm sure a married man of your standing and intelligence would always use condoms..........."

All the while I avoided looking at my hostess, the beautiful wife of one of the Governors. I could feel her frozen next to me as I spoke.

The minister had drops of sweat running down his brow despite the very efficient air conditioning system of the governor's grand living room. The honourable minister had nothing to say. He mumbled some excuse and left rather quickly.

The governor's wife placed her hand over her mouth and began to giggle after he had left the room. It is a known fact that Nigerian men are reluctant to use condoms. Some macho thing! I was not about to let him off easily after his dismissive comments.

"Patti, that was so cruel! You frightened him!" said my hostess still giggling.

"Didn't you hear what he said? And he is a Minister? How do you women put up with that kind of ignorance?"

"Now you see what we have to deal with. You should speak to all our men. It might wake them up to the HIV epidemic."

With the minister's silliness still infuriating me I was taken to the Nigerian House of Representatives. I was only able to spend a few minutes listening to a debate in the chamber before being taken to address eleven Senators in a side room on the subject of HIV. My host was a female Senator who had warned me of the arrogance of the male senators. The then Leader of the House was among them. The female Senator was right about the arrogance. Why are there so few people who are truly worthy of respect? Especially in positions of power! I was in my forties by then, but thank God, could easily pass for twenty something to those who don't know me and I knew I was looking good that day. The Leader of the House welcomed me and more or less stated how important they were and how precious their time was. I guess I was supposed to be grateful that they bothered to see me at all! I glanced at the embarrassed face of my hostess. I have never found a room full of men intimidating. I find that men cannot resist the temptation to outdo each other to impress any lady in the room, especially if she has taken great care to look good. On the contrary, I find it more "empowering", to use my pet hate word.

This bunch of fat bellied men reclined in their seats with total distain as if they had come to the meeting just to humour me, which was probably true. There is something about celebrity status that makes people think you are stupid. Sometimes it makes them want to compete with you. My favourite is when those lacking in confidence attempt to belittle you so that they can feel more important. By the time the toad-faced Leader of the House had finished his 'we are important" speech I was raring to speak.

"Honourable Gentlemen, Senator........." I used the name of the female Senator.

"I am well aware of how important you may be in our country and among our people. As you are aware, right now I live abroad in Britain in a fair degree of notoriety. My honest and humble opinion about our country is that Nigeria's reputation in the eyes of the outside world will shock you. As leaders of a country with such a bad reputation you must all be aware that it greatly diminishes your own importance."

There was a slight uncomfortable shuffle from around the room.

You all preside over a country that has not yet deserved respect from the outside world. The only place you are guaranteed importance is within this country. If you want respect outside Nigeria, you will have to promote honesty, dignity, humility and integrity to the offices you occupy and to the people. Corruption has to go. Only then, as Senators, will you be able to hold your heads up." With that little lecture over, I went into my main theme:

"I probably have more knowledge than any of you on the subject of HIV/AIDS. That is why I am here, to try to give you some understanding of the severe and terrible threat to your people. Do not let your pride come between you and the actions that your Government needs to take"

I told them all I knew about HIV, my encounter with baby Victor was just a few hours old. I was still badly affected and in no mood to deal with nonsense and ignorance.

"You will forgive me if I do not consider any of us to be important or worthy of respect in a country, continent or even a world, where such things can happen to children. I would like to build basic healthcare clinics in your constituencies in Nigeria. I don't need money from you, just an acre or two of land, on which the Clinics can be built, the land must be donated to the local Community and to the Charity."

Somebody said "I will donate acres of land to your charity!" Soon all the senators were clamouring to make what I knew to be empty promises of land to the Charity. I thanked them politely and left with the female senator. She said;

"That was a daring speech Patti and you got them to donate land to the Charity!"

"Surely you don't think any of those men will keep to their word! They were just trying to impress. Those were empty promises. Any land donated from any one of those men would be of no value and something they couldn't make any money out of! But I know God will bring us people, whom He has chosen to bless, for the charity. There were none in that room!"

I was right. Not a single donation of land materialized. They all knew they could contact me through the female Senator, but not a word. From the minute the Leader of the House started speaking, my instinct was right. I knew in my heart, I would not hear from any of them in future. The lesson for me was to avoid wasting time and effort with local politicians!

After settling the bills from the "Reaching out" concert" at the Royal Albert Hall, we came out with enough funds to build two clinics. I turned to my older sisters for the donation of land and to help with building the first clinic in Okpanam. It opened in the third week in October 2002.

It was planned that the first clinic was to have been in Ikot Efa or near Calabar where my mother was born, but this did not happen. Despite the vital lesson I learnt about not dealing with Nigerian politicians, I felt I was safe dealing with the female Senator I mentioned earlier. There was a fire in a village near Ikot Efa that destroyed many huts, rendering many villagers homeless. When we heard about this we wanted to purchase land and build our first basic healthcare clinic near those who had lost so much. The female senator had located a piece of land in the village. Out of his personal account, Stephen sent a deposit for the land, which vanished into thin air. It was an expensive, but good lesson! Not even the female senator could be trusted! When we raised funds I became extremely careful, patient and meticulous with the charity funds. Patience was the key! If you rushed the projects you played into the hands of crooks.

I established a chosen method of carrying out the building of the clinics. First we ask for land to be donated. With the exception of the one donated by my family, land given to the charity was normally a piece of land deemed useless by the donor.

For instance, our second clinic was built on a piece of land where the surrounding villages had dumped their rubbish and human excrement. The land is located in a very needy area near Port Harcourt. Clearing the land was an arduous task! Naturally, the men employed as builders were reluctant to clear the filth from the land. It took my sister Grace, who was supervising the works, to get things going when she picked up a shovel herself and started clearing and burying the excrement. She told them;
"Building this Clinic is not ordinary work. It is an offering to God!" Her action shamed the men into clearing the land for building.

For all the clinics the building process was worked out between Grace in Nigeria and myself in London under the "good cop, bad cop" routine. We both donated our time to the charity in memory of our Mother. We paid for our own expenses and passed no personal costs on to the charity.

During the building process, Grace would negotiate the initial cost for clearing the land. As an experienced developer herself, she knew how much building materials should cost and she was great at negotiating. As soon as the builders became aware that the Charity was based in London and that Sir John Major was a Patron, they would assume that the Charity was on the UN level and had money to burn. This gave Grace some negotiating problems and sometimes her negotiations would reach a stalemate! At this point she would hand them my number in London so that I could do my "Bad Cop" routine. When I received a call from the builder I knew the man at the other end of the line had delusions about the charity's wealth. He thought that I would think his inflated charges reasonable and an agreeable sum. Grace being a developer would tell me exactly how much the job should cost in Nigeria. This is how the phone conversation went for the first Clinic, but this would be typical of such conversations for most of the buildings;

"Hello, good afternoon. Please may I speak to Madame Patti Boulaye." The word "Madame" immediately sets up my hackles because I know they want something.

"Yes Patti speaking, can I help you?"

"Ah! Madame, Good Afternoon." The surprise of getting directly through to me produces a nervous high-pitched giggle from the other end.

"I was not expecting to get you straight away!"

"Well you have, what can I do for you?"

"I am working with Mrs Coker (Sister Grace) to build the Support for Africa Clinic." There is then a pause. erhaps he is waiting for a word of encouragement or appreciation. I remain silent.

"Ma, I hope I am not disturbing you! Mrs Coker gave me your number to call you about the cost of clearing the land. You see Ma, it is very expensive to get the right people to do the job and because this is charity work, I have decided not to charge my normal fee..........."

"How much are you charging the Charity?" I interrupted his flow, which had the desired effect. He is beginning to feel my cold and no nonsense approach over the phone.

"You see Ma, where the land is........"

"How much is it to clear the land and lay the foundation?"

"Ma, the building that you are planning will cost....."

"That is not your concern at the moment: I want to know how much you want to charge up to foundations level. Your charge will tell me whether you are the right man for the job or not."

"Ma, to clear the land will cost £3,500 because............"

"Too much! I don't want to hear your reasons. We are not planning to build Buckingham Palace in Nigeria. Please don't take me for a fool because I live in England. I grew up in villages in Nigeria, so I know I can build eight large huts in any villages, each with three or four rooms for that amount of money. Mrs Coker is giving her services free, how do you expect me to tell her I am wasting the charity's money on greedy builders who think charities are Banks! This is a very small charity respected by people who lend their good names to it................."

I won't repeat all of the words, I did not swear, but I spent the next 5 minutes telling him off. After that, he would usually be speechless and his delusions spiked. I later found out that amongst the builders I had earned the nickname "The wicked witch of England"! As long as they complete the job within the charity's budget and do not give Grace too much grief, they can call me any name they like! At least now they don't try to cheat the charity or go over Grace's authority to get to me. To them Grace is easier to deal with and she is a lot less cutting with her words.

Two weeks later, in the case of the first Clinic I got a call from Grace, the cost had dropped to about £600 from the same man. Now that's more like it! She laughed and wanted to know what I had said to him.

This was just one of the problems we had to deal with to build the clinics. There are five steps.

(1) Clearing the land (cutting down trees etc),
(2) Laying the foundation and then building up to the window level.
(3) The rest of the structure including toilets, doors, windows etc.
(4) Roofing
(5) Plastering and painting

The cost of each step of the building process was haggled for step by step in this way. We would only have twenty five to thirty five thousand pounds to spend on putting up each building. The same building would normally cost four or five times that amount, if you were any other visiting charity or a western company. We had to bluster, bully, charm and tug at the heartstrings with great patience to get the buildings built for this amount.

The building of the charity's healthcare clinics from the clearing of land to the opening, varied in timescale. Whenever Grace was in charge, she gave up a lot of time, effort and money to complete the project. She would take no stragglers or greedy men and would both cajole and bully the men into completing the project in record time. This was so important, because with the two projects we left to the local men (as we were forced to do in Cameroon), the building work took not months, but years. I think that they hoped this would force my hand to part with more than the funds we had raised.

If you want something done on time in West Africa, have a strong and honest woman in charge! That is the lesson we have learnt. The women seem to be more organized and to have more integrity. Of course, there are always the few exceptions to that rule like the Senator I mentioned earlier.

Cameroon, Bayangam and Bafia Clinics

The Opening of our first clinic in Bayangam, Cameroon, which was solely sponsored by Unite Group PLC, was a trip I'll never forget. My local church had a Cameroon Committee whose leaflet Stephen had picked up. We had just had one of our Royal Albert Hall events and we already had three clinics open in Nigeria. I was praying for direction as to where to build next. The leaflet got us thinking of building in Cameroon. I had wrongly assumed that our church committee had local Cameroons contacts they could trust. As it turned out, they were just being used as a money supply from England. Poor Grace went to meet with the Cameroons, being sponsored by our church in a place called Tofu. It took her four days to cross the border from Nigeria into Cameroon, which is the neighbouring country to Nigeria. When Grace finally got to Tofu after another uncomfortable days' journey, she only met with local corruption. Even the local Bishop would not believe that we only had twenty five thousand pounds for the building project. He went behind Grace's back to email a proposal to me. He more or less demanded we build a hospital (not clinic) at the cost of a hundred and fifteen thousand pounds! The cheque was to be sent over for the building project to his personal account! Oh yeah?

I panicked when I got the email demanding a hospital. I don't know why, but the dubious and almost threatening tone of the Email got me worried about my sister's safety. After many tries I finally got Grace on her cell phone. I was just getting ready to leave for a show in Brighton with Stephen. I told her about the email regarding a hospital. I could tell she was worried, but I know she is very diplomatic. I went up to our bedroom and fell on my knees in prayer for help guidance. As I was praying a thought came to my mind. I remembered being introduced to a professor from Cameroon by a friend, Prof Fenwick of Imperial College London. I could not recall the Cameroon professor's name! Stopping in the middle of my prayer I got up, went down to the study, opened the large box in which I kept business cards. There were so many cards! Grace had given up her time and money for my charity project in Cameroon and now she was in a hostile situation in a foreign land and I may have endangered her. She was never one to complain, but I could hear in her voice how tired she was. She is so caring and would do anything to bring help to the villagers and at the same time make life easier for the charity.

My hands were shaking as I picked up the box and opened it: "Please help me Lord! Please, please help me! If Cameroon is where You want the next clinic, then help my sister who is trying to serve You. Let the card be here."

Just then Stephen called out to me. "Darling we've got to leave!" It made me jump. I dropped the box full of cards. The cards were everywhere! I knelt down to put the cards back into the box. The first one I picked up read Prof Louis-Albert Tchuem Tchuenté, Cameroon! He is the founder and national coordinator of the National Programme for the Control of Schistosomiasis and Intestinal Helminthiasis in Cameroon, which at the time was one of the priority programmes of the Ministry of Public Health. I rang the number on the card and got through. He remembered meeting me! Thank You Lord! I explained Graces arduous journey to Cameroon, the charity's work and Grace's voluntary role. I explained that if he could not help we would have to build elsewhere. I gave him her number and thanked him. Louis Albert said he would not want the charity to give up on building our next clinic in Cameroon where the need for such help is great. He offered to look after Grace and suggested that she get to Douala where he would send a car for her.

Relieved that Grace now had somewhere where she could at least spend the night, I rang her back. This time I got through easily and gave her the professor's number. She had to make another three or four hours' journey south on a bus to get to Douala. Just as we were arriving at Brighton, I got a call from Grace. She was on her way to see Louis Albert. Later on, just before nightfall, she was in Douala, showered, watered and fed. The next day when I spoke to Grace, they were on their way to see a piece of land in the professor's village, Bayangam. Grace had bought and taken customary gifts for the head of the village. She does all of this out of her own pocket. In the twelve years as a volunteer building supervisor and Vice President of the charity, we have never received a bill from Grace for expenses. But we insisted we paid for her flight to Cameroon for the opening of the Bayangam Clinic.

The infrastructure in Cameroon is generally far superior to that in Nigeria. Cameroon is a smaller country to manage. There was regular electricity and, therefore, easier access into the website from Cameroon. Once again, when the builders saw Sir John Major was a Patron of the charity, the level of greed went up. They wanted total control of the project. Cameroon was another country and they were too proud to let Nigerian builders help them. At least that was their excuse. It was too long and tiresome a journey for Grace to keep travelling to Cameroon, but she did sneak in a few visits to speed up the process.

The local politics meant that the builders had to answer to the local head of the village, who was convinced, as is usual, that there was a lot more money for the project and wanted to get his cut, or he would not let the building work be completed. After a long waiting time; something I've learnt as good practice with the charity's very limited funds, never give in! Then there were intercessions by the kindly, soft spoken and likeable Professor Louis-Albert Tchuem Tchuenté. The building work continued. But it soon stalled again for a few months. When it came to be time for the opening ceremony, we travelled to Yaounde for a few days, to take in the ceremony and to visit the CBCHS centre, where we stayed, to hear their ideas for the future administration of our Cameroon Clinics.

Thankfully, the Cameroon Baptist Convention Health Services (CBCHS), which is USA funded, was introduced to the project through a friend, Susan Lugard. Susan was planning to adopt a child from Cameroon and eventually did so after seeing the child on a UK TV programme. With CBCHS I had to part with more money than I had planned, just so that we could get the Clinic open. Nevertheless, we agreed with CBCHS that they would provide medical cover for the clinics, providing doctors and nurses and helpers. We also agreed to build a clinic in another village, Bafia where the need was great. CBCHS had out-reach projects in villages. Their modus operandi suited perfectly our plans for our charity's building projects.

Once every two weeks the Baptist health services would send out nurses to treat villagers. The nurse would travel before daybreak, but would only spend a few hours treating the villagers before he/she would have to head back to the town through the forest before dark. Doctors would visit the Villages periodically.

With regard to the second Clinic in Bafia, one of the nurses explained how heart breaking their job was. For example, they would treat a baby or patients with a simple ailment, before the wet season, when Bafia was not reachable. But when they returned, after the wet season the baby or patients they were treating would often have died needlessly. If they had a building where they could treat patients and spend the night, or sleep over for periods, they could continue to monitor the patients and many more lives could be saved. Our building projects in Cameroon would not only provide a basic healthcare centre, but would also provide a living area for the nurses to spend more time administering treatment to the sick. We were sold on the idea.

I still have not recovered from our trip to see the village of Bafia at the top of rocky mountain. It was a four hours' journey on a treacherous, narrow and dangerously bumpy track in a sturdy truck. During the journey I had to hold on to the side of the vehicle all the time, but I let go to pick up a bottle of water and my head hit the truck window so hard I saw stars for a few minutes. Parts of the track had disappeared in the rainy season and the holes were so huge I could not believe that we could enter one end and actually come out the other! Most of the ride was up steep hills. Meeting the people at the other end was worth it all, and explaining to the headman what we wanted to do was important, as we would need his blessing. Stephen, as always, was handing out little toys he brought from England to the dozens of children. Then we had to face the journey back down the mountain!

In Yaounde we stayed at the Baptist Centre in modest rooms with showers. On the day of the opening of the Clinic in Bayangam, we travelled through Bafoussam to Bamenda and thence to the Clinic in Bayangam. We drove through towns and villages with the roads winding upward as we went. On the way we stopped for some fresh pineapples, which we bought from a street vendor. They were the best I have ever tasted.

When we arrived at the Clinic we found that the borehole was not dug in time for the opening and so there was no water! If you wanted to use the loo, you had to go into the bushes. At the Ceremony the local dignitaries, who were all men, of course, dominated the opening ceremony with their lengthy, boring and incomprehensible speeches. I got the feeling we were caught up in a local election campaign. CBCHS who were supposed to have organised the event left no seats for Grace, Stephen staff members of the sponsoring company Unite Group PLC and Louis-Albert Tchuem Tchuenté! Stephen had to bully everyone to get all the seats organised. This was so different from our usual snappy openings organized by Grace. But this was a different country, language, and culture. We let them get on with it. As long as they provided the services promised to the villagers, I didn't care what they did after that. It was a different experience for us and when it came to building the second Cameroons Clinic at Bafia, I did not want Grace to go through the hassle of travelling all the way from Nigeria through dangerous roads to babysit grown men, so CBCHS agreed to do the supervising. However, the building work of the Bafia Clinic took over two years instead of the usual three months under Grace.

Chapter Thirty Five: The Queen's Golden Jubilee

Two days after the triumph of the first Albert Hall concert for Support for Africa I got a call from Dougie Squires. There was to be a Presentation by the Steering Committee for the Queen's Golden Jubilee at the P&O building at 10.00am the next day. I didn't know I was on such a Steering Committee, but Dougie said Sir Michael wanted me there.

Thank God I arrived early! I greeted Dougie and Sir Michael and thanked them for inviting me. "What is the presentation for?" I asked.
"Didn't Michael tell you?"
"Tell me what?"
"About this morning."
"I was told to be here and here I am."
"You were supposed to prepare a two minutes speech about the 5000 strong Gospel choir you are organising for the Jubilee."
The blood rushed to my head and my lips went dry, as always happens when I'm nervous. I heard myself thinking, "Thank God it's only two minutes!"
"Who am I speaking to?"
"People from top businesses, the Palace, the Government, the Press, everything that makes Britain tick, about 200 of them."
"Dougie, I didn't know. I have not prepared a speech."
"Well, luckily you are early so you have time to think of something!"

Dougie took me to the next room set with rows of over 200 gold painted chairs with dark red velvet seats. In front was a screen on which various images flashed up one after the other. I suddenly saw my name, Patti Boulaye with '5000 Gospel Singers' blazoned underneath in a large font. My heart sank even further. The Pyrotechnics team and such like flashed up on the screen, the floats, the Carnival etc. I went numb.
"This is all real!" I thought.
"Who are the people attending from the Government?" I asked trying to disguise my petrified state. Dougie's answer provided me with my two minutes presentation. Dougie explained the Government's reluctance about having any celebrations for the Queen's Golden Jubilee at all. Those representing the government at the presentation were there in principle to stop the celebrations planned. They believed it would be a waste of money as there was, in their opinion, widespread apathy towards the Royal family. They wanted to spare her Majesty the embarrassment of too few people

turning out for the celebrations. My blood boiled as I returned to the room, where the tea and coffee were laid out to map, out my two minutes.

Within minutes the main room with its guilded seats was filled, I took a seat four rows back from the recognizable faces from the Government. I repeated over and over again to myself "It's only two minute, just speak from the heart! Lord, please speak for me!" Someone started the presentation. Suddenly without warning, I was to go first. "Oh no! There was no time to control the nerves. There was my name on the screen; Patti Boulaye '5000 Gospel Singers'. Shaking from head to toe I floated to the front with a blank piece of paper in my hand.

"Good morning ladies and gentlemen. As it says on the screen behind me, I am in charge of getting together five thousand Gospel singers for the Jubilee celebrations. We had three thousand at the Royal Albert Hall two nights ago. But in just over two months' time their number will be five thousand for the Jubilee celebrations. But that is not what I would like to talk about. I want to speak as an African who has lived in Britain for many years. Outside Britain, Her Majesty is loved and respected. I was a child when she visited Nigeria, my country of birth. I have never forgotten it even though I was very young. I remember waving the British flag and the euphoria that her visit generated. Her Majesty represents everything that is good about this country to the outside world. Britain has always led the world in almost every aspect of life..... The world has just cried as one sad family after the evil that was perpetrated on 11th September last year, we are all still trying to come to terms with the terrorist attacks on the twin towers in New York. Britain has been handed a great opportunity and is well placed to put a smile back on the face of the world through the Queen's Jubilee celebrations. Britain will get the world to share some good news and laugh together again and enjoy Her Majesty's fifty years on the throne. Fifty years on the throne! No other country can celebrate better than Britain. No other country can beat the British when it comes to putting on a great party! Fifty years on the throne is God-given. No one in this room will have another opportunity or live long enough to celebrate a monarch who has served so well and tirelessly for fifty years. I know I won't! I hear there are people who want to stop this celebration. I think it would be evil not to celebrate such a unique and happy occasion that will definitely bring that smile back to us all. I am so excited and can't wait to celebrate Her Majesty's Golden Jubilee, neither can my five thousand gospel singers whose numbers I could easily and gladly increase to ten thousand if Sir Michael could accommodate them. Thank you!"

I floated back to my seat; "There goes my British passport or do they still send people to The Tower of London?" I sat down my mouth was dry, my lips glued to my teeth, my hands and legs still shaking with nerves. From behind me a hand rested on my right shoulder and someone whispered in my ear; "Well done! You brave girl, you have just said what the rest of us weren't allowed to say. Thank you!" I did not turn around to see who it was. I thought I would do that at the end. It was Lord Stirling, Chairman of the Golden Jubilee Celebrations! Anyway, after all that, the three government representatives did not speak at the presentation.

It was 12th March 2002, I had just over two months to prepare the choirs for the celebrations on 2nd June. Without funding, except what Stephen could spare and without a secretary it was incredibly hard getting the recording done. I had to attend the committee meetings, some of which were held at Buckingham Palace. The whole thing was an awe-inspiring experience and so much fun! I persuaded Sir Michael, who was partial to another children's charity, to use Stagecoach as the children welcoming The Queen. I thought this would serve as a "thank you" for Stagecoach's help at The Royal Albert Hall.

During the final meeting in Buckingham Palace, which involved the press, there were light-hearted comments about Ozzie Osborne appearing at the Jubilee. We all knew our roles. If anyone was nervous it did not show. There was a feeling of everything being in place. Every detail was covered at the committee meetings. Sir Michael, the producer, had a way about him that created an efficient, relaxed atmosphere. I went mentally through the day in my head to make sure my 5000 not only looked great, but would not let the side down. Everything had been perfectly organized by the logistic company, Unusual Services led by the MD Alan Jacobi, the celebrations' director, Dougie Squires, Sir Michael and their various teams. Her Majesty's main concern was "Will the Palace still be standing?" She asked this question several times, owing to the planned fireworks that were to be wired to the Palace itself for the spectacular waterfall effect set to music. This was the brainchild of brilliant pyrotechnic designer Wilf Scott. Her Majesty's concerns about the fireworks wired to the Palace, sent me on a 'Prayer Fast', that all would be well. Later Lord Stirling, and Sir Michael Executive Producer of the Golden Jubilee Weekend Festival joked; "If the Palace catches fire, I'll be on a flight heading east!" The other said; "And I'll be on one heading west!"

With no secretary or sponsors, I relied on help in kind from people like Viv, the owner of the Premier Studios in Hackney for studio time. I had to choose, time and record twenty-five minutes' worth of tracks for the choir to sing during the parade. The tracks would be played very loudly to the public through the speakers on either side of the Mall, as we all swayed down the wide boulevard. The beat of the track would make sure that the 5000 singers kept to time. Nicky Brown very kindly produced the tracks for me. Sir Michael had allocated 25 minutes for each parade. I took this timing seriously. The day before the celebrations I went to The Mall with Stephen. We walked up and down The Mall from the Admiralty Arch to Buckingham Palace thirteen times. I timed how fast the first 500 and the last 500 singers would have to walk in order to get to the Palace in 25 minutes.

I had the names of anyone who helped me, even in the smallest way, added to my page on the official brochure for the Golden Jubilee. I was moved to tears when Sir Michael mentioned me on his introduction and foreword on the brochure in glowing terms. My own page ended up being the centre page of the brochure. Sir Michael was the only one who knew how hard I had worked on the Committee without any outside help, but I loved every minute of it. It was a great honour to work with such a team learning from the best in the world. That was enough for me!

I chose seven old gospel songs like 'Amen', 'This Little Light of Mine', 'He's Got the Whole World in His Hand', but also my own "Celebrate Good News', a song I had written for the day and which we called 'The Jubilee Song'. I wrote 'Celebrate Good News' to help move the mass choir faster. The arrangement for the song was in the style of the South African Swinging Safari and set a steady upbeat pace. Each of the songs was segued together with 'Amens' in between, designed to encourage the crowd to sing along with us. 'The Jubilee Song' was simple, we repeated it twice and the people in the crowd picked it up easily, they were all so excited and enjoying themselves. It all worked!

For appearances' sake, and to separate the choir from the others, I asked everyone in the choir to bring red, blue and white ribbons, each a metre long, which they all waved. This was very effective visually. We all met in St James Square very early in the morning. I tried to circulate among the choirs, but only got round to about half of them. At about 1.30pm we all moved into position from St James Square to Pall Mall and waited there for instructions to move on to The Admiralty Arch. I still did not know whether I was to lead the Choir or go to the dais at the Palace to sing "Amazing Grace" At 2.30pm a message came through the Walkie-Talkie from Sir Michael saying I would have to lead the choir down the Mall. He wanted me to be on the stage outside the Palace ready to sing "Amazing Grace". The easiest way to get me there was in front of the Choir, because two million people had arrived for the celebrations and were crowding the Mall. There were just so many people, that you could not get to the palace except through the heavily guarded open road, the Mall itself. Thank God that was the arrangement! In the end it turned out to be a godsend for which I am very grateful. While we waited, I went about trying to imagine what we would look like from the front and from the helicopters hovering over our heads. I had requested, the young people from Stage Coach wear yellow instead of their favoured black T-Shirts. I had them arranged in the middle of the five thousand so they would spell out the letters HM from a bird's eye view. In the front I arranged my Sun Dance dancers from the Royal Albert Hall "Support for Africa" concert in a chevron (V) shape. I had personally made them eye catching bright red/orange costumes on which they wore a white sash that said 'Sun Dance Gospel Choir'. Behind them were the 100 strong Metropolitan Police Gospel Choir in uniform. At first they had their black jackets over their white shirts and I wondered how I could broach the idea that they take the jackets off. Just before we moved into position under The Admiralty Arch, I decided it was now or never. I approached the officers in the choir, but before I could ask, three of them said;

"Would you mind if we take off our jackets?" It was a warm day.

"Would I mind? You would look fantastic and at least in white you won't look as though you are policing us! Thank you!"

Everything had fallen into place! They did look fantastic in white shirts behind the Dancers' V shape. Behind the Metropolitan Police Gospel Choir were the Yellow T-Shirts of stage Coach. I felt very proud! Sir Michael had given me the permission to fly two flags with my Support for Africa Charity logo on them. (This was later to prove to be the only complaint about the Choir, which was contained in a letter to 10 Downing Street, stating I had used the Jubilee to promote myself!) I should not have been surprised that someone would complain!

Unbeknown to me, during the Choir's procession, a total stranger, one of the staff members from *'Songs of Praise'* was being given the credit for all my hard work, on the Dimbleby live coverage! I had not even met the man. While I was on The Mall, David Dimbleby was presented with a man I did not even know, and who had nothing to do with the Choir or the Jubilee Committee. Being black and from 'Songs of Praise', they assumed he must have something to do with the choir, though 75 percent of the choir was white! The man sat there and accepted the credit, as the words were put into his mouth! Still, it was a small price to pay for the great honour of being on the Jubilee Committee!

The crowd was amazing! The atmosphere was electrifying! I was disappointed not to have been able to see their Royal Highnesses waving from their seats just outside Buckingham Palace as we approached. I was as blind as a bat having left my glasses at home! But nothing could dampen my spirits. I had to pinch myself several times! Here I am, this little girl from Africa! Oh! If only my mother could see me now! I couldn't stop praying and giving thanks. I should have been exhausted, not even my high heel shoes hurt until it was all over! Sir Michael was standing in the middle of The Mall gesticulating madly, trying to get the Parades to move faster and stay on time. Being a military man, he felt it was crucial to have everything on time. But I was proud to have had part of the Choir singing with me on the main stage outside the Palace. I was overwhelmed and emotional, during the Concord's Flight over us. It was just so great! I willed the rain to hold off a little longer and gave thanks for being allowed to be a part of the day. While two million people were singing in The Mall and two hundred million were watching on TV, I was praying for The Queen, Dougie, Sir Michael, Princess Diana and the Queen Mother. I wasn't aware of anything else, not even of the microphone in front of me!

During 'God Save the Queen' I was holding back tears and mouthing a prayer of thanksgiving for the smooth running of the whole day, for the crowd that gathered, the rain that held off, I had no idea the TV cameras would pick me out as I prayed!

I was thrilled with the reviews and pre-promotion by the BBC and others. I have the Golden Jubilee official brochure with my centre page for a keepsake and to remind me of my contribution to the Queen's Golden Jubilee. *"Celebrate Good News"* got noticed and mentioned in articles. Here are some of them:

"Patti Boulaye's 5,000-strong gospel choir were a highlight, making a glorious noise." (By The BBC's arts and media correspondent Nick Higham who followed the Queen on her Jubilee tour of the UK)

"Singer Patti Boulaye helped warm up the masses as she led a march of 5,000 dancers from Admiralty Arch down to the Palace grounds. A chorus of gospel singers provided the uplifting soundtrack. "Celebrate the Good News," they sang, "It's been so long since we felt so strong." The sentiment said it all." (By Jonathan Duffy BBC News Online, in central London)

"The gospel choir was led by Patti Boulaye, singing a special Jubilee song she had written for the occasion." (BBC)

*"And adding a note of wonder for the first stage of the procession will be the largest ever choir of gospel singers. Five thousand people led by Patti Boulaye will give the Quee*n a rousing chorus for her appearance at the Queen Victoria memorial at 15.45."* (BBC)

Chapter Thirty Six: Radhanath Swami

A call came in from Dr Joy Philippou MBE. She would like Stephen and me to speak at one of her many events at the House of Lords. Joy is in her 80s.

She's a very energetic intellectual, who encouraged me to write this book about my life. She is the kind of motherly character that is difficult to say no to. I first met Joy at Hanna and Uri Geller's 25th wedding anniversary and renewal of vows cerebrations at their house. Michael Jackson was the best man. I had the chance to renew my friendship with him on this day. Michael had a leg injury and had to go to the hospital on the way to the ceremony. He was almost two hours late and during that time I had the good fortune of getting to know Joy. It turned out she was Uri Geller's teacher when he was about 10yrs old. She told me a story about Uri at that age. Joy would release her class at 4.00pm each day, but one of the other teachers asked her why she persistently released her class 15 minutes early. She denied this until she realised that her classroom clock seemed to always be 15 minutes fast when it came to going home time and not otherwise. Finally she noticed that the hands on the clock would move by themselves close to the end of class and she turned to see Uri directing the hands with his hand!

The event at the House of Lords was in the Lord Chamberlain's Private Rooms. It was organized by Joy Philippou, who had invited Stephen, HRH Princess Katarina and me. Surinder Shandilya, VP of Global Private Bank HSBC was the MC. The evening was intended to celebrate the 40th Anniversary of Bhaktivedante Manor, the UK headquarters of the Krishna religion. I was to speak for 10mins on 'Spirituality' and Stephen was to prepare a speech on 'Spirituality and Finance'. Stephen and I parked in the car park just opposite the Black Rod's Entrance of the House of Lords. We were just entering the gates when we bumped into the cheerful Surinder, waiting for the arrival of His Holiness, Radhanath Swami who is the leader of the Krishna movement. Surinder introduced himself and asked Stephen and me to wait to be introduced to His Holiness. Few minutes later His Holiness arrived accompanied by a group of men. He was dressed in the saffron yellow colour associated with the Krishna religion. I asked,
"How do we address him?"
"His Holiness." was the reply.

I had no problems with that. This is indeed a holy man! I thought to myself. I shook his hand and bowed respectfully. He clasped my hand in both his, smiled a very warm smile and bowed. Not wanting his to be the last bow, I clasped both his hands and did the same in return. The Swami's handshake was gentle, but firm. There was great warmth in his arresting smile. At our first meeting, I wasn't sure if the glow around him was from his saffron attire or the bright daylight. Here was a very humble, but powerful man, the leader of the Krishna section of the Hindu religion. Stephen and I joined the group that lead His Holiness to the lift that lead to the Lord Chamberlain's Room. The Swami is a small man in stature and a great leader, who made everyone feel special.

Stephen was told that His Holiness had just flown in to London, on his way to India after a meeting with the newly elected President Obama. My friend Her Royal Highness, the lovely Princess Katarina of Yugoslavia was one of the speakers. Surinder introduced each speaker with great reverence. His Holiness spoke after Princess Katarina. Naturally, his speech was on 'Spirituality'. There went the subject of my speech! How could I follow a holy man who has just delivered a riveting hour on Spirituality? He covered everything I was going to say and more. I decided to talk about my career in show business instead. I had not done my research on the Bhaktivedanta Manor. Joy had not mentioned that it was the 40th Anniversary of the Manor, which was donated by George Harrison of the Beatles to the Krishna movement. Maybe she did, but I had not focused on it. I knew there were different arms of the Hindu religion. Just to be sure, I asked Srutidharma Das (Bhaktivedanta Manor Temple President) if it would be appropriate to include the 'Hare Krishna' in my story.

I was nervous! There were now only ten minutes left of the time allowed in the Lord Chamberlain's room. I decided to introduce Stephen. I began with how I got into show business. When I got to the part of me being hired in 'Hair' to sing the Maha Mantra, to my surprise the whole room started singing with me. I was encouraged and realized then that the room was filled with people of the Hindu religion. By the time Stephen began his speech there was five minutes left. In those five minutes he had the room in fits of laughter with his take on 'Spirituality and Finance'. Better still when some House of Lords jobsworth rudely interrupted him mid-speech and practically threw him off the stage shouting that the time was up, he took it well, as only Stephen can. His Holiness was impressed by Stephen's humility in the way he handled the interruption with jokes and laughter. Stephen and I received signed copies of His Holiness Radhanath Swami memoir "The Journey Home - Autobiography of an American Swami".

We also received an invitation to the 'Krishna Janmashtami Festival' at the Manor for the following 1st September 2013.

A few months later, His Holiness made another short visit to London and asked Surinder Shandilya to invite Stephen and me to a private dinner. Our daughter Aret was pregnant and due to give birth to our grandson, Dante. During our private evening with His Holiness, there were just the four of us, His Holiness chose me to say grace at mealtime. I did this nervously, humbled to have been asked by a holy man to say grace. As we ate the special vegetarian meal prepared for him, I asked questions about his spellbinding memoirs. The Journey Home recounts his travels from the US to India. We talked about Lord Jesus and we talked about His Holy Mother Mary and Lord Krishna. He explained that since he has been the head of the Krishna movement he has organised that his Krishna movement feeds 350,000, yes 350,000 poor children every day in Mumbai and they are building schools and housing.

The search for enlightenment had led Radhanath Swami as a 19 years old Jewish teenager all the way from America, trekking across Europe to India. The difficulties he survived to get there in an extraordinary journey filled with dangerous adventures, peculiar characters and mystical experiences. I wanted to know what drove him to put himself through this incredibly dangerous journey, especially not knowing what answers he would find. I already knew the answer to that. Every Catholic saint whose life I admire had made a similar journey. The Swami lived in India for many years as a sadhu (wandering monk) before returning to America. There he shared the sacred knowledge and wisdom he had learned from the many holy men and women he had met. He emerged from his travels wanting to explain to others the rewards and beauty of a life that is dedicated to God.

The beginning of 2014 brought great news through Surinder that his Holiness would be passing through London specially to bless our grandson on April 29th. At first I thought he was teasing me! But it was true! His Holiness was really coming to our home to meet family, friends and bless our Dante! We worried about what we would feed him and what the protocol would be. We needn't have worried, three women including Surinder's wife, prepared the delicious vegetarian food, which must contain no onions. Family members and friends gathered, including our favourite Benedictine Monk Fr Andrew Hughes, HRH Princess Katarina and Dr Joy Philippou. They all loved His Holiness! Dante climbed up and sat on his knee as he spoke to all those gathered, about the importance of children and family. Everyone received a private hearing and a signed copy of his memoirs. My teenage step grandchildren were very taken by him.

He inspired all of us with his wisdom, selflessness and humility. The officials who came with him including Srutidharma Das were anxious to get him away after three hours so he would get enough rest before his dawn prayers. After everyone had left, His Holiness stayed with us another three hours. It was an incredibly humbling and life changing experience! Stephen and I keep wondering if His Holiness has us mixed up with some other better deserving couple! We feel blessed by him.

On the 6th of Dec 2014, His Holiness was in London to recover from an illness caused by exhaustion. He had just spoken at the Oxford Union and again Surinder sent a message that his Holiness would like to see us. The dinner was arranged. It was a delightful evening with eight guests. After the dinner he took us aside to whisper that His Holiness' birthday was in a few days' time. We were invited as surprise guests. Now we definitely felt we were being mistaken for someone else. It was getting unreal and we are waiting to wake up from the dream! Why would such an obviously holy man have the time of day for Stephen and me? We went to the temple in Wembley, where His holiness was addressing hundreds of people. As we walked towards the raised and beautifully decorated stage, he looked up and saw us. That wonderful smile filled his face and my heart. He was surprised and pleased to see us. He got up from his meditation position, left the stage and came down to greet us. My head was in a spin! Something told me this was not the usual protocol with His Holiness. He went back on to his stage and we sat down on chairs with Surinder and his wife. I was grateful for the chair because my left knee was swollen and painful from an injury. As I sat there listening to his every word about spirituality and the teachings of Christ, I prayed and gave thanks to God for such a privilege. The atmosphere was wonderful I didn't want to leave. I wanted to speak to everyone I could. I watched as families went to him for blessings. Their faces said it all. The reverence, gentleness and love they gave and received from this holy man who had put his obvious illness aside to attend to everyone in the room. What a life changing experience that was, for Stephen and me!

"Angels in My Hair" - Lorna Byrne

I am always amazed at the way God touches our lives. Our neighbour Ruby Kaur who lived opposite us, gave me a book "Angels in My Hair" as a thankyou present.
"You will love this book, Patti. When I read it, I knew I had to get you a copy."
I don't enjoy reading as much as I should. It's probably because I like to be active and hate being still for too long. If I get to read, it's usually at

bedtime. Unfortunately, Stephen and I go to bed very late and we read the Bible together, maybe discuss the contents of the night's reading before prayers. After which, I am too tired to read a book.

"I don't have time to read a book, not now!" I thought. I was up to my neck preparing lessons for my BIPADA Academy's private clients. I personalize each training session and I often spend most of the evenings up to 3.00am preparing for the next day's training sessions.

I had told Ruby about the angels that guard the four corners of our home. When she gave me Lorna's book, she also told me that for about five nights, when they first moved into the street, she and her husband had noticed a 3-D figure standing at the corner of our front garden. The shape would become visible each time car headlights were pointing at our house. Ruby told her husband;

"That must be one of Patti's angels."

Handing me the book, she added. "I have a feeling you will meet the author. If she comes to England, let's go and see her together."

I laughed at the idea. It was a few weeks before I got round to reading the book which I had kept by my bedside. I was riveted as soon as I started it!

Lorna Byrne is an Irish author. She is best known for her bestselling memoirs, "Angels in My Hair" (2008), "A Message of Hope from the Angels" (2012) and "Love from Heaven" (2014) "Angels in My Hair" debuted at No. 1 on the UK Sunday Times best sellers Book Chart. Her books have been translated into 30 languages and published in over 50 countries.

Lorna was born into a poor family in Dublin in March 1955. Long before she could talk Lorna was seeing and talking with angels. She sees them as physically as the rest of us see someone standing in front of us. The angels impart great wisdom and insight to her. They asked her to write her million best-selling book about them even though she could neither read nor write at the time and even introduced her to her publisher. As a child, her lack of interest in the material world and conversations with apparently empty rooms led to concerns about her health, and she was diagnosed as being 'retarded'.

The book confirmed everything I had imagined about God's angels, my Guardian Angel and the ones I had requested in prayer to guard our home. I have since given away more than forty copies of her first book and many copies of the subsequent books. I sent a copy with the Christmas presents to members of my family; my stepdaughters, friends and anyone I was moved to send it to. When Lorna was booked to appear in Birmingham, Ruby was keen that we should go together, but I wasn't free.

My sister Maggie came to visit us in London. She had a skin problem that the specialists could not diagnose for a long time and which they were unable to cure. She was distraught, as nothing they gave her worked and the remedies suggested only seemed to make it worse. I felt helpless. She works too hard and takes on more than I could ever cope with (that's saying something). She runs a nursery, two schools and a pharmacy.

A friend mentioned to me that Lorna Byrne had visited their women's group in Ireland. I got on to the organiser of the group, but she was not helpful. I went on Lorna's own site and noticed that prayer requests were left on a special section. So I left a prayer request. Then I got lucky, perhaps helped by the angels, I found the name of Lorna's agent and contacted her leaving a message, requesting a prayer for Maggie in the hope that Lorna would receive it. I also left some information about Maggie including her phone number in Lagos.

A few days later, Maggie told me she had received a call from Lorna. She was somewhat taken aback, but very elated. I had not told Maggie that I had been in touch with Lorna's office. I could hear the difference in Maggie's voice. When you are down, it is always uplifting for the soul to know that somebody cares. I left another message to thank Lorna for being so kind as to actually call my sister personally.

Sometime later, I received a message that Lorna was coming to London to be publicly interviewed by a top newspaper reporter at the Friends Headquarters in Euston. She had arranged for Stephen and me to be invited. We were asked to visit her in her dressing room before the event to meet this charming and gentle person. The interview on stage went really well and it made for a most tangibly profound and enlightening evening. The audience of nine hundred people were so engrossed that they all waited in an orderly queue to have the chance to speak to her personally and all of them were individually blessed by her. Lorna is a petite bundle of innocence, love and goodness all rolled into one. Tall men in the queue would drop their heads on to her shoulder in meek submission as she blessed them with the sign of the cross on the forehead. There were families, couples, young and old people, people from all over the world and from all walks of life. Stephen and I wanted to show our appreciation and so we waited our turn to be blessed at the end of the incredibly long queue. We offered her and her agent a lift to their hotel. We felt we had truly met one of God's real angels. Our friendship with Lorna has grown exponentially from that day and we have been privileged to stay at her tranquil home in Ireland for some blissful and memorable days.

Freedom of the City of London Dec 2014.

What an honour to have received the Freedom of the City of London on 9th December 2014! In attendance at the ceremony were my lovely husband, our wonderful children and grandson. We were joined by some special friends, who attended even though they were all given two days' notice. I was so busy with so many things that I had forgotten to tell everyone even our children about the date. I was sponsored for my charitable work in Britain and Africa. You have to read the Declaration at the ceremony, but I decided to sing mine so that it would be special to me. I sang it making up a tune as I went along. It must have sounded like a Gregorian chant! At least I was the first to sing the Declaration, or so I was told by the Clerk of the Court, who conducted the ceremony. He was funny and put the whole event into its historical perspective with great stories of past recipients. He made it such a special day for me.

OBE

2016 started with a bang! In the same week chosen for the Kindle Store launch of this book was the first showing of my BBC TWO series "The Real Marigold Hotel", filmed brilliantly in India by Two Four Group. I had participated in the series with eight other celebrities. In the same week, this was followed by my visit to Buckingham Palace to receive an O.B.E ('Officer of The Most Excellent Order of The British Empire'), which, I was very proud to know, was awarded for my charity work in the UK and Sub-Saharan Africa. HRH Prince Charles made the presentation to me. It was the experience of a lifetime, not just because of the great honour of being a recipient, but because I had the support of my husband and children, Aret and Sebastian at the ceremony. I had a warm welcome by HRH Prince Charles and the Royal Staff, which made me feel as though I was the only one there, but I'm sure it was the same for all the other recipients. After the ceremony our children went back to work. I had a quick interview with Joyce Ohaja of TVC and then a mad dash with Stephen to Gerrards Cross to be in time to pick up our grandson from the nursery. A perfect and wonderful week!

For you, who have just read my story, I pray that all your prayers will be answered. T.T.G.O.G